FULL
MOON
FEAST

FULL MOON FEAST

Food and the Hunger for Connection

JESSICA PRENTICE

FOREWORD BY DEBORAH MADISON

CHELSEA GREEN PUBLISHING
WHITE RIVER JUNCTION, VERMONT

Editor: Mary Bahr
Managing Editor: Marcy Brant
Copy Editor: Laura Jorstad
Proofreader: Collette Leonard
Indexer: Beth Nauman-Montana, Salmon Bay Indexing
Designer: Peter Holm, Sterling Hill Productions
Design Assistant: Daria Hoak, Sterling Hill Productions
Illustrations by Sara Love

Printed in the United States
First printing, March 2006
10 9 8 7 6 5 4 3 2 1

Our Commitment to Green Publishing
Chelsea Green sees publishing as a tool for cultural change and ecological stewardship.
We strive to align our book manufacturing practices with our editorial mission, and to
reduce the impact of our business enterprise on the environment. We print our books
and catalogs on chlorine-free recycled paper, using soy-based inks, whenever possible.
Chelsea Green is a member of the Green Press Initiative (www.greenpressinitiative.org),
a nonprofit coalition of publishers, manufacturers, and authors working to protect the
world's endangered forests and conserve natural resources.
   Full Moon Feast was printed on Nature's Book Natural, a 50 percent post-consumer
waste recycled, old growth forest-free paper supplied by Maple Vail.

Library of Congress Cataloging-in-Publication Data

Prentice, Jessica, 1968-
Full moon feast : food and the hunger for connection / Jessica Prentice.
      p. cm.
ISBN-13 978-1-933392-00-4
ISBN-10 1-933392-00-2
1. Cookery (Natural foods) 2. Natural foods. I. Title.
TX741.P74 2006
641.5'63—dc22

                              2005036540

Chelsea Green Publishing Company
Post Office Box 428
White River Junction, VT 05001
(800) 639-4099
www.chelseagreen.com

Text on pp. 57-58, 71-72, 77, 98, 168, 250, and 286 is used with permission
from the Price-Pottenger Nutrition Foundation. You are encouraged to join
and support this nonprofit organization. See Resources for contact
information.

To the ancestors
and
the animals

World-Come-to-an-End Food

From a dialogue between two Karuk elders, recorded during the first quarter of the twentieth century. Translated from the Karuk by Julian Lang.

Vaa vúra kích pakunmáharatihanik Peekxaréeyavsa.
Koovúra vaa kunkupítihanik; pahûut Peekxaréyav
    kunkupítihanik, vaa kunkupíti.
Xás pávaa pakun'áamtihanik Peekxaréeyav, víri vaa kích
    pakun'áamti.
Vaa kinípeeranik, "Véek páy ku'áamtiheesh.
Peekxaréeyav áama kun'áamtihanik, xuun kunpátatihanik,
    áama xákaan xuun. Káru pufich'iich kun'áamti-
    hanik."
Vaa vúra pakunfúhishtihanik, Peekxaréeyav
    axakyâanich vúra kun'ípamtihanik,
Vaa vúra kích pakunkupítihanik.
Pa'apxantínihich pakunivyíhukanik, xás vaa kunípaanik,
    "Kêemish pakun'áamti,
Kemisha'ávaha, ithivthaneentaniha'ávaha."
Achíphan vúra va'áraaras vaa kích papishîich kun'á-
    vanik pa'apxantiich'ávaha.
Víri pakunvíshtar, vúra kunvíshtar. Puráan kunipêer,
    "Vúra uum amáyav."
Xás tákunpiip, "Ník'áta vúra uum pu'íimtihara. Naa
    táni'av, pasára."
Xás vaa koovúra papihnîichas káru pakéevniikichas
    xára xás kun'ávanik.
Nuu ta'ifuchtîimichas pávaa nu'áapunmuti
    pávaa Peekxaréeyav pakunkupítihanik; vaa
    kunáamtihaak.
Pámitva kinípeentihat pananutaat îin.
Víri vaa vúra nuu káru vaa tapukin'áamtihara,
    pámtiva kinípeerat, "Veek ku'áamtiheesh."
Hûutheesh pananu'ífuth va'ífapuhsa?

The Old People were following the Ikxaréeyavs, the
      Spirit People, all the time.
All the People did the same long ago; whatever the
      Ikxaréeyavs did, the People did.
And the things that the Spirit People ate, that was all
      the Old People ate.
That's what they were told, "You must eat this kind of
      food.
The Spirit People ate salmon and they spooned up acorn
      soup, eating salmon along with acorn soup. And they
      ate deermeat."
And the Old People claimed that the Spirit People ate
      two meals a day,
And so that's the way the Old People did as well.
When the white people all came, the Old People said
      that they were eating food poisonous to Indians.
It was poison food, world-come-to-an-end food.
The middle-aged people were the first to eat the white
      man's food.
When they liked it, they really liked it. Then they told
      each other, "It's good tasting food."
They said, "He never died. I'm going to eat it, that
      white man's bread."
It was a long time before the Old Men and Old Women
      ate the white man's food.
We are the last ones that know
      how the Spirit People used to do, all that they used to eat.
Our mothers told us that.
And even we do not eat anymore,
      what they told us before "You must eat this kind."
      And what will they who are raised after us do?

ACKNOWLEDGMENTS

I have been so blessed, and there are so many people to thank . . .

First, I want to acknowledge the communities that have so supported me: The loved ones in the Washington, DC, area who have known me since childhood; the communities at the Center for Ecoliteracy, the Headlands Center for the Arts, the Ferry Plaza Farmers Market, and the Brick Hut Café—thank you so much for your support over the years. The programmers at KPFA radio in Berkeley who saved me the cost of an advanced degree, and whose influence is on every page of this book. (A special thanks to Layna Berman.) The sustainable agriculture communities here in the Bay Area and nationally—I hope I have made a contribution to this crucial work. The nourishing traditions communities here in the Bay Area, as well as all my fellow chapter leaders for the Weston A. Price Foundation—let's keep it up! Peter Barnes and the staff and fellow writers at the Mesa Refuge, where I wrote the bulk of this book—what a gift! The Colley clan—I am proud to be a part of you. And to the community of Saint Francis Lutheran Church—my spiritual home, my precious village—I am so glad I found you.

Thank you to all those writers and thinkers who have so deeply influenced my work: Jeanette Armstrong, Wendell Berry, Marcus Borg, Caroline Casey, Annemarie Colbin, Wade Davis, Sally Fallon, Lewis Hyde, Sandor Katz, Helena Norberg-Hodge, Martín Prechtel, Weston Price, Joel Salatin, Vandana Shiva, Malidoma Patrice Somé, Maya Tiwari, Marilyn Waring, Alice Waters.

Thanks to my wonderful family: My mother, Dinah, who shared with me her love of human culture in all its diversity, a deep respect for the traditions of everyone in the human family, a hunger for the spiritual life, and who took me traveling—thank you! My father, Patrick, who shared with me his passion for clear thinking and the written word, and who has always believed I had something worth saying—thank you! My stepfather, Foster, whose quiet and steady support of my work has been a great gift to me—thank you! And to the rest of my extended family, with great gratitude for their presence in my life: Josh and Ketaki, Brett and Sarah, John and Marie, Lynn, Linda, Bill, Grandma, my cousins, nieces, and nephews, and those who are with us now only in Spirit—each one of you is a precious blessing to me. And to O. Z. Tully, with gratitude for his generosity and wisdom, and to the rest of my Tully family.

Thank you to all the wonderful friends and home cooks who tested my recipes: Christina Abuelo, Vanessa Barrington, Daphne Blumenthal, Teresa Brown, Jean Cherie, Porsche Combash, Jane Evans, Sarah Klein, Marilyn Fisher, Darcey Blue French, Maggie Gosselin, Linda Harrour, Michael Hiller, Ulrich Honighausen, Holly Howe, Stephanie Johnson, Misa Koketsu, Julia Kurtzer, Nicole Leong, Sharon Lutz, Luana Lyons, Kate Mendenhall, Arthur Morris, Natalie Peck, Sienna Potts, Yoko Sato, Bonnie Scott, Lynda Smith-Cowan, Joan Stear, Helen Tadeo, Erika Trayer, Denise Wilson, Larry Wisch, Krista Wood, Layne Zimmerman.

Friends and comrades who supported me in other ways: Julie Amberg, Naomi Baer, Sarah Beaton, Krys Bobrowski, Ruth Conniff, Tom Cowan, Gabrielle Dean, Christine Farren, Tamsen Finn, Margrit Haeberlin, Carol Karasik, David Kwan, Kirsten Marshall, Tara Massarsky, Eduardo Morell, Sandrine Hahn, Sarah Hall, Laurent Pouget, Julie Quinton, Dev Rana, Janie Riley, Samantha Smith, Catherine Spanger, Chien Wang, Anja Weber, Adam Wilson, Katie Whitmer, Nobuko Yamada, Daphne Zepos, and most especially my dear friend Kristin Nelson.

I am full of gratitude for the farmers, ranchers, and fisherfolk who both teach me and feed me: Janet Brown and Marty Jacobson, Wallace and Nancy Condon, Stephen and Gloria Decatur, Pascal Destandau and Eric Smith, Dave Evans, Ted Fuller, Mike Gale, Robin and Nancy Gammons, Andy Griffin and Julia Wiley, Jean Harrah and Bob Thorson, John Lagier, David Little, Annabelle Lenderink, Ben and Karen Lucero, Liz Milazzo, Larry and Roz Miyamura, Judith Redmond, Dru Rivers, Brandon and Michelle Ross, Lloyd and Nancy Stueve, Nigel Walker, David Winsberg, and many others.

A huge thank-you to my editor Mary Bahr, who has made my writing so much better and has been a true pleasure to work with. And to Margo Baldwin for believing in me and my idea from the beginning. To John Barstow, Marcy Brant, Alice Blackmer, and the entire Chelsea Green team for taking such good care of my work.

The memory of Daniel Glos was much with me as I wrote this book—you were gone from us many moons too soon. So, too, Tammy Bruce, Margaret Kilgallen, and Jeff Young. You are all missed.

And last but not least, my deepest gratitude to Debora Tully. I don't know where I would be without your love, support, and wisdom. Thank you.

CONTENTS

RECIPE LIST   xii

FOREWORD   xv

INTRODUCTION
   LUNAR CALENDARS AND
   TRADITIONAL FOOD WAYS   xxi

1.   HUNGER MOON   1

2.   SAP MOON   24

3.   EGG MOON   48

4.   MILK MOON   70

5.   MOON OF MAKING FAT   95

6.   MEAD MOON   119

7.   WORT MOON   141

8.   CORN MOON   164

9.   MOON WHEN SALMON RETURN TO EARTH   187

10.   BLOOD MOON   209

11.   SNOW MOON   233

12.   MOON OF LONG NIGHTS   259

13.   WOLF MOON   284

EPILOGUE
   ON THE CUSP OF ANOTHER MOON   304

RESOURCES   309

NOTES   326

INDEX   337

RECIPE LIST

Cream of Parsnip Soup 18
Beet Borscht 19
Oyster Plant Chowder 20
Winter Minestrone 21
Golden Vegetable Bisque 22
Roasted Root Vegetables 23
Coconut and Palm Sugar Semifreddi 43
Maple-vanilla Panna Cruda 43
Cardamom and Jaggery Rice Pudding 44
Maple-roasted Nuts 45
Hot Coco Cocoa 46
After-dinner Mints 46
Asparagus Frittata 66
Stracciatella (Roman Egg Drop Soup) 67
Asian Egg Drop Soup 67
Spring Tonic Nettle Soup 68
Avocado and Hard-cooked Eggs with a Lemony Dressing 69
Yogurt 89
Warm Frothed Milk with Saffron and Cardamom 90
Yogurt Cheese Peras with Rosewater Syrup 91
Kefir 92
Clabbered Cottage Cheese 93
Creamy Salad Dressing 94
Superfood and Kefir Shake 114
Coconut-date Energy Balls 115
Rendering Lard 116
Niter Qibbeh (Ethiopian Spiced Ghee) 117
Olive Oil Mayonnaise 118
Mellow Mead 138
Honeybee Lemonade 139
I Dream of Peaches and Cream 139
Honeybee Yogurt 140
Summer Berries with Lavender Crème Anglaise 140
Lemon Verbena Ale 158
Root Beer 159
Herbal Latte 160
Hibiscus and Rose Hip Soda 161
Yarrow Ale 162

Birch Beer or Sorghum Ale   163
Suffer-free Succotash   182
Calabacitas with Herbed Crema   183
Potato-corn Chowder   184
Sourdough Corn Fritters   184
Sourdough Crumpets   185
Budín de Maíz   186
Whole Roast Salmon   204
Salmon Cured with Maple and Juniper   205
Simple Salmon Fillets   206
Easy Hollandaise   207
Salmon Poached in a Lemongrass and Coconut Milk Sauce   208
Simplest Roast Chicken   226
Swedish Meatballs   227
Beef Liver with Browned Onions   228
Stir-fry of Pork and Vegetables with Ginger   229
Lamb Chops with Meyer Lemon and Mint Gelée   230
Beef Broth   231
Sauerkraut and Rot Kohl   252
Quick and Simple Kimchi   254
Lacto-fermented Raita   255
Lacto-fermented Tabbouleh   256
Lacto-fermented Corn Relish   257
Lacto-fermented Peach Chutney   258
Sausage with Potatoes and Cabbage   278
Pot Roast   279
Pumpkin Mashed Potatoes   280
Cranberry Sauce   281
Shchi (Russian Peasant Soup)   281
New England Clam Chowder   282
Cream of Butternut Squash Soup   298
Chicken Stock   299
Chicken Soup with Wild Rice   300
Dungeness Crab Cakes   301
Sourdough Cheese Herb Scones   301
Homemade Sourdough Crackers   302
Sourdough Pancakes   303

FOREWORD

After reading *Full Moon Feast: Food and the Hunger for Connection*, I took
a look at my library of cookbooks to see if there was anything that
came as close to embracing the scope of the human relationship to
food.

First, there are my favorites, classics published from the 1950s
through the 1970s, the books that got me started in cooking—
Elizabeth David's slim books and Jane Grigson's two plump volumes,
one on fruit and the other on vegetables. Both authors greatly enriched
their work with erudition, and their recipes are peppered generously
with scholarly tidbits both botanical and literary. Memories and recol-
lections of dishes, places, and the people who knew and cooked them
provide a heady stew of context for the recipes, which are breezy and
relaxed in their telling; tea cups, wine glasses, and butter "the size of a
nut" do for measurements. Waverly Root's two volumes on France and
Italy, which also date from the 1950s, depict a geography of food as he
portrays dishes that are eaten in mountainous regions or by the sea;
recipes that are products of rich areas and poor; food cultures that are
based on butter or olive oil or lard.

Twenty years later Richard Olney wrote a marvelous book called
Simple French Food in which he portrays not just how to make a dish, but
the culture and context in which the dish dwells. He does give recipes,
which are fairly precise, but years later he wrote, "I don't like recipes.
They keep cooks from using their intuition, and intuition is precisely
what so much of cooking is about." Perhaps that's why he often followed the specifics of a recipe with a long verbal ramble that considers
all the other possibilities, should you have leftovers or something other
than what's called for, as is so often the case. There were other writers
of this ilk, authors who dove into a culture perhaps not their own and
explored its food. What connects them is the sense of connection itself
that they can't help but communicate: a dish and its recipe don't stand
apart from place and season, history, and people. To me this sense of a
recipe existing in a web of connections is an enormous part of these

authors' appeal. I've also noticed in my travels that the more a culture is intact, the fewer cookbooks it produces. *Full Moon Feast* also seeks connection and culture, but it reaches back farther in time to ancient peoples and practices that illustrate a more fundamental relationship to food, and food's relationship to life.

In our ever-fracturing world everything has changed, including food writing and cookbooks. Most of my cookbooks, the ones accumulated over the past twenty years, speak not of geography, tradition, and culture, but exist in service to pursuits peculiar to America—the pursuit of speed and efficiency, for example, or for ways around commitment, time, and the pleasures of cooking and sharing meals. There are a myriad of single-subject cookbooks that vary thematically from chicken to eggs, from meat to muffins, and rice to roots. There are gigantic all-purpose cookbooks as well as guides to putting food up and keeping food fresh. And of course there are books that promise health or weight loss or cater to a diet that involves eliminating something—meat, dairy, wheat, fat. In stark contrast to these books are those glossy tomes in which chefs reveal their often intricate and costly recipes. Cookbook writing dwells in a wild territory, a place where worthy traditions are freely flaunted in order to cater to the desires of a particular audience. Foods are combined with no regard for their season or attributes; dairy that would be rich and full of good fat in its original culture is reduced to nonfat in this one, yet the promise of goodness is not withdrawn. A vegetarian might claim that nutritional yeast tastes "just like chicken stock" or act as if a cheese made from rice milk has all the complex, mysterious attributes of raw cows' milk cheese. Recipes are executed in an exacting style and the free, open gestures of those earlier writers who pointed us to rich cultural traditions are gone. Recipes float on the page. They aren't anchored to a greater whole.

But recently books have been looking different. They haven't gone back to the world of exploring cultures that exist elsewhere (although some very good ones do), but they have gone on to reveal the larger context in which we need to consider eating and cooking in our consumer-driven culture. They may include recipes, as does *Full Moon Feast*, but at the same time they thread a path through such issues as provenance, toxicity, animal welfare, sustainability, seasonality, and more. *The Ethical Gourmet* wants to show us how "to enjoy great food that is humanely raised, sustainable, non-endangered, and that replenishes the earth." Tall order. *The Real Food Revival* is "an A to Z guide for interacting with the multi-faceted, often convoluted business of food." Jane Goodall has written about food and the shape of food practices in America, and Andrew Weil speaks to our health by connecting what we eat to how we live in the world. A farmer writes about raising peaches in California. From England, *The River Cottage Cookbook* touts real home cooking and includes a paragraph on owning a shotgun and another on slaughtering a pig—a truly whole-foods approach that considers a world of self-sufficiency and intimacy with animals.

Like Jessica Prentice's, my library doesn't include cookbooks alone. I too have Dr. Weston Price's book on nutrition and physical degeneration; collections of folktales; books on the ethics of eating meat; others on botany, plant origins and histories; memoirs of cooks; books on food chemistry, on wild fermentation, and others on the dangers of modern food. But the difference between Jessica Prentice and me is that these books live in her home, whereas my cookbooks live in my office, as if home and office occupy different worlds. In *Full Moon Feast*, Prentice deftly shows that they clearly are of one world. It takes someone with a wide vision to bring all these facets of human thought and experience together into a rich and unified whole, which Prentice has.

The moons in the title refer to food times, times of the year when certain foods assume prominence, and they make perfect sense, if you can imagine—and with this author's help, you can—a world in which human cultures are exactly in tune with the places they occupy on the planet. This was once a universal human experience, but for modern Americans especially, it is not easy to imagine how it feels to live such a vital connection between season and food, let alone experience it. *Full Moon Feast* takes us far from the mechanistic bent of our "everything all the time" culture and shows us how we might see ourselves as members of a human community that ranges far back in time and wide in place, much farther and wider than the world of the authors I've mentioned. This is not about fashion or style on the plate; it's not about trendy new foods or amazing equipment. Nor is it just about how cruel and disconnected our ways of raising, cooking, and consuming food are. Closer to *Walden Pond* than *The Joy of Cooking*, *Full Moon Feast* puts aside what isn't important to realize a more fundamental relationship to food, one that weaves history, anthropology, folk life, myth, medicine, a personal journey and, of course, food itself into a whole.

Full Moon Feast picks up the whole cloth of our human world, not just the rag that is our food-as-fuel (but not too much fat, please) approach. Rather than telling us only what's horrific about something, it digs down to those fundamental attitudes that have produced our now-trying relationships to food and shows us what other possibilities might exist, have existed, for deeper connection and joy in our life. The cost of replacing our intuition and connection with such things as the desires for speed, thinness, the constant availability of foodstuffs, is the vitality and joy of life itself. Not just about the right or wrongness of a situation, *Full Moon Feast* brings together the threads of human culture that we might look more deeply at the nature of the collective self and ask the question: What kind of a human animal do we want to be, really? Amazingly, preachiness is avoided, even in the heartfelt offerings that conclude each chapter. And the recipes, which in most cases appear to be for familiar foods (sauerkraut, sourdough fritters, taboulleh), are recast as foods that are alive with cultures other than human—beneficial bacteria, yeasts, things causing fermentation that makes foods alive and probiotic. You can taste the difference in food that is alive, and feel it, too.

It hasn't happened often, but on a few occasions I have had profound encounters with food. One was eating honey, collected from an orchard in Hawaii, that had never been heated in its making; another was eating bison that was shot in its field then blessed by the Native American rancher; and just recently, savoring a piece of beef cooked in Barolo, both from the Piedmont. The breed was an old one, still loved and raised by a few wise farmers in that area. It was more than simply good. On these occasions I experienced something I can only think of as deep nourishment; food as sacramental sustenance that went far beyond everything we usually make food into. These were foods that were whole in the deepest sense, foods that were alive, and foods you could *feel;* foods that came from human hands, hearts and minds at work. As soon as I tasted them, I felt something was different, and a feeling of reverence arose spontaneously. This was physical and spiritual nourishment, food that expressed webs and layers of connections. It was, in each case, astonishing. I believe that we are nourished by foods that come out of wholeness or, in other words, foods that have integrity, that come from a place where things are connected. For me, *Full Moon Feast: Food and the Hunger for Connection* is ultimately about this deep nourishment and the lives we might live that include it. Reading it, you sense that this might, just might, be possible.

DEBORAH MADISON
Author of *Local Flavors: Cooking and Eating
from America's Farmers' Markets*

INTRODUCTION

LUNAR CALENDARS AND TRADITIONAL FOOD WAYS

stars around the beautiful moon
hide back their luminous form
whenever all full she shines
    on the earth
      silvery

—Sappho, translated from the ancient Greek

Our sense of time and the seasons is based on the rhythms of life on planet Earth. Darkness gives way to daylight; the sun moves through the sky until its setting blankets the Earth in darkness again. At night the moon and stars shine clear against the black canopy of the sky, and they appear to move until daylight overtakes them.

We live our lives, literally, day by day: waking in the morning, working through the day, resting in the evening, and sleeping at night. While we know that the spinning of the Earth on its axis accounts for this rhythm—it takes twenty-four hours for the planet to spin once around—beautiful sunrises and sunsets still have the power to take our breath away, and to make us aware of the miracle of life on our planet.

Throughout most of human history, the activities of the nighttime sky were much more visible and more a part of human consciousness than they are now. With our cities lit up by electric lights, with televisions, computers, and movies to claim our attention, and with bedside lamps to read by, most of us are distracted from what is happening in the night sky. Our ancestors, however, watched the rhythm of the heavenly bodies with great interest.

Each night marks a subtle but discernible change in the shape of the moon. Sometimes the moon is not visible at all. And then it seems to magically reappear, as a slender crescent, getting bigger and bigger each night until finally it is a complete sphere of light. And then it begins to shrink until once again it disappears. This cycle, from new moon to new moon, is called a lunation. Lunations vary somewhat in length, but average twenty-nine and a half days. We now know that a lunation is the period of time it takes for the moon to orbit the Earth.

We have evidence that humans kept track of lunar cycles as early as 25,000 BCE. Lunar calendars were probably the first calendars developed throughout the world, underscoring how intimately the moon is connected to our concepts of time and measurement. Our ancestors connected the cyclical rhythm of the waxing and waning of the moon to the changes in seasons of the world around them. Ancient and traditional cultures often developed evocative names for the different lunations that corresponded to the seasons, and to the natural phenomena that nature replayed in their environment year after year.

Many of these old moon names are hard to find, and even harder to verify once you do find them. They are part of the oral traditions of hunter-gatherer and agrarian peoples from around the world, and almost everywhere they have been replaced by our modern Gregorian calendar. But some of these names were written down, and can be found if you look for them. It would take extensive field research to verify the authenticity of some of these names—and it may not be possible anyway, since so much of this traditional knowledge and language has been lost. But if we listen to them for their poetry, and for the way of life they recollect, they resonate with meaning with or without proof of their perfect accuracy.

Naturally, each culture's moon names related to the seasons as they experienced them. The Saanich (Wsanec) people of the Pacific Northwest named the moon that fell around our month of October *Pekelánew*, which can be translated as the Moon That Turns the Leaves White. An old Japanese name for the moon that fell around May was *SaTsuki*, the Moon When Rice Sprouts. An ancient Babylonian name for a moon in early spring was *Addaru*, the Moon of Threshing. A Cree name for a moon that fell roughly around our month of May was

Sakipakawpicim, or the Leaves Appear Moon. A moon in the Islamic Hijrah calendar is *Jumaada Awal*, the Moon of the First Freeze. An old German springtime moon was *Winnemanoth*, the Grazing Moon; and the lunation that corresponds to our July was—to the Maasai of East Africa—the Moon When Women Wrangle and Squabble Because the Cows Give but Little Milk.

Many cultures had names for the moon that fell around the time of year that their primary food source was harvested. Many of us have heard of the Harvest Moon, a name that has been preserved by the *Old Farmer's Almanac*. The Hopi had a moon called *Tuho'osmuya*, which has been translated as the Moon of Harvesting. An ancient Norse name for a moon was *Kornskurdarmánudr*, or Corn-Cutting Moon. There was an ancient Hebrew moon named *Hodesh ha-Aviv*, which can be translated as the Moon of the Harvest. The old Anglo Saxon calendar had a *Hærfestmo:nath*, the old Dutch calendar had a *Herstmaand*, and the old German had a *Herbistmanoth*. In all of these names can be heard the ancient importance of the harvest.

About four years ago I began writing a monthly e-letter that I send out to a list of subscribers around each new moon. I used an old moon name for that lunar cycle as my starting point for writing about food, cooking, health, and culture. I discovered that these moon names gave me a deeper sense of seasonality, and of what each time of year meant for my own ancestors as well as other cultures living in the same physical place I do (North America). They helped me to connect modern foods to culinary history and agricultural traditions. I mostly used names from the *Old Farmer's Almanac*, from indigenous North American traditions, and from Old European calendars. Writing an e-letter that comes out on the new moon, rather than once a month, has helped me to reconnect to the lunar cycles that were once so important in people's daily lives. The discipline of having a lunar deadline has actually been a great blessing in my life, and I feel more drawn than ever to living in a way that takes into account the cycles of nature and the cosmos.

This book grew out of that experience. For any moon at any time of year there are many names in many languages. I chose the names that resonate for me, and introduce topics that matter to me. In other words, these moon names do not reflect one particular culture's calendar. They are a collage of names from various calendars of peoples that have lived in the northern half of the Western Hemisphere. (I have avoided using the lunar names of peoples that lived in places dramatically different in terms of climate and geography from North America so that I could talk about issues and seasons familiar to me.) I might have called chapter 9 Harvest Moon, but I wanted to write about salmon, and so chose instead Moon When Salmon Return to Earth. Each moon name does, however, reflect a particular time of year, and the moons move through the seasons just as they do in nature.

Why are there thirteen moons? It is nearly impossible to synchronize a lunar calendar with a solar calendar. There are more than twelve lunations in a year, but fewer than thirteen. Many peoples that used a lunar calendar had thirteen moon names, one of which was used only once every three years or so (similar to our leap day), as a way to recalibrate their lunar calendar to the seasons of the solar year. In the *Old Farmer's Almanac* there were twelve regular moon names. The term *Blue Moon* was used when a month had more than one full moon, or a season had more than three. This thirteenth moon name enabled the keepers of the almanac to bring their lunar calendar into sync with the solar one. These extra moon names are called intercalary months.

According to one observer, the Maasai also had twelve regular moon names. When their moon name didn't correspond to what was happening in nature, they would recalibrate their calendar by repeating the moon name just passed. If they reached what should be the Moon When the Lesser Rains Fall (December), but the hot season was not yet actually over, they would say, "We have forgotten, it is the Moon When the Clouds Become White" (November), even though that moon had just ended. This is similar to the Chinese lunar calendar, which has occasional leap months that share the name of the previous moon.

The Islamic calendar is lunar, but is not calibrated to the solar calendar. Because it has only twelve moon names, the months rotate backward a bit each year. This means that even though one Islamic moon name is *Rabia Awal*—the Moon of First Spring—this month could fall at any time of year. Interestingly, the new lunar month in the Islamic calendar begins not at the point of the astronomical new moon, but at the point when the first crescent of moon is visible in the sky—a day, or two, or even three days later. The first sighting of the new crescent moon would be announced to the community, and the new month would begin. A similar process happened throughout the ancient Mediterranean, and in fact our English word *calendar* comes from the Latin verb *calare*, to call out.

The Hebrew calendar is also lunar. Like many other lunar calendars it uses twelve regular moon names, and then an intercalary month every few years to synchronize the moons with the solar seasons. Jewish holidays are still determined based on this traditional lunar calendar. The major holiday in the Christian liturgical calendar—Easter—is also still determined by lunar cycles. Easter falls on the first Sunday after the first full moon after the spring equinox. The word *Easter* itself appears to be a reference to the Germanic fertility goddess Eostre, who was celebrated in times of old with a lunar festival—on the vernal equinox full moon.

Most American Indian calendars had thirteen moon names, one of which wouldn't be used every year. Some cultures taught the moon names as a series described by the thirteen sections on a turtle's back. A lovely children's book called *Thirteen Moons on Turtle's Back* shows how this worked.

Although thirteen is sometimes thought to be a dangerous or unlucky number—while twelve is considered a more holy or wholesome number—I think this is a misreading. Thirteen is twelve plus one, which is holy even in the Christian context. There were twelve apostles *plus Jesus*. That makes thirteen. There are twelve moons in a year *plus one* added every few years. Some claim that the fact that the value ration between gold and silver—which has remained around one-to-thirteen since antiquity—is based on the relationship between the sun (gold) and the moon (silver). The number thirteen was sacred to the ancient Maya and remains so among modern Mayan peoples. I think there is good reason for this. Thirteen is a powerful number.

I chose to use thirteen moons as a way to draw on this power, to honor indigenous traditions, and to make the distinction between months and moons. Although the idea of a month as a unit of time is directly descended from the word for moon, and our months are roughly similar in length to the period of a lunation, our modern months have now lost all correlation to the phases of the moon. Twelve months are of course easier to manage than thirteen moons, but they have lost their connection to the waxing and waning of a heavenly body, and their names no longer resonate with what is happening in the natural world.

Naturally, because food was so important in the lives of traditional peoples, many moon names reflect what was happening on farms at a particular time of year, or what people were doing to secure food for the community. Many lunations were named for a food abundant during that moon. This makes old lunar calendars a good fit for writing about food and culinary traditions.

In my own life's journey of discovery, food has been a great guide and teacher. I've spent countless hours over the years in my kitchen—cooking or engaged in other culinary projects and pursuits. I've also read extensively about traditional foodways, health, nutrition, and culinary history. My fascination has led me to learn more about agriculture, visit many farms and ranches, get to know farmers, and shop at farmer's markets—where I ask lots of questions and get inspired over and over to try something new. All of these pursuits have opened up a world of connections between the deep spirituality of this fundamental necessity—food—and the benefits of recovering a whole relationship to it.

Life is a great mystery and an enormous blessing. I am honored to share with you this taste of life as I've experienced it. May it be sweet.

FULL
MOON
FEAST

1

HUNGER MOON

In want and hunger was their lot,
  They who fled to the parched wastelands:
They plucked saltwort and shrubs;
  The roots of the broom plant were their food.

—JOB 30:3–4, TRANSLATED FROM THE HEBREW

In the deep of winter, when the earth in the North has been covered with snow and ice for many moons already, comes the Hunger Moon. This late-winter lunar cycle was called the Hunger Moon by many peoples in various languages, but always for the same reason—the frozen land yielded little to eat, and game was often scarce.

European American settlers in the New England area adopted the name as one of the full-moon names used in the *Old Farmer's Almanac*. They adapted it from Native American calendars, particularly the ones used by the various Algonquin peoples that lived in the northeastern areas of what is now the United States, from New England to the Great Lakes.

Indigenous names for the moon were as varied as the languages that they came from, but often carried similar meanings. The Choctaw name for this moon is translated Little Famine Moon; a Cherokee name is the Bony Moon or the Bone Moon because it was said that there was so little food, people gnawed on bones and ate bone marrow soup to survive. All of these names lament the scarcity of food. In the days before refrigeration and wide-scale shipping of produce and staples, hunger often became a real threat by the end of a long winter. Both hunter-gatherer societies and farming peoples subsisted on very little after months of bitter cold.

For the agrarian peoples in the Northern Hemisphere such as the new European American farmsteaders, fresh produce was unavailable when the fields were covered with snow and ice. Farmers worked hard to prepare for the season, and this final stretch of freezing weather tested their reserves. The root cellar of a well-prepared farmhouse might still hold some beets, potatoes, turnips, onions, winter squash, and root vegetables. The barrel of dry beans wouldn't be quite empty yet. There would still be some smoked ham, salt pork, or corned beef. Fresh green vegetables would be nearly impossible to find, but a crock of sauerkraut might still be yielding. Wheat, rye, dried corn, and other grains could be ground for baking into bread, or soaked for porridge, or cooked into pancakes and other quick meals.

Few of us in the United States today ever experienced seasonal shortages of food. Insufficient income is more likely to be the reason for any scarcity. As long as we have the money, we can get just about any kind of food whenever we want it. Food is no less readily available during the late-winter Hunger Moon than it is during the late-summer Harvest Moon when agricultural production is at its peak. We no longer experience the annual cycle of scarcity and abundance familiar to our ancestors.

Growing up in the land of plenty, long after the Great Depression and World War II rationing were things of the past, I have never witnessed a time of widespread lack of food. Instead, all I saw around me as I was growing up was more, more, more. Myriad packaged products on the shelf competed for my attention. A full fridge, a full

Buried Treasure

Thirteen vegetable foods from the old-fashioned root cellar:

1. Beets
2. Celery Root
3. Parsnips
4. Rutabaga
5. Turnips
6. Carrots
7. Potatoes
8. Onions
9. Garlic
10. Pumpkins
11. Sweet Potatoes
12. Dry Beans
13. Cabbage

freezer, a full pantry, full grocery stores, full candy machines, full cafe-
terias, a full bowl every morning and a full plate every night, day after
day, month after month, year after year—that's the America I grew up
in. My trick-or-treat bag brimmed every Halloween, and my stocking
was stuffed every Christmas. We had candies galore at Easter and pic-
nics on the Fourth of July. On our birthdays we got to choose what we
wanted for dinner, and it always appeared.

We were not rich. My mother worked at a low-paying office job, and
my dad stayed home to write and take care of us. We lived in small
rentals and then a small fixer-upper. New clothes were considered luxuries; there were plenty of things we couldn't have because we couldn't
afford them. But there were no Hunger Moons in my childhood.

As I reached adolescence, something began to shift in my relationship to food. When I was fourteen I became a vegetarian, convinced
by an older student that eating meat was wrong in a world where
people still suffered from hunger, and animals died cruelly and unnec-
essarily. It was a decision that ultimately had some negative consequences, but at the time I was proud of myself for taking a stand.

By the time I was fifteen I had learned that not only was meat bad,
but fat was bad, salt was bad, and sugar was bad. I put myself on a no-
fat, no-sugar, no-salt vegetarian diet and stuck to it for as long as I
could, despite my constant hunger—and for a long time afterward still
considered it an ideal diet. In high school I began to bring to school
every day a lunch that consisted of a whole wheat pita bread stuffed
with chopped dry raw vegetables: carrots, peppers, celery, sprouts. No
cheese, no sauce, no oil or mayonnaise. Eating that during my lunch
break at school, I felt virtuous and healthy—but I was still hungry. In
fact I was ravenous. But going to the candy machine or the cafeteria
would, I felt, spoil my healthful lunch. And yet I had hours of classes
yet to go, tests to take, rehearsals to attend. I found myself in a conundrum—should I eat more and blow my diet, or should I press on fam-
ished and try to make it through the afternoon without a snack?

I felt guilty for being hungry. I had eaten. I was surrounded by food.
I lived in America. I was privileged. Compared with the rest of the
world I was rich. Why should I want more? Why should I crave french
fries and candy? I would often give in to my cravings and binge on junk

food—ice cream, potato chips, cookies, whatever. Then I became filled with self-disgust. I felt overfull. I was stuffed. I felt sick. Why had I eaten that? Why had I done that? What was wrong with me? Didn't holy people fast? Didn't holy people need hardly any food? Didn't I want to be thin? Wasn't I putting on weight? Wasn't my skin breaking out? Probably the french fries had done that! Why was I worrying about food? Weren't there more important things? Shouldn't I be writing poetry or falling in love or doing something—anything—more profound than worrying about what I ate?

Regardless of what I actually ate—whether it was salads or pizzas or Thanksgiving dinner—I never felt satisfied or truly nourished. I was in a continual state of either hunger or overfullness, often experiencing both at the same time. It would be years before I figured out why this was so. But at the time, my worry about what I was eating gave way to worry over worrying about what I was eating. My obsession with food seemed unhealthy, pathological, and I needed to get over it.

But I didn't. On and on it went like that: dieting, bingeing, feeling hungry, feeling stuffed, feeling sick, making resolutions to do better, failing to do better, hating myself for failing, hating myself for hating myself. It went on for years. By the time I was nineteen and in college I wrote in my diary:

> It is time for change . . .
>
> It is time to establish a positive relationship to food—to form new habits. This is going to involve discipline and that hated but very useful mechanism—a system.
>
> I want firm goals—
>
> By my twentieth birthday I want to have firmly established an effective system for coping with my negative relationship to food.
>
> By my twenty-first birthday I want to have ingrained this system into my lifestyle to the extent that it's almost second nature.
>
> The most important ritual of coming of age that I could go through during this period (the next sixteen

months) would be to truly overcome my compulsive eating and my obsessive thoughts about it.

This will be an arduous and painful process—both the development of a system and its carrying out. But the time has come to grow up; to move beyond this.

I find it hard now to read what I wrote as a suffering youth. I have to shake my head when I think about my desire for a system, for an answer, or about my belief in discipline to solve problems. I am struck by the fact that I so clearly viewed the problem as a problem with me—it was *my* negative relationship with food; it was my job to cure myself. It was my job to embark on an arduous and painful process to move beyond what I viewed as a shallow preoccupation. It never occurred to me that all of America might be suffering from what journalist Michael Pollan would later call "our national eating disorder."

Here I am, seventeen years later. Did I ever develop a system? No. Did I ever move beyond a preoccupation with food? No. But that wasn't really what I wanted, even then, at nineteen. I just wanted to stop suffering in my relationship with food. And that indeed happened. I finally just stopped fighting against food, and dived into it headlong. And I found it, after all, a fascinating and profound place to be. Food grabbed my attention, forcing me to study it, meditate on it, and finally to appreciate the depths of meaning and spirituality it entails. Food, as a topic, engages the body, mind, and soul. Working with it and thinking about it teaches me, day after day, moon after moon, how to be a human being. It has opened me to the world of politics, of history, of art, of pleasure, of anger, of grief, of faith—all the profound things I thought food was keeping me from. It has helped me to feel God's healing presence in my life, and taught me how to be vulnerable, how to love, and how to let go.

When I was still in college—probably not long after I wrote that diary entry—I read a book called *The Obsession* by Kim Chernin. In it she discusses eating disorders, putting them in a social and historical context, and looking at them from a feminist perspective. The book precipitated a breakthrough in my relationship with food: I realized that I wasn't alone. Although I had heard of eating disorders, I didn't think I had one. I wasn't bulimic, and I wasn't anorexic; I was just obsessed. Sometimes, in fact, I had wished that I *did* have an eating disorder, because then someone might intervene, check me into a program, and help me get healthy. But reading Chernin's book I began to see that my dysfunctional relationship with food existed on a continuum—one that included anorexics and bulimics and me—and millions of other Americans, many of them young women, who might not have had anything as diagnosable as an eating disorder but still struggled and felt miserable in their hunger, in their bingeing, in their bodies. All of a sudden I saw my own issues as something other than a personal failing. Something was happening culturally and societally. I began to wonder if our individual struggles with food could be reflecting a failure in how we handle food in this country. I was not looking for a place to lay the blame for my pain—I had been taking the blame for years. But I suddenly realized that my pain had a certain social and historical context, and that I could never sort out my own troubles with food without understanding the way my people related to food. I was not an island; I was part of a whole. I belonged to a place and time.

Still, my problems with food were far from over. Gradually I moved from a place of emotional suffering to a place of physical suffering. While my teens were full of angst, my twenties were marked by a series of frightening illnesses. I think my dietary choices had no small part to play in my poor health, and I continued to look to food as key to my own healing. I eventually had to let go of almost everything I thought I knew about food, and let myself be led to a deeper place, a deeper understanding, a knowledge that came not so much from my head as from the cells of my body. It has been a long journey that has brought me now, in my thirties, to a place of recovery and true nourishment. As my body heals, so, too, do my soul and my aching heart. I am learning to eat in a way that feeds not only my physical hunger, but also my hunger for connection.

Although bookstores are full of advice on how to be healthy or thin or both, and there is a constant stream of media telling us which foods are good for us and which are bad, I have found very little of what I hear about food in contemporary America to be useful to me. The surfeit of information doesn't help me eat well—in fact, it confuses me and sets me back—and it doesn't help me to feed any other hunger either. To do that, I have had to look outside my own time and place (contemporary America), to the way people have, in other times and places, related to food. How did they explain, understand, and resolve questions about where food comes from, how it grows, when and how we should eat and prepare it? I find that looking at traditional, indigenous, and historical foodways has fed me in a deep and meaningful way, and led me out of my self-referential conundrum around food.

Our first experience of food is often synonymous with love: We are held, we are fed, and we are cared for—all at the same moment, by our mothers. In Hindu tradition the first rite of passage occurs when a baby reaches six months old—when he or she eats a mouthful of rice, the first food that is not mother's milk. The rice-eating ceremony is celebrated in the presence of a priest, often in a temple, with a gathering of relatives to witness this important transition in the child's life. Mantras and prayers are said. Such a ceremony reflects a worldview where food is sacred—a blessing and a gift—and being fed is not to be taken for granted.

Our culture doesn't express this worldview. We look at food as fuel, as something we need to keep going—our Energizer battery. We view food as a commodity, something that people need and so a thing that can generate a profit. Of course food *is* fuel and it *is* a commodity, but that is not all it is. I think that many of my teenage struggles with food came as a reaction against the commodification, commercialization, and overall undervaluation of food in our culture. If my grandparents had displayed what is often called a Depression-era mentality, maybe I displayed an Excess-era mentality. Maybe all those boxes on the supermarket shelves, the continual bombardment of commercials from the

TV, and the abundance of the food itself played a part in the way I felt about what I ate and what I refused to eat.

The Excess-era mentality that I grew up around, along with the widespread adulteration of food with preservatives, chemicals, colors, flavors, and textures that originated in a laboratory instead of a kitchen, made food feel like something that was tainted, something unclean, fake, and artificial. I reacted by trying to be a food purist. Hence my lunch of pita bread filled with dry diced vegetables and sprouts. I thought eating that way would make me pure.

The Hopi have called this late-winter moon, which falls around February, *Powamuya*—the Purification Moon. It is interesting that the word *February* comes from the Latin phrase *Februarius mensis*, meaning "the month of Februa." Februa was a Roman festival of purification that was celebrated every February 15, and so February was the month (moon) of *februa* (purification). In the Christian calendar, the period of Lent begins on Ash Wednesday, which falls in the beginning of February and lasts for forty days leading up to Easter. That is also a time of purification, of fasting, and of prayer. It is a time of intentional, conscious hunger.

I wonder how different my teenage years would have been if I had lived in a culture in which fasting, hunger, or purification were ritualized by the community, and were part of an annual cycle. Would I have spent years depriving myself of nourishment if there had been a Hunger Moon or Purification Moon in my calendar? Or if I had grown up in a time when my community observed the period of Lent through repentance and prayer? Or if my village held a purification festival at the end of winter?

And what if these practices were not about punishment, but about celebration and acknowledgment? Scarcity can be ritualized as a way of acknowledging it without having to actually suffer it. It can be seen as part of a cyclical whole, a new moon's darkness to the full moon's light.

Or what if I had simply grown up in a time when food was seasonal? When there was, in each year, a time of more and a time of less? When food was not just there in packages on the supermarket shelf all year? What if I had grown up watching the planting, watering, and harvesting of crops, the threshing and winnowing of grains and beans, the drying of corn, and the careful calculations involved in making sure there would be enough food to last until springtime? Would I have inflicted unnecessary hunger on myself, privately and painfully, if hunger had been honored and ritualized in my culture, and food considered precious and holy?

Teacher and thinker Jeanette Armstrong has shared a model of a healthy community that is drawn from her indigenous Okanagan culture. In this model, a thriving community balances four societies: the Fathers, the Mothers, the Youth, and the Elders. Each of these societies embodies a set of strengths and values that don't necessarily have to do with gender or age. The Fathers are those who take action to ensure the safety and security of the community. The Mothers are those who take care of the relationships within a village or tribe, and tend to the community's day-to-day needs. The Youth are those who have a vision for the future of the community—of what can be changed, reformed, or improved. And the Elders are the ones who keep traditions alive, holding the wisdom of generations and connection to the land. All four of these elements—Action, Relationship, Vision, and Tradition/Place—are essential to a thriving society.

Armstrong points out that European American culture emphasizes Action and Vision, and undervalues Relationship and Tradition. I see this feature of our society very clearly with regard to food. Proponents of our current food system argue that its industrialization is necessary to ensure Americans an ample, safe supply of food. And much has been accomplished along these lines. We grow a lot of food in this country (Action). The USDA, the FDA, and our state departments of health compose an elaborate system that aims to keep our food supply safe (Action). All of this is the result of a vision to feed a lot of people in a safe and efficient manner and to ensure economic growth (Vision).

Unfortunately the equally important areas of Relationship and Tradition/Place have not informed our Action and Vision plans. Our current food system has virtually severed our citizenry's relationship to the Earth and to the processes of planting, tending, and harvesting. Farmers themselves do little actual fieldwork, most of it now handled by big machinery. Planting is a matter of driving one machine that releases seeds; harvesting means driving another machine that cuts the plants. Tending the fields often involves little more than flying overhead in a plane that drops chemicals onto the plants to kill the pests that would normally afflict them. Feeding the soil is accomplished at a distance by injecting chemical fertilizers into an automated irrigation supply.

Processing agricultural products into meals has undergone a similar severing of relationship. Commercial factories now produce canned, frozen, dried, and other processed foodstuffs using heavy equipment and machinery and a minimum of low-paid labor. These packaged products line shelf after shelf of our grocery stores, while advertising campaigns make a feeble attempt to create some sense of relationship among the product, the ingredients it was made from, and the people who consume it. But it is a fabricated relationship—an image of a relationship, not the real thing.

In the rush to industrialize our food system, tradition has not only been ignored, it has been actively shunned. We make the assumption that the new thing is the better thing, indicating progress and vision, and that the old thing is obsolete. But vision, to be healthy, must be balanced by tradition. Unfortunately our country neglects tradition. Activities that were commonplace aspects of our food system during my grandmother's generation less than a century ago are now completely antiquated: milking the family cow, pressing apples for cider, threshing and winnowing grain, making bread, churning butter, pickling cucumbers, curing meat. These tasks were regularly done at home on a human scale in the context of relationship until widespread industrialization.

The loss of traditions has resulted in an incalculable sacrifice in food quality, and I believe that all of our modern diseases—heart disease, cancer, diabetes, autoimmune disorders, allergies, and addictions—can be linked, at least to some extent, to a lack of vitality in the food we grow, process, and eat. This lack results from a food system that has sacrificed relationship and tradition in the pursuit of its vision for action.

Fortunately a few people have seen the dangers of a chemically dependent, factory-dominated food supply, and have worked to keep

agricultural and culinary traditions alive. The organic farming movement has helped to preserve the knowledge of composting and cover
cropping, of interplanting and crop rotation. The Slow Food movement
acknowledges and rewards artisanal and traditional food processing on
a community scale. The native nutrition movement is keeping alive the
nutritional wisdom of our ancestors and of healthy indigenous peoples
from around the world. But we still have a long way to go if we wish to
create a sense of balance of the four societies in our food system. Until
that time, Mothers and others will have to find ways to restore
Relationship, Tradition, and a sense of Place to our daily nourishment.

One of the simplest and yet most profound changes that I made in my
diet after I moved to California thirteen years ago was that I began to
eat seasonally and shop at farmer's markets. This turned out to be a
huge step toward recovering relationship and tradition in my life. Just
visiting a farmer's market gives me a sense of the season and a direct
connection with the people who spend their days growing food.
Eating seasonally reconnects me to the natural pulse of life, the
Earth's annual cycle of cold and heat, wet and dry, long nights and
then long days as it makes its journey around the sun. These annual
cycles make me more mindful of the eternal realities of birth, growth,
death, decay, and rebirth. They keep me aware of my humanness and
my mortality as well as my kinship and interdependence with all other
life on Earth.

For many of us, our interest in seasonality is somewhat selective.
We want the warmth without the cold; we want the long days without
the long nights; we want the abundance without the scarcity; we want
the birth and growth without the death and decay. But without the
death and decay there is no rebirth. Abundance is a subjective experience, not an objective reality. It is something that we *feel*, not something that we *have*. Those of us who have gone traveling to a so-called
poor country and encountered an amazing spirit of generosity and a
true sense of abundance can attest to this. We find it surprising and
charming and quite exotic.

Without the sense of scarcity, there is no sense of abundance, because there is no perspective. At the height of the summer, when there are bountiful fresh juicy tomatoes, sweet corn, crisp green beans, and peaches that are bursting with flavor, we may flock to the farmer's markets and celebrate the joys of the harvest. But our enthusiasm doesn't last through the Hunger Moon. Beets, dry beans, ham, and sauerkraut don't have the same sex appeal as the sweet juicy offerings of summer. Around the country most farmer's markets close during the winter due to lack of produce or customers when the weather is cold. During the Hunger Moon we return to the supermarkets to buy produce imported from tropical countries where the sun still shines. Our interest in seasonality is seasonal.

Where I live in the San Francisco Bay Area, many farmer's markets are open year-round, and our Mediterranean climate means that the Hunger Moon still yields a cornucopia of fresh produce: lettuces, winter greens, herbs, cabbages, root vegetables, winter squash, and citrus fruit. But there are also many things that aren't available from local fields at this time of year, not only tomatoes, corn, green beans, and peaches, but also peppers, eggplant, grapes, zucchinis, plums, and berries. Even apples, pears, pomegranates, and sweet potatoes are past their prime and difficult to find in good form.

After years of eating seasonally, I find that I no longer have any interest in summer foods during wintertime. Knowing there will be delicious and beautiful tomatoes galore come August, I hold that expectation in private delight. It feeds my hunger for connection, my deep desire to be in touch with the planet and its cycles and phases, the profound intelligence that is at work in the universe. A tomato on my table at this time of year would be disconcerting and out of place. Life would feel out of whack, disrupted, disturbed. Eating a tomato in February would be like opening your Christmas presents at Thanksgiving. It would spoil the fun and kill the anticipation.

Eating seasonally, even during the heart of winter, has also let me discover truly unexpected pleasures and joys. It has pushed me to explore the ignored or forgotten gems of the old-fashioned root cellar: parsnips, beets, rutabagas, turnips, parsley root, celeriac, salsify. If these names make your nose turn up, you may not have enjoyed well-prepared dishes made with these vegetables. If some of them are new to you, you have a treat in store. These foods lend themselves to warming meals like creamed soups and chowders. There's hardly anything I'd rather eat on a cold winter day than a bowl of thick soup.

Nevertheless, it took me years to figure out how to cook salsify, and to really enjoy it and look forward to it. I still haven't achieved a fondness for Jerusalem artichokes. They are earthy and intriguing and someday I certainly hope to.

A dashing, blue-eyed farmer named David is part of the reason I'm not giving up on Jerusalem artichokes, also known as sunchokes. David grows organic potatoes in Marin County (just a few miles from San Francisco) and is one of my favorite farmers. Phone conversations with him are a bit like counseling sessions. He vacillates about whether or not he should stick with farming and whether or not the work he does is really worth the trouble. He has a family—a wife and two adolescent children—and making ends meet as a small farmer is challenging. He doesn't own land suitable for potato farming, and so each year he rents different small parcels of land from landowners in the county—usually acreage that has been fallow for a while. In the spring he drives his tractor to these spots and tills and plants potatoes using a tillage technique called dry farming. Rainfall is scarce in these parts in the summer, so David tills the soil with a tractor and then presses the top layer down with a roller in such a way that moisture from winter rains gets trapped in the soil under a top layer of dry crust. This way he doesn't have to do any irrigating, making wise use of the winter's rainfall. By autumn he has twenty or more varieties of heirloom and hybrid potatoes—pink skinned, purple fleshed, Yukon gold,

Be a Locavore!

Thirteen plant foods that can be grown successfully anywhere in the continental United States, and so can be eaten locally and in season without any need for importation:

1. Apples
2. Lettuce
3. Carrots
4. Potatoes
5. Onions
6. Tomatoes
7. Strawberries
8. Corn
9. Peppers
10. Raspberries and blackberries
11. Greens (spinach, collards, kale)
12. Herbs (thyme, sage, oregano, basil)
13. Root vegetables (beets, turnips, rutabaga)

fingerling, russets, and many more that he sells at area farmer's markets throughout the fall and winter.

When I directed the education programs for the large Ferry Plaza Farmers Market in downtown San Francisco, I led a number of farm tours. One of them took us to a one-acre parcel of land that David had recently harvested. He had been nice enough to leave a row of potatoes in the ground for us to harvest. I wanted the people on the tour to have the experience of digging up potatoes for themselves. While David harvests his potatoes mechanically for market, they are actually quite easy to dig without a tool. We dug our bare hands into the rich, loose ground to find the hidden treasure buried there underneath the straggly brown stems that still stuck out into the air. You could hear cries of delight as people found each new potato, dug it up, and put it into their paper bags. We felt just as good as a dog that has found a precious buried bone. It was such a pleasure to watch forty urbanites digging in the dirt on a day full of magical sunshine while David's little dog Dottie Mae jumped and yipped and helped dig. If I could show you that scene, I would have to do nothing more to convince you that people (even sophisticated city folk) are hungry for relationship with their food source. They long to know where their food comes from and to have the opportunity to play in the dirt every once in a while. One woman told me after digging those potatoes that she'd had the most fun she could remember ever having. I'm not surprised. Some days are magical like that.

We can feed our hunger for connection by eating seasonally and also by buying directly from small farmers at the farmer's market. Forming relationships with the people who grow our food, and taking up opportunities to visit their farms, is a healing practice. It is important for the farmers as well. The majority of small farmers are not in it for the money—farming is no longer lucrative. They do it because they have a love of independence, because they love working with the land, and often because they believe in building a food system that is based on relationship. They get immense satisfaction when their customers take an interest in their farming practices and in how and why they grow their produce.

But what does all of this have to do with Jerusalem artichokes? Well, it happens that David doesn't grow just potatoes, but also a few other crops: some winter squash, onions, garlic, and Jerusalem artichokes. Recently I was at the farmer's market shopping quickly for a catering job, and stopped briefly at his stand to say hello. He wouldn't let me leave without handing me a large bag of the sunchokes and telling me to cook them. "How should I cook them?" I asked. "Just boiled with salt and butter." *Easy enough*, I thought, *I'll give it a try*.

I took them to the catering job and as I cooked the meal, I debated whether or not I should serve the sunchokes as well. I'd tried them once before, as part of a recipe for a vegetarian potpie, and remembered finding the flavor obtrusive. But I wanted to branch out; I wanted to like them. I boiled them right there at the catering job and then cut into a steaming hot, knobby little nugget and plopped it in my mouth, hoping to fall in love. I didn't. *Yuck*, I thought, and decided against serving them. Back at the market the next week, I relayed my findings to David. He said he was going to try growing a different variety next year and asked if I would give them another chance. "Of course," I assured him. If I hadn't kept trying to like salsify or rutabaga I certainly wouldn't love them now. When you don't grow up with a memory of something tasting wonderful, you sometimes have to work a little bit to learn to love it. There's always a chance that you'll never learn to like a thing, but you don't know that until you really try. My relationship with David inspires me to try again.

Until I began working at a farmer's market I hadn't really understood that, from a monetary point of view, all produce is not created equal. Some produce has good press or current vogue and can therefore fetch a good price and help support a farmer. Heirloom tomatoes are a perfect example. Customers pay top dollar for them. Berries are another such crop. One farmer I know, a charming young grower named Brandon, farms year-round, growing winter produce such as broccoli and leeks when it is cold, and tomatoes, strawberries, and raspberries when it is warm. But out of his whole year of farming, he claims that he makes up to 90 percent of his annual income in a six-week period during July and August, from his high-volume, high-profit sales of tomatoes and berries. The broccoli and leeks don't even really pay for themselves, it turns out. So why does he even grow them?

He grows non-income-producing crops because they improve the quality of his soil and the vitality of his high-earning crops. He plants the broccoli in a field where he just harvested strawberries because it helps keep the field from harboring fungi and pests that would ruin the strawberries in the second or third year. Growing winter crops also enables him to employ his farm workers year-round, rather than just seasonally. He has seen firsthand the havoc that having only seasonal work can have both on migrant workers and on their communities. Workers are unable to build stability in their family lives, and this impacts communities where large segments of the population come and go with the annual harvest season. Elementary school classes swell and shrink, schools have a hard time getting adequate funding, and it becomes hard for teachers to teach and students to learn with so much inconsistency. Brandon wants his workers to be able to support their families year-round and keep their kids in the same school from September until June. He grows winter crops to help make this possible.

Many small farmers are committed to having diversified crops that provide good food year-round. They plant broccoli so that people will have broccoli. If farmers only planted the crops that were highly profitable, it would be like saying, *Let them eat cake!* Or rather *Let them eat berries!* Many farmers don't farm just for money; they farm to grow food. And food is a lot more than the crops that are popular because they are sweet and easy to eat such as grapes, peaches, tomatoes, plums, berries, and apricots—all of which fetch a high price in the farmer's market economy.

If heirloom tomatoes are on the top of the produce hierarchy, rutabagas are on the bottom. It's hard to get people to buy them, period, much less pay enough to support the farmer who's growing them. Turnips and Jerusalem artichokes suffer the same problem. While summer crops are the candy crops, winter vegetables are the old-fashioned staples—starchy roots that would see a family through the Hunger Moon. With a seasonless array of imported vegetables and fruits available almost any time of day or night at a grocery store within a few minutes of our homes, these hardy survivors of an earlier era are a hard sell.

But there are many reasons to celebrate and enjoy winter produce. They taste wonderful. (Try some of the following recipes and tell me if that's not so.) They are nutritious and make your diet more biodiverse and interesting. They are affordable. (I get a lot of food value for my dollar with winter produce.) And buying such produce from local farmers helps them to farm year-round (or at least for a longer season), maintaining the integrated, small-scale farming systems and stable work environments that are about feeding people and sustaining community rather than just making a buck.

And of course eating winter produce in winter helps me reconnect with the Earth's rhythms and with the seasonal reality of my forebears. It reminds me that to everything there is a season and a time. It helps me let go of my desire to have whatever I want, whenever I want it, instantly. It helps me appreciate that which I have been given and to accept it gratefully. A long night in the Hunger Moon will be warmed immeasurably by a thick, creamy bowl of Cream of Parsnip Soup. Eating it with a chunk of good aged cheddar on a slice of dark bread, it is a little bit of Heaven on Earth. It is no sacrifice at all, just a return to the simplicity and beauty of eating with wisdom and appreciation.

I have discovered that I am not the only one in this land of plenty who is hungry, deeply hungry. And I have also come to discover that there actually is food on Earth that will feed our hunger; that will leave us feeling satisfied, well fed, and blessed. Even so, our hunger will return, day after day, moon after moon, until our moons upon the Earth are over. This cycle of hunger and satiety is as natural as the ebbing and flowing of the tides, the waxing and waning of the moon.

On the Hunger Moon, I send out a prayer that our food system may begin to shift some of its energy from offering us *quantity* to offering us *quality*. May we acknowledge that there is a time of purification and hunger and want, and yet be comforted with the knowledge that spring will soon be here, that the Earth will flower again, and the abundance of the harvest will follow behind. May we be full of gratitude to the Earth that feeds us. May we remember that after the Hunger Moon comes the Sap Moon, and that is sweet consolation indeed.

HUNGER MOON RECIPES

Cream of Parsnip Soup
Serves 3–4

2 tablespoons butter or olive oil

2–3 leeks, sliced into rounds and well rinsed

4 medium or 1–2 large parsnips, cut into chunks

1 quart chicken stock (preferably a light-colored stock; page 299) or filtered water

1 bouquet garni (page 309)

1 cup whole milk (preferably raw) or half-and-half (also preferably raw) or

¾ cup raw cream, crème fraîche, yogurt, or buttermilk

Salt and pepper to taste

Dollop of crème fraîche or yogurt, for garnish

Finely minced rosemary, thyme, sage, or parsley leaves (or a combination of these herbs); or a grating of nutmeg; or a grind of black pepper, for garnish

1. Heat the butter or oil in a medium-sized soup pot. Add the leeks and sauté until soft.
2. Add the parsnips and sauté for a minute or so.
3. Add the stock or water to cover the vegetables by about ½ inch. Add the bouquet garni, cover, and bring the pot to a boil.
4. Reduce the heat and simmer, covered, until all is tender.
5. Turn off the heat. At this point you can let the soup cool a little by letting it sit, uncovered, or transferring it to a serving bowl. If you are using raw or cultured dairy, this will help to preserve the enzymes.
6. Remove the bouquet garni.
7. Puree the soup with an immersion blender (or in a standard blender), adding the milk or other dairy until the soup is the consistency you like, and adding salt and pepper generously as you blend. Taste the soup and adjust the seasonings.
8. Serve with a dollop of crème fraîche or yogurt and a sprinkling of herbs, nutmeg, or pepper.

Beet Borscht
Serves 4

Borscht is great served with a dark, whole-grain bread—especially one with rye in it, spread thick with butter and perhaps a hunk of cheese. A salad of crisp lettuce with hard-cooked eggs is also a great accompaniment.

2 tablespoons butter, ghee, or olive oil

1 onion, sliced or chopped small

½ teaspoon (or more, to taste) caraway seeds (optional)

1 carrot, thinly sliced

1 stalk celery or 1 parsley root, thinly sliced

1 small can (14.5 oz) diced tomatoes or tomato puree, or 1 tablespoon tomato paste (optional)

1 bunch medium red beets (or one very large red beet), peeled and thinly sliced

1 quart beef stock (page 231) or filtered water

1 bay leaf

Salt and pepper to taste

½ cup beet kvass or rusell (see page 309), ¼ cup brine from homemade pickles (see page 312), or a teaspoon of apple cider vinegar or other vinegar, to taste

Sauerkraut, made from either red or green cabbage (page 252)—or add a handful shredded fresh cabbage after the carrots

Crème fraîche, sour cream, or yogurt, for garnish

Fresh dill, chives, or scallions for garnish (optional)

1. Heat the butter or oil in a medium-sized soup pot. Add the onions with the caraway seeds and sauté for a moment. Add the carrot and celery, and sauté until soft. (If you are using fresh cabbage instead of sauerkraut, add it now.)
2. Add the tomatoes, puree, or paste and heat through.
3. Add the beets and the stock or water. It is good to cover the vegetables with liquid by about ½ inch. You may need to add a bit more water or stock to make sure this is the case.
4. Add the bay leaf and bring the pot to a boil.
5. Reduce the heat, cover, and simmer until all is tender.
6. Turn off the heat and remove the bay leaf.
7. Add a big pinch of salt and a grind of pepper to the pot. Taste the soup and adjust the seasonings by adding salt, pepper, and kvass, brine, or vinegar to taste.
8. Put a spoonful of sauerkraut in the middle of a shallow bowl and then ladle the soup over it.
9. Serve with a dollop of crème fraîche, sour cream, or yogurt and a sprinkling of fresh dill, chives, or scallions if desired.

Oyster Plant Chowder (Salsify Soup)
Serves 3–4

3 tablespoons butter

1 small white or yellow onion, diced

3–4 stalks celery, diced

4–6 salsify roots, scrubbed, cut into ½-inch rounds and tossed immediately into lemon water

2 small potatoes, diced

1 bay leaf

1 sprig of thyme

Filtered water or chicken stock (page 299) to cover, about a quart

½ cup cream or crème fraîche, or 1 cup milk or half-and-half

Salt and pepper to taste

1. Melt the butter in a heavy-bottomed pot or saucepan over medium heat.
2. Add the onion and sauté until soft and translucent, then add the celery and sauté for a few moments.
3. Add the salsify, potatoes, bay leaf, sprig of thyme, and enough water or stock to cover the vegetables.
4. Turn the heat to high, cover the pot, and bring to a boil. Reduce the heat and simmer until the salsify and potato are fork-tender.
5. Remove bay leaf and thyme sprig, then add the cream, crème fraîche, milk, or half-and-half.
6. Use an immersion blender to partially puree the soup, leaving some chunks. (If you use a regular blender, blend about half the soup and leave the other half as is.)
7. Turn off the heat. Add a generous pinch of salt and a few grinds of black pepper.
8. Stir and taste. Add salt until the chowder is savory and delicious.
9. Serve with a sprinkling of paprika, cracked pepper, or a dollop of crème fraîche, and maybe a few oyster crackers just for fun.

Winter Minestrone
Serves 4–5

2 tablespoons extra-virgin olive oil, beef tallow, or other fat

1 large onion or 2 leeks, chopped

1 large carrot, diced small

2–3 stalks celery (or use celery root, parsley root, or parsley stems), chopped

1–2 root vegetables such as turnip, rutabaga, golden beet, or salsify, peeled and diced

Shredded leaves of a small bunch of winter greens such as escarole, lacinato kale, collards, chard, or cabbage (or a combination of these)

1 small can (14.5 oz) chopped tomatoes, or a dollop of tomato paste, or some tomato sauce

1 cup or more well-cooked chickpeas, or kidney, gigante, or cannellini beans (optional)

1 quart filtered water, beef broth (page 231), or a combination

1 bouquet garni (page 309)

Salt and pepper to taste

A splash of red wine vinegar or pickle brine (see page 312) if more acidity is needed

A grating of hard aged cheese such as Parmesan or a sprinkle of minced herbs (any of the herbs in the bouquet garni would work), for garnish

1. Heat the oil in a heavy-bottomed stainless-steel pan over medium-high heat.
2. When the oil is hot, add the onion and sauté, then add the carrot, celery, root vegetable, and greens in turn, sautéing each for a minute or two before adding the next.
3. Add the tomatoes, paste, or sauce and sauté until warmed through.
4. Add the beans or chickpeas, if using.
5. Add the water or broth and the bouquet garni.
6. Cover and bring to a boil, then lower the heat and simmer until all is tender.
7. Add the salt and pepper and then taste for salt, acidity, and spiciness. Add a splash of vinegar if desired. If the soup is too thick, add filtered water as needed.
8 Serve with a grating of cheese on top, or a sprinkling of fresh herbs, or a grating of black pepper, or a drizzle of olive oil. (Or all of the above!)

Golden Vegetable Bisque
Serves 4–5

2 tablespoons butter or olive oil

2–3 leeks, sliced into rounds
and well rinsed

1 small celery root (aka celeriac),
peeled and cut into chunks

1 parsnip, cut into chunks

1 rutabaga, cut into chunks, and/or
1 golden turnip, cut into chunks

1 carrot, cut into chunks

1 bouquet garni (page 309)

1 quart chicken stock (preferably a
light-colored stock; page 299)
or filtered water

¾ cup raw cream, crème fraîche,
yogurt, buttermilk, raw whole milk,
or half-and-half (or more as needed)

Salt and pepper to taste

A dollop of crème fraîche, for garnish

Finely minced rosemary, thyme, sage,
or parsley leaves (or a combination of
these herbs); or a grating of nutmeg;
or a grind of black pepper, for garnish

1. Heat the butter or oil in a medium-sized soup pot. Add the leeks and sauté until tender.
2. Add the vegetables one by one, sautéing each for a moment.
3. Add the stock or water to cover the vegetables by about ½ inch. Add the bouquet garni, cover, and bring to a boil.
4. Reduce the heat and simmer, covered, until all is tender, about 15 minutes.
5. Turn off the heat. At this point you can let the soup cool a little by letting it sit uncovered or transferring it to a serving bowl. If you are using raw or cultured dairy, this will help to preserve the enzymes.
6. Remove the bouquet garni.
7. Puree the soup with an immersion blender (or in a standard blender), adding the cream, or other dairy, until the soup is the consistency you like. Add a big pinch of salt and pepper as you blend. Taste the soup and adjust the seasonings.
8. Serve with any of the garnishes above.

Roasted Root Vegetables
Serves 1 person for every ¾ cup of vegetables

You can use any of the following vegetables, in any combination:

Celery root (aka celeriac), peeled
Parsnip
Rutabaga
Turnip (either white, purple, or
   golden)
Beets (either red, golden,
   or chiogga), peeled

Carrots
Potatoes (any color)
Sweet potatoes
Olive oil
Salt
Pepper

1. Preheat the oven to 475° F.
2. Peel any vegetables that have thick or blemished skin. Cut the vegetables into a uniform dice—½-inch dice, ¾-inch dice, or 1-inch dice—or just quarter or half the vegetables, if they are on the small side. The only important thing is that all the pieces are about the same size. The smaller the size, the faster they will cook. The larger the size, the longer they will take. Half-inch-dice vegetables can roast in 20 minutes or so. Figure about I cup of vegetables per person as a side dish.
3. Coat all the vegetables with olive oil. I do this by getting the pan I am going to use—a cast-iron pan, sheet pan, or roasting pan, preferably metal—and pouring in a generous amount of oil. I put my hands right in the oil and spread it all around the bottom of the pan, getting my hands oily. Then I pick up the vegetables in handfuls, rub them with my hands to cover them in a thin layer of olive oil, and drop them in the pan.
4. Ideally, prepare enough vegetables for a single layer in the pan you are using. You do not want to pile up the vegetables. If you have too many to fit in a single layer, get another pan, grease it with olive oil, and put the rest of the vegetables in there.
5. Sprinkle salt and freshly ground black pepper over the vegetables. It is hard to say how much salt to use. It is better to use too little than too much, because you can add more later. You also don't want to overwhelm the flavor of the vegetables with salt. So just sprinkle lightly at this stage, until you've roasted vegetables often enough to know what you are doing.
6. Put the pan in the oven on the top rack and leave for at least 15 minutes before opening the oven, then check them. They should be starting to brown. You can use a spatula to mix and flip the vegetables in the pan, or just shake the pan. Stick a fork in the vegetables to see how tender they are. If they feel pretty tender, try eating one. Check them regularly like this until you are happy with the results. Add more salt and pepper if you like and serve with fish, meat, or egg dishes, and a fresh salad.

2
SAP MOON

Once again we shall
See the snow melt
Taste the flowing sap
Touch the budding seeds.
Smell the whitening flowers
Know the renewal of life.

—FROM AN ANISHNABEG (OJIBWAY) THANKSGIVING FOR SPRING,
TRANSLATED FROM THE ANISHNABEG

Following the Hunger Moon, just before the first thaw after the cold winter, comes the Sap Moon. Though snow and ice still cover the ground throughout the North, the very first movements of spring stir within the forest trees. The sap of renewed life begins to rise up through the trunks, making its slow and steady way to the outermost tips of the branches where it will nurture the buds that will become new leaves.

While all northern trees produce sap at this time of year, the sugar maple in particular inspired the naming of the Sap Moon. Maple sap runs from the first sign of thaw until the first buds appear on the trees—a period of four to six weeks, depending on the weather. During this phase of the year, in times past, the northern dwellers of the eastern part of this continent would begin to check the maple trees for the sweet sap that was an important source of food. When the sap was running it was time to head for your nearest grove of sugar maples, called a sugar bush, begin tapping the trees, collecting sap, and pouring it into large pots for sugaring. What a lovely thing to contemplate: people stirring huge cauldrons of boiling maple sap with a wooden spoon over a fire in the midst of a snowy wood. The fragrance of the sap as it evaporated slowly into thick, sweet syrup must have been intoxicating.

The first peoples to harvest maple sap were the indigenous peoples of the northern woodlands, where the sugar maple, *Acer saccharum*, is both native and prodigious. For many cultures—the Anishnabeg (or Ojibway or Chippewa), Abenaki, Mi'kmaq, Passamaquody, Penobscot, Potawatomi, and Iroquois, to name a few—tapping maple trees was an annual ritual. The sap is watery and clear; Native peoples drank it as a spring tonic beverage and used it to make vinegar. European colonists often called it maple water. An Iroquois legend explains how the secret of maple sugaring was discovered. A chief named Woksis threw his tomahawk into a tree before leaving on a hunt. As the weather warmed, the sap began to flow from the gash into a container that happened to be sitting by the tree. The woman of the house found the container full of liquid, assumed her thoughtful husband had already been to the stream to fetch it full of water, and used it to boil the evening's meat. As the meat stewed, the sap cooked down into syrup, and thus the secret of maple sugaring was revealed.

The Sap Moon was also often called the Sugar Moon. The process of reducing maple sap is called sugaring, and most indigenous peoples that relied on maple sap as a primary source of carbohydrate, flavor, and nutrition cooked the sap down past the syrup stage and into the sugar stage, at which point it crystallizes. Solid sugar was much easier to transport than liquid syrup, and was conveniently packaged in birch-bark containers often called *mokuks*, which held from twenty to thirty pounds each.

Indigenous communities often moved camp during the sap season to be close to a sugar bush, and passed the entirety of the month or so while the sap ran there, engaged full-time in making sugar. They kept enough sugar for the community and then traded, sold, or gave away the rest. In 1896 a European American observer of indigenous culture wrote:

> The season of sugar-making came when the first crow appeared. This happened about the beginning or middle of March, while there was yet snow on the ground. This

period of the season was looked forward to with great interest, and, as among the Minnesota Ojibwa today, became a holiday for everybody. Each female head of a household had her own sugar hut, built in a locality abounding in maple trees which might or might not have been convenient to her camp, but which was the place always resorted to by her, and claimed by right of descent through her mother's family and totem.

Early American colonists quickly adapted sugaring techniques to their own technologies. They used spouts, buckets, and huge iron cauldrons to boil the sap down into sugar. Farmers in the northern regions added sugaring to their repertoire of homesteading skills. Benjamin Rush, in 1792, wrote:

> No more knowledge is necessary for making this sugar than is required to make soap, cyder, beer, sour crout, etc., and yet one or all of these are made in most of the farm houses of the United States. The kettles and other utensils of a farmer's kitchen, will serve most of the purposes of making sugar and the time required for the labor, (if it deserve that name) is at a season when it is impossible for the farmer to employ himself in any species of agriculture.

For homesteading farmers and indigenous peoples alike, maple sugaring was the main contribution that could be made to the food supply at this time of year, and the products are utterly delicious. Another note made about the indigenous northerners was: "Generally, they prefer their maple sugar to the West Indian cane sugar, and say that it tastes more fragrant—more of the forest."

It is interesting to note that as the outrage over slavery grew among northern settlers in the late eighteenth and early nineteenth centuries, maple sugar came to be seen as a socially responsible alternative to the refined cane sugar being imported from the Caribbean. An 1803 farmer's almanac exhorts: "Prepare for making maple sugar, which is more pleasant and patriotic than that ground by the hand of slavery, and boiled down by the heat of misery"; and in 1805: "Make your own sugar, and send not to the Indies for it. Feast not on the toil, pain and misery of the wretched." A historian of Vermont said of maple sugar that it had "two important recommendations. It is the product of our own state, and it is never tinctured with the sweat, and the groans, and the tears, and the blood of the poor slave." Choosing food based on social conscience and with a preference for locally grown ingredients is nothing new.

Like many people, I got turned on to maple syrup as part of my journey through health foods and various diets, when I learned about all of the health problems associated with white sugar. I have tried to avoid refined white sugar throughout my life. This quest pushed me to explore natural sweeteners such as maple syrup. At some point I began to wonder if the sap of the maple tree is the only sap we use for food. I couldn't immediately think of another example of a foodstuff derived from tree sap, but with all the billions of plants on the planet, each having its own sap running through its stems, trunks, and leaves, I reasoned that there had to be another sap somewhere that we harvested for food. I started to keep my eyes open.

During my meandering readings on food and health over the years, I found this little morsel among the wonderful writings of Ayurvedic teacher Maya Tiwari: "The earth offers us *soma*, symbolic of the nectar of the gods, from the bark of the maple tree, from the coconut, from the fruit, from the grain, from the bee, from the cow, from the buffalo, from the goat, and from the tiger. . . ." Yes, I thought, maple syrup is a bit like the milk of the tree, and a bit like the nectar of the gods: It is a true gift.

It intrigued me that Tiwari also referred to the coconut, and I wondered which gift of the coconut tree is the *soma*, the symbol of the nectar of the gods. Food scholar Alan Davidson calls the coconut palm—*Cocos nucifera*—the "most useful tree in the world." He goes on to explain that "it provides not only food and drink, but also vessels to serve them in and fuel to cook them, as well as textile fibre, thatching and basket materials, timber, medicines, chemicals, and many other valuable or useful products." Tiwari is undoubtedly speaking of a foodstuff, but even so there are many good candidates to be the coconut's symbolic *soma*. It could be the juice, drunk straight from green coconuts throughout the tropics. Or it could be the milk made from the flesh of the nut, an ingredient that makes Thai curries and soups taste like the nectar of the gods. It could be the rich white fragrant oil, widely used for cooking. Or could it be the sap?

After taking a closer look at coconut, I found that we do indeed tap another sap—one that is used by many more peoples and throughout more lands than maple sap: that of palm trees, including the coconut palm. Few of us here in North America realize that in a manner not dissimilar to the tapping and reducing of the sap of maple trees, the people of Southeast Asia tap palm trees for their sap, which they then cook down into a universal natural sweetener: palm sugar. The Thai food writer Kasma Loha-unchit describes making sugar from the sap of the coconut palm in her book, *It Rains Fishes*:

> Near the colorful Damnoen Saduak floating market in Rajburi province southwest of Bangkok, there is a small coconut sugar plantation run by an energetic old man. . . .
>
> Very early every morning, he climbs the many coconut trees on his plantation to make cuts in the flower buds, under which he straps cylindrical plastic containers to catch the sweet nectar dripping from the cuts. A couple of hours later, he returns and climbs the trees again with great agility to collect the filled containers.
>
> The lightly cloudy fluid is poured into huge woks over an old earthen stove at the edge of the nearby canal. A helper gathers dried coconut husks and leaf ribs for fuel and builds a fire to boil the watery fluid down to a thick, concentrated syrup. Attracted by the fragrance

and sweetness of the nectar, honey bees swarm around the woks, dozens giving in to a sweet death in the hot syrup. They are skimmed off before the gooey sugar is whipped to a smooth creamy texture with a beater attached to a long wooden stick. The light brown coconut sugar is then dropped onto wax paper in small lumps, or spooned onto shallow round molds, and left to set and harden. . . .

I have been using palm sugar as an ingredient in Thai curries for years without knowing that it was made from sap. It surprised me to learn how similar the process used to make palm sugar is to that of maple sugar. While it is hard to imagine a tree more quintessentially northern woodlands than the maple, and one more perfectly tropical than the palm, they are both prodigious producers of a sweet sap ideally suited to being turned into healthful, local sugar. Maple syrup and palm sugar are steeped in history and are still used extensively today.

My father-in-law, who grew up on a farm in Texas during the 1920s and 1930s, describes a similar process for making syrup on his family's old-fashioned self-sufficient ranch. In this case, the sap did not come from a tree, but from a cereal grass called sorghum that his family grew for this purpose. I love to listen to him describe how they would cook down the sap on a tray set above a fire. The large tray had a series of troughs connected with narrow openings between them. The trough closest to the fire would burn the hottest, and as the sap cooked someone would push it through the openings into the troughs that were farther away from the fire. The process required some expertise. The person pushing it had to know just how thick it should be—if it was cooked too long it would burn; too little and it would spoil. When the syrup was at that perfect stage, it was poured out of the last trough and into a large can. This sorghum molasses was used over the course of the year whenever some sweetness was called for.

Sweet Somethings

Thirteen traditional and unrefined sources of sweetness:

1. Maple syrup or sugar
2. Palm sugar
3. Birch syrup
4. Sorghum molasses
5. Jaggery or gur
6. Piloncillo
7. Dates or date sugar
8. Honey
9. Fresh sweet fruits and berries
10. Dried fruits such as raisins, prunes, and dried apricots
11. Fruit juices such as apple, orange, or grape
12. Agave nectar
13. Barley malt and other malted grains

Ah, sweetness—that great metaphor for goodness, comfort, and joy. When I was a perpetually hungry teenager, fighting what seemed like endless cravings, one of my primary urges was for sweetness. When I was miserable, I had a vague notion that a candy bar or some other sweet thing would put everything to right, would solve all my problems. But I did not crave maple syrup or palm sugar or sorghum molasses during those dark nights of the hungry soul. I craved white sugar. I craved one of the endless array of baked, boxed, packaged, and frozen confections sold everywhere in this country.

The primary physical effects of eating refined sugars are twofold. First, refined sugars actually deprive our bodies of minerals. As Sally Fallon explains in *Nourishing Traditions*:

> Only during the last century has man's diet included a high percentage of refined carbohydrates. Our ancestors ate fruits and grains in their whole, unrefined state. In nature, sugars and carbohydrates—the energy providers—are linked together with vitamins, minerals, enzymes, protein, fat and fiber—the bodybuilding and digestion-regulating components of the diet. In whole form, sugars and starches support life, but refined carbohydrates are inimical to life because they are devoid of bodybuilding elements. Digestion of refined carbohydrates calls on the body's own store of vitamins, minerals and enzymes for proper metabolization. . . . Refined carbohydrates have been called "empty" calories. "Negative" calories is a more appropriate term because consumption of refined calories depletes the body's precious reserves.

Second, the way that refined sugar floods the bloodstream with sucrose puts repeated stress on our metabolic balance by giving us a sense of instantaneous—and false—energy. As Fallon explains,

> When we consume refined sugars and starches, particularly alone, without fats or protein, they enter the blood stream in a rush, causing a sudden increase in blood sugar. The body regulation mechanism kicks into high gear, flooding the bloodstream with insulin and other hormones to bring blood sugar levels down to acceptable levels. Repeated onslaughts of sugar eventually disrupt this finely tuned process, causing some elements to remain in a constant state of activity and others to become worn out and inadequate to do the job.

Sugar acts on the body like a drug, and can be similarly addictive. It is no wonder that as a hungry, struggling teenager I turned again and again to sugared sweets for comfort and pleasure. Like much of America, I was hooked.

In the 1920s an American dentist from Cleveland, Dr. Weston A. Price, became alarmed by what he was seeing in his practice. Not only did young Americans seem to have more cavities than ever, but he noticed a steady rise in what he called dental deformities (what we would call crooked teeth, or needing braces). An increasing number of his patients did not have room in their mouths for all their teeth, and so needed to have some pulled. Few patients made it to adulthood with all thirty-two natural teeth (which includes the wisdom teeth) intact. Dr. Price heard reports that isolated, traditional peoples that had never before had contact with Western civilization often had perfect teeth. He decided to do some research on his own. He had two primary questions on his mind: Do groups of people with healthy teeth exist, and if so, what are they doing differently than us?

Price began an eccentric journey that would take him more than a decade and to many far corners of the Earth. Upon hearing that a certain group of people had perfect teeth, he would travel to that part of the world and spend some time getting to know the community before asking them if he might have a look at their teeth. What he found amazed him: whole villages and communities of people with almost no cavities. Furthermore, he found that they had wide faces with plenty of room for all their teeth, each of which lined up beautifully in their faces. They didn't need braces, or teeth pulled, or cavities filled. These communities had no dentists, practiced very limited oral hygiene, and had no access to modern medicine. The people also struck him as unusually healthy and happy.

Before the development of braces and other modern dental procedures, examining teeth was common for evaluating a person's intrinsic health. In cultures where women were considered property and their primary function was to bear children, an adolescent girl's teeth would be investigated as a way of predicting her potential as a breeder. Enslaved Africans and others would be similarly examined to judge how strong and vigorous their constitutions were and to predict their potential as physical laborers. The sexist and racist contexts for these practices don't negate the fact that the practiced eye could learn much about overall health from a discerning look at the teeth and dental structure. Our phrase "don't look a gift horse in the mouth" has ancient origins and came from the practice of investigating the teeth of a horse before you purchased it to get a sense of both its age and how healthy and vigorous it might be. Price undertook his work in a different spirit with a different purpose: to find the cause of the increasingly poor dental health he was seeing in his own patients and community.

Price's process was the same in each community he visited. He examined the teeth, made copious notes as to the people's dental health, and took photographs of their dental arches. He inquired about the overall health of the people as well. He wanted to know whether they suffered from degenerative or contagious diseases, what they died of, how long they lived, whether the women had difficulty getting pregnant or giving birth, and the rate of birth defects. He asked many questions about diet, the source of their food, how they prepared foods, and their rituals and values around the foods they ate. He wrote all of this down. In order to eliminate factors that could be considered genetic, he then would locate a community of people from the same ethnic group who no longer ate their traditional diet. These would be people living in cities, or in missions, or on reservations. He asked them the same questions about their health and diet, and examined and photographed their teeth. In 1939 he published his findings and his photographs in a book called *Nutrition and Physical Degeneration*.

The photographs and text of his book are both shocking and fascinating. In it he profiles fourteen different communities of people who had consistently beautiful teeth. The faces he photographed are round and radiant. Not only were their teeth healthy, but these same groups also enjoyed long, vigorous life spans characterized by a lack of degenerative diseases, a resistance to contagious diseases that they had been exposed to, ease of childbirth, and generally strong and hearty constitutions. Price was struck by the lack of social ills within their societies. Juxtaposed with these faces are those of the same groups—but the people no longer ate their traditional diet. The faces are narrow and sallow; the teeth are rotten, crooked, or deformed. Without access to dentists, their dental decay went unchecked, often within only a few years of abandoning (or being deprived of) their indigenous diet.

Unlike their traditional diets, however different, their new diet was always high in the foods that Price referred to as "the displacing foods of modern commerce." Chief among these was white sugar. While most of us have been taught that "sugar rots the teeth," Price's work went much farther. He found that sugar's propensity to rob the body of its minerals and vitamins contributed to a *general and universal* deficiency whereby the body simply doesn't have the nutrients it needs to build healthy bones, teeth, and organ systems. Teeth are only the most visible and easily studied aspect of a whole process of physical degeneration that our modern diet precipitates. Not having enough room in the skull for the teeth often indicated that the pelvic cavity might be incompletely formed (causing painful and difficult childbirth), the skeleton would be weak overall, and the body's lack of nutrition would eventually make it susceptible to degenerative diseases, compromised immunity, and cognitive, mental, and emotional difficulties. We are watching this correlation play out in our modern culture.

There are many important differences between the sweetness in indigenous diets and that in our contemporary diets. One has to do with whether the sugar is in a more natural or a more refined state—maple sugar versus white sugar, for instance. Another has to do with how it is made use of in the food system—what it is combined with and when it is eaten.

The concept of dessert—of a whole sweet course in a meal—was a culinary notion popularized during the eighteenth century in Northern Europe. This was exactly when white sugar was in need of a rapidly expanding market. Desserts came to Europe riding on the tail of the juggernaut of white sugar, and then to the rest of the world on the tail of the juggernaut of European influence.

This fact was brought home to me when I worked as a chef at a residential arts center. Each evening, I prepared dinner for anywhere from ten to a hundred people. As a cook interested in cuisines from around the world, I usually made a meal that reflected a particular part of the world and its special culinary traditions. One night dinner might be North African, the next night East Asian, and the next southern United States. I found that in my quest for creating authentic meals, I was often stymied when it came to preparing desserts. For European or American meals, there was never any difficulty finding the perfect sweet thing to end the meal, but with other cuisines it was a bit harder. As I scoured cookbooks, I often found few authentic desserts within a given culinary heritage. I found Chinese desserts a particular challenge. We think of fortune cookies as the classic end to a Chinese dinner, but they were developed here in San Francisco and are not at all authentic to the cuisines of China.

My contract actually stipulated that I had to make dessert, and at one point I protested to my boss about it—not because I am a killjoy, or against dessert, or lazy, but because for people to have dessert every night seemed, in my view, excessive. I guess my feeling about dessert is a little old-fashioned. I think of it as a special treat. She demurred. The dessert could be simple—a cookie, for instance—but it was part of the deal. Occasionally the dessert could be a piece of good fruit, but this was frowned upon. An artist had once complained that a previous cook had tried to pass off fruit as dessert. I got the message.

How did traditional and indigenous diets use the sweet things they had, whether from sap, fruit, honey, or other source? Mainly they combined them with the other elements of the meal. One European who lived and ate with a maple-sugar-eating indigenous community noted in 1755, "The way we commonly used our sugar while encamped was by putting it in bear's fat until the fat was almost as sweet as the sugar itself, and in this we dipped our roasted venison." *Pemmican* was a northern woodlands indigenous staple made from dried and pulverized meat combined with melted fat, berries, and often maple sugar. In Thai cuisine, cooks use palm sugar in curries, where they combine small quantities with coconut milk, meat, fish sauce, and herbs and spices. Throughout South and West Asia people use sweet dried fruits in pilafs and other dishes that are served with meats and pulses. Chutneys and other relishes that are served with the main meal contain fresh and dried sweet fruits. In Morocco the classic dish *tagine* is a deliciously sweet and aromatic stew of meat, fruits, and spices. (Interestingly, in many sub-Saharan African cultures, sweet foods are seen as feminine, and men eschew them in honor of their masculinity.)

In East Asian cooking, sweet flavors are combined with salty and spicy to make such classic Japanese sauces as *teriyaki*, *yakitori*, and *ponzu*, which are used with vegetables, rice, meat, and fish. The sauces on Chinese dishes almost always contain a sweet element. Even European cuisine, before the influx of white sugar, took this approach. Old-fashioned British cuisine included such now despised dishes as mincemeat pie, in which beef suet is mixed with dried fruits and spices and baked in a shell; and Lombard tart, which combines eggs, cream, dates, and beef marrow. A look at culinary traditions reveals this phenomenon again and again. The sweetness is *woven into the larger meal*, not a course of its own. This makes sense when you look at it from the point of view of health and wholeness. Sweetness, when it is accompanied by protein, fat, and vitamin-rich vegetables, and balanced by mineral-rich salt, soy sauce, fish sauce, or broth, is absorbed by the body slowly and evenly, without the usual spike and crash.

The development of dessert, on the other hand, was based on a particularly lopsided equation. When white sugar came to Europe, cooks began to combine it with another new refined carbohydrate—white flour, the other primary displacing food of modern commerce. A whole cuisine of confectionary grew up around this unbalanced marriage. If the sugar-and-flour combination had stayed limited to desserts following a complete meal, its effect on worldwide health might not have been so deleterious. But this unfortunate combination soon became a substitute for the morning meal—sugar-sweetened muffins, pastries, and pancakes became popular, and eventually cold cereals, Pop-Tarts, and doughnuts took over where they left off.

People also began to use sugar in tea, coffee, and chocolate. While traditional peoples had made beverages from these stimulant plants, with their enlivening substances teine, caffeine, and theobromine, they took on a whole new compulsion when mixed with sugar. This refined carbohydrate, white sugar, and stimulant trio would eventually also become the British high tea and the American coffee break, the thing we crave in the afternoon to get us through the rest of the day. Such daily fare is very depleting to the body.

In the twentieth century, sugar was combined with two other ancient stimulants in an entirely new formula. A company combined coca leaves from the Amazon, kola nuts from Africa, and sugar from the islands to create a beverage that would eventually rot the teeth and deplete the health of countless millions throughout the world: Coca-Cola.

At the same time, the modern candy industry grew up around the marriage of chocolate to sugar, and expanded to include all manner of new sugared confections. One of them, interestingly, combined sugar with another ancient tree sap known to the indigenous peoples of the Central American rain forest. The *chicle* tree, *Manilkara zapota*, is tapped in the rain forests of Mexico, Guatemala, Honduras, and Belize for its sticky sap. This sap is cooked down into a chewy latex that is used in chewing gum.

As harmful as white sugar has been to human bodies, it has also been devastating to human communities. While people almost always write about maple sugaring in poetic, even nostalgic terms, this is not at all the case with refined cane sugar. Even in the seventeenth century, a Barbadian colonist wrote of the sugar mills on that island:

> In short, 'tis to live in a perpetual Noise and Hurry, and the only way to render a person Angry, and Tyrannical, too; since the Climate is so hot, and the labor so constant, that the Servants night and day stand in great Boyling Houses, where there are Six or Seven large Coppers or Furnaces kept perpetually Boyling; and from which with heavy Ladles and Scummers they Skim off the excrementitious parts of the Canes, till it comes to its perfection and cleanness, while other as Stoakers, Broil as it were, alive, in managing the Fires; and one part is constantly at the Mill, to supply it with Canes, night and day, during the whole Season of making Sugar, which is about six Months of the year. . . .

Descriptions (even old ones) of white sugar production always seem to ring of the hellish and infernal. A historian of sugar production writes:

> So rapid was the motion of the mill, and so rapid also the combustion of the dried canes or trash used as fuel in the boiling house that the work of the millers and firemen, though light enough in itself, was exhausting. . . . Those who fed the mill were liable, especially when tired or half-asleep, to have their fingers caught between the rollers. A hatchet was kept in readiness to sever the arm, which in such cases was always drawn in; and this no doubt explains the number of maimed watchmen.

The subtle and yet profound difference between the beautiful descriptions of maple, palm, and sorghum sugaring, and the exploitation involved in refining cane sugar, are striking. It's not that sugarcane can't be sugared in a small-scale, artisanal way; it can. In India people boil down the juice into unrefined blocks of golden-brown cane sugar called *jaggery* or *gur* (which is also sometimes made from palm sap). In parts of Latin America, brown loaf sugar is called *panela* or *piloncillo*. But as anthropologist Sidney Mintz points out in his book *Sweetness and Power*, "There are great differences between families using ancient wooden machinery and iron cauldrons to boil up a quantity of sugar to sell to their neighbors in picturesque loaves, and the massed men and machinery employed in producing thousands of tons of sugar cane (and, eventually, of sugar) on modern plantations for export elsewhere." The heart of the difference has to do with wholeness versus fragmentation.

Both maple and palm sugar are traditional foods that have been made in similar fashion for many centuries. Certainly people traded and exported it, but the people who made the sugar also consumed the sugar as part of their cuisine, and had an ancestral relationship to it. The trees that it comes from were part of their native landscapes, part of the place they called home. Everything about the sugar was imbued with culture, tradition, history, place, landscape. The same is true of small-scale production of unrefined cane sugar, or the sorghum molasses that my father-in-law's family used to make.

But everything about the production of refined white sugar broke down communities and wiped out traditions. This fragmentation started with the removal of people from the places of their ancestors. The peoples indigenous to the islands where cane is grown industrially were enslaved, and their cultures were in most cases completely destroyed. The Africans who were used to do the labor of production, once the natives were wiped out, were captured and transported from their birthplace to the sugar islands. Once placed in the fields where they were to work, they were intentionally grouped with Africans from disparate cultures and language groups—further alienation. Many Europeans also ended up as indentured servants in the sugar mills. These were debt servants, petty criminals, religious nonconformists, labor organizers, Irish revolutionaries, and other political prisoners. Many were simply kidnapped; according to Mintz, "to 'Barbados' someone became a seventeenth-century verb for stealing humans." The people who now grew the sugar (enslaved blacks, indentured whites, the few remaining island indigenous, and—in the case of Hawaii—East Asians) had no ancestral relationship to either the cane or the sugar it produced. It played no part in their indigenous cuisines, and they had little access to the product in any case, as it was all grown for export to Europe and the United States. Sugar production was one of the early models of an exploitative, globalized food system.

I cannot think of sugar without remembering its tragic history and its enduring disconnect from both people and place. When I went to Maui, I visited a sugar museum located next to the last remaining area of sugarcane cultivation on the Hawaiian Islands, where sugar was once the primary crop. The museum sits across the road from a processing facility that takes the sugar through the primary stages of evaporation to create raw sugar. The factory smelled terrible, and I marveled that the museum could survive downwind of such a stench. There I learned that the raw sugar processed on Maui would be shipped by tanker to California, where it would be refined in a plant less than half an hour's drive from where I live. It is a factory I have often passed on the freeway, and I find its huge smokestacks and their black emissions dismaying. Although I knew that it was a C&H sugar factory, I didn't realize that this stood for "California and Hawaii" after the states where it is processed and grown. After the sugar is refined in Northern California, it is shipped all the way to New York to be packaged. From New York, packages such as the little teaspoon packets that sit on café tables everywhere are shipped to their myriad destinations, including back to Hawaii. After the museum tour I drove a mile from the sugar plantation to a coffee shop and noticed the sugar packets on the table. I now knew that they had traveled halfway around the world and back again (more than ten thousand miles) to make a trip that had taken me fewer than ten minutes.

To make traditional sugars from sugarcane, you simply evaporate the juice until it crystallizes, the way you do with maple, palm, or sorghum. But in order to refine cane sugar into its "perfection and cleanness," you have to take it through a series of repetitive processes that extract from the once wholesome cane all of its complex flavors, minerals, and energies until there is nothing left but sucrose. After centuries of sugarcane production, Northern Europeans began to refine white sugar from sugar beets to create a similarly "pure" refined, white sugar. From a chemist's perspective, the two forms of white sugar—cane and beet—are indistinguishable. They are both 99 percent sucrose. Everything else is gone. It is no surprise that eating such a fragmented, broken food has such a negative physiological effect on our bodies.

I believe that the preponderance of refined white sugar—and its newer counterparts, high-fructose corn syrup and artificial sweeteners—is among the worst problems with our modern diet. Although I can't say that I completely avoid sugar (a task that would be Herculean, if not Sisyphean, in this food system), I try not to eat too much of it, and I don't use it in my own cooking. When making sweet things, I experiment with less refined, more old-fashioned sweeteners that have been in use for millennia.

You may find it odd, after a whole chapter dedicated to eating locally and seasonally, to find me endorsing maple syrup and palm sugar, since both of these have to be shipped over distances. There are no sugar maple trees or coconut palms where I live in California, nor any sorghum growing that I know of. Maple syrup, palm sugar, and sorghum molasses are regional foods, filled with the *terroir* of the places they grow. But they are not part of my region; theirs is not the *terroir* of the place I live.

Still, I believe there are foods that it makes more sense to ship long-distance than others. While I don't think we should be importing apples when we can grow them right here, it seems to me that historic, natural sweeteners are exactly the kinds of foods it makes sense to transport: They are healthy, traditional, naturally preserved foods that can't be grown or produced locally. The point is to be wise, not rigid.

White sugar made from cane or beets has already displaced traditional sugars in many parts of the world, and continues to do so. I learned recently that many Thai cooks now replace palm sugar with white sugar when making their curries. I think this is a great loss. Some foods will always travel long distances to foreign ports. Let these be the flavors and foodstuffs that have endured from ancient times, foods with great cultural pedigrees, foods that can't be grown or made where we live—cinnamon and cloves, palm sugar and coconut milk, maple syrup and cocoa powder.

I also don't want to give an unreasonably black-and-white picture of refined versus natural sugars. The occasional homemade chocolate chip cookie might be just too good and too full of love to pass up, despite the refined sugar it contains. Maple syrup production has been taken over by European American companies, and many indigenous peoples were driven from their sugar bushes in the process. Industrial production of maple syrup often includes formaldehyde, and to avoid that you have to buy an organic brand. Sugar maples can be overtapped; care must be taken for their health. And of course maple and palm sugars are still very high in sucrose, and need to be eaten in moderation and balanced with proteins and fats. But in many places, tapping sap from trees is still a ritual of community embedded in place, and that is something to celebrate.

> ### Worth the Trip
>
> Thirteen foods that I use in my kitchen that are imported or shipped:
>
> 1. Spices that only grow in tropical climates, such as cinnamon, pepper, and nutmeg
> 2. Sea salt
> 3. Parmesan cheese
> 4. Maple syrup
> 5. Natural cane sugars
> 6. Coconut milk and oil
> 7. Fish sauce
> 8. Cocoa
> 9. Palm oil
> 10. Cashews
> 11. Palm sugar
> 12. Bananas
> 13. Kuzu and arrowroot

Perhaps it is because of all I have learned about sugar, its history, and its effect on the body, but I find that I do not much relish desserts after meals anymore. I do like the festivity of it, and when I go out to eat I often find myself hoping that dessert will be ordered in order to prolong the occasion. But it is not the food itself that I want—I am so unaccustomed to sugary sweets now that I usually find little to enjoy in the cake, pie, ice cream, or custard that we order. It almost always tastes too sweet.

At home I do often have a little something sweet to end a meal, but it is less sweet and richer in fat or protein than typical desserts. Often it is one of the recipes at the end of this chapter. Sometimes just a piece of fresh fruit or a pot of a relaxing herbal tisane can give a wonderful sense of completion after dinner.

We all need sweetness—goodness, comfort, and joy—in our lives. We need it in our mouths sometimes, and we need it in our hearts and souls even more often. Maybe if we lived in a culture that really fed us, on a deep level, every day, we wouldn't crave those boxes and cartons and plates of sugared things so much. Maybe if we spent the Sap Moon stirring our cauldrons in the snowy woods, intoxicated by the smells of simmering maple syrup, this would feed us even more than the sugar we were making. Maybe it is really our hunger for connection that is calling out to be fed when we find ourselves reaching for cookies, cake, or candy.

On the Sap Moon, may we all be reminded of our enduring connection to the trees and plants of landscapes that are part of our planet's web of life and cultural heritage. May we hold in our hearts all those whose lives and communities were devastated by slavery. May we give thanks for sap, which is to plants what blood is to animals and water is to earth—that liquid movement of life, growth, and return. May we all be blessed with the sweetness of life, and may we sometimes find it somewhere other than dessert!

SAP MOON RECIPES

Coconut and Palm Sugar Semifreddi
Serves 3–4

1 can (13.5 oz) organic coconut milk

½ cup palm sugar (see page 311)

A couple of pieces of star anise and/or orange peel, or other exotic sweet spice (optional)

1 tablespoon Bernard Jensen's gelatin (see page 315) or 2 teaspoons Knox gelatin

Pinch of salt

1. Heat the coconut milk gently over medium-low heat.
2. Add the palm sugar and star anise or other spice. Stir gently with a whisk or wooden spoon to break up the sugar.
3. When the liquid is hot, stir in the gelatin and add a pinch of salt.
4. When the sugar has dissolved, pour the liquid through a strainer into three or four wineglasses, ice cream dishes, or little parfait cups.
5. Let the mixture cool for a few minutes before placing the dishes in the freezer for about half an hour, or until just gelled. Transfer them to the fridge if you're not ready to eat.

Note: Depending on the coconut milk, the dessert may separate into two layers, one with coconut cream on top and a coconut gelée on the bottom, or it might just have a uniform creamy texture. It is delicious either way. Eat with a spoon and remember the old man with his wokful of palm sap, cooking it down to sugar.

Maple-vanilla Panna Cruda
Serves 3–4

1 cup raw cream or crème fraîche

1 teaspoon vanilla extract

½ cup filtered water

1 tablespoon Bernard Jensen's gelatin (see page 315) or 2 teaspoons Knox gelatin

Tiny pinch of salt

¼ cup maple syrup, or to taste (this amount may be too sweet for some palates—start with 2 tablespoons and then taste)

(continued)

Maple-vanilla Panna Cruda
continued

1. Put the cream or crème fraîche into a bowl with the vanilla extract.
2. In a very small pan, heat the water until almost boiling. Add the gelatin and tiny pinch of salt.
3. Simmer the water for a minute or so until the gelatin is dissolved. Remove from the heat and allow to cool for a couple of minutes.
4. Stir the gelatin-water mixture into the cream.
5. Add the maple syrup to the cream mixture, and taste it. You want it sweet but not too sweet.
6. Pour into three or four wineglasses, ice cream dishes, or little parfait cups. Place in the freezer for about half an hour or until just gelled. Transfer to the fridge if you're not ready to eat. Alternatively, just put the dishes straight into the fridge and allow a couple of hours for the mixture to gel.
7. Serve as is, or with fresh seasonal berries or other fruit.

Cardamom and Jaggery Rice Pudding
Serves 4–6

This is a great way to use up leftover rice for a quick and satisfying dessert—especially rice that turned out a little gummy or soft! The recipe can easily be halved if you have less rice to use up.

1 can (13.5 oz) organic coconut milk— or substitute 1½ cups milk or half-and-half

¼ teaspoon ground cardamom

¼ cup jaggery or gur (available at Indian groceries or markets)

2½ cups leftover well-cooked rice (I usually use brown)

½ teaspoon vanilla extract

Pinch of salt

Slivered pistachios or almonds, or a sprinkling of cardamom, for garnish (optional)

1. Heat the coconut milk (or dairy milk) gently over medium-low heat.
2. Add the cardamom.
3. Add the jaggery, breaking it up into the liquid with a wooden spoon or whisk. When the liquid is hot, the jaggery should dissolve into it.
4. When the jaggery has dissolved, add the rice, vanilla, and pinch of salt (if the rice was salted when it was cooked, you don't need to add more).

5. Break up the rice into the milk using a wooden spoon or whisk. Stir the mixture and bring it to a low simmer. Cook, stirring occasionally, for 5 to 10 minutes or until the whole mixture is flavorful and somewhat thickened.

6. Serve warm in small bowls or parfait dishes with a dusting of cardamom and/or slivered nuts on top.

Note: You can also make this dessert with palm sugar, maple syrup, or other natural sweeteners, but jaggery gives an authentic, lovely flavor.

Maple-roasted Nuts
Makes 1 cup

1 cup walnuts or pecans

3 tablespoons maple syrup

1. Place the nuts in a colander and shake to remove any powdery bits that might burn.
2. Transfer the nuts to a cast-iron skillet and toast over medium-high heat, stirring constantly with a wooden spoon, until they begin to change color and smell fragrant (just a few minutes).
3. Pour the maple syrup over the nuts in the hot pan. Stir and shake for a minute until all the nuts are coated and the syrup has evaporated.
4. Pour the nuts onto a wooden cutting board. Immediately fill the skillet with water and place it in the sink. (This prevents the sugar from sticking to the pan and becoming hard to clean!)
5. Use a spatula or other tool to scrape and stir the nuts on the cutting board and keep them moving for a minute or so while they cool (otherwise they'll stick to the cutting board).
6. Transfer the nuts to a bowl and put the cutting board under hot water.
7. Eat and enjoy as a snack, or serve with fruit, or put on a salad.

Hot Coco Cocoa
Serves 1–2

I make this hot cocoa at least once a week! Sometimes I like to froth it in my milk frother until it is foamy (do this between steps 4 and 5).

¼ cup filtered water

1 tablespoon palm sugar

1 tablespoon cocoa powder, or to taste

¼ teaspoon vanilla extract

1½ cups raw whole milk

Few grains of sea salt

1. Heat the water in a small, heavy-bottomed saucepan over medium heat.
2. Add the palm sugar and cocoa powder. Whisk vigorously as the mixture comes to a simmer until both sugar and cocoa are dissolved.
3. Add the remaining ingredients.
4. Heat gently until the cocoa feels hot to the touch, but not so hot that you can't keep your finger there (about 110° F).
5. Remove from heat and pour into warm cups or mugs.

After-dinner Mints
Makes about 20 mints

I have always loved mints with a chocolate coating. These healthful mints are delicious and easy and satisfy that craving. They can substitute for dessert. I think kids would love to help you roll them.

½ cup coconut spread (available from Wilderness Family Naturals)

1 tablespoon palm sugar

1 tablespoon honey, preferably crystallized

1 tablespoon coconut oil

4–5 drops organic peppermint essential oil

Cocoa powder for dusting—1–2 tablespoons (you can substitute carob powder)

1. In a bain-marie or small heavy-bottomed pot, very gently warm together the coconut spread, palm sugar, honey, coconut oil, and peppermint oil.
2. When all is warm and pliable, transfer the mixture to a food processor and process into a smooth paste, or transfer to a bowl and mix together thoroughly with a spoon.

3. Transfer the paste to a bowl and cool completely. You can put the bowl in the fridge for 5 to 10 minutes.
4. Place the cocoa powder in another small bowl.
5. Roll the mints by taking about a half-teaspoon of paste and rolling it into a ball in the palm of your hands, then rolling each ball in the cocoa powder until coated, and transferring to a plate.
6. Place the plate of balls in the fridge until firm, then transfer to a tin or airtight container and store in the fridge.
7. To serve, you can allow the mints to come to room temperature or eat them cold, as they are.

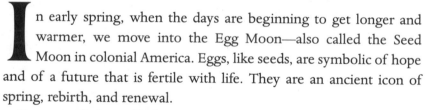

3

EGG MOON

I only remember my grandfather would put the
egg up like this, looking towards Heaven and
thanking the birds for the food that he found. . . .
He'd call the birds just like they were people,
. . . and he said,
"Thank you for letting me find the egg for my meal today."

—Huna Tlingit memory of springtime gull-egg harvesting

In early spring, when the days are beginning to get longer and warmer, we move into the Egg Moon—also called the Seed Moon in colonial America. Eggs, like seeds, are symbolic of hope and of a future that is fertile with life. They are an ancient icon of spring, rebirth, and renewal.

Eggs symbolize wholeness, completeness, and often serve as metaphors for the universe. Many diverse ancient cultures had a sacred story in which Creation was born from a cosmic egg. In the Chinese mythos, a being named P'an-gu grew within a great egg for eighteen thousand years, then woke from a long sleep. He felt suffocated, so he broke out of the egg with an ax. The light, clear part of the egg floated up and formed the heavens; the cold, heavy matter stayed below to form earth. P'an-gu began to grow and push apart the heavens and the earth, and continued to do this for another eighteen thousand years. Finally the earth and heavens drew far apart, and P'an-gu, having spent all of his energy, died.

When P'an-gu died, his breath became the wind and clouds, his voice the thunder. One eye became the sun and the other, the moon.

His body and limbs turned into mountains, and his blood became the waters of the Earth. His veins transformed into far-stretching roads and his muscles turned into fertile land. The stars in the sky came from his hair and beard, flowers and trees from his skin and the fine hairs on his body. His marrow turned to jade and pearls. His sweat flowed like the good rain and the sweet dew that nurtures all things on Earth. His tears flowed to make rivers, and the brightness of his eyes turned into lightning that lights up the night. When he was happy the sun shone, but when he was angry the sky would fill with black clouds. One version of the legend has it that the fleas and lice on P'an-gu's body became the ancestors of mankind—an unsettling pair of antecedents.

This story makes me contemplate for a moment the amazing thing that happens inside an egg. That the yolk and white of a hen's egg so familiar to a cook should, with warmth and time, turn into a baby chick, with beak, eyes, feathers, and little clawed feet, is miraculous. That this story takes the image a step further and has a full-fledged humanlike deity crack out of the egg seems a logical next step. When P'an-gu's body becomes the visible universe, it creates a world in which all of Creation is alive, where the microcosm reflects the macrocosm and vice versa.

The Egg Moon comes in the spring. On old-fashioned farms the hens start producing more eggs at this time of year: Chickens respond to longer days with increased laying. It is part of their natural cycle. When hens see light, it stimulates their pituitary gland to produce a hormone that stimulates their ovaries to produce eggs. So spring signaled the return of eggs to the farmhouse diet.

Shopping in the grocery store, where eggs are plentiful year-round, this seasonal pattern is not evident. Factory farming of eggs maximizes production by artificially lighting the egg factory, sometimes twenty-four hours a day, tricking the hens' bodies into thinking it's always summer. Antibiotics stimulate production even further—as if to make the Egg Moon last all year long.

But I know when egg season is here by checking out the eggs at a vendor at my local farmer's market. Mr. Davis is an elderly, old-fashioned farmer who raises poultry and a few vegetables and nuts about an hour away from where I live. In early spring he begins to bring goose eggs—enormous white eggs with a thick shell and a large yolk. I love these rich eggs. One goose egg, scrambled, will feed two people. The taste is very similar to chicken eggs, but a bit richer (and the color is yellower), since the proportion of yolk to white is higher. This is just the way I like my eggs to be. The geese don't lay much in wintertime—or in summer or fall, for that matter—so goose eggs are very seasonal around here. Sometimes Mr. Davis has duck eggs as well, which are larger than hen's eggs but smaller than goose eggs, and also feature very large, rich yolks. He also brings lots of Araucana eggs in the spring—pale blue-green eggs from a small breed of chicken that is not a strong egg layer. He charges more for all of these eggs, but I have no trouble paying for the pleasure of a goose egg in spring, and for the knowledge that the eggs are from birds that live on a farm, rather than in a factory.

A good egg is hard to find. Most eggs in this country are produced by large corporations that subcontract production out to farmers who used to be independent, but now live in a system that one rancher I know compared to indentured servitude. Male chicks are immediately killed, sometimes ground up into pet food. Female chicks may have a worse fate: beaks burned or sliced off to keep them from pecking one another to death; fed a standardized commercial mixture laced with antibiotics and generally containing GMOs; housed in crowded buildings without sunlight or access to the outdoors; force-molted by food deprivation to increase egg production; and then killed when production begins to fall off even slightly. These hens are so overbred, so confined, and so sedentary during their short, miserable lives that they don't have use of their legs or wings. The factory-farmed eggs sell for rock-bottom prices. It is a terrible thing to do a living being, and a disgraceful defilement of this symbol of life, hope, and fertility—the egg.

The answer to the old question, "Which came first, the chicken or the egg?" is obviously the egg. Not only do few of the ancient stories mention chickens, but also we know from science that eggs were part of Creation long before chickens were, or even their wild ancestors. Archaeologists have postulated that humans domesticated chickens around 3200 BCE in India from a wild jungle fowl, *Gallus gallus*, and that this new species spread rapidly from there to other parts of the world.

But prehistoric humans, and perhaps even prehuman hominids, were collecting and eating wild eggs many millennia before that. Some historians believe that eggs were one of humanity's very first foods— before game, right after water and salt. This would make sense, as eggs are a complete animal food that can be eaten raw without any preparation whatsoever, and without the need for weapons, stalking, or any of the other tools or skills of the hunter. Wild carnivores and omnivores will eat eggs if they find them, and we certainly did the same. It wouldn't have taken much for us to realize that it was worth doing a little extra work to look for them, and so wild eggs became a prized source of nutrition for hunter-gatherer societies around the world.

Nor did we limit ourselves to birds' eggs. Human communities have eaten almost any kind of egg they could get their hands on, including those of reptiles and fish. Among the Andanamese Islanders in the Bay of Bengal, turtles' eggs have long been one of their most precious foods. Similarly, the Kuna of what is now Panama prized turtles' eggs. Many Mayan communities traditionally eat iguana eggs. The Inuit have long gathered the eggs of wild migrating ducks and of a marine diver bird called the murre that resembles a penguin. At least two of the groups that Dr. Weston Price studied valued fish eggs as a sacred food, one that was essential for children, pregnant women, and nursing mothers. In the far northern part of the Americas, the Inuit dried salmon eggs during the season for use throughout the year. In the far southern part, the indigenous peoples of the Pacific coast in Peru would harvest and dry the eggs of the *angelote*, or angel shark, which looks similar to a stingray or a skate. These eggs were traded way up into the mountainous and dry regions to people who had no direct access to seafoods. They prized these eggs as a nutritional supplement.

While wild eggs provided a reliable and important source of nutrition for hunter-gatherer societies and small agrarian communities, as

Not All in the Same Basket

Thirteen sources for eggs in human nutrition:

1. Chicken
2. Goose
3. Duck
4. Quail
5. Salmon
6. Sturgeon (caviar)
7. Murre
8. Angel shark
9. Ostrich
10. Emu
11. Guinea hen
12. Turtle
13. Iguana

populations grew wild eggs were often over-harvested. In many places now, regulations control or prohibit collection of wild eggs from birds, reptiles, and fish to ensure the survival of the species. It is the domesticated chicken that has come to be a worldwide source for eggs in human diets.

Over the course of the past five thousand years, chickens have become an essential part of agricultural systems in all temperate areas throughout the world. The chicken has been bred to be a highly productive component of a small-scale, subsistence farm and local food system. A chicken will lay between one and two eggs per day, about as many eggs as one person will eat. Chickens need space, but not as large an amount of pasture as a cow or other larger mammal requires. With a small coop and a bit of fenced-in yard, a chicken is content. Even when given free range, chickens do not stray far from their homes. On my father-in-law's Texas farm, the chickens had a house with a door and were allowed to range freely throughout the property. I asked him if it was someone's job to herd the chickens up into their coop at the end of the day. "Nope," he answered, "they would go up there on their own." The coop offers chickens safety from predators, shelter from the elements, comfortable roosts where they like to sleep perched up off the ground in the dark, and the padded nests where they lay their eggs. Being omnivores, chickens aren't too picky about what they eat. They love bugs, snails, worms, grasses and other leaves. They need a small amount of feed, usually a mixture of grain and legume. They will eat kitchen waste and compost, including raw, cooked, and baked leftovers from animals, vegetables, and grains.

There are manifold benefits to having chickens on a small family farm. They eat many of the pests that eat the vegetables in the garden, as well as flies that can breed disease. They eat weeds. More important, their manure is a rich fertilizer for vegetables, fruit, grains, and other crops. Chickens don't absorb all of the nutrients out of their food, and thus many remain in their manure. The soil absorbs these nutrients easily, and so do the plants that are grown in the soil enriched by the manure. For millennia this has been one of the easiest ways to keep a family farm's topsoil fertile and rich. What the plants take out of the earth in the course of a year can be replaced by manure so that the soil is not depleted by farming year after year, but is actually enriched.

And of course, the chickens provide the family with both eggs and meat. But of these two foodstuffs, the eggs are usually the more critical piece on a subsistence farm. Many farming families eat their chickens infrequently or only on special occasions—their eggs are just too valuable as a reliable, steady, easily obtained source of daily nutrition. On a small family farm, the roosters would often go into the stewpot and form the basis for the famously healing and comforting chicken soups of the world.

On ranches that raise cows on pasture, chickens play an important role to play in the ecosystem of the farm. Visionary rancher Joel Salatin has developed a system for using cows and laying hens synergistically to raise food humanely, nutritiously, and ecologically. A few months ago I toured Salatin's ranch, which he calls Polyface Farm (the Farm of Many Faces) in the Shenendoah Valley of Virginia—about a three-hour drive from where I grew up. Joel drove the tour group out into the fields on a wagon that he pulled with his tractor. After visiting his hogs, broilers, and turkeys, he brought us to see his "eggmobile"—a large chicken coop on wheels set out in the middle of a lush, expansive green field, surrounded by about a hundred chickens that were pecking around in the grass but gathered pretty close to the coop. A lightweight movable fence surrounded the field.

Salatin explained that this pasture was the field that had been, a day or two before, occupied by the cattle, which were now behind us in another demarcated area of green grass. Salatin moves his cattle onto a piece of land that has been allowed to rest for a while, and lets the cattle eat the rich, biodiverse grasses that are growing there. This fresh pasture is highly nutritious food for the cows. Before the cattle start overgrazing the grass, Salatin moves them onto a fresh piece of land, and brings his eggmobile onto the pasture that the cattle have just left, opens the door, and lets the chickens loose.

In addition to enjoying the grass that has been courteously mowed down for them by the cattle (chickens don't like to eat grasses that are too high), they peck through the cow pies, eating the larvae of flies that lay their eggs in the dung. This disinfects the cow pies and breaks the cycle of bovine stomach parasites, eliminating the need for synthetic worm medicines for the cattle. Their pecking also breaks up the cow pies and spreads them out over a larger area. This means that the manure recycles into the soil much more readily. Otherwise, the nitrogen in the manure would concentrate in certain spots, creating overly rich bunches of grass that cows refuse to eat. Instead, evenly fertilized grasses grow throughout the pasture and offer a wonderful diet to the cattle when they are eventually returned to that piece of land.

This mimics what happens in nature. Flocks of birds often follow large herds of herbivores—such as bison—picking through their dung, feasting, and doing important work at the same time. Salatin is always looking for ways to integrate multiple species to create a farming model that works ecologically and to the benefit of all the species involved. His rich, green pastures are striking next to those of his neighbors. He jokes that his neighbors refuse to admit that his system increases soil fertility this much, and prefer to believe that Salatin's land gets more rain.

The chickens, meanwhile, have everything they need to thrive: shelter, freedom, ample room, a balanced diet of bugs, green grasses, and a grain-and-legume feed that they can eat whenever they want, fresh water, plenty of sunlight and the outdoors. The naturally healthy chickens require little or no treatment with antibiotics or other medications.

Salatin's farm is in a stark contrast with what he calls "inhumane, fecal-factory, concentration-camp mausoleum houses." In addition to leading brutish, short lives, their eggs carry the antibiotics that the hens were fed. This constant supply of antibiotics in our food can have a dangerous effect on humans: antibiotic resistance. People who eat antibiotic-laden foods can become less responsive to medical anti-biotics when they are needed to fight disease or even save lives.

In addition to the antibiotics, how can these eggs not carry with them the misery of the hens that lay them? How can we, if we eat these eggs, not be affected by the negative energy of the conditions under which they were laid? How can they truly nourish us? Like the abolitionists who avoided sugar because it was "tinctured with the sweat, and the groans, and the tears, and the blood of the poor slave," and exhorted others to "Feast not on the toil, pain and misery of the wretched," I avoid eating eggs that come from factory farms as much as possible. (It is impossible to do it completely, as I occasionally eat somewhere other than my own home, and these are the eggs of commerce, the eggs of our culture, the eggs used in baking and cooking an endless array of foods.)

I buy my eggs from small farms directly at the farmer's market. Whenever possible, I buy eggs from a local rancher named Dave who follows Salatin's principle of moving chickens behind cattle on open pasture in a portable coop. I've been to visit his ranch, and seen the chickens pecking around in the grass and breaking up the cow pies. I've walked through the mobile coop and seen the eggs lying in their bedded nests. I've watched the coop being moved to a new piece of pasture, and seen the chickens run after it, disliking to be too far away from their comfortable home. Dave sells these eggs for six dollars a dozen, more than twice what most people are used to paying. But I am happy to pay extra for the humane treatment of chickens, the ecological preservation of the pastureland, and an egg that is full of nourishment for me and anyone who eats at my table.

I generally avoid buying grocery store eggs because any producer large enough to distribute eggs to grocery stores arouses my suspicion. I know of at least one large battery-hen egg producer that also has a line of so-called organic, humane, free-range eggs. The chickens still have their beaks burned and are still crowded, but their pens have screens rather than walls, allowing the air to flow through and qualifying them as free range. They don't get to eat bugs or snails or greens on open pasture, though; they are limited to chicken feed.

Unfortunately, there is a lot of green-washing when it comes to eggs—packaging and marketing that makes eggs sound more humane than they really are for the purpose of making a profit. The organic regulations adopted in 2000 make it relatively easy to produce eggs that are certified organic. As Joel Salatin points out:

> It is amazing when people find out the truth of what the new livestock standards, which require access to range, really mean. To the average consumer this is "home on the range," blue skies and wildlife. Not for Wall Streetified organics. "Access to range" refers to an 11,000-bird layer house with a 30-by-30 foot corral next to it that the chickens can step out on. Instead of pushing to a maximum quality and artisanal designation, everything becomes minimalized as we move toward a commodity base. It's a pass/fail, what-can-we-do-just-to-get-by system. It does not ask, "How can I do the very best?"

Some people may ask why—given the rampant abuse of laying hens and the difficulty of finding a truly humane egg—eat eggs at all? Why don't we just become vegans and eliminate eggs from our diet altogether? There are several reasons that I don't do so, or recommend it.

The eggs produced by healthy, free-roaming chickens such as those on Salatin's farm are among the most nutrient-dense foods available. This is a major reason the domesticated chicken has become part of agricultural communities around the globe, and why the egg is a part of every major cuisine in the world.

When Weston Price studied the traditional diets of the healthy isolated peoples he located in the 1920s and 1930s, one of the most striking differences between their diets and our modern counterparts had to do with nutrient density. Everything they put into their mouths was rich in something that the body needs on a daily basis—one or more of the most necessary vitamins, minerals, enzymes, amino acids, or essential fatty acids. Arrangements were made to make sure that members of the community had access to even rare nutrients not readily available in the area where the community lived. Trade or travel would accomplish this.

One example was on the South Pacific island of Viti Levu, which is part of the Fiji Islands. By the time Price reached this stage of his research, in 1934, he noticed that all of the healthy indigenous groups he studied ate some form of animal food in order to meet their needs for nutrient density. He was interested to see if he could find a healthful, traditional diet that didn't make use of animal foods—in other words, a vegan diet that supported healthy humans generation after generation. As Dr. Price writes:

> Since Viti Levu, one of the islands of this group, is one
> of the larger islands of the Pacific Ocean, I had hoped to
> find on it a district far enough from the sea to make it
> necessary for the natives to have lived entirely on land
> foods. Accordingly, with the assistance of the govern-
> ment officials and by using a recently opened govern-
> ment road I was able to get well into the interior of the
> island by motor vehicle, and from this point to proceed
> farther inland on foot with two guides. I was not able,
> however, to get beyond the piles of sea shells which had
> been carried into the interior. My guide told me that it
> had always been essential, as it is today, for the people of
> the interior to obtain some food from the sea, and that
> even during the times of most bitter warfare between
> the inland or hill tribes and the coast tribes, those of the
> interior would bring down during the night choice plant
> foods from the mountain areas and place them in caches
> and return the following night and obtain the sea foods
> that had been placed in those depositories by the shore
> tribes. The individuals who carried these foods were
> never molested, not even during active warfare. He told
> me further that they require food from the sea at least
> every three months, even to this day. This was a matter
> of keen interest, and at the same time disappointment
> since one of the purposes of the expedition to the South
> Seas was to find, if possible, plants or fruits which
> together, without the use of animal products, were

capable of providing all of the requirements of the body for growth and for maintenance of good health and a high state of physical efficiency. . . . Land animal foods, however, are not abundant in the mountainous interior, and no places were found where the native plant foods were not supplemented by sea foods.

As far as I know, there is no evidence of a thriving, vegan culture that has been able to provide adequate nutrition to its people generation after generation. Every group Price studied not only valued animal products for their nutrient density, but also made special arrangements, such as those on Viti Levu, to ensure that all members of the community had at least periodic access to them that would not be interrupted by war or weather.

Eggs are nutritional powerhouses, designed by nature to contain all the food that an embryo would need to grow into a full-fledged bird, fish, or reptile. As Sally Fallon and lipid expert Mary Enig write:

> Eggs have provided mankind with high-quality protein and fat-soluble vitamins for millennia. Properly produced eggs are rich in just about every nutrient we have yet discovered, especially fat-soluble vitamins A and D. Eggs also provide sulphur-containing proteins, necessary for the integrity of cell membranes. They are an excellent source of special long-chain fatty acids called EPA and DHA, which play a vital role in the development of the nervous system in the infant and the maintenance of mental acuity in the adult—no wonder Asians value eggs as a brain food. Egg yolk is the most concentrated source known of choline, a B vitamin found in lecithin that is necessary for keeping the cholesterol moving in the blood stream.
>
> It pays to buy the best-quality eggs you can find—eggs from chickens fed flax or fish meal or, better yet, pasture-fed so they can eat bugs and worms. Their nutritional

qualities are far superior to those of battery-raised eggs and even many so-called free-range eggs. In particular, they contain a better fatty acid profile, one in which the omega-3 and omega-6 fatty acids exist in an almost one-to-one ratio; but in eggs from chickens fed only grains, the omega-6 content can be as much as nineteen times greater than that of the all-important omega-3. Other very-long-chain and highly unsaturated fatty acids—necessary for the development of the brain—are found in properly produced eggs but are almost wholly absent in most commercial eggs.

Like many Americans I was, at one point, hoodwinked into believing that eggs were bad for me. I bought the line that eating cholesterol would clog my arteries; succumbed to the macrobiotic belief that eggs were so *yang* that they would throw my system off-balance; and fretted over the alternative-health notion that eating eggs would somehow disrupt my reproductive system. Luckily these notions didn't hold me in thrall for long, as I began to notice that they didn't in any way jive with traditional wisdom about eggs. The more I studied about eggs and nutrition, the more I understood that the real problems with today's eggs are the results of the production model used by factory farms and not inherent in the egg.

I don't think it is an accident that an egg from a chicken out on pasture eating bugs and grasses is so much better for our health than a "fecal-factory" egg. Why should it surprise us that what is good for the chicken is good for us, too? It also happens to be good for the soil and good for the cow. And it is good for our society—a decentralized, local, small-scale food system where independent farmers can thrive and express their values and creativity. The story of poultry farmer Jimmy Johnson is a poignant example of how our agribusiness model of factory farming is not working for small farmers. The *Winston-Salem Journal* told his story in an article in 2004:

> Johnson started with two chicken houses and a contract with Piedmont Poultry in 1987. He built another in

1988 and two more in 1990. In 1996, Mountaire Farms, with headquarters in Delaware, bought Piedmont and renamed it Mountaire Farms of North Carolina. Johnson and his wife, Sheralyn Johnson, refinanced their operation and made improvements. . . . Over the years, they had put in new feeders, new water systems, new heaters and new curtains, then more fans, gas meters and a computer to monitor the curtains, fans and cool cells. "Whatever they asked us to do," she said. She said that in October 2002 her husband told her that a company official had asked him for more upgrades. The Johnsons applied for a $50,000 loan from Carolina Farm Credit and lost a flock of 18,000 chickens the following Sunday, she said. That Tuesday, Sheralyn Johnson said, the same company official told her husband that he could only have three more flocks—less than a six-month contract. . . . Nearly $300,000 in debt and convinced that he was facing the end of his contract to grow broiler chickens, Jimmy Johnson walked into an empty chicken house on October 27, 2002, and committed suicide.

Johnson was raising chickens for meat, but the system is the same whether the chickens are broilers or layers: Farmers who are under contract to one of the few large poultry companies are vulnerable to bankruptcy. You may ask why they don't just farm independently like Joel Salatin does. Well, what Salatin does isn't easy—there's no "just" about farming independently. He has come up with not only his own farming system—one that fits the terrain and climate of his land—but his own distribution and marketing systems as well. He writes books and speaks at conferences and has built up over decades a following for his products. Much of what he does flouts the regulations of the health department, the FDA, and the USDA. He wrote one article called "Everything I Want to Do Is Illegal." But one thing is clear: When consumers like you and me refuse to eat fecal-factory eggs and are willing to spend more for healthy eggs, other farmers will follow

Salatin's lead. And we will find that when it comes to eggs, what is good for the chicken is good for the eater, for the farm, for the soil, and for the farmer—and all of this is good for the society at large.

Many people are wary of egg consumption due to fear of salmonella and other pathogens. Recently a proposal to mandate in-the-shell pasteurization of all eggs was put forth on a national level. A terrible idea for a number of reasons, the proposal gained some support because of people's fear of eggborne diseases. The USDA now urges people never to eat uncooked or undercooked eggs, although they have been a part of diets and cuisines around the world for many millennia and are full of healthful live enzymes. To clear up a few misunderstandings: First of all, a healthy individual with a strong immune system can eat an egg containing salmonella and not get sick. Second, most eggborne salmonella poisoning comes from commercial eggs, which makes sense since the crowded conditions contribute to the spread of the disease. Unfortunately, fears of salmonella have been used by the egg industry to discourage regulations for organic certification that require access to the outdoors. The director of farming for the National Humane Society explains in a paper on the subject:

> Large farming businesses, reluctant to provide outdoor access, are using the threat of salmonella as a scare tactic to exempt farmers from being required to raise poultry outdoors by the National Organic Program. In fact, there is even the possibility that not only would organic farmers be affected, but that all farmers wishing to allow chickens outdoor access would be prohibited. The arguments for greater susceptibility of outdoor chickens are unproven since there haven't been any scientific studies to show this. What is apparent, however, is that birds raised by the large commercial poultry companies have had significant problems with salmonella in their "protected environments." This casts doubt both on the

arguments about outdoor access and the motivation of such companies in raising them.

I eat farm-fresh, free-range eggs raw almost daily and have never had a problem with salmonella or any other eggborne disease. I serve these eggs raw without fear. I do not, however, eat or serve commercial eggs raw; there may be some reason to be concerned about the wholesomeness of eggs that come from chickens with compromised immune systems grown under fecal-factory conditions. Joel Salatin relates a story about salmonella and his eggs:

> One of the restaurants we used to sell to had a salmonella outbreak. The bureaucrats went in, confiscated some of our eggs, and claimed they were the problem. We quickly grabbed the eggs and sent them to Brookside Laboratory and paid a couple of hundred bucks—we even sent samples of the chicken manure from our farm—it all came back one hundred percent clean, zero salmonella. We were waiting on pins and needles for the state cultures to come back. Finally, I got tired of waiting, called the inspector in charge, and asked what they found. She said, "We never cultured it." I asked, why not? She said, "Culture doesn't mean anything, it's just a point in time. That species of salmonella has been found in the past, in some cases, on eggs, so we just assumed it was from your eggs because they are unwashed." If our eggs are not dirty, we don't wash them because it preserves their bacterial film and keeps them fresher longer. We have customers who don't want washed eggs. This inspector said, "As far as I'm concerned an unwashed egg is inedible." . . . An interesting sidenote to that story occurred the very next day, when a friend who had just toured France called me up and was telling me about his trip. He said, "In France it is illegal to sell a washed egg." They figure an egg that needs to be washed is so dirty that it has to be pasteur-

ized, because the shell is porous, and if you wash it, it is
going to accept bits and pieces of the dirty exterior.

I think the best way to approach egg safety is to buy eggs fresh from
a small farmer who practices free-range agriculture, and to enjoy them
any way you like. Either that or raise your own laying hens—which is
legal in most areas, even many cities.

For those of you who may balk at paying more for eggs than you
are used to, remember that truly free-range eggs from outdoor
chickens require a more expensive and labor-intensive production
process than do than the factory-farmed eggs in the supermarket.
Even at the high-end price of six dollars a dozen, eggs at fifty cents
apiece are still affordable. A two-egg breakfast costs only a dollar, and
you know that your egg contains all the life-giving nutrient density it
was meant to have. Remember that eggs from pastured chickens have
more vitamin E, B_{12}, carotenes, antioxidants, and omega-3 fatty acids
than factory-farmed eggs. How many people eat cheap battery eggs
and then go spend a lot of money buying supplements such as antioxidants, vitamins E or B_{12}, carotenes, or oils containing omega-3 fatty
acids? The nutritional supplement industry is a huge and growing
worldwide business, despite many indications that we are better able
to assimilate nutrients from the foods we eat than from pills containing isolated nutrients. The sugar industry and others have frac-
tured our foods and taken the nutrients out. Now another industry
seeks to sell us the pure nutrients, again taken out of context of our
foods. Why don't we instead invest in supporting independent farmers
and getting our nutrients the way our ancestors did, through nutrient-
dense whole foods from small farms?

I love to eat eggs because they are a culinary expression of cultures
across the globe. While we tend to think of eggs as breakfast food, in
most of the world they are lunch and dinner fare. Hard-cooked eggs
are used in countless ways other than the familiar egg salad or deviled
eggs. In much of South and West Asia they are served in curries, often

rich with coconut milk, or with rice dishes or meat stews. In Ethiopia they are added to the country's best-known specialty, *doro wat*, a spiced stew of chicken and onions typically eaten with *injera* bread. In the Yucatán they are diced and wrapped in corn tortillas, and then covered with a sauce of pumpkin seeds and topped with tomato sauce for a Mayan dish called *papadzules*. In Scotland they are surrounded by fresh sausage, rolled in bread crumbs, and then fried.

In Japan egg pancakes are cooked thin and sliced into ribbons, or cooked thick and then cut into strips or cubes. They are then combined with rice for sushi rolls or added to other dishes such as soups. In China raw eggs are added at the last minute to simmering chicken broth to make *don far tong*—egg flower soup, aka egg drop soup. A similar soup, called *stracciatella*, is made in Rome, with the addition of Parmesan cheese. In Greece eggs and lemon juice are used to thicken *avgolemono*, the classic egg-lemon chicken soup. This technique is common in Turkey and other Mediterranean countries as well. The Japanese *chawanmushi* is a cross between an egg-thickened soup and a savory custard. Many cuisines feature a soup with a poached egg floating in the middle: the Portuguese *açordas* made with bread, garlic, and broth; the Japanese noodle-and-egg soup, *miso nikomi udon*; the Azorean tomato soup with a poached egg, *sopa de tomate com ovos escalfados*; the Nicaraguan *sopa de frijoles*, a puree of red beans with a poached egg; and on, and on.

The Pennsylvania Dutch pickle hard-cooked eggs in a salty brine made from beets, turning them a rosy pink. The Chinese preserve raw eggs with salt and tea leaves, turning them a translucent greenish brown, the famous "thousand-year eggs." They also hard-cook them, then gently crack the shells and steep them in soy sauce, tea, and star anise to marble them with a copper color and infuse them with flavor.

Eggs are indispensable in baking, and without them we would forgo our most common desserts, including most cookies, cakes, and ice creams. The yolks are used to thicken sauces such as mayonnaise, hollandaise, and crème anglaise. The whites are whipped, sweetened, and flavored to make meringues. Add coconut and they are macaroons, or almonds and they are amaretti. The famous soufflé, whether sweet or savory, is impossible without eggs. So is flan or crème brûlée.

All of these dishes appeal to me. And the authentic main ingredient doesn't need to be imported from afar, but can be grown almost any-where—as close as your own backyard. Eggs are the original fast food, and my kitchen would be bereft without them. I could not whip up frittatas for a quick supper as I often do, or soft-boil, fry, or scramble them for a quick breakfast with toast. I couldn't make the sauces that make so many other dishes delicious. My cooking would be impover-ished indeed.

So I offer here just a very few of the recipes that I love to make in my kitchen, with great gratitude for the gift of eggs. On the Egg Moon, I say a prayer for all the chickens living in confinement. May we humans see the errors of our ways and dismantle the egg factories in favor of free-range, integrated, ecological farms. May each one of us find a source for eggs that we can be proud of, so that we can eat eggs without fear or hesitation, but with relish, pleasure, and respect.

EGG MOON RECIPES

Asparagus Frittata
Serves 3–4

I make frittatas all the time, using whatever produce I find in season at the farmer's market. Asparagus is the herald of spring, and so this is a perfect Egg Moon recipe.

1 small bunch asparagus, about ¾ pound

1 large or 2 small leeks

2 tablespoons butter

4–5 hen's eggs from family farm chickens, or 1–2 goose eggs, or 3–4 duck eggs

¼ cup cream, half-and-half, or whole milk (from a family dairy, if possible)

¼–½ teaspoon sea salt, or to taste (you might want to use the lesser amount if you are adding cheese; more if you are not)

Pepper, freshly ground

Nutmeg—a little grated fresh, or ⅛ teaspoon powdered

¼ cup grated cheese such as cheddar or Monterey Jack, or crumbled feta (optional)

1. Preheat the oven to 300° F.
2. Break off the tough ends of the asparagus. Cut the spears into 1-inch pieces on the diagonal.
3. Slice the leeks into thick rounds. Put them into a bowl of cold water and mix to get the dirt out.
4. Melt the butter in an oven-safe skillet (cast iron or stainless steel). When it's hot, lift the leeks out of the water in handfuls, shaking off any excess water, and put into the pan. Sauté over medium heat until just tender.
5. Add the asparagus pieces to the pan along with about a tablespoon of water. Cover the pan and allow the asparagus to steam for 1 to 3 minutes, until just tender.
6. Meanwhile, mix together the eggs with cream, milk, or combination.
7. Add the salt, pepper, and nutmeg.

(Note: Because I trust my source for eggs, I always taste my raw egg mixture to check if it's salty enough. For my palate, the egg mixture should be salty enough to taste the salt, yet not overly salty.)

8. Add the asparagus to the pan and pour the egg mixture over, then add the cheese, pressing it gently into the eggs. Let this cook on the stovetop over low heat for a minute or two, and then transfer to the oven and bake until the eggs are just set—this may be as little as 5 minutes. (You can also finish under a broiler, as long as the pan isn't too deep and you keep a close eye to make sure it doesn't burn.)
9. Remove from the oven, cool for a few minutes, and slice and eat. Serve with salad and good bread, and maybe a few steamed new potatoes.

Stracciatella (Roman Egg Drop Soup)
Makes 2 cups

This is one of my favorite quick lunches. You can easily multiply the recipe to feed more people.

2 cups or so chicken broth (page 299)

Sea salt or fish sauce to taste

1–2 leaves Swiss chard, spinach, or other leafy green

Parmesan cheese

1 egg

Black pepper

Nutmeg

1. Bring the chicken broth to a boil in a small pan. Season with fish sauce or salt to taste. Chop the chard leaves finely and add to the boiling broth.
2. Grate the Parmesan on the finest grater you have (it's best to get it as close to powder as possible) until you have about a tablespoon; you can also use pre-grated Parmesan if you have that around. In a bowl, whisk the egg together with the cheese.
3. Beat the soup with the whisk while you pour in the egg mixture in a thin stream. The egg should cook immediately. It will be more fully dispersed than in Asian egg drop soup, due to the Parmesan.
4. Pour the soup into a bowl, grind some black pepper on top, grate on some nutmeg, and eat.

Asian Egg Drop Soup
Serves 2 as a starter or side

3 cups or so chicken broth (page 299)

1 tablespoon plus 1 teaspoon fish sauce, or to taste

1 teaspoon soy sauce, or to taste

1 egg

2–3 scallions, sliced thinly

1. Bring the chicken broth to a boil in a small pan. Season with 1 tablespoon of the fish sauce and 1 teaspoon of the soy sauce, and taste. If you'd like it saltier, add a little more of either.
2. In a bowl, whisk the egg together with the remaining teaspoon of fish sauce.
3. Beat the broth with the whisk while you pour in the egg mixture in a thin stream. The egg should cook immediately. Remove from the heat.
4. Pour the soup into a bowl and top with scallions.

Spring Tonic Nettle Soup
Serves 3–4

Some important notes about nettles: If you're picking wild nettles for eating, don't touch them with your bare hands, and harvest only the top four inches of the plant. In the kitchen use tongs or a large fork to pick them up. You may want to remove the thick stems from the nettle tops before cooking. Always cook nettles until they're soggy or completely wilted before eating; a quick sauté is not sufficient to deactivate the sting. If you're making nettle tea with fresh nettles, be sure to strain the nettles out, and don't eat the leaves unless they've been thoroughly cooked.

2 leeks, cut into rounds

3 tablespoons butter or olive oil

¼ pound stinging nettle tops

1 bouquet garni (page 309)

1 quart chicken stock (page 299), filtered water, or other light chicken stock made without vegetables or herbs (a strong stock will overwhelm the flavor of the nettles)

2 egg yolks

½ cup crème fraîche

Salt and pepper to taste

Nutmeg to taste

1. Sauté the leeks in the butter or olive oil. Add the stock or water and bring to a boil.
2. Add the nettles (being careful not to touch them with your bare hands!), bouquet garni, and stock or water.
3. Cover, bring to a boil, and simmer until the nettles are very soft.
4. Meanwhile, in a bowl, whisk together the egg yolks and crème fraîche.
5. Remove the bouquet garni from the soup, turn the heat to low, and puree using an immersion blender, adding a generous pinch of salt and a grind of pepper.
6. Take a ladleful of soup and stir it into the egg mixture.
7. Return the egg-nettle mixture to the soup and stir gently over very low heat (do not let it boil again).
8. Grate some fresh nutmeg into the soup, taste, and add more salt as necessary to make it savory and delicious.

Variation: Add a handful of sorrel leaves to the soup for a lemony flavor.

Avocado and Hard-cooked Eggs with a Lemony Dressing
Serves 2

This simple composed salad can be a quick meal. The amounts are subjective, depending on whether you're serving this as an appetizer, meal, or side salad. To prepare as an appetizer for three to four people, cut the eggs into quarters and the avocado into eighths.

4–6 small eggs (2–3 per person)*

1 egg yolk from a free-range, farm-fresh egg

⅓ cup olive oil

¼ teaspoon mustard

Juice of ½–1 whole lemon

Sea salt and freshly ground pepper

2 small ripe avocados (1 per person)

Red leaf (or other) lettuce, or radicchio (optional)

1. Place the eggs in a pan and cover with water. Bring to a simmer, cover the pan, and simmer for 3 minutes. Then turn off the heat and allow the eggs to sit, covered, for 7 more minutes (10 minutes if you're using large eggs).
2. Meanwhile, make the lemony dressing. Put the yolk in a bowl and whisk while you slowly pour in the olive oil. Add the mustard, and lemon juice to taste. Add salt and pepper to taste.
3. Pour the hot water off the eggs and transfer them to cold water to soak for a few minutes. Then peel and cut each egg in half lengthwise.
4. Cut each avocado like this: Cut in half and around the pit, then split in two. Carefully remove the pit. Cut each long-way half into halves (if two eggs per person) or thirds (if three eggs per person).
5. To assemble: You can either dress the lettuce with the lemony dressing and place a bed of that on the plate, or just put the dressing directly on the plate and spread it in a circle in the center. Reserve a little dressing to drizzle on top.
6. Arrange the avocado and egg slices alternately in a ring radiating out from the center of the plate (or the bed of lettuce). Drizzle the remaining dressing over everything.
7. Sprinkle sea salt over the dish, and grind fresh pepper on the egg halves. (I sometimes like to put a dollop of *rot kohl*—red sauerkraut—in the very center of the arrangement. It looks pretty and tastes good, too.)

*Note: Very fresh eggs are harder to peel. You can allow them to sit at room temperature for a day or two to age them before cooking.

4

MILK MOON

My speckled heifer will give me her milk,
And her female calf before her.
*   Ho my heifer! heifer! heifer!*
*   Ho my heifer! kindly, calm,*
*   My heifer gentle, gentle, beloved,*
*   Thou art the love of thy mother.*

—From a Gaelic milking song, translated from the Gaelic

I love you, my favorite cow
You provide us with everything!

—From a Maasai milking song, translated from the Maasai

The Milk Moon falls right around Beltane—May Day—the first day of summer in the old Celtic calendar. On Beltane, Celtic people left their winter homes and drove their herds up onto summer pasture. According to tradition, a procession would form for the journey up into the hills. The sheep went first, followed by the cattle in order of their ages, then the goats, and finally the horses. The animals were kept on the summer pasture until Samhain, six months later, when they would be brought back down for the winter.

This annual ritual evolved from considerations of climate and geography. Higher pastures get more snow in wintertime. So in autumn, people would bring pastured animals down to winter homes where they could feed them cut hay—or allow them to graze on grass when it was available—and house them in stables to protect them from the weather. As the hills warmed in spring, the green grass on these higher pastures began to grow once again, fed by the water of the melting snow. This rapidly growing fresh grass was an especially nutritious food for cows and other ruminants, and so they were led back up into the hills to feast on this quality pasture.

A similar pattern was followed in the remote Alpine villages of Switzerland. The Swiss villagers of the Loetschental Valley were among the first isolated traditional groups that Weston Price studied in his search for people with strong health and bone structure. The high mountains surrounding the valley permitted limited trade into or out of many of the villages. The people in some villages grew all their own food (except salt) and the fiber for their clothing. Price found them to have exceptionally healthy teeth and bodies and a high level of resistance to tuberculosis—a major killer at the time. After observing many aspects of their pastoral, agricultural, and culinary traditions, he wrote:

> Almost every household has goats or cows or both. In the summer the cattle seek the higher pasturage lands and follow the retreating snow which leaves the lower valley free for the harvesting of the hay and rye. The turning of the soil is done by hand since there are neither plows nor draft animals to drag the plows, in preparation for the next year's rye crop. A limited amount of garden stuff is grown, chiefly green foods for summer use. While the cows spend the warm summer on the verdant knolls and wooded slopes near the glaciers and fields of perpetual snow, they have a period of high and rich productivity of milk. The milk constitutes an important part of the summer's harvesting. While the men and boys gather in the hay and rye, the women and children go in large numbers with the cattle to collect the milk and make and store cheese for the following winter's use. This cheese contains the natural butter fat and minerals of the splendid milk and is a virtual storehouse of life for the coming winter.
>
> From Dr. Siegen [a village pastor], I learned much about the life and customs of these people. He told me that they recognize the presence of Divinity in the life-giving qualities of the butter made in June when the cows have arrived for pasturage near the glaciers. He gathers the people together to thank the kind Father for

the evidence of his Being in the life-giving qualities of butter and cheese made when the cows eat the grass near the snow line. This worshipful program includes the lighting of a wick in a bowl of the first butter made after the cows have reached the luscious summer pasturage. This wick is permitted to burn in a special sanctuary built for the purpose.

Reading Price's chapter on the isolated Swiss reminds me of my favorite childhood book, *Heidi*—Johanna Spyri's story of a young orphan sent to live on a mountainside in the Alps with her cranky and solitary grandfather, the Alm-Uncle. He makes a little three-legged stool and a bed of hay in a loft to accommodate his new charge. Heidi spends her days following her friend Peter, the goatherd, up high into the mountains, where they keep watch over the village goats and play among the wildflowers. Each day they eat their lunch of dark rye bread, homemade cheese, and fresh raw goat's milk, exactly the daily fare of the Swiss villagers Price studied.

Heidi conjures a vision that I found endlessly romantic as a child. When I reread it recently as an adult, I found much culinary wisdom between the lines. The story is a paean to the healing powers of milk, a traditional diet, and a rugged way of life.

Although Heidi is happy with her grandfather, she is taken away to the city to be a companion to the disabled daughter of a wealthy urban businessman. Heidi is ever cheerful and a good companion to Klara, but is so homesick that she begins sleepwalking, dreaming of the snow-topped mountains of her home. Eventually Heidi is returned to the Alps out of concern for her health. Not long afterward it is decided that the country air might do Klara some good as well, and she is sent to the country to visit Heidi. She is carried up the mountain in her wheelchair, and must be lifted up into the hayloft at bedtime. The Alm-Uncle puts her on a healing regimen of milk from one of his two goats. He feeds this goat special herbs, and all her milk is reserved for Klara, who drinks bowl after foaming bowl of it—raw, of course. After a number of weeks of this healing food, Klara is able to walk for the first time.

Perhaps it was my love of this story as a child that made me skeptical of the many negative accusations I heard about milk and dairy products over the years. I aspired to veganism for a time, won over briefly to the notion that dairy was, after all, a bad thing. But I hated life without animal products. Cream, yogurt, butter, cheese, and milk—these are among my favorite things. I was sulky without them. None of the popular substitutes satisfied me. I've always found the taste of soy milk to be chalky, fake, and oversweet. Rice milk is thin, anemic, with unpleasant overtones. Almond milk is kind of tasty, but it tastes like almonds, not like milk. Soy "cheezes" taste like the rubbery imitations that they are, and I'd rather have my toast dry than spread it with margarine, which is awful. I am always amused when someone hands me one of these knockoffs and professes that it tastes "actually pretty good." I can never concur.

Nevertheless, I can see why they have garnered a following. The conventional dairy industry is a disaster. Veganism and the yucky fake-dairy products seem preferable to miserable cows and overprocessed milk. Heidi, those free-ranging goats munching on wild herbs, the healing milk—these are things of the past, we assume, or merely fictional. They are a distant memory nearly forgotten.

But when I was in Switzerland two years ago, I took a hike in the Alps. Climbing over an incline, I heard the gentle ringing of bells break through the vast quiet, filling the air with their persistent chiming. And then I saw them—a herd of cows munching on grass, the large bells around their necks clanging as they chewed their cuds. Tears welled up in my eyes. I had a fierce sense of homecoming. We climbed higher and saw a small herd of goats making their way over a crag. We were so high, I felt we could touch the clouds. After a long and sometimes frightening hike along a narrow ridge, we descended. At the mountain's base there was a small café where we ordered a drink. Sitting there, we again heard the clanging of bells. At first the sound was far off, then closer. Looking up into the sunset, we saw the herd of cows returning to the farmhouse after their day up the mountain. We sat and watched the old phrase come to life: *the cows come home*. The cowherd and his dog followed, making sure no one ran astray. The cowherd was on a motorbike, but other than that it could have been a hundred years ago—or five hundred, for that matter. The ranch hung out a hand-written sign that read LAIT CRU—raw milk. I realized that the world of my childhood fantasy, the world that Price wrote about in the 1930s, had persevered—at least to some degree—in this place.

I have never understood the argument against milk that asserts that because humans are the only species to drink milk after weaning, it somehow isn't a natural food. Those who saw the movie *Microcosmos* about the fascinating world of insects may remember a scene featuring ants and aphids. After the movie, I inquired about what was going on in that scene, and was informed that ants do something that could be described as keeping herds of aphids and milking them—a kind of entomological ranching. Yet no one points to ants and says, *Well, they're the only species that milks aphids, so they should stop.* It would be ludicrous.

Humans evolved over thousands of years in relation to other species on the planet, including dairy animals and many others. We are not the only species that drinks milk after adulthood (dogs and cats are proof of that), just the only species that developed the practice of keeping dairy animals and milking them. This was a wise and elegant survival strategy in places rich in pastureland where ruminant animals could be domesticated or followed for their milk.

Another argument made against milk is that it is somehow a colonial or even racist food. This is based on the erroneous notion that dairy products are inextricably tied to

Mammalian Mamas

Thirteen breeds of dairy animals that have been milked in traditional cultures:

1. Jersey cows
2. La Mancha goats
3. Sarakatsan sheep (ewes)
4. Bashkir horses (mares)
5. Kachchhi camels
6. Reindeer
7. Water buffalo
8. Zebu cows
9. Yaks (dris)
10. Ankole-watusi cows
11. Dzomo (yaks crossed with cattle)
12. N'Dama cows
13. Nigerian dwarf goats

Europeans and European history. Yes, Heidi was European, and her very local and indigenous diet of milk, cheese, and dark rye bread was a part of that cultural heritage. But Europeans are certainly not the only people that traditionally herd cattle and milk them. Bri Maya Tiwari, who grew up in an Indian community in British Guiana, writes of the milk of her childhood:

> I grew up in an idyllic village not far from the sea. In the still afternoons, women gathered on their kitchen verandas and sifted through grains and dhals. . . . The lithe ebony milkman, whose feet were always in flight, would arrive before tea and fill the milk buckets that were waiting for him on the landing below. The milk was delivered, buff-colored and foaming, within the hour of the milking. It was never preboiled. Milk was a vital and living food for as long as the ancestry could remember. The cows were gentle and happy. They grazed in the green pastures of fertile and rich land. They roamed by instinct, with their own rhythm. No one questioned why they should seek shelter from the blazing sun, or why they sat and gazed with those stupendous lotus eyes. . . . No child ever felt threatened by the presence of the cows. They were part of the dynamism of our life. A field without grazing cows would have been inconceivable in those evanescent afternoons.

Milk is an indigenous food in the diets of many diverse traditions. In Ladakh, a Himalayan region sometimes called Little Tibet, the people depend on their dairy animals for survival. Helena Norberg-Hodge, in her book *Ancient Futures*, writes of the pastoral lifestyle of the Ladakhis that she has lived among for more than thirty years:

> Some of my best memories of living closer to nature come from experiences at the high pastures, or *phu*. . . .
> Sheeps, goats, cows, yaks, and *dzo* all spend their summer at Nyimaling. The sheep and goats are taken to

the hillsides above the valley, every day to a different area so as to avoid overgrazing. Meanwhile, the cows wander along the floor of the valley. The *dzo* and yak, always independent, forage up high near the glaciers. . . .

Nyimaling: a 21,000-foot peak towering above the bowl of the valley; patches of green, carpets of wild flowers, marmots whistling to each other; the air ringing with the sounds of flutes and young shepherds' songs. For those few days at the *phu*, I glimpsed what life must have been like for thousands of years. The closeness between the people and the land and the animals they depended on was deeply touching—something that had never been part of my life, yet something that felt familiar.

She describes that haunting sense of familiarity that I felt in the Swiss Alps when I saw the cows with their bells high up in the fields. Is it an ancestral memory of our pastoral existence? The similarities between the lifestyle of the Ladakhis and that of the old Celts and Swiss villagers are striking to me—a common wisdom in how people relate to animals and the land. The way that the Ladakhis use the milk of their animals is also similar to that of the Swiss villagers Price studied. Norberg-Hodge again:

Most milk, *oma*, is made into butter, *mar*. None of the Ladakhi animals produces very much milk, but it is very rich. Yak milk is exceptionally rich, and its butter is a deep creamy yellow. The remaining buttermilk makes a low-fat cheese, *churpe*, that is dried and hardened in the sun. *Churpe*, along with a few vegetables, apricots (the only sweet treat), and dried meat, can be stored for more than a year without spoiling.

While dairy products have been a crucial part of the diets of peoples that live in cold mountainous regions such as the Alps and the

Himalayas, herding has not been limited to these landscapes. Among the most famous dairying people in the world are the pastoralist cultures of eastern and southern Africa. The Maasai live in what is now Kenya and Tanzania and are renowned for their height, their strength, and their skill as warriors. Price studied this cow-herding, pastoralist people and profiled them in his book because of their excellent health. Fresh raw milk is a major source of calories, and their cow herds are considered both a sacred trust and a sign of wealth. Price observes:

> Their estimate of a desirable dairy stock is based on quality not quantity [of milk]. They judge the value of a cow for keeping in their herd by the length of time it takes her calf to stand on its feet and run after it is born, which is only a very few minutes. This is in striking contrast with the practice of our modern dairymen who are chiefly concerned with the quantity of milk and quantity of butter fat rather than with its value as a source of special factors for nutrition. Many of the calves of the modern high-production cows of civilized countries are not able to stand for many hours after birth, frequently twenty-four. This ability to stand is very important in a country infested with predatory animals; such as lions, leopards, hyenas, jackals and vultures.

The Maasai also keep goats. Other dairying cultures of Africa include the Kalenjin people—also in Kenya—for whom milk and milk products form a major part of the diet. Some Kalenjins obtain more than half of their daily calories from one cheeselike fermented milk product called *mursik*. In recent years the dairy-loving Kalenjins have famously dominated the world of track-and-field distance events, winning Olympic medals and leaving competitors in the dust in the Boston Marathon and other races. Other African peoples that use dairy products extensively include the Xhosa, Tutsi, Muhima, Watusi, Karamajong, Fulani, Antandroy, Bara, Peulh, Borana, and many, many others.

To portray milk as an oppressive white man's food is to misrepresent reality. The true culprits of culinary colonialism are white sugar, white flour, soft drinks, fast food, and the panoply of prepackaged industrially manufactured products. These foods have invaded and colonized the diets of people around the world. They are the foods we should be campaigning against, not milk. Raw, fermented milk has been a staple for countless Europeans, Africans, and Asians for millennia.

Others argue that the ability to digest milk is a genetic mutation. Even if this is true, eye color, hair color, and skin color—none of which are considered unnatural—are also genetic mutations. Interestingly, the ability to digest lactose is a dominant trait, so where one parent can digest lactose and the other can't, the children will usually be lactose-tolerant. In cultures where milk is not only a staple but in fact a survival food, everyone is lactose-tolerant.

Widespread milk allergies and lactose intolerance are often cited as proof of the ill effects of dairy consumption. There are of course people who have trouble digesting dairy products, and others who are allergic to them. But some people will die if they eat peanuts, and others, shellfish. I can't eat mangoes without getting violently ill. This doesn't mean that peanuts, shellfish, and mangoes are bad foods.

Furthermore, we cannot look at the problem of lactose intolerance without considering the widespread pasteurization of milk in our country. Pasteurization cooks the milk—a process that kills bacteria but also kills enzymes. Primary among these is lactase, the enzyme naturally occurring in milk that digests lactose. Pasteurization destroys lactase but not lactose. Is it any wonder that so many people are lactose-intolerant when we have destroyed in the milk the enzyme

---

Gut Milk?

Thirteen traditional cultured dairy products:

1. Kefir (Balkans)
2. Mursik (Kenya)
3. Dahi (India)
4. Chura loenpa (Tibet)
5. Omashikwa (northern Namibia—Owamboland)
6. Koumiss (Mongolia)
7. Leban (Middle East)
8. Skyr (Iceland)
9. Yogurt (originally from the Middle East, now throughout the world)
10. Irgo (Ethiopia)
11. Jocoque (Mexico)
12. Crème fraîche (France)
13. Shubat (Kazakhstan)

that digests it? All of the peoples throughout the world that have thrived generation after generation on dairy products have eaten their dairy products either raw, or cultured, or both. Culturing is a process that increases the beneficial bacteria and predigests many of the sugars (lactose is a sugar).

Indigenous and traditional peoples culture their milk in a few ways. One is to simply leave it at a warm temperature to let the bacteria multiply and naturally sour (or clabber) it. Another is to add a culture such as kefir grains to the milk to better control the fermentation and create a distinctive flavor. The cultured dairy product most familiar to Americans is yogurt. It is made by heating the milk to sterilize it, adding a culture rich in particular strains of *lactobacilli* (beneficial bacteria) back into the milk, and then allowing it to culture at a warm temperature. Yogurt is also a central part of the diet throughout South Asia, West Asia, and Europe.

In America the automatic pasteurization of milk is a recent development—even my grandmother grew up on raw milk from the family cow on their farm in Minnesota, and the extra milk was sold to city folk. When the farm was foreclosed and the family moved to town, it was hard for my grandmother to learn to like pasteurized milk. By this time pasteurization was becoming popular as a result of widespread fears of tainted milk. These fears had some basis in fact. With industrialization, milk began to be produced under increasingly crowded and unclean conditions. In his book *The Untold Story of Milk*, Ron Schmidt describes the dairies that grew up around alcohol distilleries:

> The War of 1812 with England resulted in the permanent cutting off of America's whiskey supply from the British West Indies. As a result, the domestic liquor industry was born, and by 1814 grain distilleries began to spring up in the cities as well as in the country.
>
> Soon every major city had one or more distilleries, where grains were turned into whiskey. As the cities grew, readily available pasturage shrank, while the demand for milk—as well as for whiskey—rapidly increased. The processes of fermentation and distillation

extracted the starch and the alcohol from grains, and produced an acid refuse of chemically changed grain and water known as distillery slop. This waste product was then fed to cows by individuals who cared nothing about the animals or the quality of the milk thus produced.

Distillery owners then began housing cows next to the distilleries and feeding the hot slop directly to the animals as it poured off the stills. Thus was born the slop or swill milk system. . . .

Slop is of little value in fattening cattle; it is unnatural food for them and makes them diseased and emaciated. But when slop was plentifully supplied, cows yielded an abundance of milk. The milk was so defective in the properties essential to good milk that it could not be made into butter or cheese, and was good for nothing—except to sell.

The decline in the quality of milk and the increasingly unhealthy conditions of cows in unnatural conditions on unnatural feed meant increasing outbreaks of milkborne diseases and problems with the milk supply. Fears of unhealthy milk—combined with the dairy industry's desire to lengthen its shelf life—created a strong push for pasteurization. Once widespread pasteurization of milk began, the stage was set for a dairy industry that put a minimum of emphasis on the health of cows and the nutritional quality of milk and a maximum on quantity of milk at the lowest cost of production. Milk that contains pus and blood from sick animals can be pasteurized and then sold. While distillery dairies were eventually closed, the production model they created lives on. Ron Schmidt again:

Today in confinement dairies throughout America cows are living in stalls they never leave, stalls literally welded shut, where they are fed "scientific" diets devoid of fresh grass, diets designed to maximize milk production. These diets include grains, soybeans, "bakery waste" (bread, cakes, pastries and even candy bars) and citrus peel cake loaded with pesticides. Some will die in place, and the rest will live only a quarter of their natural lives. While some of the grossest excesses of the distillery dairies have been eliminated, confinement cows today are not healthy animals, and they are not producing the kind of milk America's children and adults need and deserve.

We have abused milk, both in production and in processing, tainting its goodness. Then we reject it because it is unhealthful. But the milk of Maya Tiwari's tropical childhood was an Ayurvedic healing food. The milk of Kenya's Kalenjin people produces the fastest long-distance runners in the world. The milk of the Alpine Swiss whom Price studied built a strong, hearty people resistant to the plague of their time. And the milk of the Himalayan Ladakhis has nourished a thriving, self-sufficient, ecologically wise culture for generations.

Milk is the original comfort food. If we were lucky, we had the opportunity to suckle the milk of our mothers for the first moons of our lives. When we cried, we were taken to the breast and comforted with sweet milk. The books of Martín Prechtel chronicle his experiences living and being trained as a shaman among the Tzutujil Maya in Guatemala. Among the Tzutujil, the major transitions in a person's life were celebrated with ritual, ceremony, and tradition. Prechtel describes these movingly, including what took place after his first son was born to his wife, Ya Lur:

> At the midwife's bidding and Ya Lur's command, I placed the little bound up nestling into the arms of Ya Tzimai, Corn Silk Woman, my first client as a shaman. She had been unable to have a baby, but after our ceremonies she was nursing my own boy, who suckled milk from her breasts brought down by the birth of her own child two months before.

Then he was passed to the next woman, and the next and the next and the next. Every woman who was lactating, who wanted to bless the new mother, my wife, came to let the newborn suckle so that he would never feel like a stranger in any compound of the village. In the minds of the Tzutujil, having suckled from the breasts of women from every clan in the village, my son would now be related to the whole village in the deepest way possible. This was the beginning of initiation because the Tzutujil knew that the smell of one's mother was strong, and that the sweet animal smell of all the village mothers huddled together lived in your memory like the house in the village where you were born. Once more this made you feel even more intensely received and at home in your village and welcome to come through every doorway.

Adults sometimes had to stop quarrels among their peers by reminding them how they had suckled from the other's mother or grandmother. This milk-giving was a peacemaking thing.

Among the Maasai, if two clans have been warring and decide to make peace, their agreement is sealed with mother's milk. Each side brings a lactating mother and her baby to a neutral place, and the mothers exchange babies and suckle the other's child. This is how they sign their treaty. Milk is a messenger of peace.

Milk is profoundly intimate. Just contemplating it makes us feel vulnerable. On a spiritual level, it is symbolic of so much that we are uncomfortable with: our animal nature; our dependence on and love for women, feminine sexuality and sensuality; our birth and thus our death and mortality.

I think this is part of why we have such a love–hate relationship with milk. Historian Felipe Fernandez-Armesto says, in his scholarly history of food *Near a Thousand Tables*, "I find the very idea of drinking unmodified milk disgusting." While he writes at length and with neutrality about cannibalism, not to mention appetites for creatures such as worms, snails, bugs, and dogs, it is for unmodified milk that he retains his disgust. He is not alone in this—many with sophisticated palates turn up their noses at milk. Why are our feelings for this first food so laced with repugnance? Is it because milk belongs to the realm of that Earth-bound femininity that we seek either to dominate or to transcend? Is it the desire for control over the sacred feminine that causes us to overbreed our cows, treating them not as creatures but as units of production?

In our factory-farming system, cows are taken off grass when the single greatest gift they offer us is to turn that inedible grass into nourishing milk and cream. They are milked in factories where we no longer have to touch the teats. Then we boil the milk and homogenize it to make it less distinctively itself, to kill its life-giving and digestive enzymes. We bottle it in plastic and ship it across the country, labeling it a commodity so that we can control its price and ensure that it will be cheap and expendable. We make certain that what we end up with is as little like the precious mother's milk that it once was as possible. And we make sure that its profound relationship to an animal, to the Earth, to open space, to the season and the rain and the growing of wild, natural grass is severed.

In the Asian system of *yin* and *yang*, milk is a very *yin* food. *Yin* energy is the energy of the moon, of the Earth, of the divine feminine, of darkness, of water, of receptivity, of emotion. Milk is like these things. But our culture is much more comfortable with what is *yang* than what is *yin*. *Yang* energy is the energy of the sun, of the heavens, of the divine masculine, of light, of fire, of action, of reason. We cut ourselves off from much that is *yin*, and seem especially keen to exert control over it. We see the moon and then we must get into a rocket and go there and walk on it so we can say *Ha! Moon, I've got you! I've put my flag on you—you're not so special.* We look at milk and we say *Ha! Milk, I've got you! I've boiled you and bottled you and stuck a low price on you—you're not so special.* We look at women and we say *Ha! Women, I've got you! I've devalued your gifts and skills, commodified your beauty, and stuck you with a low wage—you're not so special.* We look at water and we say *Ha! Water, I've got you! I've dammed you and pushed you through pipes to where I want you to go and treated you with chemicals—you're not so special.*

But these things *are* special. Traditional cultures held each of them as sacred—carriers of part of what is divine and mysterious in life. The moon pulls the tides, makes them rise and fall as it waxes and wanes and pulls on the cycles of women, who bleed and ovulate and then get pregnant and give birth and then lactate and give milk. All these things are connected through the mystery of nature.

Once upon a time I, too, had a low opinion of milk. I went back to reread the book that most convinced me to give it up, to try to find the argument that had so influenced me. The book was *Food and Healing* by Annemarie Colbin. There were lots of scientific analyses of the problems of milk—most of which had to do with the modern mode of production. But there was also a spiritual argument. Colbin writes:

> I find that on the spiritual level, milk reunites us with the Mother energy, and supports all the feelings associated with childhood: emotions close to the surface, easy laughter, easy tears, contentedness, dependency. It keeps us in innocent bliss and lacking in conscious awareness. In effect, as long as we consume milk or milk products regularly, we have not been fully weaned—thus, regardless of chronological age, we remain unable to attain our full potential as adults.

At one point I swore off milk in the effort to become a full adult. I have reason to believe that Colbin has changed her view on milk. I have, too. Now I read this passage and think: Is it so bad to be reunited with Mother energy? Is it so bad to have emotions close to the surface, easy laughter, easy tears, contentedness, even dependency? Are we ever fully weaned from our mother the Earth? Is that even desirable?

In Tzutujil Mayan culture Martín Prechtel witnessed the ornate ritual that turned boys into men—a process that took many moons. The rite served to wean the boy from his earthly mother, but in the process he was married to the Earth Mother. As the young men went through the ritual, it was crucial that they brought their emotions close to the surface: "They wept and wept for life, for the grief of being a person destined to die, a person whose friends and relatives died, a person who suffered in so many ways. They wept for any of the many griefs that men and women knew and began to speak it all out loud in a way that began to sound holy."

The initiation ritual took the boys through a series of tasks that involved rescuing the Goddess of the Flowering Earth from the Underworld and from Death, thereby making the Earth live again. Initiation was considered a process of cooking. After being cooked by the rituals, a boy became an *Acha*, an initiated man. Prechtel describes how important it was to go through this before marrying a woman of the village:

> Only an initiated man or *Acha* could marry a woman and not be miserable and disappointed. An uninitiated man was one who didn't know that his first love was a divine being, a being that lived and kissed him in nature, as a village, in the landscape of the world. If he tried to find her first in a human woman, he would become angry or depressed because she could not be that Goddess. It was the same for the girls, since the husband of an uninitiated woman would have to be a God or he would be trivialized and discarded as a failure, or, worse yet, start believing that he was one!
>
> Uninitiated men beat women for not being Goddesses. They left women behind who turned out to have thoughts and opinions of their own, or they allowed themselves to be ground to dust, year by year, by women whom they wanted and hoped would miraculously turn into a Goddess later on. Women had the same experiences with their husbands, men who disappointed them

when they refused to be the Gods the women longed to be loved by. . . .

The by-product, of course, was that each man got his own heart back. When his hollowness had been filled with the small Goddess of his own heart, then when he married a woman, she could see that he could see her seeing him seeing her, and both looking at the little piece of God and Goddess that resided in the other's "Heart Throne" and they were free to love each other properly, as themselves. Having understood and risked one's life for the delicate survival of the divine, one would not readily or willingly destroy it, especially in the heart of the human being who can really love you.

I fear we lack such spiritual intelligence. We lash out at all we don't understand, instead of embracing, saving, and defending the mystery. True heroism is not about killing and destroying, nor is it about rising above or maturing beyond the messiness of existence. It is about having the courage to love and respect all that is sacred in this earthly life. To weep and laugh and dance and worship and believe, and to know that there is no such thing as weaning from the Great Mother, is a path of wisdom. We *are* dependent. If we find a few moments of contentedness in that dependence, it is nothing to run from. Rather, it is something to soak up with every cell of our being. We can and should drink that milk of comfort.

We live in a country founded and built on the ideal of independence. Our national heroes are rebels, frontiersmen, and self-made men. The Puritans, immigrants, refugees, and slaves from whom so many of us are descended all sought freedom, and we celebrate that deep and abiding urge. Our ancestors either left behind, or were separated from, their long-standing traditions, their connection to place, the ties that bound them—in pursuit of liberty. And yet, ironically, the industrialism that went hand in glove with the desire to be independent is rendering us increasingly unable to provide for ourselves, and ultimately dangerously dependent on resources that are finite and nonrenewing.

The Ladakhis, who acknowledge and celebrate their dependence on the land and on their animals, live largely self-sufficient lives. They grow all their own food. Their animals pull their plows and turn their mills, provide them with milk, butter, cheese, and meat, and even provide them with their source of energy and an important building material in the form of their dung. Traditionally, the only trade Ladakhis conducted was for luxury items such as jewels. Otherwise they provided for *all* their material needs from the land and their animals. Hence the people developed a wide range of skills—farming, animal husbandry, dairying, cheese making, milling, cooking, weaving, sewing, building, irrigating, and regulating their own society. Now, that's true independence—based on a profound spiritual acknowledgment of dependence.

How many of us could grow our own food, grind our own flour, make our own cheese, weave our own cloth, sew our own clothes, build our own houses, and create a physical and social infrastructure without any heavy machinery, computers, electricity, or petroleum? What we've created in the industrialized West is functional dependence, based on a petulant, shallow notion of independence. Like twelve-year-olds who have run away from home but have no skills or resources, no real idea of how to survive, we assert our freedom from our mothers and fathers (our Mother Earth and our fatherlands) but in the end are dependent anyway. Like homeless teenagers whose so-called independence means forming gangs, depending on handouts, and becoming addicted to drugs, our so-called independence has become about forming monopolistic corporations, depending on modern technology, and becoming addicted to petroleum. We are weaned, but are we really free?

This paradox is similar to that embodied by the dairy cow. She represents human dependence on the Earth, the sacred feminine, connectedness, and the reciprocity of giving and receiving. At the same time, she is an emblem of self-sufficiency, wealth, and status. She was the original stock in the stock market. All dairying cultures prize their livestock, and if a family has cattle of its own, it is able to provide for itself. Note the words of the Maasai milking song at the beginning of this chapter: "I love you, my favorite cow—*you provide us with everything.*"

A family, clan, or culture with dairy animals is blessed with milk, meat, horsepower, fuel, leather—and all the products that can be made from these raw materials. The cow *is* the horn of plenty.

There is a song from the Scottish group Mouth Music that I often find running through my head. It is called "Milking the Cow," and the lyrics are based on a Xhosa chant, *"Ah senginkomo."* The Xhosa are a people of South Africa who hold their cows as sacred; the cattle pen, or *Kraal*, is the center of their village politics and life. Milk is a staple in the diet, drunk raw and slightly soured. Nelson Mandela, that great peacemaker of our time, is Xhosa. The lyrics go like this:

> *To milk the cow is to praise the hand of God that moves before us*
> *To feed the cow is to worship the spirit that breathes within us*
> *To kill the cow is to accept the darkness deep within us*
> *To spurn the cow is to spurn the gift of God that gives us life*
> *Milk the cow and feel the rhythm that beats inside us*
> *Touch the cow and feel the spirit that breathes within us*
> *Kill the cow and feel the sorrow that lies before us*
> *In blood we are born . . . blood of the cow redeems us*

On the Milk Moon, may we move beyond our petulant rejection of the things that make us feel vulnerable, and understand that only when we accept our utter dependency can we know the true meaning of freedom and power. May we honor the cow and the Earth and the Great Mother as well as our own mothers, who brought us into the world with tears and blood and a great messy thrust toward life. And may we also honor all those metaphorical mothers—those who may not have suckled us at their own breast, but who offered us the milk of human kindness. May we find within ourselves the heroism to seek out all that is *yin* and holy and rescue it from the forces of destruction. Maybe if we do that, we will get our own hearts back.

MILK MOON RECIPES

Yogurt
Makes 1 quart

Making yogurt at home is easy and satisfying. This is how I do it. It is a magical culinary process to experience with children.

3½ cups whole milk, preferably raw

1 tablespoon yogurt with live active
cultures

1. Heat the milk in a heavy-bottomed pan over medium-low heat, stirring occasionally, until it reaches 180° F. I use a milk thermometer to check this, but you can also heat it until it is steaming and ready to boil but not boiling.
2. Turn off the heat and allow the milk to cool, stirring occasionally so a film doesn't form on top.
3. Put the yogurt in the bottom of a 1-quart mason jar.
4. When the milk cools to 110° F or lower on a milk thermometer—or when it is quite warm to the touch but not so hot that you can't comfortably keep your finger there—pour a ladleful of milk over the yogurt and whisk to combine. Pour the rest of the milk into the jar and screw the lid on. Put the jar in a *warm* place to culture. I put mine on top of the pilot light on my gas stove. You can also use an electric heating pad, or set it on top of your water heater. It should stay between 80° F and 100° F overnight, or for at least 8 hours.
5. The yogurt should now be thick. Transfer to the fridge and let it cool before eating.

Warm Frothed Milk with Saffron and Cardamom
Makes 1 generous cup

This is based on a common breakfast drink in India. I usually make it before bedtime, however, as I find it soothing and soporific to drink while I read in bed before going to sleep.

¼ cup filtered water

A pinch (about 10 strands) of saffron

A generous pinch (about ⅛ teaspoon) of ground cardamom

1 cup milk, preferably raw

Honey to taste, if desired

1. In a small pot or stainless-steel stovetop milk frother, heat the water, saffron, and cardamom together until the water begins to simmer.
2. Simmer the water and spices together for a few minutes.
3. Add the milk and heat the mixture until it's quite warm to the touch but not too hot to hold your finger in—about 110° F. If you are using pasteurized milk, it doesn't matter if the milk gets really hot—it's already cooked. Heat over low heat and make sure not to scald (boil) the milk—it's okay if it simmers for a minute or two at low temperature.
4. Now you need to make the milk frothy. There are several ways to do this:
   - In India, the hot milk is poured from one glass to another, back and forth, from a height to create the froth. This is a bit of an art; some people can do it from as high as 3 feet. I tried doing this once but spilled a lot of milk and accomplished little froth!
   - I have a cappuccino milk creamer made by Nissan. This is a stainless-steel pot with a top that has a built-in frothing screen. (It looks sort of like a French press coffeepot.) Milk (whether hot or cold) can be frothed by just pumping the screen up and down until frothy. It is easy, takes just a minute, and requires no electricity. I love this gadget, and it really helped me to break my cappuccino habit. You can heat the milk right in the pot—this is what I always do. There are also many glass versions of this, and they work the same, but you have to do all your heating in another vessel, then transfer the hot milk to the glass frother and pump.
   - You can use an immersion blender right in the pot where you heated the milk, blending the milk at the surface. Or you can transfer the hot milk to a blender and blend on high speed to create froth.
   - Battery-operated, whisk-type frothers are widely available now. I haven't tried them.
   - If you have a steam cappuccino machine, you can combine the cold milk and the hot water–spice mixture in a steaming pitcher and then steam it.
5. Pour the frothy milk into a glass. If you want the drink a bit sweet, put a little honey into the bottom of the glass first, then stir the milk in. In India the drink is often garnished with slivered pistachio nuts on top. I prefer to just sprinkle on a little cardamom.

Yogurt Cheese Peras with Rosewater Syrup
Serves 4

Peras are a traditional Indian sweet—little rich, sweet balls, fresh not fried. The rose-water syrup makes them divine! Try to find real rosewater—most of what's on the market is synthetic.

Peras

1 quart yogurt

⅓ cup coconut spread (available at Wilderness Family Naturals)

1 tablespoon coconut oil

2 tablespoons palm sugar

1 tablespoon raw honey

A few grains of salt

Syrup

¼ cup raw honey

2 tablespoons real rosewater or rose hydrosol

1. Make the yogurt cheese: Pour the quart of yogurt into a strainer that is lined with a few layers of cheese-cloth and sits over a receptacle. Transfer to the fridge. Let this drip for about 12 hours, then gather the cheesecloth over the top of the yogurt cream and place a gentle weight (such as a clean rock or a jar full of beans) on top of that. Let it drip for another 12 hours or more.
2. Use 1 cup of the yogurt cheese for this recipe; the rest you can use as you would cream cheese.
3. Put the cup of yogurt cheese in a food processor.
4. In a bain-marie (double-boiler)—over water that is hot but not simmering—combine the coconut spread, coconut oil, palm sugar, honey, and salt. Break up this mixture gently with a whisk or a wooden spoon until all is soft.

5. Add the coconut mixture to the yogurt cheese in the food processor and process for 1 minute until combined. Put this paste into a bowl and put in the fridge for at least an hour to cool.
6. Roll the yogurt mixture into balls about 1 inch in diameter and put on a plate. Transfer the plate to the fridge for at least another hour to cool.
7. Mix the honey and rosewater to make the syrup.
8. To serve, put a tablespoon or so of syrup in the bottom of a dish, and put three *peras* into the dish. Decorate with rose blossoms if you have them. Serve with a spoon.

Note: If you can't get the mixture to roll into balls because it is too moist, you can serve a scoop in a dish with the syrup poured over it.

Kefir
Makes 1½ cups

Pronounced kef-EER, this is an easy cultured drink that can be made from raw milk. You can get kefir grains online or from someone else who makes kefir. As you culture the milk, the grains reproduce. You can harvest the extra grains and use for making the ales, beers, or mead in this book. This is how I make kefir at home. I use it for my daily kefir shake.

1½ cups raw whole milk

1 scant tablespoon kefir grains

1. Put the grains into a clean 1-pint jar. Pour the milk over the grains. Put the jar in a warm place and let it culture for 24 hours or more, depending on the temperature.

2. In my experience, kefir goes through a few predictable stages: First it stays liquid but gets a little slimy. Then it thickens into an almost yogurtlike consistency. Then it separates into a cottage-cheese-like thickness floating in clear whey. I like to use mine when it is yogurtlike (which usually takes about 24 hours), but will still use it when it is cheesy. If it is getting thick but I am not able to use it, sometimes I stick it in the fridge.

3. Strain the kefir through a sieve (some people advise not using a metal strainer, but I have never had a problem doing so) into a bowl to remove the grains. Sometimes I use a spatula to gently press the kefir through the sieve (not including the grains).

4. I usually transfer the grains directly back to the jar without rinsing them or the jar. Then I pour more milk over the grains and so get the next day's kefir started. Since the grains reproduce, every few days I will harvest some of the grains to make ales. About once every 10 days or so I will wash out the jar or use a clean one. I don't ever rinse the grains unless I am harvesting them for ales.

I use the kefir to make my Kefir and Superfood Shake (page 114). That is pretty much the only way I drink it, though some people enjoy drinking it straight.

Your grains always need to be immersed in milk to stay alive. If I go away for up to a week, I cover the grains with fresh milk as above, but instead of leaving it in a warm place, I put the jar in the fridge. This always works fine. If you're going away for longer, you might want to ask whoever is watering your plants to change the milk on your grains!

Clabbered Cottage Cheese
Makes about 2 cups

Sometimes I make clabbered, raw-milk cottage cheese from scratch. This is how I do it.

1 quart raw milk

1 teaspoon sea salt, or to taste

1. First, find a glass or ceramic bowl or dish that will hold the quart of milk and will also fit comfortably on top of a Crock-Pot or pan in your kitchen. I use a glass bowl that fits comfortably on top of my 5½-quart Crock-Pot.

2. Put the milk into the bowl you choose and put it in a *warm* place. I put it above the pilot light on my gas stove. Any place that will keep it above 80° F and below 110° F will work.

3. Allow the milk to "clabber"—to separate into a thick white cheese on top and a clear whey on the bottom. This could take anywhere from 1 to 4 days. You can check whether it has clabbered by cutting into the top with a sharp knife and seeing if it is solid enough to cut.

4. When the milk has clabbered, use a sharp knife to cut the curd. Make parallel cuts going in one direction, making ½-inch strips, from one end of the bowl to the other. Then rotate the bowl and make parallel cuts going perpendicular to the first cuts, also ½-inch strips, forming a crisscross pattern on top.

5. Fill a Crock-Pot or pan with very hot water and set over very low heat; put the bowl on top of the Crock-Pot or pan so that the hot water goes up its sides. Put a milk thermometer in the curds. Raise the temperature of the curds to 110° F slowly, stirring occasionally.

6. When the curd has reached 110° F, hold it there for at least an hour to set the curd. You will probably need to turn off the heat, then turn it back on again, a couple of times. The longer you hold it at 110° F, the firmer the curd your cheese will have. I usually hold mine for a few hours. If the temperature goes above 110° F, you have not ruined the cottage cheese, but you may have killed some (or most) of the enzymes. The curd will be firmer, and may be more like a feta than a cottage cheese.

7. Line a strainer with several layers of cheesecloth and pour the curds and whey through. Remove the whey. Allow the curd to drain until most of the liquid is gone, then pour about ½ cup filtered water over the curd and drain some more. You can move the cheesecloth back and forth gently to help the cheese to drain.

8. Sprinkle the salt over the curds a bit at a time and stir gently to combine. Taste as you go along so you can salt to suit. Transfer the cottage cheese to a jar in the fridge and eat within a week. You can pour a little fresh cream over the cheese before serving if you'd like.

Creamy Salad Dressing
Makes ½ cup

This is one of my favorite salad dressings to make at home. It suits a crispy lettuce with some body to it, such as romaine or little gem. You can also use this recipe to make Blue Cheese Dressing by adding ¼ cup of crumbled blue cheese to it before tossing the salad.

¼ cup crème fraîche (see Resources)

1 egg yolk (optional)

¼ cup olive oil

½ teaspoon white wine or apple cider

vinegar

A generous pinch of salt

Plenty of freshly ground pepper

1. In a large bowl, whisk the crème fraîche into the egg yolk, and then whisk in the olive oil.
2. Add the vinegar, salt, and pepper.
3. Put the cleaned lettuce leaves directly into the bowl and toss before serving.

5

MOON OF MAKING FAT

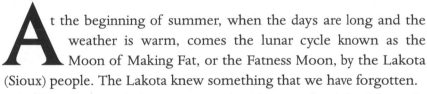

*Dekar, don't get excited, be a little bit calm
    and collected.
Right now I will give you enough meat and rice to
    stuff you,
sweet buttered rice like rolling eyes, and noodle soup like swaying hips.
I will give you momos like a pleated chupa.
Wish-fulfilling Dekar, I will fill your mouth with fat!*

—FROM A TRADITIONAL TIBETAN NEW YEAR SONG,
TRANSLATED FROM THE TIBETAN

At the beginning of summer, when the days are long and the weather is warm, comes the lunar cycle known as the Moon of Making Fat, or the Fatness Moon, by the Lakota (Sioux) people. The Lakota knew something that we have forgotten.

Before the twentieth century, most cultures valued fat. Not only was it precious, but those animals and plants that yielded it were precious as well. Fat was used as food, and also for lighting, for religious ceremony, and for anointing the body. Indigenous people of all continents made use of the fat from the wild game, seafood, or nuts that they hunted or gathered. The bison, sacred to the Plains Indians such as the Lakota who hunted it, provided the fat they rendered and used in staples such as *pemmican*—dried pounded meat mixed with rendered fat. The Inuit used seal oil, whale blubber, and other fats as staple foods and sources of light. Northern Europeans prized lard from pigs, tallow from sheep and cows, schmaltz from chickens, and fat from ducks and geese.

Throughout Europe cream and sour cream were coveted, as was the butter churned from the cream. Skimmed milk—milk stripped of most of its fat—was fed to the pigs, which would turn it into fat on their bodies. In India *ghee*, a form of clarified butter, is ceremonial and medicinal, and considered extremely *sattvic* or spiritual. The word for fat in Sanskrit, *sneha*, also means "lavish love." In many parts of South and Southeast Asia the fat of the coconut forms a critical part of the cuisine, in the form of both oil and coconut milk. In Mediterranean countries olives and olive oil are treasured. In West Africa red palm oil and the meat of the palm nut are used in stews, soups, and other dishes, greatly enriching the diet. In the Himalayas yak butter, cheese, and milk are valued for their fat. In the healthy indigenous cultures that Weston Price studied, the percentage of calories in the diet that came from fat ranged from 30 to 80 percent. None of these cultures ate what we would call a low-fat diet.

But recently (relatively speaking), here in America, the theory was propagated that fat causes heart disease—despite ample evidence to the contrary. In southern France, generous amounts of saturated animal fats were routinely eaten, yet heart disease rates were very low. The experts didn't know how to explain this, so they called it the French Paradox. The Inuit people had for many centuries eaten a diet high in saturated fat—in some cases 80 percent of the total calories consumed—with no incidence of heart disease and glowing good health. That became the Eskimo Paradox. Then it was noted that the Maasai of East Africa had a diet that consisted of mostly full-fat milk, blood drawn from their living cattle, and meat, supplemented by honey and some vegetables and fruits. Yet the people were tall, thin, athletic, full of energy, and without heart disease. That became the Maasai Paradox. Few, I suppose, wondered if maybe the rise in heart disease in our country—which corresponded statistically to a *decrease* in our intake of saturated, traditional fats—might have something to do with the things we *were* eating much more of: white sugar, white flour, processed foods, preservatives, and hydrogenated vegetable fats. Traditional fats, once prized and hoarded, became despised and avoided.

The notion that fat is bad for us has been so pervasive in recent years, many of us hardly question it. We scrimp on butter, avoid buying cream, order our omelet with egg whites only, buy nonfat milk, and believe that by thus depriving ourselves, we are being healthy, virtuous, and good. But as Sally Fallon points out in *Nourishing Traditions*:

> Fats from animal and vegetable sources provide a concentrated source of energy in the diet; they also provide the building blocks for cell membranes and a variety of hormones and hormone-like substances. Fats, as part of a meal, slow down nutrient absorption so that we can go longer without feeling hungry. In addition, they act as carriers for important fat-soluble vitamins A, D, E, and K. Dietary fats are needed for the conversion of carotene to vitamin A, for mineral absorption and for a host of other processes. . . .
>
> The theory—called the lipid hypothesis—that there is a direct relationship between the amount of saturated fat and cholesterol in the diet and the incidence of coronary heart disease was proposed by a researcher named Ancel Keys in the late 1950s. Numerous subsequent researchers have pointed out the flaws in his data and conclusions. Nevertheless, Keys received far more publicity than those presenting alternative views. The vegetable oil and food processing industries, the main beneficiaries of any research that could be used to demonize competing traditional foods, worked behind the scenes to promote further research that would support the lipid hypothesis.

Of course, the quality of the traditional fats valued by traditional peoples was high. Fats from animals that grazed on pasture growing in mineral-rich topsoil on expansive plains or pristine mountainsides were concentrated with vitamins and nutrients. These fats contained the life of the soil and the energy of the sun harnessed by the grasses through photosynthesis. Carotenes in the grass, concentrated in butter, give it a naturally yellow color. On old-fashioned farms the family enjoys deep yellow butter in the springtime when the April showers have fed the pastures that the cows are eating. In the middle of winter, when the cattle feed on stored hay, the butter is a pale yellow. Many butter producers now use annatto or other colorings to give their butter a yellow color, since the cattle are kept in feedlots without access to green grass.

The same principle applies to the fats of wild sea animals eaten by people in northern coastal climes. These animals were at the top of a food chain that started with plankton and other sea plants that harvested solar energy and grew in the mineral-rich waters of the ancient ocean. Today we might wonder how a people like the Inuit, who ate a diet made up largely of animal fat and meat with very few vegetables, could have an adequate supply of vitamins in their diet— because we don't understand that vitamins concentrate in the fats of animals that eat high on the food chain. Dr. Weston Price studied the Inuit diet as part of his travels, and he notes:

> Seal oil provides a very important part of their nutrition. As each piece of fish is broken off, it is dipped in seal oil. I obtained some seal oil from them and brought it to my laboratory for analyzing its vitamin content. It proved to be one of the richest foods in vitamin A that I have found.

Price also emphasizes the vitamin content of the butter and other dairy products he found in use by the traditional pastoralists he studied. He considers this factor crucial in enabling the human body to absorb and utilize other nutrients that are in our foods:

> I have referred to the importance of a high vitamin butter for providing the fat-soluble activators to make possible the utilization of the minerals in the foods. In this connection, it is of interest that butter constitutes the principal source of these essential factors for many primitive groups throughout the world. In the high mountain and plateau district in northern India, and in Tibet, the inhabitants depend largely upon butter made from the milk of the yak and sheep for these activators. The butter is eaten mixed with roasted cereals, is used in

tea, and in a porridge made of tea, butter and roasted grains. In Sudan, Egypt, I found considerable traffic in high vitamin butter which came from the higher lands a few miles from the Nile Basin. This was being exchanged for and used with varieties of millet grown in other districts. This butter, at the temperature of that area, which ranged from 90 to 110° Fahrenheit, was, of course, always in liquid form. Its brilliant orange color testified to the splendid pasture of the dairy animals. The people in Sudan, including the Arabs, had exceptionally fine teeth with exceedingly little tooth decay.

This yellow color can also be found in the body fat of animals that have eaten a grass-based diet. We have all heard of how much steak is eaten by the Argentines, and we may marvel at how such a diet produces the stunning, slender, active, and healthy population we see in tango films. We are rarely informed that the cattle of Argentina are not raised in feedlots, but rather on the grasses of the plains. I have heard stories of Argentines coming to the United States and being dismayed to see the white marbling of the steaks, since back home the sign of a good piece of meat is the yellow color of the fat. American consumers, on the other hand, have been hoodwinked into thinking that the white marbling is preferable and that yellow fat means something is wrong with the meat—when it really indicates the presence of nutrients.

Although I have not been able to confirm it, I believe the Lakota called this the Moon of Making Fat because the bison (and perhaps the elk and other prey animals) were beginning to make fat on their bodies as they ate the late-spring and early-summer grasses flourishing on the prairies as the weather warmed. The principal hunting season immediately followed. All the hunting peoples of the Great Plains sought out animals that had put on enough body fat to be tender and nutritious.

The high vitamin content of fats serves two purposes: It nourishes us, and it helps us to absorb other nutrients in what we eat. This is part of why side vegetables are traditionally served with butter—butter not only makes them taste better, but also helps us to absorb the nutrients they contain. Carrots are commonly reputed to contain vitamin A, but this is not the case. They contain carotenes, which we can convert to vitamin A. It isn't easy for our bodies to make this conversion, however; we require dietary fats to help us. If we serve carrots with good grass-fed butter, not only do we get vitamin A from the butter itself, but the butter also contains fat-soluble activators that help our bodies to convert the carotenes in carrots into this crucial vitamin. If we eat carrots without butter, or drink too much carrot juice, we are simply ingesting a plant nutrient (carotene) that our animal bodies can't absorb. In fact, if you drink large quantities of carrot juice without having enough fat in your diet to help in the absorption of carotene, your skin can take on an orange hue.

Adult bodies have considerable trouble converting plant nutrients into usable vitamins, but children's bodies fare even worse. I often teach workshops with Dr. Thomas Cowan, an anthroposophic doctor in San Francisco who wrote the book *The Fourfold Path to Healing*. Tom tells a story at these workshops relevant to this topic. One day one of his sons asked him, "Do you know the definition of an adult?" Tom asked him what it was. The son said, "A person who likes vegetables." Instead of dismissing this apparently self-serving analysis, Tom decided to look into it. It turns out that when we hit puberty, our bodies' ability to process plant nutrients into usable vitamins increases greatly. So perhaps there actually is a physiological reason that kids don't favor vegetables. One alternative way to get those crucial plant nutrients into a child is, as Tom puts it, to run them through a cow. He points out that there are very few children who don't like butter or cream.

Running the plant material through an animal was, in fact, a general strategy of many indigenous peoples. It was especially important for those who lived in cold climates with few plant foods. The Inuit did this by eating the oil of seals high up on the plankton-based food chain. The Swiss villagers Price studied had fresh vegetables only in summer. Butter, cheese, and the fat in meat were their consistent sources of nutrients. The Saami people of northern Scandinavia and Russia have a traditional diet consisting almost entirely of meat, fish, and reindeer dairy products. As they have Westernized and begun eating more carbohydrates, the nutrient content of their diet is decreasing.

Many traditional fats from plant sources have important nutrients as well. The red palm oil and palm butter used extensively in Africa get their coloring from high levels of carotenes. Because they are carried in a fat, they are easier to convert into vitamin A than the carotenes in carrots. Red palm oil is also such a rich source of vitamin E and antioxidants that some people are using it as a supplement. It is also apparently a source of vitamin D, because of the interaction between the oil and the sun. Unfiltered olive oil is full of antioxidants. The yellow oil made from ripe olives is rich in carotenes, and the green oil made from unripe olives is rich in chlorophyll. Mustard seed oil ranges from yellow to orange in color, and has long been in common use in India. There it would be pressed in very small batches in a village mill and used for cooking and pickling. This tradition is now being threatened as people have been convinced that it is safer to use imported oils such as soy.

Fat doesn't have to have color to be nutritious. Coconut oil is white, but it is rich in lauric acid, a potent antiviral that greatly boosts immunity. It is being hailed as one of the new superfoods. Some people with HIV are using it as a supplement to strengthen their immune systems. Lard contains high levels of vitamin D if it comes from hogs that lived outdoors. In tropical countries where the pigs get to eat coconuts, the lard may also supply lauric acid. Goat milk, cheese, and butterfat are white because goats are so good at converting beta-carotene into vitamin A, and goat dairy products are rich in it.

> ## Lavish Love
>
> Thirteen nourishing traditional fats that people have eaten in good health for millennia:
>
> 1. Butter from cow's milk
> 2. Coconut oil
> 3. Duck fat
> 4. Ghee
> 5. Lard
> 6. Olive oil
> 7. Chicken fat (Yiddish schmaltz)
> 8. Palm oil
> 9. Yak butter
> 10. Seal oil
> 11. Mustard seed oil
> 12. Tallow
> 13. Sesame seed oil

Traditional fats are crucial sources of essential fatty acids. These are now so lacking in our diet of processed foods that many people are buying supplemental fatty acids in pill form to correct the deficiencies that are causing their health problems. Once again, these acids will be found in higher concentrations and with a better balance of omega-3s and omega-6s in fats from animals that have eaten an appropriate diet and had ample access to the outdoors than fats that come from factory-raised animals. Traditional fats are far from being the empty fillers that we often think them to be—things that fill us up and taste good but don't actually provide us with essential nutrition. They are in fact nutritional powerhouses.

Contributing to our negative belief system about fat is the notion that eating fat will make us fat. And becoming overweight is one of our greatest fears. We all know that America is experiencing a dramatic rise in obesity, and that this disease is linked to our lifestyle. We work hard to avoid even the suggestion that we might be overweight. But what is overweight? Is there one ideal body type that we should all aspire to?

About fifteen years ago, I spent a year as the only white student at an African American college in Mississippi. Coming from a northern, urban, European American background, I was continually struck by differences between the culture I had grown up in and that in which I was suddenly immersed. One small example was my fellow students' much greater acceptance of different body types. Their southern politeness made saying anything derogatory about someone's weight taboo. They described someone who was what I would have called heavyset or plump as healthy. Similarly, they never called anyone skinny, but rather tiny. (Where I came from, no one would hesitate to call someone skinny, which is a huge compliment because "You can never be too rich or too thin.") It wasn't just that people didn't want to be rude; all sorts of body types were considered natural and even sexy. Larger women were often proud of their size, and were looked on as desirable.

Before that year in Mississippi, I had already had another eye-opening experience regarding body types: traveling in Europe and looking at Renaissance paintings. I was shocked, at the tender age of fifteen, to see women portrayed as irresistible goddesses who were—

by modern American standards—overweight. Even the dimples in their skin from generous flesh were considered attractive. At that time I was spending considerable energy (as so many young American women do at that age) obsessing about my weight and my body. Convinced I was too fat, I swung on the pendulum between dieting and bingeing, with a full dose of guilt, self-recrimination, and self-disgust thrown in. Seeing these women painted so exquisitely, so erotically, in their bountiful largeness rocked my world. I began to consider the possibility of a more inclusive view of feminine beauty, one that encompassed a greater range of diversity than what I had been brought up seeing.

Years later still, studying about Ayurveda, I came across drawings showing the three different body types of the three Ayurvedic *doshas*. The *Vata dosha* is thin, flat chested, narrow hipped, angular. The *Kapha dosha* is big boned, ample bosomed, wide hipped, fleshy. The *Pitta dosha* is in between, medium sized and muscular. The three doshas are not just body types, but energetic elemental types: Vata is air and space, Pitta is fire and water, Kapha is water and earth. Each dosha has its tendencies, excesses, shortcomings, and longings. I am a fire–air type (Pitta–Vata) born under an air sign (Libra), and I find that I am always reaching for the moon and longing for the Earth. I have to struggle to pay attention to the physical world around me. I long to feel connected to the plants, animals, and other earthy and earthly things of life. I work hard to stay grounded because it is not my natural tendency.

Cultures have doshic tendencies as well. Our American culture is very Pitta, action-oriented, strong, muscular, quick to anger, fiery. The form of feminine beauty we celebrate is in a range from Pitta to Vata, with slenderness a priority. The extremely Vata imagery of the fashion industry tends toward an ethereal, unearthly ideal that most Ayurvedic doctors would recognize as either undernourished or young and unformed. The culture of the Renaissance celebrated the Kapha, the earthy, the maternal seduction of mature womanhood— what we sometimes call Rubenesque or zaftig. It is an ideal of beauty that we rarely see appreciated in our modern society, but it has been a powerful symbol of the sacred feminine throughout human history.

In the best-selling series of books set in Botswana, *The Ladies' No 1 Detective Agency*, the heroine, Precious Ramotswe, is proud of being a "traditionally-built lady" and both critical and dismissive of the Western influence that makes women want to be thin. She doesn't diet or express any desire to be anything but the "traditionally-built lady" that she is, and experiences unabashed pleasure at her favorite dinner of pumpkin dripping with butter and beef stew with lots of good gravy. She sees her size as the size she was given, and considers it a blessing. She is also blessed to live in a culture that still embraces her beauty despite the encroachment of Western influence.

The Vata ideal of beauty in this country damages women. Even Vata women end up feeling that they are not Vata enough. Our adolescent girls—who are just beginning to develop into women—starve themselves, binge and purge, and spend countless hours obsessing over their weight and seeking to discipline their appetites. From experience I know that this is an appalling waste of time, of energy, and of intelligence.

We make a great mistake lumping together obesity, body fat, and the presence of fat in the diet. We think that the fat in our diet is the cause of obesity, and consider that any body fat we find on our bodies puts us on the road to obesity, none of which is true. While a person with a Kapha body type may be at a higher risk of obesity than a Vata, it by no means implies that the person is or will inevitably become obese. That person might well be healthy (as they said in Mississippi). While a Vata body type might not be courting obesity, poor nutrition might still be a problem.

Fat in the diet and obesity are not necessarily related. In America, our rates of obesity have gone up steadily in the last seventy years while our average consumption of fat has gone steadily down. Whereas once we (like all sane people everywhere) ate as much butter, cream, lard, and other nourishing fats as we could afford, we now avoid all these things and eat a diet high in sugars, refined carbohydrates, and processed foods. In fact, the sugars, carbohydrates, and processed foods are often actual substitutes for the natural fat content in things.

When you take the fat out of a foodstuff, you are left with two serious palatability issues: flavor and mouthfeel. As we liked to say in cooking school: "Fat is the messenger of flavor." Take out the fat and you take out the flavor; you have to put something back in to make it taste good. That thing is usually sugar or one of its toxic mimics. You also take away the sense of richness and goodness in the mouth—the mouthfeel. The way you make up for that is through refined carbohydrates in the form of starches and gums, and also processed, fake, and hydrogenated fatlike products—frightening chemical compounds that utterly confound our wise bodies.

Luckily for the companies that manufacture these low-fat foodstuffs, but unluckily for us, sugars, gums, fillers, and chemical compounds are much cheaper to produce than healthy fats. Healthy fats come from animals that need lots of room and good husbandry to stay healthy. They come from the fruit and nuts of trees that require expanses of land, healthy soil, and good stewardship. They come from fish that thrive in the wild only if we protect clean and well-managed marine ecosystems. In other words, good fats are still precious, challenging to obtain, and derived from nature in its most expansive, complex, interconnected form: just as they have always been. Fat substitutes can be synthesized in laboratories, patented by companies, produced for pennies, and sold at the same price as their full-fat competitors. The nutritionist and author Joan Dye Gussow made this quip: "As for butter verses margarine, I trust cows more than chemists." Me, too.

Thinking that eating fat makes us fat cheats us out of reverence for the mind-boggling complexity of Creation. As living beings, part of an intricate, subtle, and miraculous world, our bodies work in ways that are mysterious and fascinating. Plants take sunlight and transform it into leaves, petals, bulbs, fruit, roots, sap, bark, and many more vegetal forms and functions. They do this with *light*! Ruminant animals such as cows turn grass (which is virtually indigestible to people) into muscle, fat, blood, milk, horns, bones, and hooves. Chickens eat worms and grasses and snails and grains and turn them into flesh and feathers and eggs. Oysters take in plankton and build shells, bodies, and even pearls.

Do we really think that human bodies are the exception to this rule? That instead of doing something magical and mind boggling, we simply take fat in and then stick it on our hips? Not at all! Will drinking milk make us lactate or eating fertile eggs make us ovulate? Of course not. We are part of this miraculous Earth, and our bodies have a genius beyond our comprehension.

When I was a girl, my round face embarrassed me. I wanted to have the high-cheekboned, chiseled, slender face I admired in fashion magazines. My family would tease me about my "moonface." Then, when I lived in Thailand as a young woman, the people with whom I worked often complimented me on the shape of my face, explaining that a round face is a sign of beauty in their culture: the ideal being a face the shape of the full moon. This struck me as a bit ironic, and made me feel better. Years later, as I read the work of Weston Price, my feeling about the round-ness of my face changed again. He found direct correlations among healthy people, healthy dental structure, and wide faces, as well as direct correlations among ill health, rotting teeth, and narrow faces. He also found that one common denominator in the diets of all the people with good health, broad faces with plenty of room for teeth, and an absence of tooth decay was that they all ate diets rich in traditional fats.

Over time I have come to be proud of my broad face—and only wish it had been broad enough that I didn't need to have my wisdom teeth pulled! I have also let go of the notion that we should avoid fat because it will make us fat, and now understand that our bodies work with a deep intelligence. Somehow, through a series of intricate phys-iological processes, we take in fat and turn it into strong and healthy bones and teeth. We take in carbohydrates and turn them into fat—a wise system of stored energy that evolved during the ice age to help us live through times of deprivation.

Our fat phobia has had some bad consequences for farm animals as well, particularly pigs. As Temple Grandin writes in her book *Animals in Translation*:

> American breeders have started selecting for much leaner pigs, because Americans want to eat leaner cuts of meat. So far the leaner pigs are healthy, but their personalities are completely different. They're super-nervous and high-strung. No one knows why this happens, although it might have to do with myelin, which is the fatty sheath surrounding the nerve cell axons that helps signals pass from one brain cell to another. Myelin is made of pure fat, so it's possible that when you breed a pig to have less fat you interfere with myelin production in some way. Lower myelin levels could produce jumpy animals because inhibitory signals—the chemical signals that tell other neurons *not* to fire—don't get through from one neuron to another. The animal can't calm itself down. That's one theory, anyway.
>
> Lean pigs are also a lot less sexual. In China the pigs are all fat, and the mama pig makes way more piglets. A fat Chinese mother pig will have a litter of twenty-one piglets compared to just ten or twelve piglets in a lean American sow's litter. And the fat Chinese boars are super-sexy. When they brought them to the University of Illinois the boars would magically slip out of their pens and breed the sows whenever the staff wasn't around, something no American pig would ever do. They had nonstop sex on their minds and they turned into Houdini to have sex. All the fat Chinese pigs were super-calm and super-sexy. The females were really good mamas, too.

What a shame for American pigs—high-strung, supernervous, jumpy, less sexual, less fertile, lacking in drive that would turn them into Houdini—all because of American people's unfounded fear of fat. I can't help but compare those too-skinny American pigs to many too-skinny American people who suffer some of the same problems. We so often think of the American stereotype of the overweight couch potato munching compulsively on cheap processed junk foods that we forget about the underweight neurotic overachiever munching compulsively on expensive processed junk foods packaged as health foods. They are two sides of the same coin.

Another aspect of our fat phobia is our disgust at gluttony. We have imprinted in our cultural imagery the idea of the fat, gluttonous rich European man—usually a noble or a king—chewing on a leg of meat dripping with fat and slurping his wine. Again, the gluttony is associated with the body fat, which is in turn associated with eating fatty food. But again, all of these things are separate. Eating a diet rich in fats and eating to excess are actually more physiologically incompatible than not. As Dr. Tom Cowan writes in *The Fourfold Path to Healing*:

> One of the most important food components the body needs to feel satisfied is animal fat. That is why I never recommend lowfat diets for weight loss, even though the vast majority of books on weight loss promote a lowfat regimen. *Our brain is specifically designed to sense the fat content of our food and to tell us to stop eating when the proper amount of fat has been ingested. When the need for fats and the nutrients they contain is satisfied, we stop eating.* [Emphasis added.]

In other words, it is a lot easier to overeat carbohydrates than it is to overeat traditional fats. Fats make us feel satisfied—they tell us when we have eaten enough, and we are not drawn to overeat. But if we eat lots of unrefined carbohydrates, we never feel satisfied. (This is why the dry pita-bread-and-raw-vegetable sandwiches I ate in high school never satisfied me.) Dr. Cowan also points out:

> The feeling of satiety is designed to tell us when we have taken in enough to nourish the body. Weston Price was the first to note that primitive diets were relatively low in calories but high in nutrients. The food was highly nourishing and therefore completely satisfying, whereas most modern food is high in calories and low in nutrients. Modern processed food satisfies only momentarily because the body continues to signal the brain that it needs more nourishment. Ironically, overweight is actually a symptom of malnutrition, a sign that the appestat never receives the signal to turn off.

I don't think the importance of eating traditional, nourishing fats derived from healthy animals living in healthful environments can be overstated. Human beings need these fats and the nutrients they contain in abundance in order to thrive. Although many experiments are under way to create, through genetic engineering, artificial substitutes—"pharmafoods" and "nutraceuticals" such as rice with genetically added carotenes—I believe these attempts will either fail or have grave unforeseen side effects. Better to protect the availability of vitamin-rich, traditional fats and protect people's access to them.

Traditional animal fats *do* need protection. While the Inuit were among the healthiest people Weston Price found and studied, in the seven decades since he visited them a new and unforeseen culprit is jeopardizing the health of a people that thrived for millennia in one of nature's most challenging environments. Despite our pristine image of the Earth's northern climates, toxic pollution is beginning to wreak havoc on the very people who have been most steadfast in upholding their traditional way of life. This is happening through the degradation of traditional fats in their diet. As Marla Cone writes in her important article, "Dozens of Words for Snow, None for Pollution":

> Traditionally, this marine diet has made the people of the Arctic Circle among the world's healthiest. Beluga whale, for example, has ten times the iron of beef, twice the protein, and five times the vitamin A. Omega-3 fatty acids in the seafood protect the indigenous people from heart disease. A 70-year-old Inuit in Greenland has coronary arteries as elastic as those of a 20-year-old Dane eating Western foods. . . .
>
> Yet the ocean diet that gives these people life and defines their culture also threatens them. Despite living amid pristine ice and glacier-carved bedrock, [Inuit] people . . . are more vulnerable to pollution than anyone else on earth. Mercury concentrations in Qaanaaq mothers are the highest ever recorded, twelve times greater than the level that poses neurological risks to fetuses, according to U.S. government standards. . . .
>
> The Arctic has been transformed into the planet's chemical trash can, the final destination for toxic waste that originates thousands of miles away. Atmospheric and oceanic currents conspire to send industrial chemicals, pesticides, and power-plant emissions on a journey to the Far North. Many airborne chemicals tend to migrate to, and precipitate in, cold climates, where they then endure for decades, perhaps centuries, slow to break down in the frigid temperatures and low sunlight. The Arctic Ocean is a deep-freeze archive, holding the memories of the world's past and present mistakes. Its wildlife, too, are archives, as poisonous chemicals accumulate in the fat that Arctic animals need to survive. Polar bears denning in Norway and Russia near the North Pole carry some of the highest levels of toxic compounds ever found in living animals.

Perched at the top of the Arctic food chain, eating a diet similar to a polar bear's, the Inuit also play unwilling host to some 200 toxic pesticides and industrial compounds.

Once we acknowledge the benefits of traditional fats in diets throughout the world, we see the widespread presence of industrial toxins in our environment in its most insidious light. We understand how important it is to eliminate harmful chemicals from our industrial and technological systems. Just as minerals, vitamins, carotenes, and chlorophyll concentrate in the fats of animals higher on the food chain, so, too, do poisons. The animals that the Inuit traditionally rely upon for food are no longer living in pristine waters; they are living in waters polluted by our industrial lifestyle. The sources of the pollutants that are poisoning the Inuit are such common items as flame retardants used in mattresses and computers, Teflon used to coat pots and pans, and insecticides used in farming.

Healthy fats are based on healthy ecosystems. Period. There is no substitute, no replacement, no other option. Life on Earth has as its basis one source: the Earth herself. And though she is abundant and intricate, and though she operates from an intelligence beyond our comprehension, she is not infinite. The universe may be, God may be, but the Earth is, like a mother, a finite being. She has a great deal to offer, but we cannot continue to view our relationship with her as a one-way street. All indigenous cultures knew, all of our ancestors knew, that we must each do our part to honor and protect this relationship, our source of life.

The problem of pollution in the Inuit diet was discovered due to the contamination of the breast milk of Inuit mothers. As Cone points out, "The average levels of PCBs and mercury in newborn babies' cord blood and women's breast milk are a staggering twenty to fifty times higher in Greenland than in urban areas of the United States and Europe." I can't help but be reminded of the story Martín Prechtel tells of his newborn baby being passed from Mayan mother to Mayan mother to breast-feed. How tragic that the trust involved in that ancient ritual is nearly unthinkable in today's tainted world. Who would be willing to let her baby suckle at the breast of an Inuit woman, once she saw the chemical analysis charts? And yet it is *our* trash—*our* poisons—that have caused the problem. Though it may not have been intentional, it is our responsibility to clean up the mess we have made.

It is hard not to find the toxicity of our planet profoundly depressing. But I believe in miracles. I take hope from the experiments currently being conducted by fungus expert Paul Stamets. His work has revealed that mushrooms may have enormous potential to clean up toxic wastes. He has inoculated piles of toxic garbage with oyster mushroom mycelia and recorded that, after a period of time, the garbage is no longer toxic and there is a flourishing patch of oyster mushrooms—which are themselves free of toxins and edible! He describes one such experiment:

> We inoculated three mounds of soil, each contaminated with a different mixture of diesel fuel, motor oil, gasoline, and other petroleum hydrocarbons.
>
> After four weeks, the tarps were pulled back from each test pile. The first piles, employing the other techniques, were unremarkable. Then the tarp was pulled from our piles, and gasps of astonishment and laughter welled up from the observers. The hydrocarbon-laden pile was bursting with mushrooms! Oyster mushrooms up to twelve inches in diameter had formed across the pile. Based on our earlier tests, we estimated that most of the PAHs and alkanes had been broken down by this time. The mushrooms were tested and shown to be free of any petroleum products.
>
> After eight weeks, the mushrooms had rotted away, and then came another startling revelation. As the mushrooms rotted, flies were attracted. . . . The flies became a magnet for other insects, which in turn brought in

birds. Apparently the birds brought in seeds. Soon ours
was an oasis, the only pile teeming with life! We think ·
we have found what is called a "keystone" organism, one
that facilitates a cascade of other biological processes
that contribute to habitat remediation.

If that's not something approaching a miracle, I don't know what is.
And it brings us back to what I was saying earlier about food, fat, and
the nature of living things: Life moves in mysterious ways. Bison can
eat grass and their bodies make fat, people can eat fat and their bodies
make bones, mycelia can eat petroleum-based waste products and
their bodies make mushrooms. Now, who would have guessed that?

On the Moon of Making Fat, may we be free of the oppressive ideal
of thinness, as well as the disease of obesity. May adolescent girls be
nourished—body and soul—and know that they, too, are precious.
May cultures such as the Lakota and Inuit thrive and renew, along with
the populations of American buffalo on the Great Plains and the seals
and whales of the Arctic. May we all do our part to protect and restore
the ecosystems of planet Earth, who offers us her lavish love in the
form of nutrient-dense traditional fats. And may we send our blessings
to the mushrooms. They might yet save us all.

MOON OF MAKING FAT RECIPES

Superfood and Kefir Shake
Serves 1–2

This delicious shake is a nutritional and digestive powerhouse. It is an easy way to get those who don't like supplemental oils to take them and enjoy them. Children will most likely love it, though it is not appropriate for babies or toddlers. You can try using other brands of cod liver oil—but it might not work. This brand has a light, delicate flavor.

1 pint homemade milk kefir (page 92), chilled or at room temperature

1 banana (preferably organic and Fair Trade)

½ teaspoon bee pollen (optional; see page 309)

1 teaspoon Nordic Naturals orange flavor cod liver oil (or adjust for daily dose)

½ teaspoon vanilla extract

1 egg yolk from a free-range chicken

2 tablespoons unrefined coconut oil

1 tablespoon raw butter

1 tablespoon raw honey

Ice cubes (optional)

1. Strain the milk kefir into a bowl or blender. Peel the banana and break it up into pieces in the kefir. Add the bee pollen, cod liver oil, vanilla extract, and egg yolk to the bowl or blender.
2. Gently melt together the coconut oil, butter, and honey. I do this by putting them in a very small pan set inside a larger pan that has about an inch of water in it and is on the stove over a medium-low flame. As the water begins to simmer, the oils and honey melt together. You could also use a small, stovetop bain-marie (double boiler). Or you could put the oils and honey in a small metal bowl and set that into a larger bowl into which you have poured boiling water. The point is, you don't want to cook the oils or the honey; you just want to melt them gently.
3. Blend the kefir-banana mixture together in the blender, or by using an immersion blender in the bowl. Once the banana is completely blended into the kefir, as are the pollen, the oils, and the vanilla, slowly pour in the melted coconut oil mixture while continuing to blend.
4. Pour into one or two glasses and enjoy. If your kefir was warm, you might want to pour it over ice, or add ice cubes while you are blending. It is best drunk right away. You can refrigerate it for later in the day, but you might need to eat it with a spoon or thin it out with milk or water.

Coconut-date Energy Balls
Makes about 20

I love these little balls—they are sweet without being too sweet, and are rich with coconut meat and coconut oil. I store them in a cookie tin and sometimes bring them in the car with me when I know I'm going to be running around doing errands or other busyness. Their balance of good fats with natural sugars means they give both an immediate lift but also sustained energy until the next real meal. They also make a nice sweet for after a meal, a good snack during a meeting, or a welcome addition to a lunchbox. They are great for kids to both roll and eat! They need to be kept cool or they will soften or melt.

1 cup date paste or 1½ cups pitted dates

½ cup coconut spread (available from Wilderness Family Naturals)

Zest of 1 lemon or small orange (optional)

3 tablespoons coconut oil

¼ cup finely shredded dried coconut, plus more for rolling the balls in

1. In a food processor, process the date paste or dates for a few seconds or a minute or so. If you're using dates, they should be processed into a chunky paste.
2. Add the coconut spread (and the optional zest, if using) and pulse a few times until the ingredients are mixed.
3. Melt 1 tablespoon of the coconut oil in a very small pan. Then start the processor and pour the melted oil in through the top while the processor is running. Add the dried coconut and process for 5 or 10 seconds more.
4. To roll the balls, pick up a very small handful of paste and press it in your hand. It should stick together. Then take the paste and press and roll it into a little ball, about 1 inch in diameter—a little smaller than a walnut. Put the balls on a plate as you roll them.
5. When you have finished rolling all the balls, melt the remaining 2 tablespoons of coconut oil and remove from the heat.
6. Now take each ball and do this: Put it in the little pan with the melted coconut oil. Shake the little pan so that the ball gets covered with coconut oil. Take the warm oiled ball and immerse it in the dried coconut flakes so that it gets covered with coconut. I do this by just putting the ball into the bag of dried coconut and rolling it around. Put the ball back onto a clean plate or straight into a cookie tin. Repeat with all the balls until they are all covered with coconut. Store in a cool place and eat as desired!

Rendering Lard
Yield depends on quantity of fat you start with

Most of the lard you can find in stores is from confined hogs and contains preservatives. This is the real thing.

2–6 pounds pork fat from free-range, pastured pigs, cut into small pieces, approximately 1"x1"

¼–½ cup filtered water, depending on how much fat you're rendering

I like to render the lard in a Crock-Pot (slow cooker)—this gives perfect long, slow heat. You can also do it in a heavy pan, either on top of the stove or in the oven. I give directions all three ways:

Crock-Pot
1. Put the pieces of fat in the Crock-Pot, then pour in the water. Put the lid on the Crock-Pot and turn it on to low.
2. Cook for 4 to 5 hours or until much of the fat has liquefied, and you have small pieces of solid floating in liquid.
3. Remove the cover and cook for another hour or so—this will finish rendering the lard and also allow the water to evaporate.
4. When almost all the fat has liquefied, and the solids that remain seem empty, strain the fat into quart mason jars and cool to room temperature before transferring it to the freezer (for long-term storage) or fridge (to start using immediately).

Stovetop
1. Put the pieces of fat in a heavy-bottomed pot—stainless steel or cast iron—and pour in the water. Turn the heat to medium until the pan gets hot and the fat begins to cook, then turn the heat down to low.
2. Cook for 2 to 4 hours (depending on the amount of fat and the temperature) over very low heat. You might want to use a flame tamer. Be careful—the fat may sputter some.
3. When almost all the fat has liquefied, and the solids that remain seem empty, strain the fat into quart mason jars and cool to room temperature before transferring it to the freezer (for long-term storage) or fridge (to start using immediately).

Oven
1. Preheat the oven to 275° F.
2. Put the pieces of fat in a heavy-bottomed pot—stainless steel or cast iron—and pour in the water. Put on top of a stove burner and turn the heat to medium until the pan gets hot and the fat begins to cook.
3. Transfer the pan to the oven.
4. Cook for 2 to 4 hours (depending on the amount of fat and how hot your oven runs).
5. When almost all the fat has liquefied, and the solids that remain seem empty, strain the fat into quart mason jars and cool to room temperature before transferring it to the freezer (for long-term storage) or fridge (to start using immediately).

Note: Lard will keep for months in the fridge and more than a year in the freezer. I try to render enough for a year, put 1 quart in the fridge, and store the rest in the freezer, pulling it out as I run low of the one in the fridge. Then render again a year later. You can also keep it at room temperature if you want, but I'm not sure how long it will safely last—for weeks at least, but maybe not longer. You can save the pork rinds and eat them sprinkled with a little salt. If you have a dog or cat, these will make fabulous treats.

Niter Qibbeh (Ethiopian Spiced *Ghee*)
Makes about 2 cups

This classic cooking oil of Ethiopia is a great thing to use whenever you want to give something a more complex North African or Middle Eastern flavor. It is also a primary ingredient (along with the spice mixture berebere) of Ethiopian cooking.

1 pound butter

½ onion, cut into coarse slices

2 cloves garlic, coarsely chopped

4 slices gingerroot, each about the size of a quarter

4 slices fresh turmeric root, each about the size of a dime—or ½ teaspoon powdered turmeric

4 pods cardamom, each one pounded once so that the pod cracks open (you can do this in a mortar and pestle or on a cutting board using a meat pounder or a hammer wrapped in a towel)—or ½ teaspoon ground cardamom

1 cinnamon stick, broken into a few pieces

2 cloves

¼ teaspoon whole fenugreek seeds

1 tiny chunk of nutmeg

1. Melt the butter in a cast-iron pan over low heat until it begins to foam.
2. Add the remaining ingredients to the butter and cook over low heat until the surface is clear. This could take anywhere from 20 to 45 minutes.
3. Turn off the heat. Pour the niter qibbeh through a fine-mesh strainer or a strainer lined with cheesecloth into a jar.
4. Let it cool and then transfer to the fridge. It will keep for several months.

Olive Oil Mayonnaise
Makes a generous ½ cup

Real mayonnaise made from scratch.

1 egg yolk from a free-range farm-fresh egg

⅓–½ cup olive oil

½ teaspoon mustard

A pinch of salt

Freshly ground pepper

½ teaspoon white wine vinegar

1. Put the egg yolk in a heavy bowl. Put the bowl on a damp cloth or anything that will steady it. Whisk in a few drops of olive oil. Keep whisking in a few drops at a time until you have poured at least a tablespoon, then begin pouring in a slow stream and whisking until you have incorporated all of the olive oil.

2. Whisk in the mustard, salt, pepper, and vinegar. Taste and adjust the seasonings.

3. Depending on how slowly you added the oil, your mayo might be very thick, or it might be a little runny. Don't fret, runny mayo is still totally usable.

6

MEAD MOON

I got a drink of the precious mead,
poured from Odrerir.
Then I began to quicken and be wise,
and to grow and to prosper . . .

—FROM THE ANCIENT NORSE POEM *Rúnatal*,
TRANSLATED FROM THE NORSE

At the height of summer, when the days are long and the Earth is in bloom, we enter the lunar cycle known in sixteenth-century England as the Mead Moon. The beehives are heavy with honey made from the pollen of spring and summer flowers, and honey was the crucial ingredient for making mead—the honey wine of legend, myth, and human history brewed from the precious produce of industrious bees.

One scholar who studied this drink of old writes: "It is so ancient a beverage that the linguistic root for mead, *medhu*, is the same in all Indo-European languages where it encompasses an entire range of meanings, which include honey, sweet, intoxicating, drunk, and drunkenness. For this reason it has been suggested that fermented honey may be the oldest form of alcohol known to man." Many cultures have a version of mead: *madhu* in India and the ancient Vedas, *tej* in Ethiopia, *balche* among the Maya, *uki* in East Africa, and mead among the Norse are just a few of the traditional fermented beverages made from honey.

The practice of gathering wild honey predates agriculture—and thus our growing of wine grapes and the grains used to make beer.

Scientists estimate that bees evolved shortly before our earliest human ancestors did, and so humans and bees have been co-evolving on earth through many millennia. Honey, I've been told, is the only natural food that doesn't spoil. It has been found perfectly preserved in caves that date from ancient times.

In Ayurveda raw honey is considered medicine, whereas cooked honey is poison. Maybe this is because raw honey is teeming with active enzymes, which are deactivated when it is heated to above 117° F. Although I haven't seen any science to confirm the claim that cooked honey is poison, I tend to respect Ayurvedic tradition and avoid using honey in baking or other high-heat dishes. Raw, unfiltered honey is packed with nutrients, and has been used by traditional peoples around the world and throughout history as a health food. The pollen it contains is particularly healing. As Sally Fallon writes:

> A Russian study of the inhabitants of the province of Georgia, where many live to 100 years and a few to age 150, revealed that many of these centenarians were bee-keepers who often ate raw, unprocessed honey with all its 'impurities,' that is, with the pollen. Bee pollen contains 22 amino acids including the eight essential ones, 27 minerals and the full gamut of vitamins, hormones and fatty acids. Most importantly, bee pollen contains more than 5,000 enzymes and coenzymes . . . many of which have immediate detoxifying effects.

The Maasai of Africa, as mentioned before, eat a diet largely made up of milk and blood from their herds of cattle, supplemented by meat. But when they travel away from their herds, they subsist on honey. Our modern term *honeymoon* may stem from an ancient European practice: Newlyweds would eat nothing but honey for one moon cycle after marriage in order to increase their fertility and the possibility of an immediate pregnancy. Honey's aphrodisiacal properties probably helped, too.

Bees play a crucial role as pollinators in our farming system. When I visited an organic almond farm in bloom a few years ago, I saw rows and rows of bee boxes that had been placed there for the duration of blossoming. Standard practice among fruit and nut farmers is to hire a beekeeper to bring hives of bees to the farm while the trees or bushes are blooming. The bees pollinate the orchard or field, and then go to their next assignment. Bees are so vital to a thriving food system that it is no wonder cultures throughout human history have considered them and their honey sacred, magical, and mystical.

I did, in the past, condemn honey as unhealthy—believing it just as bad for you as sugar. But as I became convinced of its detoxifying and nourishing power, I became an enthusiastic honey eater. I buy local, raw, unfiltered honey and bee pollen from beekeepers at the farmer's market. I treasure it for its delicious taste, its health-sustaining properties, its important link to pollination and the natural world, and its timeless mythical symbolism.

I have, in the past, been even more critical of alcoholic fermentation than of honey. Having been alerted to the dangers of drinking and alcoholism while growing up, I thought of alcohol as one of the evils of human civilization. Always something of a Goody Two-shoes, from a young age I disapproved of keg parties and other youthful antics involving drunkenness. I have seen firsthand the huge accomplishment it is for alcoholics to gain sobriety, and have deep respect for those who choose to travel down this path. I think twelve-step programs have made an incalculable contribution to the physical and psychic health of modern society; I am awed by what they have been able to accomplish since their relatively recent inception.

We all know that inebriation has a shadow side. But the impulse to control drunkenness has its shadow side as well. American Prohibition ultimately glamorized intoxication rather than moderating it. Anti-alcohol sentiments can also be manipulated to assert social and economic control over indigenous drinks. We see this in the story of *uki*, a traditional honey wine in East Africa. Scholar Robert Leonard has written about *uki*'s fate in the modern context:

Food and drink in Africa transform rapidly. Many traditional foods disappear because of change from ecological degradation, population pressure, "westernized" tastes, and other agricultural and cultural change. One such food, actually a drink, is *uki* (pronounced oo-key), honey-wine made by the Kamba (Akamba in their language) people of Kenya. Its production and consumption were in the past subject to clearly defined rules that wove *uki* into the dense symbol-structure of a highly organized community. The beverage still has much traditional meaning . . . [b]ut *uki* is on the wane. As an emblem of the old, "tribal," order, *uki*'s decline was probably inevitable given the drastic upheavals of traditional society and the eagerness of young people worldwide for the new, the modern, the Western. But *uki* is a case where the demise of a traditional foodway was greatly expedited by government, specifically, the hunger of a nation-state for tax revenue. *Uki* is too hard to tax because its production is too hard to control.

Uki's use was highly regulated in the traditional context. Only men who had reached a certain level of life experience would ask their fathers for permission to drink *uki* freely. Mostly it was drunk in ritualized contexts at weddings and births. Nevertheless, the Kenyan government instituted an effective (though selective) ban against it. As Leonard points out:

> The avowed motive for the ban was to decrease drunkenness. Be that as it may, Kenyan skeptics have repeatedly pointed out to me that a very real effect of the ban was to curtail availability of *uki*, driving customers to drink expensive and highly-taxed beer, and to force what *uki* drinking remained into a public arena where it would be easier for the government to tax.

Even seemingly reasonable forms of governmental regulation can have a disastrous impact on long-standing culinary traditions.

Inebriating drinks have been a vital part of many indigenous and ancient cultures, which often revered them as gifts from the gods and used them as a sacrament. Very early on, our ancestors discovered fermentation and began to seek out sources of sweetness, because almost anything sweet can be fermented into alcohol. Alcohol was also associated with inspiration, poetry, and the arts. An ancient Norse sacred story explains the mythical origins of mead and the nature of the gift it offered:

> The gods were at war with one another for so long that they became tired of the endless fighting and agreed to meet and make peace. They took an earthen vessel and all of the gods spit into it until it was full. This was a symbol of their newfound unity, and from their joined liquids the gods formed a new creature, a man they called Kvaser, who was so wise that he knew the answers to all questions. Kvaser walked the heavens for a long time as a symbol of the peace of the gods. But then he was captured and killed by dwarfs, who collected his blood and mixed it with honey, making a new drink called Mead that would make anyone who drank it wise. The dwarfs hoarded their drink, but a giant heard about it and stole it, and gave it to his daughter to guard.
>
> Odin, one of the gods, heard about this and disguised himself as a lover and seduced the daughter. After they had spent three days and three nights together, she offered him some of the mead to slake his thirst. Just as he drank the mead, the giant returned and was enraged to find the mead bottles were empty. Odin turned himself into an eagle and flew away, and the giant turned into another eagle and followed. Just as Odin reached the realm of the gods, Asgard, the other gods gathered vessels and placed them outside so that Odin could spew the mead into

Drinks of the Gods

Thirteen traditional inebriating beverages:

1. Mead (Norse)
2. Wine (Europe)
3. Beer (Variations world-wide)
4. Gruit ale (Europe)
5. Chang (Tibet and Nepal)
6. Uki (East Africa)
7. Balche (Yucatan peninsula)
8. Sake (Japan)
9. Chicha (South America)
10. Nsa (West Africa)
11. Millet beer (Africa, South America, Asia)
12. Sahti (Scandinavia)
13. Tej (Ethiopia)

them, which he did. But he did this so hastily that three drops fell to earth, and men found these drops and tasted the Mead of the Gods. From drinking these drops, the gift of Odin, the men were given the gifts of poetry and music. Poets became known as the Bearers of the Mead of Odin and mead became the Drink of Inspiration.

The name *Kvaser* comes from the same Nordic root as the Russian *kvass*, meaning "leaven" or "beer." Leaven means yeast, and certainly some form of yeast or leaven was necessary for the making of mead. Just as Kvaser (in the form of his blood) was one of the crucial ingredients in the mythic Mead, so yeast is one of the crucial ingredients in the earthly mead. And on a metaphorical level, Kvaser was Wisdom, or the All-Wise, and the mead made from him was Inspiration. Wisdom was not enough to create poetry and art. For that, divine inspiration—the Mead of Odin—was necessary.

The connection between alcohol and the sacred is ancient and widespread. As Tamra Andrews writes in *Nectar and Ambrosia*:

Many ancient peoples viewed intoxication as an element of worship. Because the gods gave humans the gift of ecstasy, people participated in drinking much as they did in prayer. They elevated their mental state to reach that of the deities. This practice in part reflected a belief that substances capable of altering mental states had a supernatural influence, and that beverages such as wine and beer had a spirit, or perhaps were spirits in themselves.

Traditional and sacred alcoholic drinks were not only valued for spiritual reasons, but often intimately connected to cultural identity and ritual practices that created community life. Kamba *uki* is one example. Another is the Mayan drink *balche*. As Andrews describes:

> Balche is a kind of mead, an intoxicating beverage consumed by the ancient Maya and by some of their descendants today. These people make the drink in a trough or a canoe, which they fill with water and honey, adding chunks of bark and roots from the balche tree. The mixture begins to ferment immediately. It results in an inebriating drink the people consume during rituals and believe to have magic powers.
>
> The peoples of Mesoamerica have long held the balche tree and their mysterious beverage sacred. Because the drink had strong religious significance to the Maya, the Spaniards banned the beverage in an attempt to convert them to Christianity. The ban was observed until a Maya named Chi convinced the Spaniards that balche had important health benefits and that many Maya were dying as a result of the prohibition. The Spaniards then lifted their ban, and balche rituals resumed.

No doubt the history is more complicated than that, but Andrews gives us a sense of the cultural importance these traditional fermentations can have. Since we are exploring thirteen moons, I point out that the number thirteen was sacred to the Maya and played a part in their *balche* rituals:

> A typical ritual of the ancient Maya involved the ceremonial use of balche during severe droughts to encourage the rain gods to release the waters. These ceremonies lasted three days. On the third day, the participants sacrificed hens to the Chacs, who sent the rains. . . . The Maya poured balche down the throats of

the hens before they sacrificed them, and they filled thirteen gourds full of balche and offered them to the Chacs. Then everyone assembled for the ritual drank balche as well, and the shaman sprinkled it on the altar thirteen times. . . .

The Lacandon, descendants of the ancient Maya living in Chiapas along the Mexican-Guatemalan border, believe that the gods gave balche rituals to them, and that because the gods themselves first became inebriated by the beverage, the people from then on had a duty to imitate the inebriation of the gods and to experience that same exhilaration. The Lacandon chant incantations while preparing the balche. . . .

This might well sound very foreign to Westerners. But Europeans practiced similar rituals. The best-known deity to be associated with inebriation, ecstasy, and sacrifice in the Western classical tradition is the Greek god Dionysus or his Roman counterpart, Bacchus. Dionysus was originally associated with mead, and later with wine. The Maenads, or Bacchantes, were women who were votaries of Dionysus or Bacchus and who engaged in ecstatic rituals. In the fifth century BCE, the Greek playwright Euripides wrote a play about Dionysus and his devotees, called *The Bacchae*. The chorus of the play is made up of Bacchantes, and at one point they chant:

When shall I dance once more
with bare feet the all-night dances,
tossing my head for joy
in the damp air, in the dew . . .

They are chanting about a religious ritual, not a party. Drunkenness was a form of worship; it was a sacrament. Just as the Maya believed in the necessity of drinking *balche* and becoming inebriated as a sacred duty, the Maenads' intoxicated dance is about recognizing the power of God, fulfilling a sacred duty, and having the wisdom to know the limits of human power. In another passage the Bacchantes chant:

For now I raise the old, old hymn to Dionysus.
Blessed, blessed are those who know the mysteries of god.
Blessed is he who hallows his life in the worship of god,
      he whom the spirit of god possesseth, who is one
      with those who belong to the holy body of god.
Blessed are the dancers and those who are purified,
      who dance on the hill in the holy dance of god.
Blessed are they who keep the rite of Cybele the Mother.
Blessed are the thyrsus-bearers, those who wield in their hands
      the holy wand of god.
Blessed are those who wear the crown of the ivy of god.
Blessed, blessed are they: Dionysus is their god!

I cannot help but be reminded by this of the New Testament beatitudes, which were written some five hundred years later in a similar tongue. The form is nearly identical—obviously an ancient Greek hymn of praise—and both are concerned with how humans can enter into relationship with the Divine.

In *The Bacchae*, Dionysus comes to the city of Thebes and inspires a group of women, including the mother of a young king named Pentheus, to become Bacchantes and to head for the hills to dance the Dionysian rituals. Pentheus is appalled at the reports he has heard of these ancient rites and seeks a way to put a stop to them. Dionysus, dressed as a mortal man, tricks Pentheus into dressing as a woman and following him to the rituals so he can observe what the Maenads are doing. When the Maenads see him spying on their ritual, in their intoxicated frenzy they rip Pentheus limb from limb. Pentheus's mother spearheads the assault, so removed from reality that she does not recognize her son. She leads a procession into town with Pentheus's head stuck on her wand, exulting in having killed her quarry. It is only as she returns to herself that she realizes what she has done, and she leaves Thebes in exile and disgrace. In the context of the play, Pentheus was punished for his lack of reverence for the god and the traditional rituals performed in his worship.

The Bacchae springs from an ancient worldview, one that has become nearly incomprehensible to the modern mind. This is part of why it has long been a difficult play for translators and scholars to interpret. One translator observed:

> Of itself *The Bacchae* needs neither apology nor general introduction. It is, clearly and flatly, that unmistakable thing: a masterpiece. . . . Elusive, complex and compelling, the play constantly recedes before one's grasp, advancing, not retreating, steadily into deeper chaos and larger order, coming finally to rest only god knows where—which is to say, where it matters.

The same statement can be made about alcoholic fermentation in human culture and history. It is a masterpiece, a huge and important achievement. But the more we try to attach a meaning to it, to capture its essence or pin it down, the more it takes us into both "deeper chaos and larger order," and comes to rest "only god knows where," in other words, "where it matters." The figure of Dionysus in the play perhaps helps us comprehend this mystery:

> What the divinity of Dionysus represents, however, should be clear enough from the play: the incarnate life-force itself, the uncontrollable chaotic eruption of nature in individuals and cities, the thrust of the sap in the tree and the blood in the veins, the force that "through the green fuse drives the flower." As such, he is amoral, neither good nor bad, a necessity capable of blessing those who (like the Asian Bacchantes) accept him, and of destroying or maddening those who (like Pentheus) deny him. Like any necessity he is ambiguous, raw power: his thyrsus spurts honey for the bands of the blessed but becomes a killing weapon when turned against the scoffer.

Isn't this the truth of alcohol as well? That it is neither good nor bad but full of power? That it is capable of both blessing and destroying? That it is a thing to be approached with respect? Another writer makes the point this way:

In the ritual of the Maenads is the ambivalence conveyed in Euripides' *The Bacchae*: to resist Dionysus is to deny the irrational within the self, the repression of which can only lead, inevitably, to its destructive release. The human spirit demands Dionysiac ecstasy; for those who accept it, the experience offers spiritual power. For those who repress the natural force within themselves or refuse it to others, it is transformed into destruction, both of the innocent and the guilty. To have this awareness of one's own nature and, therefore, one's place in nature, is wisdom (sophia), itself.

Inebriation has long been a portal into spiritual ecstasy, into the great unanswerable mystery of life and its raw power. What traditional cultures knew and what we come dangerously close to forgetting is that this ecstasy—this moment of touching the mystery and the power—is something that the human spirit demands and cannot do without.

And yet alcohol's power can certainly be destructive, and it has perhaps never had such a negative effect in any culture as it does in modern society. Alcoholics Anonymous currently estimates its U.S. membership at almost 1.2 million, and that is only a fraction of the people who have drinking problems. Stephen Harrod Buhner, in his book *Sacred and Herbal Healing Beers*, examines this issue:

> Alcoholism, solitary drinking, and the various diseases attendant with alcohol abuse do not exist in indigenous cultures, irrespective of the amount of fermentations and drunkenness they engage in. These problems come from alcohol's separation from its sacred and ritual context, its isolation from its plant matrix, and concomitants of civilization (most especially the scientific belief that the isolated "pure" substance in a thing is better than leaving it in its matrix of origin). In all things, it seems,

our civilization has to encounter the shadow side of whatever we incorporate into it. . . .

I agree with Buhner except on one point: I believe *every* culture that has engaged in intoxication has had to encounter its shadow side. I think they simply incorporated that destructive potential into the sacred and ritual context of its consumption. They acknowledged the danger in their mythological understanding of its sacred origin, and in the practices that surrounded its use. If before being intoxicated you participate in three days of rituals, chant incantations, sacrifice chickens, and pour out libations to the gods, you are taking that intoxication pretty seriously. It is not the same as having a highball after a difficult day at work. It is not about escape. It is not about one person trying to get away from pain. It is about a community of people entering more deeply into the profundity of living, including its inevitable difficulties. This is a huge difference.

I cannot write about Dionysian symbolism and ritual without telling the painful story of my thirtieth birthday party. I viewed turning thirty as a momentous occasion in my life, a transition between youth and adulthood, and I wanted to mark it well. I decided, along with my partner and friends, to have a big celebration. One friend suggested that the party should have a theme, and we settled on Greek mythology: Guests would be invited to come dressed as a Greek god, goddess, or other figure from mythology.

I asked a friend of mine—I'll call her Max—if she would prepare food for the party along the Grecian theme. I had met Max a couple of years before when she was working as a chef at a restaurant where I was working as a waitress. More recently I had occasionally invited her to be a guest chef at the residential arts center where I was working as the chef. She had cooked for my wedding and for other special events in my life. I considered Max a culinary genius whose creations were truly inspired. It was a gift that I envied, and sought to learn from whenever I had the opportunity to cook with her.

But Max had some foibles that held her back in her career. She was a bit of a pleasure seeker, and indulged in drugs a bit more than was good for her. She was from the Caribbean, from the Bahamas, and we used to joke that she operated on Bahamas-time. She was not very punctual, and she lived in the moment—some people considered her unreliable. But she always seemed to come through in the end. And I loved her and admired her. There was no one whose food I would rather have to celebrate my coming of age.

On the day of the party I was dressed up as Hestia, the goddess of the hearth. My partner was the Telamonian Ajax, a hero of myth. One of my friends, who has a passion for sewing and fabric, came as Ariadne, a master weaver who was turned into a spider for comparing her talents to those of a goddess. Another friend showed up as Hephaestus, a god of metalwork, and had built me a fire pit in the backyard that I was planning to tend in my role as Hestia. Another friend was Astraea, a goddess of the stars. And there were nymphs and other figures arriving in beautiful costumes.

Max was late with the food, which I had expected. When she arrived I was so hungry that I grabbed one of the stuffed phyllo triangles off her platter and put it right into my mouth, even as I started grilling chicken and polenta over the fire pit. About twenty minutes later I began to have a strange feeling. The world began to shift, reality receded, and suddenly my mind was no longer my own. I was confused for a few minutes, and then it came to me. I was high. I'd been drugged. I immediately sought out Max and asked her if she had slipped something into a cigarette I'd been smoking.

She laughed, and I laughed, too, but she didn't answer. A few minutes later I began to feel even more strange, and suddenly it began to occur to me that maybe there were drugs in Max's appetizers. I was suddenly extremely concerned about my loved ones at the party, especially those who were clean and sober. I confronted Max again, asking her if there was marijuana in the food. She nodded.

I was distraught. Soon those who had eaten those delicious phyllo triangles were going to feel as disoriented as I did, and I knew without a doubt that all hell would break loose.

And so it did. My partner and I, both high as kites, began circulating to tell guests the horrible news. People were dancing, music was playing, candles were flickering. Before we could reach them, some people started to freak out as the drugs hit their bloodstreams. As bad luck would have it, a group of foreign artists from the arts center where I worked seemed to have eaten the most of the phyllos. And one of them was a tiny Brazilian, weighing not a hundred pounds, who became violently ill. Within moments her dancing went from expressive to crazed, and then she collapsed. Her friends, in only slightly better shape, ushered her into the bedroom, which soon became a vomitorium. The violent illness of the Brazilian artist and her terror began to scare us all. She started ripping off her clothes. Through all the drugs, I was very worried.

I conferred with my partner and with Max, and with another friend, whom I'll call Rafael. We decided that the sick girl should be taken to the hospital. Rafael was completely sober, hadn't eaten any of the drugged food, and had an SUV that was big enough to carry all the sick party guests, as well as Max, to the hospital. The Brazilian was admitted and hooked up to an IV in order to rehydrate her. The other artists were examined but not admitted. The police conducted an inquiry, interviewed Max, and asked everyone if they wanted to press charges against her. They all declined.

They were not the only ones who had eaten the appetizers, however. Other friends found themselves, some for the first time in their lives, feeling the effects of a mind-altering drug. None was particularly pleased, some were frightened, others were angry, and a few, once they had adjusted to the fact of their state, decided to make the best of it. One distraught mother, who had brought her infant to the party and fed him food from the table, was terrified that she had fed her child some of the drug, and at the same time felt herself incapable of tending to his needs for the rest of the night.

Needless to say the evening was ruined. But people kept arriving at the party, unaware of what had happened, and so the humiliation and terrible facts of the case were repeated over and over again.

The repercussions of this nightmare lasted for a long time, but I faced the worst of it the next day when I visited the artists who had been so violated in accepting my hospitality. I was their cook, and the tainting of food at my house involved a breach of trust that was, for some of them, profound. One artist (who hadn't been at the party) called for me to be fired. A meeting was held the following day. All of the artists, as well as the staff of the arts center—including myself—attended. It was an opportunity for people to process their anger and suggest a course of action.

In the meantime I'd had a chance to talk to Max. Her explanation was this: She had infused butter with marijuana in order to make chocolate truffles that were to be given to me as a special gift on my birthday. The butter had gone into the chocolate mixture, but there had been a bit left in the bottom of the pan. She had added fresh butter to the pan to melt for the phyllo triangles, which are brushed with butter in between each flaky layer. She had not thought she'd used enough cannabis-infused butter to have an effect. Obviously wrong, she was repentant. Once the artists and others who had been drugged understood that it hadn't been done intentionally, they could begin to move past their anger and forgive Max for her terrible judgment.

As we began to move past anger and into forgiveness, it started to become impossible to think about the event without having some strange sense that we had all been caught up in a drama that was beyond our understanding, experience, or frames of reference. Max had come in costume as well. She had, fittingly, come as Dionysus, with a crown of ivy leaves on her head and a sultry cloth wrapped around her bare body. Rafael, who saved the day by taking care of the ill group, had come dressed as Apollo. His wonderful hand-sewn costume was a pleated white with gold trim, and he carried a handmade lyre. Rafael is a tall, muscular man, beautifully built, and he chose his role well.

I could not help but be reminded, after the worst was over, of my ninth-grade English teacher who had taught a class on ancient civilizations. Tall, thin, bearded, his arms outstretched, he explained that there had been a great struggle in the ancient Greek world between the Apollonian and the Dionysian worldviews. It was, he said, a struggle between the rational and the mysterious; between the reasonable and the emotional; between the sacred masculine and the sacred feminine; between the sun and the moon; between light and darkness. I had a strange sense of all this being played out at my party. Max as Dionysus had led us into a dark place, a place of hallucinations, mystery, and irrationality. The whole night became unreal, dreamlike, full of emotion and confusion. Apollo, in the form of Rafael, had packed everyone into his SUV and driven them to the hospital, where bright lights and shiny new equipment reigned, and IVs could be used to bring people back from danger. The analogy played out on a physical level, too—Rafael was male and Max was female. Though they are both from the Caribbean (Rafael is Puerto Rican), he is very light skinned while Max's skin is very dark. Rafael's costume was carefully pleated and meticulously sewn; Max's was carelessly slung around her unclad body. All of these facts heightened the feeling of mythic resonances from the night.

I was, of course, as grateful to Rafael as I was angry with Max for the pain she had caused to others—as well as the loss of face and damage to my reputation. In the end I forgave her. Rafael did, too, as did many (but not all) people from the party. But it was one of those events that is hard to draw a moral from. Don't ask genius potheads to cook for your birthday party? Well, yes, perhaps. I can't help but feel, however, that there were strange forces at work through the whole thing—even though, practically speaking, it had been caused by a string of human decisions, some of which were clearly unwise. Something about that night was affecting, dreamlike, nightmarish, and yet deeply real. *Something happened.* I am reminded of a scene from the movie *Six Degrees of Separation* in which the Stockard Channing character, after describing the theft of her painting by a disturbed con man, tries to convey to her listeners that despite the unfortunate nature of the event it was, after all, *an experience.* I feel the same way about my party. I regret what happened, and yet another feeling lingers even more strongly, and it is an odd one: humility.

A week after the party, Max fell off her bike and broke her hand. It took surgery and many months of recovery before she was able to cook again. She seemed to mature quickly after that. Within a year or two she had settled into a long-term relationship with a very stable, rational, grounded partner. They bought a house, and then settled down into the reasonable routine of hard work and daily life.

But I am left with many questions. Did I commit the sin of pride, of hubris, in the planning of my party? Did I disrespect the power of the forces I was dealing with? Did I take things too lightly? Was I courting disaster? Was I expressing an unconscious desire for Dionysian ecstasy, ritual, and release as I set the events in motion? Was a Dionysian power answering me with a reproach to be careful what I wished for? I know that the experience taught me something new about being human.

The Christian theologian Marcus Borg writes about one of the important roles of religion being the creation of *thin places*. This concept from early Celtic Christianity refers to events, times, places, or experiences that bring us into closer relationship with God, or Spirit, or the mystery of life. They open our hearts and fill us with awe. Dionysian rituals in ancient Greece were about creating a thin place, a place where the Maenads experienced a closeness to their god, and I glimpsed how this could be so at my birthday party. Indigenous ritual throughout history and throughout the world has been about creating a thin place, an experience of the divine, a place where the veil between the rational world and the irrational is thin, and human beings can witness another level of reality. Alcohol and alcoholic fermentation in indigenous life were considered sacred because they were also about the creation of a thin place. Ritualized intoxication opened the hearts of the people who participated by diminishing the power of the analytical mind and increasing the access to the emotional body. For a period of time, entered into consciously, Apollo recedes and Dionysus is released, and people find themselves glimpsing God, and having an experience.

I don't know when, or how, or if, our "advanced civilization" will be able to reclaim a relationship to alcohol and other mind-altering substances that is sacred: one that is as much about creation as it is about consumption; one that is about enlightenment and ecstasy and not just escape; one that is about acknowledgment and not abuse; one that is as much about wisdom as it is about power.

In the past few years, the unparalleled popularity of the Harry

Potter books has shown how desperate we—and our children—are for magic and myth. We crave owls and cauldrons and goblins. We crave the ability to see things others miss, to ride on trains that others can't; we crave the knowledge that there are layers to reality, that there are mysteries to be lived, that there is more to life than meets the eye. Intoxication has long been a way that human beings could experience all this, could be brought closer to one another and to the divine.

But like any power, it is easily abused. It is a shame but not a surprise that for many it has become a thing of pain. I read somewhere that there are five reasons human beings drink alcohol:

1. To slake thirst.
2. To participate in a social situation (social drinking).
3. To become intoxicated.
4. To feed an addiction (alcoholism).
5. As a sacred act in worship or ritual.

When I drink alcohol it is usually for reason 2. I enjoy drinking socially with other people. Along with that comes for me another reason that isn't on this list—to appreciate the flavor of an alcoholic beverage, such as a fine wine. I drink to expand my palate, to experience a sensual pleasure. And I drink for reason 5 as well—each Sunday at church when I take communion. I drink a sip of wine as part of a sacrament, an act that my mind cannot fully grasp but that I experience as one of those precious thin places that brings me closer to God. The mystery of Christ's presence in the bread and wine is something I accept on a profound metaphorical level, even if not on a literal one.

And if I had the chance to participate in a similar sacrament in another ancient tradition, I don't think I would turn it down. While Apollo apparently won the struggle for power over Dionysus, and I live in a world dominated by rationality and reason, I for one will never cease to be drawn by that timeless chant of the Bacchantes:

> to dance for joy in the forest,
> to dance where the darkness is deepest . . .

On the Mead Moon, may we all honor the great mystery of life. May we be open to magic, and be humble enough to admit that there are things that we do not fully understand and never will. May we seek out thin places, and open our hearts to the divine. May we acknowledge that there is more to life than our moralistic notions of right and wrong. May we recognize the great "incarnate life-force" and the "uncontrollable chaotic eruption of nature" that pulses within each of us, and in every cultural and religious tradition. On the Mead Moon I give thanks for the masterpiece of alcoholic fermentation, even with all the questions it poses and leaves unanswered. It is the mystery itself, after all, that makes life worth living.

MEAD MOON RECIPES

Mellow Mead
Makes 2 quarts

This lacto-fermented mead has very little alcohol but showcases the flavor of honey, and is delicious. Mead was traditionally drunk on the summer solstice.

⅔ cup raw, unfiltered honey

1½ cups filtered water, very warm (about 110° F)

6 cups filtered water

½ cup kefir grains—rinsed grains from making milk kefir, or water kefir grains

1. Pour the honey into a clean, 2-quart mason jar.
2. Pour the hot water over the honey and stir to dissolve.
3. Pour the rest of the filtered water into the jar.
4. Add the kefir grains.
5. Cover the jar and put it in a warm place for 1 week.
6. Strain into two glass bottles with screw tops. I use the bottles from the mineral water Gerolsteiner. Put an even amount into both bottles. If they are 1-quart bottles, they should be full; if they are 1-liter bottles, add enough water to fill to the top. Screw the lids on tightly, label and date the bottles, and return to the warm place for another week.
7. Transfer to the fridge. Once they are cold you can enjoy them anytime! When you are ready to drink the mead, open the bottles carefully because they may have built up a lot of carbonation. Open them outside or over a sink. Turn the lid very slowly to see if the drink begins to release foam. If so, then allow it to release some of the carbon dioxide by not opening the bottle all the way and letting out some of the pressure, then opening it more and more, bit by bit. This way you won't lose your drink to its carbonation.

Honeybee Lemonade
Serves 1

This is another nutritious and delicious thing to make with or for a child, but it is a quick and refreshing summer drink for a thirsty adult, too. It is not appropriate for babies.

1 tablespoon raw honey

¾ cup filtered water

½ teaspoon bee pollen (see page 309)

Juice of 1 lemon

Ice cubes

1. Put the honey in a jar that has a tightly closing lid.
2. Warm the filtered water until not-quite-hot and pour it over the honey. Screw the lid on the jar and shake.
3. Add the bee pollen to the jar and shake again.
4. Add the lemon juice to the jar and shake again. Make sure that all the bee pollen has dissolved. It should give the drink an orange hue.
5. Put the ice in a glass, pour the lemonade over it, and drink!

I Dream of Peaches and Cream
Serves 1–3

You can find orange blossom water in specialty stores, Middle Eastern groceries, and some large supermarkets. I like to use orange blossom honey, which is fabulous in this recipe.

2 very ripe, sweet, and juicy tree-ripened peaches, peeled and cut into big chunks (pit removed)

¾ cup raw heavy cream, crème fraîche, or yogurt

1 heaping teaspoon raw, local honey

¼ teaspoon vanilla extract

½ teaspoon orange blossom water, or to taste

A few ice cubes if you like cold drinks, or if it's a hot summer night

1. Blend all the ingredients together, using a standard blender or immersion blender, until smooth.
2. Taste and adjust sweetness if necessary (add more honey if it's not sweet enough, more dairy if it's too sweet).
3. Pour into a special glass like a wineglass.
4. Drink as slowly as you can, savoring every bit.

Honeybee Yogurt
Serves 1–2

This is a delicious, nutritious, and quick treat for adults or children—though it isn't appropriate for babies. It would be a good thing to make together with a child.

1 cup whole-milk yogurt (page 89)

½ teaspoon bee pollen (see page 309)

2 teaspoons honey

1. Put the yogurt in a bowl and sprinkle the bee pollen on top. Let this sit for a couple of minutes so the pollen can begin to dissolve.
2. If the honey is crystallized or very thick, warm it by putting it in a dish set in another dish of hot water.
3. Whisk the honey and bee pollen into the yogurt until completely incorporated and serve in a bowl. It should be pale yellow in color.

Summer Berries with Lavender Crème Anglaise
Serves 4–6

This is a great recipe to celebrate summer flowers and honey.

3 pints local summer berries

1 pint half-and-half

6-inch top of 1 stem of fresh lavender such as Grosso—or ½ teaspoon dried lavender blossoms

4 egg yolks

⅓ cup raw local honey, lavender or other mild variety

Pinch of sea salt

1. Stem and clean the berries, and mix them together in a bowl. If the berries are tart, add a tablespoon of honey (gently warmed to liquefy) and stir. Set aside.
2. Heat the half-and-half together with the lavender over low heat until it steams. Cover and remove from the heat. Steep about half an hour.
3. In a bowl, beat the egg yolks. Add a ladleful of the half-and-half mixture to the yolks and whisk together. Then add the yolks back into the half-and-half and stir.
4. Turn the heat back on under the pan, keeping it medium low. Stir constantly as you cook the custard, keeping it below the boiling point, until it is just thickened.
5. Remove from the heat and strain into a bowl. Continue to stir in the bowl until the mixture is warm but not hot. Add the honey and stir until completely dissolved.
6. Allow to cool. Refrigerate until ready to serve.
7. Divide the berries into serving dishes and pour the crème anglaise over them. Decorate with a sprig of lavender and serve.

7
WORT MOON

If they would eat nettles in March,
and drink mugwort in May,
so many fine maidens would not go to the clay.

—Funeral song of a Scottish mermaid

In late summer we enter the lunar phase known in sixteenth-century England as the Wort Moon. Wort is a wonderfully old-fashioned Old English word that has fallen into disuse, one that the dictionary calls "archaic." Yet it is a word that beckons to me from history, a word that wants to be remembered.

The first definition for *wort* in the *Oxford English Dictionary* is "a plant, herb, or vegetable used for food or medicine; often = a pot-herb." As early as 1605 the word *wort* was being replaced by the word *herb*, as is shown in a quote from that year: "Woortes, for which wee now vse the French name of herbes. . . ." The word was still understood and used occasionally throughout the next centuries. In 1864: "We find the healing power of worts spoken of as a thing of course." A love poem written in 1888 includes the delectable tidbit: "And worts and pansies there which grew / Have secrets others wish they knew."

The original meaning of *wort* survives to this day in the names of many of our medicinal herbs. Saint-John's-wort, still widely used today, is a beautiful yellow plant that was traditionally harvested on Saint John's Day—which falls near the summer solstice. Many other

---

Welcome Weeds

Thirteen of my
favorite worts:

1. Nettle
2. Lovage
3. Mint
4. Chasteberry
5. Yarrow
6. Comfrey
7. Sassafras
8. Lemon verbena
9. Mugwort
10. Chamomile
11. Borage
12. Shepherd's purse
13. Passionflower

---

medicinal herbs incorporate the word *wort* in their names, including lungwort, mugwort, motherwort, gipsywort, soapwort, masterwort, Indian birthwort, figwort, rupturewort, bairnwort, banewort, bloodwort, bridewort, cankerwort, clown's woundwort, coughwort, feverwort, fleawort, glasswort, and dozens of others. In some cases the name gives a clue to how the herb is used: Lungwort makes a mucilaginous tea that soothes coughs; soapwort root is loaded with saponins, and is used in treating skin problems. But in others it can be misleading: Fleawort is so named not because it wards off fleas or cures fleabites, but because the seeds look like fleas!

The names of herbs possess much poetry. I also hear in their names a kind of ancestral memory—an ancient wisdom that wants to be remembered. The plants seem to be calling to me through their names. They remind me that once upon a time they were honored and valued; they were the primary source of healing. The herbs themselves and the gardens they grew in were our medicine chests, instead of today's brand-named plastic bottles filled with pharmaceutical pills. Herbs were a part of daily life—a familiar, everyday, working knowledge—just as aspirin and vitamin C are to us today. The World Health Organization recently estimated that 80 percent of the world's population still relies on botanical medicine for a majority of health problems. I find that statistic a potent reminder of how important plants are in treating illness.

I must admit that I have had my skeptical moments about the healing power of herbs. I have been dubious that the leaves of a certain plant could really cure a cough, or that the flowers of another could treat depression, or that the root of still one more could clear up the skin. Plants seem like such mild, simple, common things to have such powers. But everyone who was at my thirtieth birthday party and anyone else who has ever smoked marijuana knows that a plant can have a very powerful effect. So does anyone who's ever gotten poison oak or poison ivy. And of course we all know that certain plants can be fatal if eaten. So whenever I find myself doubting the power of plants, I remember that if plants can make us hallucinate, or make us itch like crazy, or kill us, it is only logical that they can heal us as well.

But for me, the proof is in the pudding—and I have seen firsthand the healing power of herbs in my own body. When I was about twenty years old I had my first case of a rash that covered most of my body, including my face. Not only did the rash look horrible, but it also itched unrelentingly. I felt like my body was on fire; I wished I could crawl out of my skin. After a string of misdiagnoses made by a campus doctor ranging from pinworm to lupus, my mother had me fly home from college and took me to a prominent dermatologist. Within less than a minute of seeing the rash he was able to tell me the correct medical term for it: eczema. He could not, however, tell me its cause. He promptly wrote out a prescription for a heavy course of hydrocortisone (both internal and external) to be taken over the following two weeks. Taking that drug had an immediate effect. It seemed like my entire epidermis peeled off, and my skin was clear again. But six months later the rash was back with a vengeance, and once again it was spreading rapidly.

In the interim I had graduated from college and gotten my own apartment and my first full-time job. It no longer seemed appropriate to expect my parents to handle this recurring health crisis. Also, as I began to research hydrocortisone, it became clear that it is an addictive drug: The more you take it, the more your skin needs it to stay clear. It does not address the systemic cause of the eczema, just its manifestation in a rash. It also has some nasty side effects. The prospect of taking a drug for the rest of my life to keep this rash at bay did not appeal to me. I began to consider alternatives.

I lived on the East Coast at the time, and I had never known anyone who'd tried acupuncture. But I had read about it in magazines as a miraculous cure for health problems Western medicine was not equipped to solve. I saw an ad in a paper for a Chinese acupuncturist in my area, and she listed dermatological problems as one of her areas of expertise. I called her. She immediately scheduled me for an appointment. Though I told her I wasn't sure if I could go ahead with the treatment and was scared of the needles, I figured it couldn't hurt to talk to her.

In her office I showed Dr. Wang the spreading rash. "I can help you," she said. The treatment would involve acupuncture treatments and drinking a tea made of herbs every day. I was scared and skeptical, but I was also desperate. The rash was nearly unbearable, and the terror of it once again taking over my body was greater than the terror of needles and foreign treatments. She had me lie down on a doctor's table, and administered some needles. I hardly felt them. Then she burned a strange-smelling incense in a small dish that she laid on my skin. She told me to tell her when it got too hot. I later learned that this ancient remedy was called moxibution and that the herb she was burning was mugwort. She then disappeared into the back and pre-pared some paper bags full of bizarre-looking natural items: white barks and shriveled red berries, black nuts and translucent powder.

Dr. Wang gave me the bags at the end of the session and encour-aged me to buy a strangely shaped black clay pot. "You must cook these herbs in a ceramic pot," she told me, "or glass would work, but never a metal one." She gave me detailed instructions on how much water I should use with the herbs, how long to cook them for, how to store and reheat the tea, when to drink it in relation to meals—a com-plete regimen. I bought the pot and the bags of herbs, and made an appointment for the following week.

Once at home I began to cook the herbs. They filled the house with an indescribably strange smell—like the floor of a distant forest—and tasted indescribably terrible, like drinking a cup of water that has been used as an ashtray. Still, I diligently boiled the herbs in the earthen pot for hours on end, downed the acrid tea, and watched to see what would happen.

My eczema got worse. It spread over more parts of my body. At my following appointment I showed Dr. Wang in panic my rash running rampant, after a week of swallowing her intolerable brew. She smiled and told me it was okay, that my symptoms would get worse before they got better, but that inside my body was already starting to heal. Then there were more needles, more smelly smoke and hot pots on my skin, more mysterious bags of bark. After a couple of weeks of treatment, the spreading rash stopped spreading. Then it began clearing up. I had been on the regimen at least a month when I was in her office one day to pick up my herbs. She had forgotten to prepare them and began hastily doing so right in front of me. I saw her take an enormous handful of what looked like bugs and put them in my bag. "Wait a second! I've never had those before!" She explained to me that she usually crushed them up; those dried shells or carcasses or whatevers were the source of the translucent powder I was used to seeing in my bag. "I didn't want to scare you," she said. Now, I was a vegetarian at this time, and was not particularly attracted to the idea of stewed bugs. She went into a long explanation of why it was so important for me to have this particular medicine, in part because my vegetarianism was weakening my system at a certain level, and this particular "herb" would strengthen and purify my blood. I decided that I had already been drinking the stewed bug juice for over a month already, and it was helping, so I'd go ahead with the program.

Pouring those little creaturelike forms into my black earthenware pot, I couldn't help but think about those three witches in Shakespeare's *Macbeth*:

> *Double, double toil and trouble;*
> *Fire, burn; and, caldron, bubble.*
> *Fillet of a fenny snake,*
> *In the cauldron boil and bake;*
> *Eye of newt, and toe of frog,*
> *Wool of bat, and tongue of dog,*
> *Adder's fork, and blind-worm's sting,*
> *Lizard's leg, and howlet's wing, —*
> *For a charm of powerful trouble,*
> *Like a hell-broth boil and bubble . . .*

Some herbalists have postulated that each of these phrases was actually derived from the descriptive names of plants. "Tongue of dog" may have referred to an herb now called hound's tongue (*Cynoglossum officinale*), "adder's fork" was what is now known as serpent's tongue (*Erythronium americanum*), and "fillet of a fenny snake" was probably chickweed (*Stellaria holostea*). This may be. But I know for a fact that a healing cauldron can contain remedies derived from the animal kingdom, just as my very first prescription included "shell of Chinese cicada" or somesuch.

Many years after that first experience with acupuncture I was traveling in India and had a mild but spreading recurrence of eczema. I went to see a traditional Ayurvedic herbalist in a small town in the north of the country—a place famous for its healers, where I happened to be staying overnight. The Indian doctor examined the rash, asked me a few questions about it, and then began to prepare the treatment. He broke up what looked like thin metal balls into a mortar and pestle, crushed them to a powder, mixed them with some other powdered herbs, and then fed me a bit of this bizarre mixture worked into honey. He told me to take some of the powder this way each day. I did so, and again that rash cleared up. I came to realize that herbal medicine is effective, expansive, and complex—drawing at least from the animal, vegetable, and mineral worlds. Still, the heart of herbal medicine is the plant material itself—the leaves, seeds, barks, berries, roots, and flowers that can have such a powerful influence on the blood, breath, and body of a human being.

Over the fifteen years since my introduction to herbal healing, I have seen half a dozen different acupuncturists, depending on where I'm living or working, my insurance plan, and other practical considerations. Chinese medicine has become the medicine I rely upon whenever I have a health problem. While in college, I had taken repeated courses of antibiotics for chronic glandular infections; I had taken pharmaceuticals for skin problems, and pharmaceutical hormones for birth control. In too many cases these drugs ended up causing more problems than they solved. Since that first experience with the healing cauldron, I have avoided the pharmaceutical medicine chest whenever I could and stuck with traditional Chinese herbal healing.

As grateful as I am to the Chinese system, and also to Ayurveda, some years ago I began to wish that my herbal medicine chest could be made up of the herbs of my own ancestors—the herbs of continental Europe, the British Isles, and colonial America. These are the herbs whose names call to me in a language I can understand. Unfortunately, while the Chinese materia medica was being developed, researched, written down, and made increasingly precise and effective over thousands of years, many practitioners of the European materia medica were being burned as witches. Instead of being encouraged and supported, their decoctions and potions were viewed with increasing suspicion and over time were put aside in favor of practices considered more scientific. While the Chinese, Ayurvedic, and many indigenous herbal healing systems were becoming more sophisticated, many European herbal traditions struggled to survive. As the Western medical establishment became more and more powerful, pharmaceutical, chemical, and surgical approaches have become the standard of Western health care and have been exported to every corner of the Earth. I certainly believe that there is a time and place for all these approaches and I use them all, but I have been glad to see a resurgence of interest in the wise worts of yesteryear.

My own interest was piqued enough that I decided to take an introductory course at an herbology school. The class was called The Technology of Independence—a name I thought a bit odd, but I came to grasp the meaning. The idea was to help us evolve toward a kind of medical independence, an ability to treat ourselves with worts the way our ancestors did. I began to dream that someday I could grow the plants that are medicinal for me, and to know how and when to harvest them and preserve them, and to be able to keep myself well. There is an Old English phrase for the knowledge of herbs and how to use them: *wortcunning*. And there is an Old English term for an herb garden: *wortyard*. After taking that class I was able to begin planting my wortyard, and to experiment with combining herbs for teas, drying them to preserve them, and making some tinctures, salves, and capsules. I began to develop just a bit of wortcunning.

A few years ago I began seeing a new acupuncturist, and found myself in for a pleasant surprise. Dr. Yang is a Chinese woman trained in Beijing, but during our first appointment she told me that instead of using the usual dried, imported Chinese herbs in her practice, she works with a Western herbalist in Marin County who makes tinctures that include organic, locally grown and wild-crafted herbs. The herbs are drawn from the European pharmacopoeia as well as the Chinese and other herbal traditions. I was very excited to hear this.

A couple of days after Dr. Yang gave me my first needle treatment, I went back to her office to pick up my first bottle of tincture. I became even more excited when I began to read the label. The names of the ingredients were in Latin, but I had been studying and growing medicinal herbs for long enough that on first glance I recognized at least half the names as plants I already knew well: *Achillea* was yarrow; *Alchemilla* was lady's mantle; *Artemisia* was mugwort; *Capsella* was shepherd's purse; *Urtica* was nettle; *Rubus fol.* was blackberry leaf; *Vitex* was chasteberry; *Zinziberis* was ginger . . .

I knew these herbs because they were all ones that I had identified as being appropriate medicines for my constitutional weaknesses, and most of them I had tried to grow in my garden at one time or another. I began to feel that my hobbylike interest in the herbs of the Western pharmacopoeia could finally begin to come together with the lived experience of herbs healing me when I was ill. From the long list of herbs in that prescription, I have already planted yarrow, chasteberry, and lady's mantle. Blackberry leaves are plentiful in my yard, as thorny blackberry vines are an aggressive local weed. Mugwort is native to my area, and someday soon I'll try putting in shepherd's purse.

As I studied herbs and also began to be interested in fermentation, I realized the strong historic connection between these two traditions. The second definition listed for the word *wort* in the *Oxford English Dictionary* is "the infusion of malt or other grain which after fermentation becomes beer." This definition has remained common in English usage throughout the centuries among beer brewers. To make beer, you need some form of sugar—something sweet for the beer yeasts to ferment or eat. Around the world this sweetness has been obtained from myriad sources—tree sap, sweet starches, masticated roots, fruit juices, and honey, among others. But in the classical European tradition, beer is made from "malted grain"—grain, generally barley, that has been sprouted (and often roasted) to convert its starch into sugar and flavor. The malted barley is then used to sweeten the water you are going to use for the beer, and the sweetened water becomes the "sweetwort." A bitter herb is then added— in the case of classical British or German beer making, hops. This infuses the sweetwort with flavor and also the medicinal properties of the herb. What you have now is the "bitterwort." To this is added a yeast or culture. The specific family of microorganisms that create alcohol from sugars is called *Saccharomyces*; these are the ones used in classical European beer making. The wort is then fermented until it becomes beer. Then it is bottled for drinking. That's a nutshell version of how beer is made.

There is a five-hundred-year-old German law—the *Reinheitsgebot*— that regulates the ingredients in beer and permits only four: water, barley, hops, and yeast. Nothing else can legally be called beer in Germany. The *Reinheitsgebot* was at least partly the result of a hot fight between advocates for hopped ale and advocates for the (then more traditional) gruit ales made from herbs (worts) such as marsh rosemary, bog myrtle, yarrow, wormwood, and sage. For many centuries ales had been brewed by women in small quantities from the herbs in their wortyard. The ales had a wide range of properties—medicinal, stimulating, ceremonial, culinary—depending on which worts had been used in their brewing. The beer purity laws enacted in the sixteenth century in both England and Germany paved the way for the consolidation of beer brewing into the hands of a few commercial producers that would eventually put the local, artisanal, small-scale production of the alewife out of business.

An alewife was a woman who brewed and sold ale. I love the word. The ancient words *ale* and *wife* have obscure origins in West Saxon (for *ale*) and Old English (for *wife*). It was once so common for women to brew ales and beers that there are many old terms for it: *alewife, aledame, brewster* (as opposed to *brewer*, which was used for men), *brewster-wife, breweress,* and *brew-wife.* And *brewing,* of course, has another whole layer of meaning. As the *Oxford English Dictionary* puts it: "to concoct, contrive, prepare, bring about, cause" often followed by "mischief, trouble, evil, or woe." Perhaps this is part of where the notion of a dangerous witch's brew came from. The witch (medicine woman? shaman?) and the alewife were part of the same continuum.

The word *wife* has gotten some rough treatment in the modern context, with its connotations of the "second sex." But the original meaning of the word was simply "woman." It had nothing to do with marriage or a man. The term evolved a later meaning as (surprisingly, from today's perspective) a workingwoman—and, by association, a working-class woman. A wife was a woman who had to earn her own living. The word *wife* was then affixed to the work she did. So an alewife was a woman who brewed and sold beer, and she might well be single. An herb-wife was a woman who grew and dispensed herbs, and was often known for her wortcunning. Oyster-wives and fishwives were women who sold seafood. An apple-wife sold apples. The old wives referred to in the phrase *old wives' tale* were simply old women.

There is only one word in modern usage where this old meaning of *wife* is still understood: *midwife*. A midwife is a woman who assists in childbirth. While the etymology of *wife* in the phrase is clear, the etymology of the *mid* part has eluded lexicographers to this day. They think the meaning is one of two: a woman *by whose means* the delivery is affected; or, alternatively, a woman who is *with* the mother as she gives birth. Students of German will note the connection between the German word *mit* (with) and the Old English *mid* (with). But I like to ruminate on the fact that one of the earlier forms of the word *midwife* was *medewife*, which sounds to me a whole lot like *medi-wife*—that is, medical woman, or medicine woman. Unfortunately, the linguists don't seem to support this theory. No matter what the etymology of the word, however, midwifery has always involved knowledge, skill, experience, intuition, and even wortcunning. Midwives were once burned at the stake, not only because they were associated with witchcraft but also because they eased women's pain in childbirth, and church officials had interpreted (or I should say misinterpreted) passages of the Bible to mean that women *should* suffer in childbirth. How much valuable knowledge died with those wise women? Still, I am happy that the tradition of midwifery has experienced a renaissance, and that many expectant mothers choose to have a midwife lead them through this profound human experience.

Like being a midwife, being an alewife required some wortcunning. Herbal beers were commonly drunk in Old Europe, and beer is a traditional carrier for the medicinal properties of a plant. Old-fashioned ales ranged from only mildly alcoholic to highly inebriating and perhaps even psychotropic. Part of this range was a result of the kind of yeasts that were used, and part of it was the result of the properties of the herbs that were added to the sweetwort.

When we hear about our ancestors drinking beer instead of water, including during work and also including children, we are often shocked. We find ourselves contemplating what life would be like if *we* drank beer all day, every day. But we are thinking of the beers of modern commerce, not the ales and small beer that the alewife used to brew. Though some were certainly quite alcoholic, there have been throughout human history and human cultures many fermented drinks that are primarily nourishing; they can be drunk daily, even in the morning, without much inebriating effect.

When I first began to learn about traditional diets, I became intrigued by what I heard about the widespread use of "lacto-fermentation" in making beverages in indigenous cultures. This kind of fermentation process preserves a whole range of enzymes and beneficial bacteria while producing relatively little alcohol. As Sally Fallon writes in *Nourishing Traditions*:

> A survey of popular ethnic beverages will show that the fermentation of grains and fruits to make refreshing and health-promoting drinks is almost universal. Usually these drinks are very mildly alcoholic, the result of a fermentation process that is both alcoholic (by the action of yeasts on sugars) and lactic acid forming (by the action of bacteria on sugars). . . .
> Throughout the world, these lactic-acid-containing

drinks have been valued for medicinal qualities including the ability to relieve intestinal problems and constipation, promote lactation, strengthen the sick and promote overall well-being and stamina. Above all, these drinks were considered superior to plain water in their ability to relieve thirst during physical labor. Modern research has discovered that liquids containing dilute sugars and electrolytes of minerals (mineral ions) are actually absorbed faster and retained longer than plain water. This research is used to promote commercial sports drinks that are merely high-sugar concoctions containing small amounts of electrolytes. But natural lactic-acid fermented drinks contain numerous valuable minerals in ionized form and a small amount of sugar, along with lactic acid and beneficial lactobacilli, all of which promote good health in many ways while at the same time cutting the sensation of thirst.

I have found much evidence of these types of beverages as I have read about indigenous and traditional communities. While reading *One River* by ethnobotanist Wade Davis, I came across this passage in his description of the Waorani people, who live in the Amazon rain forest much as their ancient ancestors did:

> Squatting by the fire, [Tomo] drank a calabash of *tepae*, the thick and mildly fermented beverage prepared by the women from the masticated roots of manioc. Like most adult Waorani, Tomo would drink almost two gallons a day. Although *tepae* is the major source of carbohydrate in the diet, no Waorani considers it food. No matter how they are consumed, all fruits, roots, and seeds are said to be drunk. Similarly a garden is not harvested, it is drunk. Only meat is eaten, for it is the only true food in the forest.

My European ancestors drank their gardens as well. They brewed mildly fermented beverages from the herbs that they grew or gathered from the wild areas surrounding the villages. Those drinks were the healthy precursors to today's ubiquitous sweet, tangy bubbly beverages—soft drinks, colas, sodas, carbonated juice mixtures, sweetened iced teas, and flavored bubbly waters. But today's sweet bubbly products are the toxic mimics of our ancestors' lacto-fermented drinks. They lack enzymes, minerals, or beneficial bacteria, and are high in sugar, caffeine, chemicals, and artificial ingredients. Root beer and ginger ale are two familiar sodas that were, once upon a time, traditionally fermented herbal ales, but lost most of their goodness when they entered modern commerce. What our ancestors drank was the *real* real thing.

As I became enchanted with traditional lacto-fermented drinks, medicinal herbs, and the memory of the alewife, I became inspired to begin making my own herbal ales at home. I experimented with herbs, some from my own wortyard, some from one of the specialty herb stores in my area, and some from the farmer's market or grocery store. I was especially excited to begin brewing ales from the herbs that I had learned were particularly good for my constitution and the chronic health challenges I face. It is difficult to imagine anyone living in contemporary society who doesn't have some ongoing health problem. For some it may be spring allergies, for others it is indigestion, for others acne. Some women get bad PMS every moon, other people get too many colds in the winter; some people battle anxiety and others contend with depression. A small amount of an herb that is specific to these conditions, drunk daily as part of a lacto-fermented traditional ale, could go a long way toward alleviating these symptoms. What if instead of

> ## *Cauldron, Bubble!*
> Thirteen traditional lacto-fermented beverages:
>
> 1. Root beer (United States)
> 2. Ginger ale (Caribbean)
> 3. Kvass (Russia and Eastern Europe)
> 4. Kombucha (throughout the northern Eastern Hemisphere)
> 5. Tepae (Waorani, South American rain forest)
> 6. Shamita (Ethiopia)
> 7. Gamju (Korea)
> 8. Sweet potato fly (Guyana)
> 9. Munkoyo (Zambia)
> 10. Birch beer (United States and Russia)
> 11. UbuSulu (southern Africa)
> 12. Tesgüino (Tarahumara, Mexico)
> 13. Posol (Maya)

taking an over-the-counter allergy medicine, you began to drink nettle beer every day? Wouldn't drinking a lacto-fermented ginger ale be preferable to taking an antacid for your indigestion?

There are also herbal ales that are good for a seasonal transition and can be recommended to everybody as the weather changes. Others can correct a particular deficiency in the diet. George Washington made one quart of spruce beer part of the daily rations of the soldiers in the Continental army. This was likely because spruce beer was well known for preventing scurvy—always a problem for troops who are subsisting on cheap dried foods and little that is fresh or green. His choice may also have had something to do with the fact that "spruce beer does not produce drowsiness like hopped beers but rather invigorates the spirits and uplifts the energy." An energetic army must be much more effective than a sleepy one. In *Martha Washington's Cookery Book* there is a wonderful recipe for an old-fashioned birch beer, made from the sap of the birch tree, which is tapped in the same way and at nearly the same time as the maple tree. The recipe notes that "this drink is very pleasant and allsoe physicall, first for procuring an appetite, & allsoe it is an antidote against gravell and the stone." Stephen Harrod Buhner notes that birch sap was also used for brewing in Russia:

> The wonderful Russian herbalist, Rita Bykhovsky, recently shared with me her experiences with birch beer. In the 13-house village where she lived, her husband would make large quantities of this beer every spring. They considered it a refreshing spring tonic beer and wonderful thirst quencher. She calls it a traditional Russian kvass (from the same root word as Kvaser from whose blood the Mead of Inspiration was made) as it was made from birch sap, fresh mint leaves, and yeast.

Another traditional Russian kvass has become increasingly popular in the United States: *teekvass*—or, as it was known in parts of Asia and has come to be known in the United States, *kombucha*. It is a lacto-fermented drink that requires a particular yeast colony as its starter culture. This culture is often called a mother, or sometimes mistakenly referred to as a mushroom. I brew kombucha in batches of three to five gallons at a time, since we drink a lot of it in our home and my ailing father-in-law loves it. He claims that it makes him feel much better. The sweetener that is most effective in making teekvass is white sugar, and the herb that it feeds on is black tea—*Camellia sinensis*. Its origins are mysterious. I've heard that no one has been able to create a new mother in a laboratory. Apparently every kombucha mother currently circulating originated from one great mother-of-them-all, which perhaps really was a gift of the gods. Its popularity is growing because of its refreshing taste and its ability to cleanse the liver and promote health. While it may seem like a modern health fad, it is actually an old and mysterious drink—part of the noble and wide-spread tradition of the kvass brewer or the alewife. I am drinking it as I write, and enjoying its tart-sweet pungent flavor.

While I make teekvass all year, most of the other ales I make are more seasonal. Nettle is a traditional potherb (wort) of spring, which is the easiest time to find nettles growing wild or at a farmer's market and the classic time to make the delicious nettle beer. In the summer, around the Wort Moon, many of the other ale herbs are blooming. My favorite summer herbal ale is made from lemon verbena, using the strongly scented leaves of the expansive bush that grows in my wortyard. The ale is fragrant and relaxing. I also love to make yarrow ale from the flowering tops of the medicinal yarrow (*Achillea mille-folium*) that thrives near the lemon verbena. Yarrow is a bitter herb, and the resulting beverage is very ale-y and beerlike. It has a reputation for being psychotropic, but I haven't found this to be the case. I thoroughly enjoy the ales made from lavender and from rose gera-nium—which retain a hint of their floral smell but become much more complex when turned into ales. I have also experimented with making old-fashioned root beer and ginger ale and like them both. Pleasant medicine, indeed.

What if our approach to health in this country were truly preventive, holistic, integrated, and cost-effective? In more traditional societies the approach to health wasn't just about curing illnesses. Supporting the health of the community was done in subtle ways on an ongoing basis. I have heard that in the traditional Chinese system, the doctor (acupuncturist) was responsible for keeping you well, and so you paid him or her a small regular fee to keep you healthy. If you got sick, payment was suspended and your treatment was free. I carry this idea around with me as an inspiring alternative to the ineffective and inefficient model I grew up with. It sounds to me like what *real* health insurance might look like. Our bodies are always changing, and our well-being depends on a balance of dynamic energies. Herbs and healing foods, rest and acupuncture, exercise and moxibution all help to keep the energies moving toward wellness and to balance the effects of stressful situations. I love the idea of a system that helps our bodies to weather the changing seasons, stages, and stressors of life, and that is responsive to our individual excesses, weaknesses, and constitutional quirks.

Healing herbs were an important part of holistic approaches almost everywhere on Earth. Many plants have been held sacred by the communities that used them. Tobacco, for example, was thought to bring peace and a passageway to the spirit world by many cultures. Coca leaves were routinely offered to the gods by the Andean indigenous who chewed them. Both plants were used to support the health of the traditional peoples that honored them. Sadly, today they have become the vehicles of wealth accumulation, of addiction, and of criminal exploitation. But once upon a time they were vehicles to the divine, and for many people they still are.

The ways that the healing powers of herbs have been transmitted to humans are practically endless. They have been cooked into teas, brewed into beers, smoked in pipes, tinctured in alcohol. They have been fed to dairy animals whose milk was then drunk. They have been dried and powdered, and given with honey. They have been infused into ghee or other fats, cooked into soups, added to pickles, or used in sweat lodges or other healing or shamanic ceremonies. They have been steamed and inhaled, added to baths, and steeped into oil that is rubbed into the body. They have been turned into candies, syrups, and other herbal confections. Nowadays many people who are taking a medicinal herb for a health problem are simply popping a pill that is not so different from any other modern drug. But once upon a time, gardens were meant to be drunk.

Reviving the tradition of the alewife would mean a return to an eco-logical, local, artisanal model of beverage production. In *Nourishing Traditions*, Sally Fallon writes:

> The day when every town in America produces its own distinctive lactofermented brew, made from the local products of woods and fields, will be the day when Americans see the dawning of a new age of good health and well-being, as well as a new era of economic vitality based on small-scale production rather than on large-scale monopolistic control of the food-processing industry.

What an appealing vision. Until that day, we can learn more and more about the magic of plants, and begin to use them in myriad ways in our daily lives. We can emulate the alewives and brew delicious and nourishing drinks that will help keep us well.

On the Wort Moon, may we all begin to develop a little bit of wort-cunning. May we find a way to tend a small wortyard, and come to know a few plants that are healing for us. May we watch them flower, smell their fragrance, taste their leaves. May we carry on the tradition of wise cultures around the world that have looked to plants for med-icine and healing. May we remember how to drink our gardens—and brew up a little mischief while we're at it.

WORT MOON RECIPES

Lemon Verbena Ale
Makes 2 quarts

My lemon verbena plant is prodigious. This is one of my favorite things to do with its fragrant leaves.

1 cup loosely packed lemon verbena
leaves

2 quarts filtered water

⅔ cup Sucanat, Rapadura, or palm
sugar

Juice of ½ lemon

½ cup kefir grains or 1 cup yogurt
whey (page 313)

1. Put the lemon verbena leaves in a large pot and pour 1 quart of the filtered water over them.
2. Bring the pot to a boil, then turn off the heat and let it sit, covered, for about half an hour.
3. Pour the Sucanat, Rapadura, or palm sugar into a 2-quart mason jar, and strain the still-hot lemon verbena into it. Stir or whisk to dissolve.
4. Add the lemon juice to the jar, along with the remaining 1 quart of filtered water. Stir to combine.
5. Touch the liquid with your finger or use a milk thermometer to gauge the temperature. Before you add the kefir grains or whey, the liquid needs to cool to about 100° F. This was the temperature the alewife would call blood warm. It should feel just warm to the touch but not hot.
6. Add the kefir grains or whey, screw on the lid, and leave to ferment for 2 days in a warm place.
7. Strain into two glass bottles with screw tops. I use the bottles from the mineral water Gerolsteiner. Put an even amount into both bottles. If they are 1-quart bottles, they should be full; if they are 1-liter bottles, add enough water to fill to the top. Screw the lids on tightly, label and date the bottles, and return to the warm place for another 2 to 3 days.
8. Transfer to the fridge. Once they are cold you can enjoy them anytime! When you are ready to drink the ale, open the bottles carefully because they may have built up a lot of carbonation. Open them outside or over a sink. Turn the lid very slowly to see if the drink begins to release foam. If so, then allow it to release some of the carbon dioxide by not opening the bottle all the way and letting out some of the pressure, then opening it more and more, bit by bit. This way you won't lose your drink to its carbonation.

Root Beer
Makes 2 quarts

This is one of the few traditional lacto-fermented beverages modern people are familiar with—though the modern version is little like the traditional. For one thing, it is now illegal to sell root beer made from sassafras. Even though sassafras was a traditional herb long used by the peoples indigenous to southeastern North America, science experiments injecting large amounts of safrole—a compound in sassafras—into lab rats gave the animals cancer. But any compound, taken out of its plant matrix and injected in high quantities, can be toxic. Some people smell a rat: soft drink companies wanting to eliminate competition from home brewers? I make my root beer from sassafras—traditionally used as a blood cleanser—and don't fret about the trace amounts of safrole it contains.

2 tablespoons dried sassafras (the bark of the root), available at herb stores or online

1 tablespoon dried licorice root, available at herb stores or online

2 quarts filtered water

⅓ cup birch syrup

⅓ cup Sucanat or Rapadura

1 cup ginger bug, ½ cup kefir grains, or 1 cup yogurt whey (page 313)

1. Put the sassafras and licorice in a large pot and pour 1 quart of the filtered water over it.
2. Bring to a simmer and cover for 20 minutes. Turn off the heat and leave covered for about half an hour.
3. Pour the birch syrup and Sucanat or Rapadura into a 2-quart mason jar, and strain the still-hot herbal mixture over the birch syrup. Stir or whisk to dissolve.
4. Add the remaining 1 quart of filtered water. Stir to combine.
5. Touch the liquid with your finger or use a milk thermometer to gauge the temperature. Before you add the ginger bug, kefir grains, or whey, the liquid needs to cool to about 100° F. This was the temperature the alewife would call blood warm. It should feel just warm to the touch but not hot.
6. Add the ginger bug, kefir grains, or whey, screw on the lid, and leave for 2 to 4 days in a warm place.
7. Strain equal amounts into two glass bottles with screw tops. I use the bottles from Gerolsteiner mineral water. If they are 1-quart bottles, they should be full; if they are 1-liter bottles, add enough water to fill. Screw the lids on tightly, label and date the bottles, and return to the warm place for another 2 to 3 days.
8. Transfer to the fridge. Once they are cold you can enjoy them anytime! When you are ready to drink the root beer, open the bottles carefully because they may have built up a lot of carbonation. Open them outside or over a sink. Turn the lid very slowly to see if the drink begins to release foam. If so, then allow it to release some of the carbon dioxide by not opening the bottle all the way and letting out some of the pressure, then opening it more and more, bit by bit. This way you won't lose your drink to its carbonation.

Herbal Latte

Based on a formula given to me by an herbalist, this brew contains herbs that help support the adrenal glands. I drank this for months as I gave up coffee. The herbs can be found at an herb store or online, then you can follow the directions for preparing the herbal mixture. The formula is more medicinal than it is delicious. For a tastier but less medicinal blend, omit the chasteberries.

This mixture can be used over a couple of weeks. If you like it, you can double the herbs next time so that it lasts longer.

Herbal Mixture (makes 2½ cups)

½ cup dried licorice root

¼ cup dried dandelion root

¼ cup dried wild yam

¼ cup dried gingerroot

¼ cup dried sarsaparilla

¼ cup dried sassafras

¼ cup dried chasteberries

¼ cup crushed cinnamon sticks

¼ cup rooibos tea (red bush tea)

1. Heat a cast-iron skillet over low heat. Add the licorice root and toast until lightly golden-brown. Transfer to a glass bowl.
2. Repeat the process with the dandelion (which will get darker brown), wild yam, ginger, and sarsaparilla.
3. Add the sassafras, chasteberries, cinnamon, and rooibos to the bowl. Mix all the herbs together thoroughly and transfer to a mason jar.

Latte (serves 1)

2 tablespoons of the herbal mixture

1 cup filtered water

¾ cup whole milk, preferably raw

1. In a Chinese herb pot or a small pan, combine the herbal mixture with the water. Bring to a boil and simmer, covered, for 20 to 30 minutes. It is good if there is a slight wisp of steam while it cooks, so that a little of the water evaporates as the mixture simmers.
2. Just before the tea is done cooking, steam, froth, or gently heat the milk (see the information on frothing milk, page 90).
3. Strain the simmered tea mixture into a mug or latte glass, and then pour the frothed milk into it.

Note: The used herbs can be reserved and used again the next day, with the addition of a teaspoon or so of uncooked herbs to the pot.

Hibiscus and Rose Hip Soda
Makes 2 quarts or 2 liters

Hibiscus and rose hips are both full of vitamin C, which is damaged by heat. That is why I use a cold infusion. This is a delicious and beautiful drink.

¼ cup dried hibiscus flowers, available at herb stores (or in Mexican markets as jamaica)

1 tablespoon dried rose hips, available at herb stores or online

½ cup agave nectar

½ cup kefir grains or 1 cup yogurt whey (page 313)

½ organic lemon

Filtered water

1. Put the hibiscus, rose hips, agave nectar, and whey or kefir grains in a 2-quart jar. Squeeze the juice from the lemon into the jar and add the rind as well. Pour in enough filtered water to fill the jar.
2. Screw the lid onto the jar and put it in a warm place for 2 days.
3. Strain into two glass bottles with screw tops. I use the bottles from the mineral water Gerolsteiner. Put an even amount into both bottles. If they are 1-quart bottles, they should be full; if they are 1-liter bottles, add enough water to fill to the top. Screw the lids on tightly, label and date the bottles, and return to the warm place for another 2–3 days, or until the soda becomes slightly bubbly.
4. Transfer to the fridge. Once they are cold you can enjoy them anytime! When you are ready to drink the soda, open the bottles carefully because they may have built up a lot of carbonation. Open them outside or over a sink. Turn the lid very slowly to see if the drink begins to release foam. If so, then allow it to release some of the carbon dioxide by not opening the bottle all the way and letting out some of the pressure, then opening it more and more, bit by bit. This way you won't lose your drink to its carbonation.

Yarrow Ale
Makes 2 quarts

Yarrow was one of the herbs used by the medieval alewife for brewing, and also one of the worts well-known to midwives and herbwives. Alcoholic yarrow beer has a reputation for being psychoactive. I have made it but didn't find it particularly inebriating! This is a very ale-y drink, as yarrow is a bitter herb. I make it when the Achillea mille-folium in my garden is flowering.

2 cups loosely packed fresh flowering yarrow tops, or ½ cup dried (available at herb stores)

2 quarts filtered water

⅔ cup barley malt

Juice of ½ lemon

½ cup kefir grains or 1 cup yogurt whey (page 313)

1. Put the yarrow tops in a large pot and pour 1 quart of the filtered water over them.
2. Bring to a simmer and cover for 20 minutes. Turn off the heat and leave covered for about half an hour.
3. Pour the barley malt into a 2-quart mason jar, and strain the still-hot yarrow mixture over it. Stir or whisk to dissolve.
4. Add the lemon juice to the jar, along with the remaining 1 quart of filtered water. Stir to combine.
5. Touch the liquid with your finger or use a milk thermometer to gauge the temperature. Before you add the kefir grains or whey, the liquid needs to cool to about 100° F. This was the temperature the alewife would call blood warm. It should feel just warm to the touch but not hot.
6. Add the kefir grains or whey, screw on the lid, and leave to ferment for 2 days in a warm place.
7. Strain into two glass bottles with screw tops. I use the bottles from the mineral water Gerolsteiner. Put an even amount into both bottles. If they are 1-quart bottles, they should be full; if they are 1-liter bottles, add enough water to fill to the top. Screw the lids on tightly, label and date the bottles, and return to the warm place for another 2 days.
8. Transfer to the fridge. Once they are cold you can enjoy them anytime! When you are ready to drink the ale, open the bottles carefully because they may have built up a lot of carbonation. Open them outside or over a sink. Turn the lid very slowly to see if the drink begins to release foam. If so, then allow it to release some of the carbon dioxide by not opening the bottle all the way and letting out some of the pressure, then opening it more and more, bit by bit. This way you won't lose your drink to its carbonation.

Birch Beer or Sorghum Ale
Makes 2 quarts

Birch syrup can be ordered from many online retailers, which you can find by searching for "Alaskan birch syrup." Make sure it is made from 100 percent birch sap. Sorghum molasses is also available online by searching for "sweet sorghum." I order mine from www.lehmans.com.

⅔ cup birch syrup* (for birch beer) or sorghum molasses (for sorghum ale)

1½ cups filtered water, brought to a simmer

6 cups filtered water

½ cup kefir grains or 1 cup yogurt whey (page 313)

1. Pour the syrup or molasses into a clean, 2-quart mason jar.
2. Pour the hot water over the syrup or molasses, and stir to dissolve.
3. Pour the rest of the filtered water into the jar.
4. Touch the liquid with your finger or use a milk thermometer to gauge the temperature. Before you add the kefir grains or whey, the liquid needs to cool to about 110° F. This was the temperature the alewife would call blood warm. It should feel just warm to the touch but not hot.
4. Add the kefir grains or whey.
5. Cover the jar and put it in a warm place for 2 to 3 days.
6. Strain into two glass bottles with screw tops. I use the bottles from the mineral water Gerolsteiner. Put an even amount into both bottles. If they are 1-quart bottles, they should be full; if they are 1-liter bottles, add enough water to fill to the top. Screw the lids on tightly, label and date the bottles, and return to the warm place for 2 to 3 more days.
7. Transfer to the fridge. Once they are cold you can enjoy them anytime! When you are ready to drink the beer or ale, open the bottles carefully because they may have built up a lot of carbonation. Open them outside or over a sink. Turn the lid very slowly to see if the drink begins to release foam. If so, then allow it to release some of the carbon dioxide by not opening the bottle all the way and letting out some of the pressure, then opening it more and more, bit by bit. This way you won't lose your drink to its carbonation.

*Since birch syrup is expensive, you can make this recipe using ⅓ cup birch syrup and ⅓ cup mild sweetener such as maple syrup or Sucanat.

8

CORN MOON

And again he said,
"To what shall I compare the Kingdom of Heaven?
It is like Leaven
Which a woman took to knead in three measures of meal
Until the whole mass of dough began to rise."

—LUKE 13:20, TRANSLATED FROM THE GREEK

The ancient Celts and many Native American peoples called the lunar phase that fell on the cusp of summer and fall—when the grains were ripe in the field and ready to be harvested—the Corn Moon. But translating the Celtic moon name and the Native American moon names as the Corn Moon creates some confusion. Corn in North America and corn in Europe are two different things.

In the United States, the word corn refers the species *Zea mays*, the tasseled plant that produces cobs of kernels in earthy hues of yellow, white, blue, and red. In Northern Europe the Germanic word *corn* means simply "grain." When Northern European colonists first encountered the plant *Zea mays* that had been cultivated and developed over many millennia by the indigenous peoples of this continent, they named it Indian corn, meaning Indian grain. Over the centuries the plant became known simply as corn in American English, while barley, wheat, rye, and other familiar cereal crops came to be referred to as grains. Early on, many colonial dishes that made use of Indian corn were given names like Indian pudding (a dessert made of cornmeal and sweetened with molasses) and rye'n'Injun bread, which was made of rye flour and cornmeal. In most other English-speaking countries, what we call corn here in America is called either maize or sweet corn, to distinguish it from grain.

For many of us who grew up in the United States, summertime evokes images of corn—the sweet, juicy variety that can be eaten right off the cob, dripping with butter, at a barbecue or a summer beach house. I can't seem to get enough of it once the season starts. But while our associations conjure feelings of carefree, lazy days, for the peoples that called this the Corn Moon, corn was a serious affair.

Many American Indian moon names reflected what was happening in the cornfields. You can find a Planting Corn Moon, a Green Corn Moon, a Moon When Women Weed Corn, and a Moon When the Corn Is in Silk in various languages. For both American Indians and the Celts, this time of year heralded the ripening of grain. So while the Corn Moon of the Celts and the Corn Moon of indigenous peoples referred to slightly different harvests, they came down to the same thing: The Corn Moon meant survival and sustenance. It meant that the sacred, staple grain, the agricultural foundation of the community, would soon be ready for harvest. The crops ensured that there would be food to last through the winter. A year's worth of planting and tending had been successful.

Once upon a time, the meaning of the Corn Moon would have needed no explanation. In an agrarian culture, there wouldn't be anyone who wasn't intimately aware of what was happening in the fields. Community members of all ages would be keeping a close eye on the progress of the crops—and when the grain was ripe, they'd be ready to begin the hard work of gathering the food that would keep them fed for another year. Everyone knew whether the harvest was early or late or right on time, and whether it was expected to be joyfully abundant or frighteningly lean.

> ## The Sacred Grains
>
> Thirteen seeds used as staple grains:
>
> 1. Wheat
> 2. Corn
> 3. Rye
> 4. Oats
> 5. Rice
> 6. Quinoa
> 7. Barley
> 8. Millet
> 9. Amaranth
> 10. Wild Rice
> 11. Sorghum
> 12. T'eff
> 13. Buckwheat

The development of grain-based agriculture constituted a major, relatively recent shift in human history. Pulitzer Prize–winning author Jared Diamond gives us a sense of perspective about the place of agriculture. He asks us to imagine

> a 24-hour clock on which one hour represents 100,000 years of real past time. If the history of the human race began at midnight, then we would now be almost at the end of our first day. We lived as hunter-gatherers for nearly the whole of that day, from midnight through dawn, noon, and sunset. Finally, at 11:54 P.M. we adopted agriculture.

In this scheme, the time since the adoption of *industrial* agriculture— with its heavy machinery, mono-cropping, pesticides, herbicides, synthetic fertilizers, and factory farming and processing—would be a blink of an eye, and the time since the introduction of genetically modified organisms would barely register.

There is some debate about whether the development of agriculture was a positive step for humankind. In the same article Diamond refers to it as "the worst mistake in the history of the human race." One of the reasons is that the overall health of the people who made the transition declined as a result. Diamond describes the contributing factors:

> At Dickson Mounds, located near the confluence of the Spoon and Illinois rivers, archaeologists have excavated some 800 skeletons that paint a picture of the health changes that occurred when a hunter-gatherer culture gave way to intensive maize farming around A.D. 1150. Studies by George Armelagos and his colleagues then at the University of Massachusetts show these early farmers paid a price for their new-found livelihood. Compared to the hunter-gatherers who preceded them, the farmers had a nearly 50 percent increase in enamel defects indicative of malnutrition, a fourfold increase in iron-deficiency anemia (evidenced

by a bone condition called porotic hyperostosis), a
threefold rise in bone lesions reflecting infectious disease in general, and an increase in degenerative conditions of the spine, probably reflecting a lot of hard
physical labor . . .

The evidence suggests that the Indians at Dickson
Mounds, like many other primitive peoples, took up
farming not by choice but from necessity in order to feed
their constantly growing numbers. "I don't think most
hunger-gatherers farmed until they had to, and when
they switched to farming they traded quality for quantity," says Mark Cohen of the State University of New
York at Plattsburgh, co-editor with Armelagos of one of
the seminal books in the field, *Paleopathology at the
Origins of Agriculture.*

There were other changes that accompanied the switch to agriculture.
People had to work longer hours than their hunter-gatherer predeces-
sors. Societies also began to organize themselves into hierarchies, and
for the first time in history an elite class developed. Diamond again:

Hunter-gatherers have little or no stored food, and no
concentrated food sources, like an orchard or a herd of
cows: they live off the wild plants and animals they
obtain each day. Therefore, there can be no kings, no
class of social parasites who grow fat on food seized
from others. Only in a farming population could a
healthy, non-producing elite set itself above the disease-
ridden masses. Skeletons from Greek tombs at Mycenae
c. 1500 B.C. suggest that royals enjoyed a better diet than
commoners, since the royal skeletons were two or three
inches taller and had better teeth (on the average, one
instead of six cavities or missing teeth). Among Chilean
mummies from c. A.D. 1000, the elite were distinguished
not only by ornaments and gold hair clips but also by a
fourfold lower rate of bone lesions caused by disease.

Thus some people refer to grains as slave foods. Pastoralism—the practice of herding dairy animals and migrating with the herds—is in some ways a midpoint between hunting-gathering and farming. In contrast to agriculturalism, it seems to have had a relatively egalitarian influence on social structure. In her book *Keeping a Family Cow*, Joann Grohman writes:

> To produce grain in useful quantities requires rich flat land such as flood plains. It requires a huge amount of energy, available in antiquity only where complex cultures developed. This energy was provided by slaves. The more slaves you had, the more grain you could grow. And the more grain you could grow, the more slaves you could afford, thus giving rise to a wealthy class able to afford monumental tombs and other durable artifacts of civilization. Grazing animals have been around for millions of years thriving on grass. They are not dependent on grain. For many thousands of years they were herded and milked, tasks which require neither slaves nor even permanent dwellings.

While she reinforces the argument that grains are slave foods, I believe she overstates the case somewhat. Dr. Weston Price found examples of communities that grew grain in substantial quantities yet were egalitarian, spiritually connected to the land, and well nourished. These included the Swiss villagers in the Loetchental Valley who grew rye and baked it into a bread that was one of their staple foods; the Gaels of the Outer Hebrides in Scotland who grew oats that were eaten daily; Africans from a variety of ethnic groups who grew and depended upon millet, sorghum and other grains; and cultures indigenous to the Andes that regularly used parched corn as a travel food. In *Ancient Futures*, Helena Norberg-Hodge describes a civilization that has little disparity between rich and poor and a vital core culture with strong ecological and spiritual values. The staple food of these Ladakhis is barley:

Much farming work is shared, either by the whole community or by smaller subgroups like the *chutso*. During the harvest, for instance, farmers help one another to gather their crops. This works well since fields ripen at different times even in the same village. With everyone working together, the harvest can be gathered in quickly as soon as it is ripe.

Bes, as shared work of this sort is called, often incorporates more than one village, and the reasons for it are not always purely economic. Some farmers will stagger the harvest, even when two fields are ripe at the same time, just so they can work together. You almost never see people harvesting alone; instead you find groups of men, women, and children all together in the fields—always with constant laughter and song.

. . . Private property is also shared. The small stone houses up at the *phu*, though owned by one household, will be used by many, usually in exchange for some work, or milk, or cheese. In the same way, the water mills used for grinding grain are available to everyone. If you do not own one yourself, you can make arrangements to use someone else's; and only in late autumn, when the water is very scarce and everyone is trying to grind as much grain as possible for winter, might you compensate the owner with some of the ground flour.

Clearly, grain-based agricultural societies are not necessarily exploitative or feudalistic. The kind of reciprocal, community-oriented, and ecological approach to farming that Norberg-Hodge describes among the Ladakhis is part of European-American agricultural history as well. Before the advent of industrial agriculture, American farmers had small-scale integrated farms that they worked by hand as well as with mules, horses, and elegantly engineered mechanical tools. The annual harvests were a matter of shared concern, and people often came together as a group to harvest first one farm and then another. When you are used to using your hands to do the everyday work of life, you come to understand that many hands do indeed make light work. And just as important, they build bonds of reciprocity, friendship, and community.

This aspect of European-American agricultural life is poignantly captured in the fiction of Wendell Berry. His novels and short stories are set in the vividly imagined town of Port William, Kentucky. They span a century and a half of rural Southern life, stretching as far back in time as the Civil War and touching on every decade of American history to the present. In Port William the primary crops are corn and tobacco. Each year at harvesttime, groups of farmers band together to accomplish the work that needs to be done on each of their fields. They work side by side through the morning as the sun rises in the sky, eat their large midday dinner together, and then return to the fields to work through the afternoon until just before sundown. Then each returns to his own farm to do the evening chores of milking cows and feeding livestock. Throughout most of the year each works solitarily on his own land, but at harvest time they gather and do the work in groups. Although they may not have had a special word for it, it was the Kentuckian version of the Ladakhi *bes*.

In Berry's work we also find a powerful depiction of the transition from an ecological approach to agriculture to an industrial one. In the novel *Jayber Crow*, Port William's barber relates the drama that plays out on one farm and in the fortunes (or misfortunes) of one farming family. The paterfamilias is an accomplished older farmer named Athey Keith. His nemesis is his son-in-law, a youthful and arrogant would-be farmer named Troy Chatham. Athey always keeps part of his farm in cover crops, building the fertility of the soil and allowing it to rest, and rotates his crops on a yearly basis in a deliberate and conscious attempt to keep the farm in balance between production and regeneration. Troy has little patience for this approach, which he considers old-fashioned, quaint, inefficient, and overly frugal. Berry captures the essence of the difference between the traditional way of farming and the post–World War II mentality by exploring the troubled relationship between father-in-law and son-in-law:

When it came time to plan for the next year, wishing them to be friends and eventual partners before Athey would die and Troy would become the farm's farmer, Athey walked Troy over the sod ground that was to be broken for row crops, showing him the outlines of the plowlands and where the backfurrows were to run. And then he led him on to show him the next year's cropland, and then the next year's, laying the pattern before him. . . .

Such knowledge ought to have passed from Athey to Troy as a matter of course, in the process of daily work and talk. And it would have, if Troy had been willing to have Athey as a teacher, let alone a friend. . . .

Troy's sole response to that afternoon's walk with Athey was: "We need to grow more corn."

This brought Athey to a stop. The law of the farm was in the balance between crops (including hay and pasture) and livestock. The farm would have no more livestock than it could carry without strain. No more land would be plowed for grain crops than could be fertilized with manure from the animals. No more grain would be grown than the animals could eat. Except in case of unexpected surpluses or deficiencies, the farm did not sell or buy livestock feed. "I mean my grain and hay to leave my place on foot," Athey liked to say. This was a conserving principle; it strictly limited both the amount of land that would be plowed and the amount of supplies that would have to be bought. . . .

Troy's demand to grow more corn was a challenge, Athey knew, not only or even mainly to himself but to the farm and its established order. . . .

"If you raise more corn," he said, "you'll have to buy fertilizer." . . .

"Hell, I don't mind buying fertilizer!" Troy said.

And so began the shift on the Keith farm from self-sufficiency and eco-logical integration to dependence on petroleum-based inputs and bank mortgages. While Athey used draft horses and mules to work the land—animals with whom he had developed a deep and mutual understanding—Troy always used the latest machinery to plow and plant his fields—pieces of equipment that generally ended up as out-dated junk. While Athey's farming was a careful and deliberate dance between man and nature, Troy's was an endless Sisyphean struggle to dominate the land and make it conform to his own designs.

The shift from Athey's ways to Troy's ways on the Keith farm was a gradual, piecemeal process, as Troy gained control over more and more of Athey's land. After a few decades Athey's once richly fertile soil had become devoid of nutrients and difficult to farm, and so Troy built a factory hog facility. At the end of the book, after Athey has died and Troy is more deeply in debt than ever, we meet Troy cutting down the forests on the property and selling them for lumber—mining the last resource on a parcel of land that had been carefully maintained and preserved by generations of farmers before him.

What Wendell Berry witnessed in Kentucky and fictionalized so poignantly was happening throughout the United States in the decades following World War II. Corn had no small part to play in a transformation that happened so quickly in this country.

In the six decades since the United States began to apply industrial and military technology to its farms, the role that corn plays in American agriculture has become increasingly convoluted, and we would be hard-pressed to explain our policies toward corn to old-fash-ioned farmers like Athey Keith. Currently, using tax dollars, our gov-ernment heavily subsidizes the growing of corn in the Midwest, the Corn Belt. We pay large-scale farms to grow more corn than we can eat, thereby creating a cheap, abundant supply. The practice of feeding cattle grain instead of grass originated from this excess of corn. Under more natural circumstances, grass would be a more economical and practical diet for cattle than grain, but when corn costs less than the cost of grazing, a grass-based diet becomes a luxury. Corn, however, is not natural to a cow's diet, and our dairy cattle suffer from digestive diseases as a matter of course.

Furthermore, in order to feed cows corn instead of grass, it is much more efficient to put them in a building rather than out on pasture. Now the cows are not only on an unnatural diet, but they are in an unnatural environment as well—deprived of sunlight and fresh air. Their manure, instead of recycling into the pasture as a natural fertilizer, becomes concentrated within this unnatural environment and turns into a breeding ground for disease. So now the cows are eating a diet they can't digest, living in crowded conditions, and unable to escape the presence of their own feces—no wonder the animals become ill. To prevent them from getting too sick too fast, it is necessary to feed them antibiotics. These drugs are transmitted to the humans who eat their meat or milk, and eventually people build up resistance to antibiotics. One of the greatest scientific breakthroughs of the twentieth century gets undermined.

The glut of corn that taxpayers subsidize gets used in other ways as well—mainly to produce inexpensive processed foods used by large corporations to keep production costs down and profits high. High fructose corn syrup is now ubiquitous in our food supply and is contributing to many of our modern degenerative diseases. Corn oil—not a nourishing or traditional fat—is abundant and cheap on U.S. store shelves and is also exported to other countries, where it displaces nutrient-dense traditional fats. The oil is also turned into butter substitutes that have been aggressively marketed to Americans as being healthier than butter, though they are now proven to contain dangerous levels of trans-fatty acids.

Even after all these noxious uses for our excess corn, we still have too much grain. So we sign a free trade agreement with Mexico, which has—since long before it even became Mexico—grown its own corn. Because U.S. corn is subsidized by the government, it is now cheaper for Mexico to import it from us than grow it. Mexico currently imports around 70 percent of its corn from the United States even though it is more than capable of growing all that it needs itself. *Zea mays* was grown in what is now Mexico between six and eight thousand years ago, and more than fifty-nine heirloom species are indigenous to the country. The cuisine of the people has long been based on the myriad ways that dried corn can be turned into classic dishes and daily sustenance. But it is now cheaper and easier for Mexican women to buy factory-processed *maseca* (dried commercial cornmeal) to make their tortillas than it is to nixtamalize—soak corn in lime to greatly improve its nutritional profile—local heirloom corns as they have for millennia. The result? The tortillas don't taste as good, they aren't nearly as nutritious, and an ancient culinary tradition is all but wiped out in a single generation.

Meanwhile, Mexican citizens don't have enough work—partly due to their undermined economy—and so risk life and limb to cross the border to the United States and work in fields that are sprayed with pesticides. These pesticides have been marketed to farmers as a way to get higher yields. (But there is a huge glut of corn, as well as of other grains—why should we want higher yields?) People who work around pesticides have a high rate of birth defects and other problems, and pesticides travel through our food chain, damaging the health of people and animals everywhere they go.

So what solution do we propose to clean up this mess? We genetically modify corn by splicing into its DNA the gene of a bacterium that will make it produce its own insecticide to kill bugs. (Look, Ma, no pesticides!) Now, does this sound like a good idea to you? Breed a corn that produces its own poison, which will then be ingested by people and cattle? We have no clear study of the harmful effects this method might yield. One of the disadvantages that even industry acknowledges about Bt corn is that because it produces the insecticide for a longer period than a farmer would spray, the insects may become resistant to the insecticide, in which case even spraying will no longer be effective. And all of this effort is for what? To make corn even cheaper and more abundant, less revered and more abused than it already is?

Although Mexico issued a ban on genetically modified corn in 1998, between 30 and 50 percent of the corn imported from the United States has been modified, and recent studies show that almost 10 percent of the corn grown in Mexico shows evidence of GMO (genetically modified organism) gene transfer. Scientists are still trying to understand how these GMO genes get passed between crops.

Our current approach to growing, processing, and distributing corn is thoroughly lacking in common sense. It is undemocratic, destructive to the environment, disconnected from community, and undermining to our health. *Zea mays* was held sacred by the indigenous peoples who bred it over millennia into a staple grain and a sustaining core element of the culture. But we have taken this sacred grain and corrupted it at every level—social, economic, ecological, biological, and spiritual. We have abused a grain that people have, in the past, treated with the utmost respect as a great gift to humankind.

In his book *The Toe Bone and the Tooth*, Martín Prechtel weaves together his story of escape from war-torn Guatemala with a sacred Mayan story that can be heard and understood on many different levels. On one level the story recounts the way in which the gift of corn was given to the Tzutujil Maya by the divine. Corn was born as two twin babies to a divine mother and a human father. The mother—a goddess called Water-Skirted Beauty—falls in love with a young mortal called Raggedy Boy. When Water-Skirted Beauty brings her lover home to her divine parents, they are not pleased in her choice of partner. Prechtel describes their conversation:

> "What's this you brought home with you, Honey?" the cloud-haired Grandmother of all plant Growth mewed through her irritation and jealousy, which caused her to grit her carved and terraced teeth.
>
> "Isn't he beautiful, mother?" Water-Skirted Beauty replied.
>
> "If I didn't know you better I could swear that what you've got there is a, what do you call it . . ." the Mountain God fumbled, when his wife stepped in.
>
> "That's a Human Being. I swear to it. I've seen them tearing up our hills before."
>
> "But look how strange and wonderful he is, he can't even kill with his bow, he makes songs and sings

to me. I want to keep him. That would be fine, wouldn't it?"

"Keep him? What, are you crazy? Did you eat something strange; what's bitten your bottom, young lady?"

"You know full well that he must be destroyed. You can't keep humans around, they kill everything, they think they own the place after a while; they do nothing but eat, consume, burn, kill, enslave the soil, the animals, your brothers and sisters, and mostly they forget us, we who feed them and give them life through our very flesh and existence, giving us nothing in return. . . ."

Grandmother Growth's description of human beings strikes me as shamefully accurate when I contemplate our current approach to corn, and to agriculture in general. The human tendency to forget the sacred nature of the things we consume during our earthly lives transcends the particularities of culture, place, or historical time period, but we have never been so forgetful as we now are in the technological age in America. While our amnesia is seductive, it does not serve us well in the long run. If we treated corn as a sacred gift, would we splice an insecticide bacterium into its DNA? Would we feed our cows antibiotics or have to try to figure out how to contain or neutralize their methane gases? Would we have rapidly increasing rates of obesity and a huge and growing industry of low-carbohydrate diets?

It does not surprise me that the latest fad in this country is the low-carb diet. We have had so many refined carbohydrates marketed to us in the past half a century—even by the government with its carbohydrate-heavy food pyramid—that we eat way too many of them. (This was partly due to the excess of subsidized corn and wheat grown in this country.) There had to be a counter-reaction. Refined carbohydrates fill up our bellies but are almost completely devoid of nutrients, and in many cases serve to deplete our nutritional capital. Our bodies store refined carbohydrates as body fat unless they are burned off in physical labor, and I would agree that they are a major contributing cause to rising obesity rates. As Dr. Tom Cowan puts it in *The Fourfold Path to Healing*:

> [C]arbohydrate intake should be intimately related to
> our level of activity. If we run a marathon every day, a
> balanced diet would probably include about 300 grams
> of carbohydrates per day, the amount contained in 20
> potatoes or 6 brownies. If we sit on the couch all day,
> obviously our requirement for energy food will be less.
> In this case a balanced diet would include only about
> 65–70 grams of carbohydrates per day. . . . [T]he western
> diet has us eating like marathon runners, when in fact
> most of us simply sit on the couch.

Working long hours engaged in rigorous physical labor was one hall-mark of the ancient transition to agriculture; eating an increasing number of calories in the form of carbohydrates was another. Today we still eat the amount of carbohydrates that our peasant and slave ancestors did, but don't do the physical work that they did to burn those calories. So we put on weight.

But all carbohydrates are not created equal. The healthy indigenous peoples that Weston Price studied, as well as the grain-eating cultures that Norberg-Hodge and Prechtel lived among, processed their grains in particular ways according to tradition—ways that are in stark contrast with our modern approach.

Healthy indigenous or traditional cultures that relied on grains for a significant part of their sustenance all discovered something important about the nutritional potential of grains. From an evolutionary perspective, plants that bear seeds have an advantage if animals *ingest* their seeds, but don't *digest* them. Undigested seeds will still sprout after they come out the other end of the animal, and thus the plant increases its chances of reproduction. The plant therefore binds up its nutrients and protects them, making it difficult for the animal to digest and assimilate the nutrients in seeds. So what's a hungry animal to do? The answer is to trick the seed into thinking it has already been planted, allowing it to release its nutrients in the normal course of becoming a plant, and *then* eat it. Squirrels do this naturally with their acorns—they bury them for days or weeks and then dig them up and eat them. The acorn, thinking it's found a good place to become a

Heaven's Leaven

Thirteen traditional foods made by souring, sprouting, soaking or fermenting grains:

1. Sourdough bread (wheat—Europe, Middle East, United States)
2. Injera (t'eff—Ethiopia)
3. Tsampa (barley—Tibet)
4. Ogi (millet—Nigeria)
5. Kaanga-wai (corn—Maori)
6. Vollkornbrot (rye—Eastern and Northern Europe)
7. Idli (rice—India)
8. Tamales (corn—Mexico)
9. Llymru (oats—Wales)
10. Hong-qu (rice—China)
11. Sattoo (amaranth—Nepal)
12. Ting (corn—Botswana)
13. Shamsy (wheat—Egypt)

tree, begins the process of sprouting. Usually it gets retrieved and digested by the squirrel before it gets a chance to do this, but sometimes it has a great head start on fulfilling its mission of becoming a new tree. This works out well for both the squirrel and the oak.

Indigenous and traditional cultures that thrive on a diet that includes grains do something similar to the squirrel. Before eating their grains, they place them in an environment that mimics the conditions needed for a seed to sprout—they find a way to keep the grain *wet*, *warm*, and *slightly acidic* for *a period of time*, generally at least seven hours. They only eat their grains after they have been soaked, sprouted, soured, or leavened. They almost always eat every part of the whole grain. Even if it is ground into flour, it is not refined. The process of releasing nutrients and neutralizing antinutrients is a chemical one, so it works even if the seeds are ground into flour first. Let me give you a few examples.

The Mediterranean bread-making tradition always depended on natural yeast—what we would call a sourdough. Whole wheat berries would be ground in a mill to produce flour, and then the flour would be moistened with water (*wet*), sourdough yeast would be added (*slightly acidic*), the dough would be put in a *warm* place to rise, and after *a period of time*, the bread would be baked.

In West Africa a staple food in many cultures is a fermented porridge made from grains or tubers. One example is the Nigerian *ogi* made from millet. The millet is *soaked* for one or two days, ground into a slurry, sieved to produce a fine texture, and *fermented* for *at least a day* at *warm* tropical air temperature. Then it is cooked into a porridge. The Ghanaian *kenkey* is made similarly, but from cornmeal.

In Ladakh and throughout much of Tibet, roasted barley flour is the staple food. But before it is roasted, the barley is *soaked overnight* in *warm* water and then drained. While still damp it is spread out on cloth, a process used throughout the world for sprouting seeds. When it is no longer wet, but still a bit damp, it is roasted over a low temperature until it turns golden-brown. Only then is it ground into flour and used with almost every meal.

Examples of this approach to grain abound: the Indian *idli* made from rice, the Ethiopian *injera* made from t'eff, the Welsh *llymru* made from oats, the English frumenty made from wheat, and the dark sourdough bread made from rye that is common in the Alps, Scandinavia, Eastern Europe, and much of Russia. Cultures that rely on steamed rice as a staple food—such as Japan, China and India—have a tradition of soaking the rice first before steaming. All grain-based fermented beverages around the world also include similar steps.

In the Americas the indigenous approach to maize was much the same—whether making Mesoamerican *tamales*, Navaho *piki*, Cherokee *gv-no-he-nv* or Iroquois *posole*—with one important addition: Either ashes or the mineral lime was added to the soaking water. This important step, called nixtamalization, releases B vitamins bound up in the grain and prevents deficiency diseases. Many African cultures that have incorporated maize into their diets also nixtamalize their corn, as do the Maori of New Zealand.

I have no doubt that whole grains, when properly processed, can be a nourishing staple food for the masses of people who now depend on agricultural systems. They can certainly be an economical one. But for them be truly nourishing we must take a cue from traditional foodways and treat them like the seeds they are. Our approach to them needs to be wiser. Many Americans are now avoiding grains in order to reduce carbohydrates, to heal their bodies by eating foods with greater nutrient density, or because they have problems digesting gluten, starches, or other components of grain. Our ignorance about how grains should be processed has contributed to the problem.

Unfortunately, belatedly emulating the traditional approach to grains does not always solve people's negative reactions to eating them. Some people *do* need to revert to a kind of hunter-gatherer diet.

Humans have had many more millennia to adapt to it, and it seems to be the easiest one for all of us to digest and assimilate. It's hard to deny that it is the closest thing we have to a natural diet. And yet it is not a diet currently accessible to the masses of people in the world. We made the switch to agriculture and we can't go back. We must find a way to build an agricultural system that is both sustainable and sustaining—constantly replenishing the Earth even as we harvest from it.

The culinary traditions surrounding grain-based staple foods capture something quintessentially human. Though not timeless, they are certainly ancient—as ancient as sowing and reaping. One health-conscious writer warns against eating bread because "there are no bread trees" and bread does not occur in nature. But this argument does not move me.

I learned to bake bread from a French baker who used the large, wood-fired brick oven at the arts center where I was the chef for a number of years. He came twice a week bearing sacks of freshly ground, organic flour and a traditional sourdough starter that he had made a few years before. He built a fire in the oven from the wood stacked in a shed just outside the kitchen, and tended it while he fed his starter, measured out flour and water, minced rosemary, toasted sunflower seeds, and soaked polenta to be added to different loaves. Meanwhile I made dinner.

Sometimes I stayed overnight and met him back in the kitchen at three o'clock in the morning to learn how to mix the dough, knead it by hand, and use the natural leaven to make the loaves rise. He shaped each loaf by hand with a deftness and mastery that I could hardly imitate. He swept the ashes out of the oven and mopped its floor with a wet rag. Then he loaded his loaves into it with a long wooden peel and sprayed water into the oven to create the steam that would give the bread its desirable golden crust. He could fit forty loaves into the oven at a time, and it was a magical moment when we first opened the door and peered into the depths with a flashlight to see all those loaves risen and baking perfectly in the even heat held in the bricks. When it came out of the oven, I was so intoxicated by the smell that it was very hard not to cut into the bread while it was still burning hot. I had to learn to let it cool down and settle a while before having the first slice.

Eventually my friend moved back to France, but he left me some of his hearty starter, and I keep it alive to this day and use it for baking. While writing these words, I have been eating slices of toast from bread that I baked last night using wheat grown, harvested, and milled by one of my favorite local organic farms, and that precious starter I consider an heirloom. I cannot mix or knead dough without thinking about not only the friend who taught me how, but also the passage from Luke that opens this chapter. For a few moments I am that woman who kneads her leaven into three measures of meal. I live out that parable of the kingdom of heaven as I watch the mystery of its rising.

It is perhaps precisely because bread doesn't grow on trees that it carries with it an air of the sacred. Martín Prechtel teaches that among the Tzutujil Maya, the gifts that people offer to the gods to feed them are precisely the things that only humans can make, using our human hands and our dexterous opposable thumbs. This is the gift the gods find irresistible—the particular beauty that only human hands create.

On the Corn Moon may we remember how to make handmade things too beautiful to be resisted, and offer them back to the divine source of life. May we do this even when we bake bread, or steam *idlis*, or fry *injera*, or roll *tamales*. May we begin to rebuild an agricultural system that respects, honors, and replenishes the Earth, even as we beg forgiveness for all the ways in which we act like we own the place. May we feel wonder for the gift of grain, which through dying is born again, or else gives its life to us.

CORN MOON RECIPES

Suffer-free Succotash
Serves 3–4

The word succotash comes from a Narragansett word, m'sickquatash—with variants sukquttahash *and* msakwitash—*which apparently meant "fragments" and referred to a stew of various ingredients, always including corn. This is my version.*

1 cup dry or fresh shelling beans, preferably white or pale green (lima beans, butter beans, or gigante beans are ideal)

½ dried ancho chile pepper (or other mild, dried chile), without stem or seeds

½ cup boiling water

2 tablespoons butter, olive oil, lard, tallow, or other traditional fat

1 medium leek or onion, chopped or diced

1 large (or 2 small) sweet pepper(s), red, orange, or yellow, diced (bell, gipsy, or other)

3 ears of corn, kernels cut off the cob

Salt and black pepper to taste

½ cup raw cream or crème fraîche

1 or 2 scallions, minced

1. If you're using dry beans, soak overnight and then drain. I like to cook beans in a Crock-Pot (slow cooker) by covering them with fresh water (make sure there is at least an inch of water on top). Cook on low heat for 6 hours or throughout the workday. Then they should be ready to use in this recipe. Alternatively, you can simmer them in a pot *over low heat* until soft, and then use.
2. Reconstitute the ancho chile pepper in the boiling water by pouring the water over it in a bowl and letting it soak for about 20 minutes.
3. Heat a large skillet or shallow pan over medium-high heat and add the butter or other fat.
4. When the fat is hot, add the onion or leek, and sauté for about 2 minutes.
5. Add the bell pepper and continue to sauté for another couple of minutes.
6. Lift the ancho chile out of the hot water and mince. Add the minced chile to the sauté and stir.
7. Allow this to cook for a minute or so, then add the chile soaking water to the sauté (strain out any seeds).
8. Drain the beans and reserve the cooking water. Add the beans to the sauté and bring the mixture to a simmer. Add the bean cooking water as needed to keep the mixture wet and saucy.
9. After about 5 to 10 minutes, add the corn kernels and cook for another minute or two to heat through.
10. Add salt and pepper to taste.
11. Remove from the heat and stir in the cream or crème fraîche.
12. Serve as a stew with chopped scallions on top, or as a side dish to fried chicken, pork chops, or other meat.

Calabacitas with Herbed Crema
Serves 3–4

Calabacitas

2 tablespoons olive oil, butter, or other fat

2 large leeks or onions, diced

5 medium summer squash such as crookneck, yellow zucchini, or zucchini, cut in half lengthwise and sliced on the diagonal

Leaves from 1 sprig fresh marjoram or oregano; or 2 sage leaves, minced

3 ears corn, kernels cut off the cob

½ cup chicken broth (page 299) or filtered water (or more as needed)

Salt and pepper to taste

2 medium heirloom tomatoes (or 1 large, or a few small), diced into small cubes

1. Heat the olive oil (or other fat) in a heavy-bottomed shallow pan or skillet over medium heat. Add the leeks or onions and sauté until translucent but not brown.
2. Add the squash and sauté until it just begins to brown.
3. Add the minced marjoram, oregano, or sage to the pan, then immediately add the corn kernels. Stir for a minute.
4. Add the broth or water and a generous pinch each of salt and pepper. Bring to a simmer. Add more liquid if it gets too dry.
5. Simmer for 2 to 3 minutes, then add the tomatoes. Heat the tomatoes through, then taste and adjust the seasonings as necessary, and remove from the heat.

Herbed Crema

3 scallions, a small bunch of chives, or the tender inner greens of leeks

½ bunch cilantro

½ cup crème fraîche, sour cream, or Mexican crema

1. Slice the scallions, chives, or leek greens into small rounds.
2. Cut the leaves off the cilantro.
3. Mince the scallions (or chives or leek greens) and cilantro together on a cutting board, or process in a food processor.
4. Stir the minced herbs into the crème fraîche (or sour cream, or crema).
5. To serve, ladle the calabacitas into a shallow bowl and add a big dollop of herbed crema. Eat with tortillas or quesadillas, if desired. This is nice served with a salad topped with roast chicken (such as leftovers from Simplest Roast Chicken, page 226).

Potato-corn Chowder
Serves 3–4

4 ears corn on the cob

1 quart filtered water or light chicken broth (page 299)

2–3 tablespoons butter or olive oil

2 medium or 3–4 small onions or leeks, sliced into rounds

A few ribs celery, diced small—or a few parsley stems or big sprig of lovage, minced

1 carrot, diced small

2 pounds potatoes, cut into chunks

1 bouquet garni (page 309)

Salt and pepper to taste (smoked salt if you have it, or smoked paprika)

¾ cup raw cream, crème fraîche, or half-and-half

Crème fraîche, for garnish

Chives or scallions, for garnish

1. Cut the kernels off the corn cobs into a bowl and scrape the corn "milk" into the bowl as well. Reserve.
2. Make a quick corn stock by simmering the cobs in about a quart of filtered water or light chicken broth, covered, for about 20 minutes.
3. In a heavy-bottomed pan, melt the butter (or heat the olive oil) and sauté the onions or leeks until translucent. Add the celery and carrot and cook through.
4. Add the potatoes and enough corn stock to cover (if you don't have enough stock, add a little milk or water). Add the bouquet garni to the pot, bring to a boil, and simmer (covered) until the potatoes are soft.
5. Add the corn kernels, salt, and pepper. Return to a simmer.
6. Remove from the heat. Remove the bouquet garni. Add the cream, half-and-half, or crème fraîche, taste, and adjust the salt and pepper to taste.
7. Serve with a dollop of crème fraîche and some minced scallions or chives, if desired. It is also great with some crispy bacon pieces scattered on top!

Sourdough Corn Fritters
Serves 2 as a main course (3 fritters per person) or 3 as a side dish

Corn fritters were one of my favorite childhood foods. Here is my adult recipe, using sourdough.

1 egg yolk

½ cup sourdough (page 312)

1 cup fresh corn kernels cut off the cob

⅓ cup minced scallions

½ jalapeño or Anaheim pepper, seeds removed and flesh minced (optional)

¼–½ teaspoon sea salt, depending on your salt tooth

⅛ teaspoon baking soda

Freshly ground pepper to taste

2–3 tablespoons lard, bacon drippings, ghee, coconut oil, or other fat

1. In a bowl, stir the egg yolk and sourdough together with a fork. Add the
   remaining ingredients and combine
   thoroughly.
2. Heat the fat in a skillet over
   medium-high heat until hot, then
   drop the batter into the hot fat in six
   to eight generous spoonfuls. Lower
   the heat slightly.
3. When the bottom of a fritter is
   crispy brown, turn over and brown
   on the other side. Make sure the fritters are cooked all the way through
   by poking one with a very sharp
   knife. You can finish them in the
   broiler if they need some more time.
4. Remove the fritters to a plate—or
   you can drain them on a paper bag
   or paper towel for a minute if you
   find them too oily.
5. Serve with crème fraîche, salsa, gua-
   camole, cortido, salad, sauerkraut,
   or a combination.

Sourdough Crumpets
Makes about 6 crumpets

*Many Americans don't even know what a crumpet is. It is like a cross between a muffin,
a biscuit, and a pancake—eaten toasted with butter. The closest thing we are familiar
with is an English muffin. Here is my version of crumpets, made with sourdough. They
are great for tea, or breakfast, but I also make them to accompany Indian food. I use the
rings from the lids of widemouthed mason jars to form the shape and size of the crumpets, but you could use anything similar.*

1 cup sourdough (page 312)

¼ cup whole milk or half-and-half

¼ teaspoon salt

⅛ teaspoon baking soda

1 tablespoon lard, ghee, butter, or
coconut oil, plus more as needed

Butter, for serving

1. Preheat the oven to 350° F.
2. Place the sourdough in a bowl and
   stir in the milk, salt, and baking
   soda.
3. Heat an oven-safe large griddle or
   cast-iron skillet over medium heat
   with the lard, ghee, or other fat.
4. When the fat is melted, place as
   many rings (from the lids of widemouthed mason jars) as possible
   into the skillet.
5. Pour the batter into each ring slowly
   until the surface of the pan inside
   the ring is just covered with batter.
   Repeat with each ring. Reduce the
   heat to low.
6. The batter should quickly become
   full of holes. Cook for a minute or
   two and then transfer the pan to the
   oven to finish cooking, which should
   take only a few more minutes.
7. Remove the crumpets from the pan
   and repeat with the remaining
   batter. Allow the crumpets to cool.
8. Toast the crumpets under a broiler
   before eating. Serve with butter,
   honey, jam, cream cheese, or other
   toppings.

Budín de Maíz
Serves 4 as a main course, 6–8 as a side dish

Budín means "pudding" in Spanish, but often refers to a savory dish. This is a delicious way to enjoy summer's corn, and is a great thing to bring to a potluck or picnic.

Butter

½ dried ancho chile pepper, seeds and stem removed

¼ cup boiling filtered water

4 cobs fresh corn

1 small bunch scallions, minced

3 eggs

½ cup cream, half-and-half, or whole milk

½ teaspoon salt, or to taste

Freshly ground pepper

1. Butter a small, ceramic baking dish and preheat the oven to 275° F.
2. Put the ancho chile in a small dish and pour the boiling water over it.
3. Cut the kernels off the corncobs into a shallow wide-bottomed bowl or baking dish. Scrape the corn milk off the cobs by scraping with back side of the knife down the cobs toward the kernels. This should produce a milky, corny slush that will add to the flavor.
4. Add the scallions to the corn as well.
5. In a separate bowl, gently beat the eggs with the cream, salt, and pepper. I always taste my raw-egg mixture to make sure it is salty enough. It should be a little on the salty side.
6. Remove the ancho from the soaking water, mince well, add this to the corn mixture, and mix well.
7. Strain the soaking water into the egg mixture.
8. Pour the egg mixture over the corn mixture and stir well to combine. Pour this into the buttered baking dish and bake until set, which will probably take about 45 minutes.

9

MOON WHEN SALMON RETURN TO EARTH

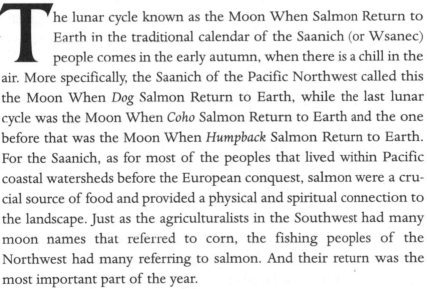

Welcome, friend Swimmer, we have met again
*   in good health.*
Welcome, Supernatural One, you, Long-Life-Maker,
for you come to set me right again
as is always done by you.

> —FROM A KWAKIUTL PRAYER SAID WHEN A JUMPING SALMON IS SEEN,
> TRANSLATED FROM THE KWAKIUTL

The lunar cycle known as the Moon When Salmon Return to Earth in the traditional calendar of the Saanich (or Wsanec) people comes in the early autumn, when there is a chill in the air. More specifically, the Saanich of the Pacific Northwest called this the Moon When *Dog* Salmon Return to Earth, while the last lunar cycle was the Moon When *Coho* Salmon Return to Earth and the one before that was the Moon When *Humpback* Salmon Return to Earth. For the Saanich, as for most of the peoples that lived within Pacific coastal watersheds before the European conquest, salmon were a crucial source of food and provided a physical and spiritual connection to the landscape. Just as the agriculturalists in the Southwest had many moon names that referred to corn, the fishing peoples of the Northwest had many referring to salmon. And their return was the most important part of the year.

But what exactly does a Return to Earth mean? In order to understand, we have to know more about the fascinating and unique life's journey that Pacific salmon—genus *Oncorhynchus*—take. Born in cool, running freshwater inland streams, they head out to live their lives in the wild, salty sea when they grow big enough to survive in the ocean. They travel incredible distances once they are far from land (Earth), eating krill and swimming freely in the ocean for three, four, or five years depending on the species and the individual fish. If they survive the sea for the length of their lives, they return—by some mysterious mechanism of DNA, or sacred knowledge, or unbelievable sense of smell—to the mouth of the exact freshwater stream where they were born. Salmon are anadromous—that is, they are born in fresh water, live the majority of their lives in salt water, and then return to spawn in fresh water—and can adapt to these two very different environments.

The spawning happens like this: The female creates a nest, called a redd, in the gravel of the shallow, cool, shaded water of the stream. In the center of the nest she digs with her tail a depression up to fifteen inches deep, called an ovipository. When she is nearly done with her work—which may have taken hours or days—a male will already have begun to hover nearby, ready for his part in the process. The two fish will then swim back and forth over the nest, quivering, in a ritual that looks to humans like a dance of courtship. Sometimes smaller males will attempt to get into the action, with the larger male chasing them off. In his book *Totem Salmon* author Freeman House describes what happens next:

> After a time, some signal passes between the two princi-
> pals that the female is ready. Side by side, both are now
> holding their jaws agape to steady themselves against the
> current. The female's tail is arched down toward the
> pocket at the bottom of the nest. Both are now trembling
> with the effort and with the gravity of the moment. The
> male releases a cloud of milt, milky and sperm-filled. At
> the same instant, the female releases a portion of her
> eggs. Often, and nearly faster than the eye can see, one or
> two other males dash over the scene and add their milt to
> the mix. For a moment, a milky cloud fills the pool.
> Another moment and it has washed away downstream. If
> we are lucky, we will have caught a glimpse of the eggs
> drifting down, slow comets dimly seen through a dense

and fertile fog. Immediately, the female will move upstream of the redd and begin to cover the eggs.

She may then go on and release her eggs two or three more times, in other nearby redds, in other showers of milt from other males. By the time she has finished building nests, releasing all of her eggs, and protecting them, she is weak and scratched and scraped by her efforts. Her life's journey is done, as is that of the primary male she mated with, and they both settle in at the edge of the stream to die. Forest animals then carry off the bodies of these majestic fish to feast on them, and their carcasses decompose and contribute to the nutrient cycle of the forest. Recent studies of West Coast conifer trees show a dramatic decrease in nitrogen levels near streams where salmon used to be plentiful but no longer are.

The life's journey of wild salmon makes the species particularly interdependent with the world around. Their survival depends on what is happening in their spawning streambeds, in the rivers and waterways they travel along to and from the sea, and what is happening out in the ocean as well. Salmon have an unusual power, but they have a special kind of vulnerability as well. When they return to the waterway where they were born, they are easy prey for the creatures that would harvest them as food. Such large fish in shallow waters are easy to grab, spear, or trap.

Historically, salmon thrived in the northern waters of both the Pacific and the Atlantic oceans. Almost all coastal northern peoples—East Asians, Northern Europeans, the Inuit peoples of both the Pacific and the Atlantic, and many other indigenous peoples of northern coastal areas—traditionally harvested them. Salmon appear in the mythologies of all the peoples that have eaten them, and are often an important part of religious rituals. The salmon, like the

Beautiful Swimmers

Thirteen words for salmon in different languages:

1. *Áama* (Karuk)
2. *Gnuibheadh* (Gaelic)
3. *Shipe* (Ainu)
4. *Leax* (Anglo-Saxon)
5. *Wy•kan•ush* (Sahaptin)
6. *Sake* (Japanese)
7. *Lachs* (German)
8. *Eog* (Old Welsh)
9. *Sceenex^w* (Saanich)
10. *Lohi* (Finnish)
11. *Taqawan* (Mi'kmaq)
12. *Laks* (Norwegian)
13. *Salmo* (Latin)

American buffalo or the whale, so nourishes the human body and spirit that whole cultures have grown up around it as a food source. By themselves, these fish are capable of providing almost all the sustenance that a culture needs to survive.

Salmon's deep interdependence with its ecosystem has made it one of the casualties of industrialization. As European cities grew, and waterways were dammed or polluted, the spawning areas of Atlantic salmon, *Salmo salar*, became destroyed. The same thing happened in European America as East Coast cities expanded and industrialized while at the same time Atlantic salmon were being overfished at sea. They differed from Pacific salmon in that they could return to spawn more than once in their lives—they could spawn and then journey back to sea, return to spawn and journey to sea again, two or three times before their death. But this fact did not make them any less vulnerable. Wild Atlantic salmon have become extremely rare; the wild fisheries are depleted; the cycle of birth in a freshwater stream, the journey to sea, and the return to spawn has ended. Except in a few remaining isolated areas, there is no moon when the Atlantic salmon return to Earth.

Fish and seafood are ancient and almost universal sources of nutrition. Hunter-gatherers were often fishers, and many agriculturalists and even pastoralists supplemented their diet with fresh- or saltwater animals. Widely considered among the most health-supportive foods on the planet, fish and seafood have been incorporated into the diets of most peoples of the world.

As a child I didn't particularly care for fish or seafood. To this day I dislike canned tuna—usually such a popular food with children. When I became a vegetarian at fourteen, fish was the last flesh that I gave up, but it was also the easiest. By the time I was seventeen I was extremely strict in my vegetarianism—I knowingly ate nothing that was made from anything that had ever been alive. Nor did I buy anything made from leather. When I was nineteen I prepared to go to Thailand, where I was going to spend six months (it ended up being a year) working in a refugee camp as an English teacher. Before leaving, I learned that the universal seasoning of Thai cooking was fish sauce—a fermented extract of whole anchovies. I was told that it was used like salt, and that if I was going to eat while I lived in Thailand, I couldn't avoid it. Once I accepted that I was going to be eating an extract of fish, I figured I might as well eat other forms of fish and seafood as well. I became a pesco-vegetarian.

I am very glad I made that decision. The seafood in Thailand is fresh, wonderful, and nourishing. For the first time in my life, I truly enjoyed and appreciated fish and seafood. I regularly ate *tom kha talee*—seafood soup with coconut milk—at a little restaurant in the village where I lived. And my friends and I often went away for the weekend to a little island just off the coast. On one of those trips we had a whole steamed fish that was so delicious, so light, and so fresh, I remember it to this day. It was caught that morning just off the coast in the Gulf of Thailand, and cooked simply and perfectly. Not a morsel was wasted.

Even though I started eating seafood again, I still considered myself a vegetarian. I'm sure that part of the reason I found this acceptable was that it is not an uncommon dietary choice in America. I didn't think too much about what eating fish might mean on a spiritual or symbolic level. More recently, I have come to understand my choice in the context of the long-standing European tradition of not considering fish to be meat, and the Catholic Church's approval of eating fish on Fridays and during Lent. Food historian Maguelonne Toussaint-Samat explores the roots of this practice:

> Why exactly was fish regarded as suitable Lenten fare for all classes, aristocrats and poor alike, from the Middle Ages onwards? People had to eat something, obviously, but why fish? Because of its associations with the Eucharist? There was more to it than that: as we have seen, meat and fat were regarded as red, rich, hot food. They were therefore likely to induce euphoria or even excitement. Fish, by association with water, was cold, and was white, lean fare, sober and soothing, and in any case pure. The church ordained Lent to make everyone

do penance between Ash Wednesday and Easter, bringing home by imitation the significance of the fast Christ observed before he began his apostolic ministry. At the same time it was a mortification of the flesh, ideally leading to asceticism, and a sacrifice made once a year in reparation for sins committed.

. . . The moral aspect of abstinence was in line with Church thinking, we are all equal before God. If only for 40 days, a highly symbolic period always associated with a cycle of purification and regeneration (and fish symbolize regeneration), everyone would eat the same kind of food—meat, the cheerful sign of wealth, being replaced by the melancholy and humble fish, so that differences in status between high and low on the social ladder were erased. That did not in fact prevent the rich from enjoying luxurious Lenten fare such as roast pike, while the poor fasted on salt herring, as many stories show us.

These attitudes, however unconsciously, contributed to my feeling that despite my commitment to vegetarianism, eating fish was permissible. Lingering from the Catholic dietary proscriptions is the notion that fish is pure, humble, moral, ascetic, healthy, and socially equalizing rather than decadent, indulgent, bloody, and aggressive. I feel that on a psychological level, much of my commitment to vegetarianism can be viewed as a form of sacrifice in reparation for sins committed. I had a sense of guilt that I felt needed atoning. Furthermore, as a younger woman, my disapproval of alcohol and meat was rooted in a yearning to be pure. One wouldn't want to do anything that might induce euphoria, or even excitement, now, would one?

Another reason we unconsciously give a higher rating of moral approval to eating fish and seafood than we do to eating other forms of meat is our impression that these creatures live their lives in the wild as they have from time immemorial. Somehow it is not so bad that we interrupt the natural order of things at the final moment, when we catch them on a hook or in a net. We believe them to be less manipulated, more free, and therefore more natural than other forms of flesh.

But this scenario does not apply to all the seafood we eat. Fish farming, or aquaculture, is actually an ancient practice, and not all fish and seafood are caught in the wild. Two forms of aquaculture were widely practiced in ancient times. One was the stocking of ponds, moats, or other small self-contained bodies of fresh water with edible fish. Often the ponds were man-made; sometimes they were naturally occurring. Such stocked ponds were a reliable source of fish, even inland.

The second primary form of ancient aquaculture was the growing of bivalve seafoods—particularly oysters and mussels—in protected tidal areas of seawater. What oysters need most to thrive is safety from the strong motion of the waves, and by installing a simple structure you could offer them that. They would latch on to a surface and stay there for the rest of their lives—until you were ready to harvest and eat them. This was a common practice in ancient Greece and Rome. China also has long-standing traditions of aquaculture. Carp is grown inland using a sophisticated polyculture that has remained ecologically sustainable over centuries. Oysters, clams, mussels, and other seafood have also long been farmed along the coasts, and so fish and seafood make up an important source of animal protein in the Chinese mainland diet to this day.

But many forms of aquaculture are post-industrial developments, and farming of salmon is one of them. I believe it to be an undertaking of quite a different order from ancient forms of aquaculture, in part because salmon are very different from other species of food fish. There is nothing cold, lean, pure, or ascetic about salmon. They invoke no sense of deprivation.

In fact, everything about salmon bespeaks a great gift—their delicious flavor, their physical majesty, their nutritional value, their inspiring journey out to sea, their annual return, even the ease with which they can be caught as they go upriver. It was only natural that people to whom they were a primary food source considered salmon a particularly sacred blessing—proof of a generous Creator. In his book *The Gift*, Lewis Hyde explores the nature and meaning of gifts in both traditional and contemporary society. He describes a ceremony that many peoples indigenous to the Pacific Northwest celebrated when that year's first salmon returned to the river to spawn:

> The first fish was treated as if it were a high-ranking chief making a visit from a neighboring tribe. The priest sprinkled its body with eagle down or red ochre and made a formal speech of welcome, mentioning, as far as politeness permitted, how much the tribe hoped the run would continue and be bountiful. The celebrants then sang the songs that welcome an honored guest. After the ceremony the priest gave everyone present a piece of the fish to eat. Finally—and this is what makes it clearly a gift cycle—the bones of the first salmon were returned to the sea. The belief was that salmon bones placed back into the water would reassemble once they had washed out to sea; the fish would then revive, return to its home, and revert to its human form. The skeleton of the first salmon had to be returned to the water intact; later fish could be cut apart, but all their bones were still put back into the water. If they were not, the salmon would be offended and might not return the following year with their gift of winter food.
>
> . . . [T]he first salmon ceremony establishes a gift relationship with nature, a formal give-and-take that acknowledges our participation in, and dependence upon, natural increase. And where we have established such a relationship we tend to respond to nature as a part of ourselves, not as a stranger or alien available for exploitation.

This passage articulates the big difference between the approaches of post-industrial Europeans and nonindustrial indigenous people who depended on salmon for food. Coastal American Indians developed technologies that took advantage of the salmon's vulnerability without exploiting it, and put it into the context of spiritual connection. Freeman House gives a wonderful example of this in *Totem Salmon*:

In all of northwestern California, the largest and most elaborate social event of the year before 1848 is said to have been the building of the fish dam at Kepel, near the confluence of the Trinity and Klamath Rivers. This highly formalized event occupied a hundred or more men and their families for ten days, exactly, and thousands of ritualized person-hours went into the construction of the weir across the river each year. Once completed, the structure was fished for just ten more days, regardless of the size of the run or the number of fish caught, and then it was opened up and abandoned, to be built anew the next year.

Each step in the process—the cutting of the poles, their placement in the river, the ceremonies required before fishing began—was informed by such complex ritual content that the role of remembering the exact procedures and supervising the event each year was invested in one man, called a formulist by the anthropologists. . . . After the structures were abandoned at the end of ten August days, he and his assistants remained in a hut above the dam site to be sure that it was washed away by early winter storms, so as not to interfere with later runs of other stocks of salmon.

House goes on to quote a Yurok woman who remembered, in 1916, the fish dams of her youth:

"In these traps, there get to be a mass of salmon, so full they make the whole structure of the fish dam quiver and tremble with their weight, by holding the water from passing through the lattice-work freely. After all have taken what they want of the salmon, which must be done in the early part of the day, Lock [the formulist] or Lock-nee [his assistant] opens the upper gates of the traps and lets the salmon pass on up the river, and at the same time great numbers are passing through the open gap at the south side of the river. This is done so the Hoopas on up the Trinity River have a chance at the salmon catching. But they keep a close watch to see that there are enough left to effect the spawning, by which the supply is kept up for the following year."

The last fish dam at Kepel was built in 1906, and then the tradition ended. That was one hundred years ago. Clearly, the relationship between human and salmon has changed drastically over the past century.

European Americans harvested salmon indiscriminately; swaths were cut out of the forests in logging operations; roads were built and streambeds made impassable by the movement of earth; hillsides were dynamited to make way for train tracks. The special conditions that salmon need to spawn—loose gravel, cool, shaded running water, continuous access from ocean to estuary to river to stream—all eroded in a matter of decades. In the nineteenth century an attempt to revive the Atlantic salmon runs by collecting Atlantic salmon eggs and hatching them on the West Coast produced none of the positive effects hoped for (Atlantic and Pacific salmon are from different genera, have different spawning patterns, and are not interchangeable), and in fact negatively impacted the native Pacific populations. And eventually, of course, huge dams were built that no salmon, no matter how strong, how determined, how majestic, could ever hope to scale. But we needed water for agriculture and for cities, and we needed electricity, and those imperatives trumped all other concerns.

The salmon no longer come to us; we have to go to them. Catching and spearing fish for food during the Moon When Salmon Return to Earth is no longer possible in most areas—there aren't enough of them. So we have a salmon fishery, and men and women go out in boats for days or weeks at a time, trolling the seas for salmon and bringing them back to shore. Here in Northern California, the season for salmon begins in the spring now, instead of the end of the summer when they are returning home. The kind of salmon that can be caught, the length, the location, and the time of year are all highly regulated by government agencies. But while the Yurok regulated their capture of salmon proactively, with religious ritual and community gathering, in order to prevent there from ever being a shortage, we regulate retroactively, with bureaucracy and policing, with fish-and-game inspectors who mount boats and measure fish, in order to protect what scarcity we have left. Which strategy has been more effective in yielding an abundance of fish? Back to *Totem Salmon*:

> That these [indigenous] cultural conservation strategies were successful and enduring cannot be denied. Conflicting estimates of annual consumption of salmon by tribes in the Klamath-Trinity basin range between half a million and two million pounds. There may have been that much variation in seasonal abundance anyway. Indigenous peoples could have taken more, but they didn't. Fishermen in the cannery-driven fishery that replaced the native one could take more, and did. The industrial fishery peaked out with a catch of 1.4 million pounds in 1912, and has been in steady decline ever since.

Over the past few decades an even newer use of an ancient technology has begun to threaten wild salmon populations. Large, open sea nets are constructed in the ocean, and then filled with hatchery-bred salmon to grow into adults. They are given feed containing soy meal and ground-up wild fish. Like their land-based, bovine counterparts, they need antibiotics to prevent diseases, and their waste is so concentrated that it creates a dead zone all around the pen. They are fed dye to make their flesh pink—otherwise it would be gray. Farmed salmon don't get to eat the crustaceans that give their wild counterparts the characteristic salmon color. Many people are concerned about the effect these fish feedlots will have on ocean ecosystems. Others are worried about the effect eating antibiotic- and dye-laden fish will have on people. Those who care about the livelihoods of independent fishermen worry that fish farming drives down the price of salmon and makes it harder than ever to make a living by fishing.

I am worried about all these things, too. But perhaps what bothers me the most about farming salmon is the way that it robs the salmon themselves of their miraculous life's journey. While it makes sense to farm bivalves like oysters that attach themselves to one place and spend the rest of their lives eating plankton from the water, or carp that thrive in a small body of fresh water, it is a totally different story with a species like salmon. Salmon embody a great spirit. They represent the part of ourselves that must be free, that must leave home and have a great and dangerous adventure, but then must just as surely find a way back home—to regenerate, to multiply and create abundance, to die, and to become nourishment for another. The life cycle of the salmon is an enduring symbol of freedom and return, death and rebirth, decay and regeneration. For millennia, humans and salmonids coexisted along the coastline such that both could flourish. Respected and honored by the people, the salmon made their epic journey year after year, and year after year they seemed to offer themselves up to nourish the people who depended on them so heavily. That relationship has been broken. Most of the salmon (and all Atlantic salmon) we eat today is farmed, and what is wild is often from fish that were hatched in hatcheries and then released.

Wild salmon stocks began to decline when people who viewed salmon as an economic commodity rather than as a sacred gift gained power over their destiny. In *The Gift*, Lewis Hyde explores the way a gift economy functions versus the way a commodity economy functions. While a gift economy operates on a model of interdependence and abundance, a commodity economy operates on a model of independence and scarcity. One of the most important aspects of giving gifts is that it brings people into relationship. As Hyde writes, "a gift makes a connection." And later: "Because of the bonding power of gifts and the detached nature of commodity exchange, gifts have become associated with community and with being obliged to others, while commodities are associated with alienation and freedom." When we give or receive a gift, we step from isolation into community, and this is a challenging idea to our Western notions of independence. Community always involves obligation; we are uncomfortable with obligation.

But Hyde asserts that this entanglement of relationships is part of why gifts tend to multiply and grow rather than diminish, which is one of the primary characteristics of a gift. How does this work? If we see salmon as a gift, we are brought into relationship with it, and it becomes something that is part of our community, part of the wholeness of our lives, not something distinct. Once we see it as a part of us, we protect it rather than destroy it—for destroying it is destroying part of ourselves. As Hyde writes:

> Gift exchange brings with it, therefore, a built-in check upon the destruction of its objects; with it we will not destroy nature's renewable wealth except where we consciously destroy ourselves. Where we wish to preserve natural increase, therefore, gift exchange is the commerce of choice, for it is a commerce that harmonizes with, or participates in, the process of that increase. . . . [W]here true, organic increase is at issue, gift exchange preserves that increase; the gift grows because living things grow.

Hyde gives examples of this pattern in European folktales—a gift is given and received, the receiver then passes on a gift, keeping the energy of the gift moving, and the new gift is received by another. Each time a gift is given and received, it offers blessings back to the giver much in excess of what that person gave away. As Hyde says, "The increase is the core of the gift, the kernel." When someone refuses a gift offered in good faith, the refuser suffers ill fortune. Like these folktale ingrates, the post-industrial mind rejects the burdens and blessings of obligation. The indigenous mind accepts obligation as a necessary and even desirable part of community, because it is also part of communion with nature. Interdependence is at the heart of Creation. Try as we might to separate ourselves from the rest of life, it is impossible to do so.

Martín Prechtel draws our attention to this crucial understanding when he describes his experiences leading the youth of his Mayan village through their ritual initiations. Having been appointed to this important role, he spent a great deal of his personal resources on the feasts and other ceremonies critical to carrying out these initiations, until finally—with many ceremonies still to go before the initiations were complete—he was completely broke. Unsure what to do, he confessed his problem to his mentor. The mentor burst out laughing and told him that it had been a source of gossip in the village that Martín seemed to have limitless resources; everyone was wondering when he would finally run out of money. Now that he had, he and his mentor went from house to house, visiting the homes of ex-chiefs and sacred ladies, and in each place they were given some money so that the initiations could continue.

It was conventional wisdom in the village that when the initiations were over, the chief who had presided over them would be blessed with unexpected abundance (the increase that comes when you give a gift), and this happened for Prechtel. An unprecedented interest in his paintings on the part of foreigners stationed in Guatemala meant that Prechtel soon found himself wealthier than he had ever been. At this point he set about going to the homes of the people he had taken money from, in order to return it. But he met an unexpected obstacle: The ladies and chiefs would not accept the repayment and in fact were profoundly insulted. He was chased through the streets with pebbles being thrown at him until he finally took shelter in the home of his mentor, who began to explain to him the problem:

> *Kas-limaal*, that's what we call it, *kas-limaal*, mutual indebtedness, mutual insparkedness.

Everything comes into this Earth hungry and inter-dependent on all other things, animals, and people, so they can eat, be warmed, not be lonely, and survive. I know you know this, but why do you push it all away now? We don't have a word for that kind of death, that isolation of not belonging to all life.

You see, every young man's chief, every initiator, every first grandchild chief has to watch his money dwindle away, has to watch the corn in his granaries empty to the bare ground until even the mice and the crickets move out. He has to watch the people in his compound holding their tongues and keeping their wor-ried eyes averted, waiting quietly. His relatives are terri-fied of starving and losing prestige, but they say nothing for fear of ruining the initiations for the village by com-plaining. The initiation which is bigger than any one of us, upon which the whole village survives, brings us rain and food and more children. . . .

After the ceremonies and struggles have ceased, and your service is finished, the spirits almost always give the chief mysterious good luck, often replacing what you've spent and distributed uncomplainingly, ten- or a hun-dred-fold, so that ex-chiefs have plenty again and then some. But this only happens if they went about their business honorably and were willing to give all.

So here you are, having had everything you exhausted replaced a hundred times more than you expected by the good graces of the spirits, the Gods, the Saints, the Many, the One, and you go around trying to give back what fed you in your time of need. But that's no good, you see. Not because you don't owe us, which you do, but because you must remain in our debt, keeping the Hole open, the wound unhealed, to be a fully initiated chief! You have to be indebted to as many ex-chiefs as possible to be part of our village. *The knowl-edge that every animal, plant, person, wind, and season is*

indebted to the fruit of everything else is an adult knowledge.
To get out of debt means you don't want to be part of life, and
you don't want to grow into an adult. [Emphasis added.]

The mentor concludes:

> The idea is to get so entangled in debt that no normal
> human can possibly remember who owes whom what,
> and how much. In our business dealings, we keep close
> tabs on all exchanges, but in sacred dealings we think just
> like nature, where all is entangled and deliciously con-
> fused, dedicated to making the Earth flower in a bigger
> plan of spirit beyond our minds and understandings.

While the indigenous people who depended on salmon considered
the annual harvest a sacred dealing, European Americans saw it as
business. And somehow, in the course of this shift from one paradigm
to another, the salmon went from abundance to scarcity.

But there is hope. The past forty years or so have seen a groundswell
of interest in protecting salmon and their habitats. Ordinary people of
many cultural backgrounds, ecologists, ranchers, marine biologists,
fishermen and -women, schoolchildren, and activists, have worked on
restoring the watersheds of the Pacific coast so that native populations
of salmon can flourish again. These efforts are informed by the notion
that the task they have undertaken is a sacred one, and that it is about
restoring a gift, not restocking a commodity. There are few teachers
on Earth that teach us as well as Salmon that everything is interdependent, everything in nature is "entangled and deliciously confused,"
and Creation involves a plan beyond our understanding. Many of the
people who have dedicated their lives and their work to salmon do so
from a place of abundance—they have experienced the presence of
wild salmon as a gift in their lives, and they want to keep the gift alive
by keeping it moving. And so salmon restoration work often operates

in a rare spirit of upwelling generosity and openhearted collaboration. The work is not just ecological, but spiritual, too.

The spirit of salmon has touched many families and young people as well. Some have spent weekends helping scientists create nesting habitats in local streams, educating schoolchildren about the life cycle of salmon, and alerting urban and suburban dwellers to the dangerous effects household products can have on waterways. I was once able to see the results. While camping in a local state park, my partner and I were told to be particularly respectful of the creek running through the area, as it was salmon spawning season. Along the creek, riparian areas had been restored. Groups of concerned citizens had placed fallen branches and other natural debris in the water to create the kinds of nooks and crannies that salmon favor to spawn in. We were told that if we watched the water closely, we might see the annual rite of return.

And so we sat on a bridge that fords the creek, and watched, and waited in the silence as the winter rains came down lightly and gently. We watched for what seemed like a long time until we saw a bit of commotion in the water upstream, and watched the turbulence closely until it was right under us. And then they were there—a pair of salmon, one more red, the other more silver, enormous, sea-sized fish in that shallow, tiny creek. We only saw them for a minute, but it was magical, truly magical, to witness the salmon's return to Earth, and to death, and to rebirth.

And it made me proud of humanity, and so grateful to all those who have dedicated decades or more of their lives to making it possible for those salmon to do the thing that makes them salmon, that makes them sacred, that makes them totem. May there always be a Moon When the Salmon Return to Earth.

SALMON MOON RECIPES

Whole Roast Salmon
Serves about 3 people per pound of fish

A whole roast salmon is a great meal for a feast—it is special when the whole party is fed by a single fish. Accompany with almost any starch and vegetable you like. To roast a whole salmon, you have to make sure it fits into your oven and that you have a sheet pan big enough for it! You might want to start with a smaller salmon.

Whole wild salmon, gutted and scaled	Sea salt
Olive oil	Freshly ground pepper
Lemon	

1. Preheat the oven to 475° F.
2. Rinse the salmon and pat it dry with a towel. Lay it on a sheet pan that has been coated thinly with olive oil.
3. Make a series of parallel diagonal slashes into the salmon at 2-inch intervals, about 1 inch deep and 2 to 4 inches long, depending on the size of the fish. Do not make the cuts so deep that they touch the bone.
4. Rub olive oil and lemon juice all over the fish, including into the slashes and the cavity. Sprinkle salt and pepper over the surface of the fish and into the cuts and cavity. Make sure you do this on both sides of the fish.
5. Place the sheet pan with the salmon into the oven and roast until just cooked through, about 12 minutes per inch of thickness of fish. A 4-pound salmon should take about 25 minutes; an 8-pounder, about 35 minutes; a 12-pounder, 45 minutes. You can use a sharp knife to cut into the deepest part of the fish to check whether it is done.
6. Use two huge spatulas to transfer the salmon to a platter.

Salmon Cured with Maple and Juniper
Makes about 2 pounds of cured salmon

This is a gravlox made with two classic flavors of North American indigenous diets—juniper and maple. Some fishmongers will try to dissuade you from using wild salmon for gravlox, citing health concerns—but people have been curing wild salmon for centuries, if not millennia. To my mind farmed salmon is far more dangerous. If you are nervous about uncooked foods, you could use fish that was frozen at sea and then thawed. Or this may not be a recipe for you. But I consider it both delicious and extremely healthful.

2 wild salmon fillets, center cut with skin still attached, about 1.5 pounds total

2 tablespoons sea salt

2 tablespoons maple sugar or syrup

1 teaspoon juniper berries, crushed coarsely in a mortar and pestle

1. Rinse the fillets gently and pat dry. Place one fillet skin-side down in a small flat ceramic or glass baking dish.
2. In a bowl, mix together the salt, maple sugar or syrup, and juniper berries. Spread most of this mixture over the fillet in the dish.
3. Put the other fillet down over the first, this time with the skin-side up. Spread the remaining small amount of salt mixture over the sides of the fillets where the pink flesh is exposed and in a thin film over the top skin.
4. Cover the fillets with a piece of parchment paper or plastic wrap, then place a weight on top of that. Put into the refrigerator.
5. Cure for 48 to 72 hours, turning the whole "sandwich" over every 12 hours or so and basting the fish with the marinade that accumulates.
6. After 48 hours, if the fillets were about 1 inch thick, or 72 hours if they were 2 or more inches thick, remove the fillets from the marinade and wipe them off with a paper towel or clean kitchen towel. You can tell the salmon is cured because it will have changed from pink to orangey red. Refrigerate until ready to serve.
7. To serve, lay the lox skin-side down on a cutting board and slice thinly on the diagonal. Wonderful with cream cheese or yogurt cheese (page 91).

Simple Salmon Fillets

Salmon is one of the easiest things to cook for supper. This is how I cook mine. You can serve it with the Easy Hollandaise (recipe following) or just by itself, or with a squeeze of lemon.

Fillets of wild salmon (figure about ⅓–½ pound per person, depending on appetites)

Olive oil, ghee, or coconut oil

Sea salt and freshly ground pepper

1. Rinse the fillets and pat dry, then set them on a plate skin-side down.
2. Spread a thin layer of oil on the top of the salmon fillets, then sprinkle the tops and sides with sea salt and freshly ground pepper.
3. Preheat the broiler.
4. Heat more of the oil or other fat in a cast-iron (or other oven-proof) skillet over medium heat.
5. When the oil is hot, put the fillets into the skillet skin-side down. Cook until you see the bottom turn pale pink, and this stretches about halfway up the fillets.
6. Stick the skillet with the fillets in it under the broiler and broil until they are done to your taste, 3 to 8 minutes depending on the thickness of the fillets and how done you like your salmon. Many people like it medium rare, with the center still bright pink. But you can also cook them more. Check the doneness by piercing a fillet at its thickest point with a sharp knife tip and looking inside.
7. Serve with a wedge of lemon, or with the Easy Hollandaise sauce. You can put the fillet on a bed of salad, or serve with potatoes or rice and a green vegetable.

Easy Hollandaise
Serves 2–3

Many people think hollandaise is an exotic and difficult sauce, but it's not. I make it all the time to serve with artichokes, potatoes, asparagus, eggs, or salmon. Hollandaise is traditionally made in a bain-marie or double boiler. I have a perfect one for this—a small saucepan with a metal insert that fits perfectly on top. But it's not absolutely necessary to use one—I sometimes make hollandaise without one. I give directions for both ways.

1 egg yolk

⅓ cup butter, melted

Juice of ½ lemon

Sea salt and freshly ground pepper

With a bain-marie

1. Put about ¾ inch of water in the bottom of a bain-marie, or anything you can jerry-rig that has a bowl on top and steaming water on the bottom. You want the water hot and steaming but not simmering, and preferably not touching the insert.
2. Put the egg yolk in the bowl and whisk while slowly adding the melted butter. As soon as you have added all the butter, squeeze the lemon juice into the mixture while continuing to whisk. Add a generous pinch of salt and pepper.
3. Remove from the heat and serve.

Without a bain-marie

1. Heat a bowl by pouring almost-boiling water into it and allowing it to sit for a minute. Pour out the water, dry it out with a towel, and set the bowl in a warm place, if possible.
2. Proceed with step 2 from the preparation with a bain-marie, but be careful to only add a few drops of butter at first, and then continue to add the butter very slowly. This will make a thicker hollandaise.

Salmon Poached in a Lemongrass and Coconut Milk Sauce
Serves 2–4

This sauce is delicious. I could eat it with a spoon like dessert! This salmon is nice served with rice and a green vegetable like broccoli, asparagus, green beans, or winter greens. Just steam the rice and cook the vegetable simply—the sauce adds flavor and richness to the rest of the meal.

1 can coconut milk (13.5 oz)

1 lemon

1 stalk lemongrass

A few strands of saffron

1 teaspoon kuzu root powder (or arrowroot powder)

1 tablespoon fish sauce

2–4 fillets wild salmon, depending on how many people you are feeding

Salt to taste

1. Pour the coconut milk into a wide-bottomed, shallow saucepan.
2. Cut a few strands of decorative zest off the lemon using a zester. Then cut the remaining zest off in big pieces with a vegetable peeler or paring knife.
3. Cut the lemongrass in 4- to 5-inch lengths, then split these in half.
4. Add the big pieces of lemon zest, the lemongrass, and the saffron to the coconut milk and bring to a simmer over medium-low heat. Simmer, covered, over low heat for 7 minutes.
5. Meanwhile, juice the lemon and dissolve the kuzu (or arrowroot) completely in the lemon juice.
6. Add the fish sauce to the coconut milk and simmer for another 5 minutes. Using a slotted spoon, remove the lemon peel and lemongrass from the coconut milk.
7. Rinse and pat dry the salmon fillets, then place them gently in the simmering sauce. Replace cover and cook until pale pink throughout. This should take 5 to 10 minutes, depending on the thickness of the salmon and how done you like it.
8. Transfer the salmon to plates.
9. Whisk the lemon juice–kuzu mixture into the coconut milk. It should thicken immediately. Taste the sauce and add salt to suit your palate. Turn off the heat and pour some of the sauce over each salmon fillet. Sprinkle the strands of zest on top and serve immediately.

Note: If left to sit, the sauce may separate some. Just whisk it again and it will come back together.

10
BLOOD MOON

Those animals which I use for riding and loading,
Which have been killed for me,
All those whose meat I have taken,
May they attain the state of Buddhahood very soon!

—LADAKHI PRAYER, TRANSLATED FROM THE LADAKHI

In midautumn, when the air is growing colder and the nights longer, comes the Blood Moon. Also called the Hunter's Moon by indigenous peoples in the eastern woodlands, it was a time when northern dwellers of many cultures would work to ensure that their store of meat would last the winter. They did this by hunting wild game or slaughtering farm animals. It was a time of year when blood was shed.

Meat eating is one of the most controversial topics among people who care about food, ecology, spirituality, human culture, and the lives of animals. Deciding not to eat meat is often either the first or the most profound decision a person makes about diet in response to political or spiritual convictions.

I was fourteen when an older friend of mine, named Sarah, converted me to vegetarianism. She was fifteen, and seemed to me infinitely wiser than I was. Throughout my childhood, I had loved eating meat. I lived in Madison, Wisconsin, as a small child, and some of my fondest memories from that time involve meals centered on meat. Once, when a tornado warning was in effect, we had to go into the

basement to wait for the threat to pass. I remember my parents frying
bacon with an electric skillet as we sat out the storm. It is a very cozy
memory, of the whole family safe together in that basement and the
delicious smells of bacon and a sense of being both nourished and protected. I also remember loving liverwurst—a popular food in
Wisconsin—and eating it in the park by the lake. After that we moved
to Virginia, and for years my favorite meal—the one I would request
on my birthday—was steak and Rice-A-Roni. Another beloved dinner
was meat fondue, where we would each cook our meat in a little
boiling cauldron and dip it into our favorite sauces. Even in ninth
grade, my first year of high school and the same year that I became a
vegetarian, my favorite treat was to go to my friend's house and make
steak-and-cheese sandwiches as an after-school snack. But all of that
soon changed.

Through conversations with Sarah I became convinced that eating
meat was wrong on many levels. She argued that eating meat was
cruel to animals, bad for the Earth, and an irresponsible indulgence in
a world that would be better fed with grains and beans. I put aside my
steak sandwiches in favor of trail mix and granola. Being a vegetarian
was clearly more evolved than being a carnivore, and what I wanted
desperately, at the age of fourteen, was to be evolved—to be more
mature, to be older, to be wiser, to be more spiritual. My vegetarianism did indeed take on a spiritual component as I came to think of
eating meat as eating death, and began to consider it a primitive, base,
and immoral thing to do. I loved life; I would not kill for my food.

While my vegetarianism started with giving up red meat, I quickly
stopped eating poultry as well, and then fish. I felt that eating death
was eating death and it didn't matter which creature had died. I soon
began to feel that it was hypocritical to be a vegetarian yet wear
leather, and so also gave up leather products. By the time I went to college, when I was almost eighteen, I was as strict a vegetarian as I knew
how to be.

During my freshman year I found myself hating the food plan. This
was basically cafeteria food, and though it was geared toward the
wealthy youth who attend Ivy League colleges, it was still pretty
awful. There were vegetarian options, but not the complete-protein

grain-and-bean combinations I favored. When I was allowed to get off the food plan my sophomore year, I did so immediately. I installed a small refrigerator in my dorm room, located a dorm kitchen on another floor, and began to shop and cook for myself along with a vegetarian friend. The *Moosewood Cookbook*s were my greatest culinary resources, and I made Mollie Katzen's vegetarian chili I don't know how many times. I would make a big pot, store it in Tupperware in the refrigerator, and heat it up using a small electric pan in my dorm room whenever I was hungry. I vastly preferred my own cooking to the institutional food my university served.

Despite all these efforts to eat nutritiously, during my first two years of college I was not very healthy. One semester was a continual cycle of glandular infections and antibiotic courses. As soon as I would get off the antibiotics, I would get sick again. A cold would turn into something worse. I would go to health services and get cultures taken; I'd be prescribed antibiotics, and feel better once I took them; but then the cycle would begin again. Whenever I went home for vacation I would collapse with an illness.

Halfway through my junor year I decided to take time off to work in a Thai refugee camp. As I mentioned earlier, Thai cooking utilizes fish sauce in almost every dish, and I decided not to attempt the impossible by trying to avoid it. I added fish to my diet. In Thailand my health improved tremendously—I had more energy and better digestion than I could remember experiencing in ages. I lived in a community with other workers from the camp, feeling happy, nourished, and fulfilled. The Thai food I ate every day tasted fresh and full of life and goodness, and while I missed cooking, the food available in small roadside eateries was delicious, and felt and tasted like homemade.

Less than a year after my return from Thailand, I moved to Mississippi to spend my last year of study at a historically black college. Once again I was on a food plan, but one even worse than in New England. My friends and I supplemented this with fast food from drive-throughs, which seemed an improvement. Occasionally a friend would bring a plate of home-cooked southern food back with her from visiting relatives, usually made by her grandmother. A paper plate of fried chicken with corn bread, black-eyed peas, collard greens, and sweet potato pie would be generously shared with the white girl from the North. I would pick through the pieces of ham to eat the collard greens, and enjoy the buttery corn bread with gusto. But all in all, my diet was bad. And that was the year that I got that first horrible case of eczema and had to be flown home for a visit to a dermatologist and a complete course of hydrocortisone.

The next year I was living on my own in Washington, DC, and returned to my supposedly healthy diet. Nevertheless, I had a recurrence of eczema and a fateful intervention of a Chinese herbalist, who added bug carcasses to my herbal brew. When I later moved to California I continued to have health difficulties. I was often exhausted; I suffered from double periods, PMS, and debilitating cramps. Finally, when I was twenty-five years old, doctors found a cyst the size of a grapefruit on my left ovary, and I had it surgically removed. Not for the first time, acupuncturists told me that I should start eating meat. One specifically suggested that I begin eating lamb. I couldn't imagine doing so! Eating a baby sheep—it was impossible. But I was desperate to get well. As I looked back, I had to admit that in ten years of vegetarianism, I had had ten years of declining health. I began to feel a powerful desire to be nourished. And it seemed that what I needed could only come from the flesh and blood, the death, of another animal.

I began to replay in my mind a story told by Annemarie Colbin in her book *Food and Healing*. Although she advocates a largely vegan, macrobiotic diet, she does acknowledge that some people may need to eat meat occasionally to maintain health, and gives as an example her husband. He had become tired and weak on a vegetarian diet, and so they decided that he should try eating meat. She describes the strange sense she had as he cooked a steak for the first time in their apartment and she took in the scent of cooking flesh. The thought filled me with longing. And so, for the first time in ten years, I ate a steak. I had never tasted anything so wonderful. I gave thanks to the cow that had died that I may live, and experienced the sense of being nourished I had been longing for.

As I began studying traditional diets, I found myself in the midst of a paradox that cast suspicion on my earlier notions of spirituality and food. I read about cultures that had an intimate relationship to the spiritual world, people for whom daily life activities were imbued with a spiritual intention and meaning, people for whom the universe and its creatures were respected, and in some cases held sacred. And yet they ate meat. I could not buy the line that these ancient cultures were primitive or unevolved. Many of their ways of life struck me as based on an understanding of life much *more* evolved than the Western industrial paradigm. It is related to the Tzutujil concept of *kas-limaal*—mutual indebtedness—that I mentioned in the last chapter when quoting Martín Prechtel: "The knowledge that every animal, plant, person, wind, and season is indebted to the fruit of everything else *is an adult knowledge*" (emphasis added). I began to see that this indebtedness inevitably involved death—it was impossible for it not to.

The more I began to learn about food and agriculture, the more I began to understand how much death is involved in the raising of food—whether grains and beans, fruits and vegetables, milk and eggs, or meat. At a popular organic farming training program here in California, one of the jokes among the students is, "If you want to be a vegetarian, you have to kill, kill, kill." To grow fruits and vegetables organically, farmers must protect their crops from the wide range of pests that attack them, till the soil so that the planting can be done, and harvest crops efficiently. All of this requires killing creatures, sometimes in large numbers. Gophers are one of the biggest pests that threaten fruit and nut trees in California, and the diligent organic farmer kills gophers by the score. A friend of mine who is a student in the program decided after years of vegetarianism to start eating meat again. His first meal of flesh consisted of stewed gophers. He figured that since he was already killing so many of them in the course of his farming, he might as well receive their nourishment. A gopher, it turns out, does not yield a lot of meat and takes a lot of work to prepare for cooking, so it is unlikely that he'll make it a regular meal. But he was very glad for the experience.

Barbara Kingsolver captures this adult knowledge beautifully in her book *Prodigal Summer*. In one passage rancher Eddie Bondo and wildlife protector Deanna Wolfe are trying to communicate to each other their perspectives on the life and death of animals:

> He shook his head, got up to collect two more logs from the woodpile, then shook his head again. "You can't be crying over every single brown-eyed life in the world."
>
> "I already told you, that's not my religion. I grew up on a farm. I've helped gut about any animal you can name, and I've watched enough harvests to know that cutting a wheat field amounts to more decapitated bunnies under the combine than you'd believe."
>
> She stopped speaking when her memory lodged on an old vision from childhood: a raccoon she found just after the hay mower ran it over. She could still see the matted gray fur, the gleaming jawbone and shock of scattered teeth so much like her own, the dark blood soaking into the ground all on one side, like a shadow of this creature's final, frightened posture. She could never explain to Eddie how it was, the undercurrent of tragedy that went with farming. And the hallelujas of it, too: the straight abundant rows, the corn tassels raised up like children who all knew the answer. The calves born slick and clean into their leggy black-and-white perfection. Life and death always right there in your line of sight. Most people lived so far from it, they thought you could just choose, carnivore or vegetarian, without knowing that the chemicals on grain and cotton killed far more butterflies and bees and bluebirds and whippoorwills than the mortal cost of a steak or a leather jacket. Just clearing the land to grow soybeans and corn had killed about everything on half the world. Every cup of coffee equaled one dead songbird in the jungle somewhere, she'd read.
>
> He was watching her, waiting for whatever was inside to come out, and she did the best she could. "Even if you never touch meat, you're costing something its

blood," she said. "Don't patronize me. I know that. Living takes life."

With this simple phrase *living takes life*, Deanna Wolfe tries to express in plain English something that is difficult for modern Americans to grasp. The concept might be more effectively communicated in the language of a mythologically literate culture. In ancient Greek, for example, there were two different words for "life": *bios* and *zoë*. As Lewis Hyde explains in *The Gift*: "*Bios* is limited life, characterized life, life that dies. *Zoë* is the life that endures; it is the thread that runs through *bios*-life and is not broken when the particular perishes." On one level, the phrase *living takes life* expresses that all living things rely on the death of other living things. On another level, it expresses that *zoë*-life, life in the biggest sense of enduring life, Life with a capital L, requires the sacrifice of *bios*-life, the particular lives of living creatures. *Zoë* takes (kills, consumes, eats, sacrifices, requires) *bios*. A core understanding of this adult knowledge lies at the heart of many spiritual practices and religious traditions worldwide. Death extinguishes a particular life, of course, but it doesn't extinguish Life. Life endures and transcends death.

When you see everything around you (animal, vegetable, mineral) as imbued with Spirit, as alive and sentient, as carrying with it a crucial part of the Whole; when you view all of life as inextricably interconnected by a thread, a spark, of something Divine; you understand that that great beautiful Creation involves death and decay just as certainly as it involves birth and resurrection. *Everything is indebted to everything else.* Every part of Creation is indebted *for its life* to the other parts of Creation that have died and decayed so that it might live.

The Western mind has developed a detachment from Earth-based and mythological worldviews; along with this it has formed a rather strict hierarchy of life-forms. We hold human life to be the most precious. In times past we consciously ranked human lives according to race, gender, religion, and social status. This is no longer socially acceptable, but we may still do it subconsciously. Nevertheless, cannibalism is our strongest taboo. It is not okay to eat other people.

We also place a high value on the life of animals we feel closer to—

dogs, cats, horses, monkeys—and often have taboos against eating them. Next down in our hierarchy are animals with which we share many biological characteristics, particularly land mammals. They have eyes and ears and noses like us, and if we are sentient then they certainly are. This unconsciously influences the decision of many people to not eat red meat. The flesh of mammals reminds us of our own flesh. Birds are another step down the hierarchy, fish and reptiles further down still, and insects below that—we give them very little value.

Once we have descended the rungs through the world of animals, we come to plants. As a culture, we place some value on trees, which seem more like us because they live longer, and so seem to have a memory. Besides, they are big. We are always impressed with size when it comes to nature, valuing whales over sardines, redwoods over oaks, and lions over bobcats. Most plants, though, fail to command our sympathy. Few people hesitate to eat a carrot, although it kills the *bios*-life of that plant.

After descending through the rungs of the vegetable world, we reach the world of microorganisms: Bacteria, yeasts, and molds are parts of the living universe that we cannot even see. If we hesitate to eat them it is only because we are afraid they may make us ill, not because we feel any moral compunction about their demise. Similarly, we give little thought to the morality or the karma of eating salt or drinking water.

But a traditional culture that lives in close and intimate relationship with the land has a very different approach to valuing life. These groups believe everything in the natural world has its own sacred nature. Water is a sacred living thing, as are trees and plants, animals, mountains, yeasts, and the moon. All are imbued with Life—*zoë*— even if their biological life—*bios*—is not perceptible. To say that it is moral to eat a root but immoral to eat an animal, then, makes little sense—both are alive.

A hierarchy may still develop in such a culture, but it will be based on how great a gift each thing is perceived to be to the community that depends on it. Where people depend upon corn for survival, it will be honored and given special importance. Where they depend upon the salmon, salmon are given an exalted status. A precious body of water may be considered a great gift, or the leaves of a particular plant, or the sap of a tree, or a deposit of metal, or stone, or salt. In Tibet, saltmen take a yearly monthlong pilgrimage to a salt lake high in the Himalayas to hand-harvest salt. Following tradition, they perform ritual prayers of gratitude to the goddess of the lake, make offerings to her, speak in a sacred, secret language during the journey, and uphold a strict standard of conduct as they near the lake.

Perceiving a part of the natural world to be a great gift does not preclude eating it, though it will always be eaten with gratitude and thanks to the spirits who bring it into the lives of the people who depend upon it. Sometimes a taboo against eating a particular animal will develop to protect another food that comes from that animal. The most common example is the taboo against eating beef—or restrictions about when it may be eaten—when a community is dependent upon the dairy products that cattle provide. Other animals come to be considered unclean or ritually proscribed for a variety of reasons, and thus there are taboos against eating them. In many indigenous cultures, certain clans are prohibited from eating particular animals that are totemic for them. To eat that animal becomes a form of cannibalism, but it is never *all* animals that are thus designated.

Of course, there are myriad reasons that people become vegetarians, but often the impulse grows out of a legitimate objection to how the animals raised for food production are treated in today's society. It is bad enough that we don't perceive corn or water to be a gift, but how much worse when it is an animal that can look at us and blink, that sleeps and eats and cries out when it is in pain, just like we do! We view our livestock not as gifts, but rather as units of production. The commodification of animal products—not only meat but eggs and dairy as well—has led to a profound devaluation of the animals we raise within our industrialized food system. They lead tragic, confined lives, cut off from the other aspects of nature—grass, earth, sunlight, sky, rain, fresh air, night, morning, day, dusk. They have been severed from the larger context of Life, of *zoë*, and of the beautiful interdependence and entanglement of existence. They are only one step removed from being machines, and so their biological death, the death of *bios*, does not echo with an affirmation of *zoë*, of Life. Its sound is hollow and cold and senseless.

All creatures live some kind of life and die some kind of death. We don't really want to look at this fact because we live in a culture that deals only indirectly with the reality of death. Because we are so divorced from nature, we are handicapped in our ability to understand the world mythically, metaphorically, or spiritually. Because we are so used to having control over our environment and being able to manipulate it, and because we rely on a literal and mechanistic understanding of how that environment functions, death seems to us a tragic and a frustrating business. We see it as a finality, as an ending, rather than a threshold or transition. The West African shaman and teacher Malidoma Patrice Somé gives us some insight into how the people of his culture—the Dagara—view death:

> For the Dagara people, death results in simply a different form of belonging to the community. It is a lesson from nature that change is the norm, that the world is defined by eternal cycles of decline and regeneration. Having journeyed adequately in this world in your life, you become much more effective to the community that contained you when you return to the world of Spirit. When my grandfather, Bakhyè, died, he told my father, "I have to go now. From where I'll be I'll be more useful to you than if I stay here." Death is not a separation but a different form of communion, a higher form of connectedness with the community, providing an opportunity for even greater service.

When we think of death as a transition, it is less tragic—in fact, it is full of Life, of *zoë*. Taking the life of another creature is not an inconsequential act in this context, but it has a much different meaning when death is viewed as part of a cycle or circle rather than the end of a line.

Many modern Americans who adopt vegetarianism for spiritual reasons do so as a way of following the doctrine of *ahimsa*, or noninjury to living creatures. The doctrine can be found in Buddhist, Jaina, Vedic, and Hindu forms. In *The Myth of the Holy Cow*, Dwinjendra Narayan Jha explores the historical development of the concept of *ahimsa* as well as that of the holy cow within the context of Hinduism and the Vedas. By looking at ancient texts and religious development, he shows that the interpretation of *ahimsa* as an injunction to vegetarianism is relatively recent:

> The [Vedic] law book of Manu (200 BC–AD 200), the most representative of the legal texts having much to say on lawful and forbidden food, . . . asserts that animals were created for the sake of sacrifice, that killing (*vadha*) on ritual occasions is non-killing (*avadha*), and injury (*himsa*) as enjoined by the Veda (*vedavihitahimsa*) is known to be non-injury (*ahimsa*). He assures that plants, cattle, trees—and birds, which have met their death in sacrifice, attain higher levels of existence. This benefit is available not only to the victim but also to the sacrificer; for he tells us that "a twice-born man who knows the true meaning of the Veda and injures animals for these purposes (hospitality, sacrifice to gods and ancestor spirits) makes himself and the animal go to the highest state of existence (in heaven)." If, however, he refuses to eat consecrated meat, he will be reborn as a beast for twenty-one existences.

Once again, this ancient text makes the *context* and *intention* in the killing of an animal the crucial factors in its spiritual impact. It is holy and sacred if it is done in order to *offer a gift*. In fact, it is unholy *not* to accept meat when it has been consecrated in this way.

I have heard that the Dalai Lama is generally a vegetarian, but when he is offered meat in the context of hospitality, he accepts it graciously.

This makes sense when you consider the sanctifying nature of hospitality in ancient texts. It also brings to mind an early experience I had as a vegetarian. When I was about sixteen years old, I went to a friend's house for dinner, along with a few other students. My friend's mother served us spaghetti with homemade tomato-and-meat sauce. I recognized immediately that the sauce had meat, but in that moment decided that to comment on it and refuse to eat it would simply be rude; I would put aside my vegetarian principles for the moment and eat as much spaghetti as I could to be polite. But one of my other friends was also a vegetarian, and she jumped up in alarm: "Does this sauce have meat in it?" she cried. "Yes," the mother answered, "why? You don't eat meat?" My friend was scandalized: "No! And Jessica, aren't you a vegetarian, too?" I nodded assent meekly, but reassured the mother that I was going to continue to eat my food while my friend's dinner was replaced with plain pasta.

This was an important experience for me because two strongly held principles of mine were at odds: gracious acceptance of gifts offered as a guest in someone's home, and vegetarianism. Something bothered me deeply about my friend's outraged response to the meat, but I also felt that she had been a better vegetarian than me—more noble and willing to stand up for what she believed. Years later I would find myself making a different choice. While I was working in the refugee camp in Thailand, on a few occasions I was invited into homes within the camp for a meal. I remember being offered the fresh spring rolls that are such a specialty of Vietnamese cooking, but I turned them down because they were stuffed with pork. I still feel some shame when I think of this—how precious that pork would have been to that family who lived on UN rations, what a generous offering it was, how much it would have meant to them to be able to offer it to the aid workers to whom they felt indebted, and how much consternation my refusal to eat it may have caused. I think Manu's law book speaks to the fact that food offered in hospitality is consecrated because it is brought into a holy realm, a realm of connectedness, mutual indebtedness, and reciprocity. I'm not sure that I'll be reborn as a beast for twenty-one existences because of my poor manners—but of course my understanding of Manu's ancient sacred text is metaphorical, not literal.

It is in fact impossible to take the doctrine of *ahimsa* literally, because we cannot live without injuring other living beings. We could devote every ounce of our energy to the task, and still fail. Even if we determine that only animals are living beings, the task would still be utterly unattainable. This is perhaps why the Buddha, although he taught *ahimsa*, continued to eat meat up until his death. His last meal was said to be pork that was "light, pleasant, full of flavour, and good for digestion." Jha points out: "As is well known, throughout its history the religion of the Buddha emphasized the Middle Path, which meant moderation: neither license nor exaggerated self-mortification. This was intended to keep life practicable for the monk as well as for the laity." The Buddha shows us by example that we can have a profound understanding of *ahimsa* without engaging in the futile exercise of trying to take it literally.

It is treacherous to read ancient sacred texts as factual truth and God-given law in the context of a post-Enlightenment, culturally diverse, scientifically oriented culture. It generally leads to one of two positions: disbelief (atheism), or fundamentalism. The atheist looks at the fact that a sacred text is contradicted by science, or by other beliefs, or by lived experience, and concludes that the sacred text must therefore be untrue, and so rejects it as false, often rejecting all religious teaching as hogwash. The fundamentalist looks at the fact that a sacred text is similarly contradicted, and then disavows the validity of the science, other beliefs, or lived experience that challenges it. The fundamentalist clings to the literality of the sacred text against all evidence to the contrary, and often becomes militant in its defense. Fundamentalist doctrine gives a person something to adhere to in a complicated and confusing world, and usually offers that person a community of others who cling to the same doctrine. It is a recent phenomenon. As theologian Marcus Borg points out, "Fundamentalism itself—whether Christian, Jewish, or Muslim—is modern. It is a response to modern culture."

In writing *The Myth of the Holy Cow*, D. N. Jha was responding to what he perceives to be an increasing fundamentalism within Hinduism, much of which attaches itself to the doctrine of the sacredness of the cow. By putting this doctrine in historical context and

Living Takes Life

Thirteen animals eaten by traditional and indigenous peoples:

1. American buffalo (bison)
2. Deer
3. Kangaroo
4. Duck
5. Reindeer
6. Llama
7. Whale
8. Seal
9. Emu
10. Goat
11. Bear
12. Rabbit
13. Antelope

showing it to be a relatively modern understanding, Jha hoped to help de-escalate the violence between Hindus and Muslims in which religious dietary doctrines have become a lightning rod. Hindu fundamentalists use the fact that they don't eat beef as a mark of moral superiority over Muslims and a justification for anti-Muslim policies. Jha's book critiques this approach, and it has been variously banned and censored in India. The author has received death threats as a result of its publication.

I see a similar strain of fundamentalism in the radical vegan movement. Unwilling to accept that *ahimsa* is a compelling but complex doctrine that needs to be understood in a spiritual and not a literal way, vegans can become rabid and unwavering in their approach to food and animals. I gave a presentation a couple of months ago, and one of the attendees approached me afterward. He said he was looking forward to posting some of my material on the fridge in the communal house where he lived because—as he said—he lived with a bunch of "fundamentalist vegans" and he wanted to provoke them. As he spoke, something clicked for me about aspects of the vegan movement that I find disheartening. Unwilling to admit that adhering to a literal understanding of *ahimsa* is impossible, they cling to the idea that we can build a food system free of the suffering and death of animals. But this is an illusion.

This fantasy is born of a hasty and unfortunate marriage among a number of factors: disconnection from nature and the cycles of life and death, pain over the commodification of animals in our modern food system, a neo-puritan longing to be free of the flesh, righteous indignation toward the powers that be, and finally an inchoate internalized guilt about the state of the world, the destruction of the planet, and the devastation of native cultures. There are good reasons to feel all these things, but I do not think that fundamentalist veganism is a Life-expanding response. It ignores the universal truth that living takes life, and further disconnects us from nature and the eternal cycles of life and death.

I do believe that vegetarianism can be a powerful and positive practice in some people's lives. Abstinence from meat under certain conditions has played a part in many spiritual traditions throughout the world for good reason—flesh and blood are powerful symbols, and abstaining from them can have a deeply focusing, enlightening, or purifying effect when entered into with that spirit. Vegetarianism certainly made a huge contribution to my own life—I can never again look at meat as simply a commodity and can no longer look the other way when I contemplate the lives of animals that are part of our inhumane factory-farming system. I offer time, energy, money, and friendship to farmers who are raising animals in ways that are ecological and humane. I am wonderfully entangled with them in a struggle to wrest animals away from the commodity market and bring them back into the gift cycle, where they always used to be.

Indigenous and traditional foodways reflected the knowledge that animal foods were a precious gift. Hunting game and slaughtering farm animals were undertaken carefully and consciously, often in a ritual context. All parts of the animal were valued and used by the community, and what couldn't be used was often gifted to some other being. It often wasn't the meat that was considered to be most valuable part of the animal by the community. Three other parts of an animal's body were most prized—the fat, the bones, and the organs—and (rightly) thought to be the most nutrient-dense. Fat is a source of vitamins and fatty acids that are critical for healthy hormonal development, as well as an important source of energy. Animal bones are primary sources of minerals in most diets—they have been used extensively by cultures around the world to make broths, or added to stews or curries, or cracked open so that the marrow could be sucked out. Organ meats are sources of vitamins, minerals, and many other vital nutrients, and so would never go to waste. The meat was sometimes the most expendable part of a food animal and might even be given to other hungry creatures. Some people think of traditional hunter-gatherer diets as being high in protein. But many of these diets were not so much high-protein as they were nutrient-dense. It wasn't protein per se that made animals so nourishing; it was all the nutrients available from their bodies. And it wasn't just hunter-gatherers who valued all parts of the animal and were focused on nutrient density, it was pastoralists and agriculturalists as well.

This is the opposite of the approach to meat in modern America—where the boneless, skinless chicken breast is a popular commodity. In any traditional chicken-eating culture, the bones were the vital ingredient in soup, curry, broth, or stew. The skin was often rendered as a stable and healthy frying fat (the famous Yiddish schmaltz) or eaten as the delicious crispy coat of a roast chicken, or used for the rich gravy that would be poured over everything else. Don't you wonder what happens to all the chicken bones and skins that are removed from all those supermarket chickens? What a terrible waste, and what a dishonor to the poor chickens!

Once we accept that living takes life, we can begin doing vitally important work: ensuring that farm animals and wild animals have the opportunity to lead a good life and die a good death. We need to approach the body of a slaughtered animal more holistically, ecologically, consciously, and spiritually. We have to witness the lives and the deaths of farm animals, and to be less squeamish about the truth of what happens to them. Last year I had the opportunity to go to a local farm and kill a chicken myself. Then I scalded it and plucked it and gutted it. The next day I ate it. I learned a great deal by doing that, and it helped me to accept the mortality of the process. I will never look at a chicken the same way again, now that I know each step involved between a feathered clucking being running around the barnyard and the pink plucked headless body you see in the store. We are so divorced in this culture from all of these steps. This disconnection is a big part of what makes it seem possible to step outside the cycle of life and death and be free from the karma of killing for our food. But a life lived on the farm or in the forest will teach you otherwise.

On the Blood Moon, may we say a heartfelt prayer for all the animals that are being raised in inhumane conditions. May we give great thanks for the farmers and ranchers who treat their animals with respect and honor and who care deeply for their welfare. May we take the time to seek out sources of animal foods that are raised with respect for the environment, for our health, and for the well-being of the animals themselves. May there come a day when factory farms have been replaced with small-scale, integrated, holistic family farms where all living things are recognized as the gifts that they surely are. May there be a day when Americans have acquired the adult knowledge that all life is dependent upon all other life in an endless circle of giving and receiving, birth and death, growth and decay, rebirth and regeneration. May we find ourselves humble as we contemplate the miracle of life, and of the Life that transcends death. That would make our ancestors proud.

BLOOD MOON RECIPES

Simplest Roast Chicken
Serves 3–4

You can add potatoes, parsnips, carrots, sweet potatoes, or other starchy vegetables to the pan before you roast the chicken. Sprinkle them also with salt and pepper. These vegetables will roast along with the chicken in its fat.

1 roasting chicken

Olive oil, if needed

Sea salt (or other high-quality salt)

Freshly ground black pepper

1. Preheat the oven to 425° F.
2. Rinse the chicken, remove the giblets, and pat dry with a paper towel.
3. Place it in a lightly oiled roasting pan or a well-seasoned cast-iron skillet that fits it well. Put it either breast-side up or breast-side down, depending on how you are going to serve it. If you are going to serve the chicken roasted as is, put it breast-side up. If you are going to remove the meat and use it another dish, you can roast it breast-side down. This will keep the breast meat a bit juicier.
4. Sprinkle sea salt over the surface of the chicken and into the cavity, then do the same with freshly ground pepper.
5. Optional: If you want additional flavor, you can stuff the cavity of the chicken with any of these: bay leaves, sage leaves, thyme sprigs, rosemary sprigs, lemon halves, orange halves, sliced gingerroot, garlic cloves, shallots, onion slices, or a combination.
6. Put the chicken in the oven on the highest rack where it will fit. Roast until the skin is rich brown and the juices run clear. You can check this by pouring out the juice from the cavity, and also by sticking a knife into the area between the leg and the body and looking at the juices. A 4-pound chicken will probably take around 50 minutes. As it roasts, you can baste the bird occasionally to keep it from drying out.
7. Remove the chicken from the oven and let it sit at room temperature about 15 minutes before serving. This allows the juices to settle into the meat.

Swedish Meatballs
Serves 3–4

Swedish meatballs are traditionally served with boiled potatoes and lingonberry jam. I often eat them with mashed potatoes, and a dollop of sauerkraut, and a fresh green vegetable. Lingonberry or another tart jam goes beautifully as well. I add liver for increased nutrition.

1 pound ground grass-fed beef or other red meat

3-ounce liver from grass-fed ruminant animal

½ onion, peeled and coarsely chopped

1 handful parsley leaves—or substitute celery leaves or a lesser quantity of lovage leaves

1 egg yolk

2–5 tablespoons sourdough bread crumbs, sprouted flour (or cereal), or stiff raw sourdough, as needed (page 312)

1 teaspoon Celtic sea salt, or other high-quality salt

½ teaspoon pepper

¼ teaspoon dried herbs such as thyme, sage, marjoram, oregano, or rosemary (optional)

1–3 tablespoons tallow, lard, or other fat

1 cup beef (or other) broth, brought to a simmer (covered) in a small pan with a few parsley stems, slices of onion, and a bay leaf

1 teaspoon kuzu or arrowroot dissolved in ¼ cup cold milk or broth

¼ cup crème fraîche

Salt and pepper to taste

1. Put the ground beef into a bowl.
2. In a food processor, place the liver, onion, and parsley leaves, and process by pulsing into a coarse texture.
3. Add the egg yolk and 2 tablespoons of the bread crumbs, flour, or sourdough to the food processor. Also add the salt, pepper, and dried herbs, then pulse until well mixed.
4. Add the contents of the food processor to the ground beef and mix thoroughly. If the mixture is too wet, add more bread crumbs or flour until you can form balls with your hands.
5. Form the meat into balls about 1½ inches in diameter.
6. Heat the tallow or other fat in a skillet over medium-high heat. When the fat is hot, add the meatballs in a single layer without crowding. (You will probably need to cook them in two batches.)
7. After the bottoms of the meatballs are cooked, gently turn them so that they can cook on another side. Continue until they are cooked on all sides and all the way through. Keep warm on a plate.
8. Strain the beef broth into the skillet and scrape up all the browned bits

(continued)

Swedish Meatballs
continued

into the broth as it cooks. Simmer for a few minutes to reduce.

9. Add the kuzu or arrowroot mixture to the pan and whisk until thick. Season to taste with salt and pepper.

Whisk in the crème fraîche.

10. If the meatballs are too cool, you can return them to the gravy to warm up. Otherwise, pour the gravy over the meatballs.

Beef Liver with Browned Onions
Serves 1–3

I often make this for a quick and nourishing lunch. I like to eat it with a big dollop of sauerkraut—the sweetness of the onions and the acidity of the kraut balance the strong flavor of the liver.

¼–½ pound beef liver

½ cup milk (optional)

½ yellow onion

2–3 tablespoons tallow, lard, or other fat

¼ cup sprouted spelt flour, arrowroot powder, or unbleached white flour

½ teaspoon sea salt

Freshly ground pepper

1 tablespoon or so brandy, wine, or beef stock

1. Cut the liver into ¼-inch-thick slices. You can soak it in milk if you like—this will make the flavor milder—though I don't usually do so. If you opt for soaking, soak in the fridge for at least an hour, as long as overnight.
2. Cut the onion into half-moon rings.
3. Heat half of the fat in a small heavy-bottomed skillet over medium-high heat.
4. When the fat is hot, add the onion and cook, stirring occasionally, until brown.
5. Meanwhile, mix the flour, salt, and pepper in a shallow bowl. (If you soaked the liver, remove it from the milk and shake off any excess.) Dip both sides of each piece of liver in the flour mixture and put on a plate.
6. When the onion is brown, add a pinch of salt and pour the brandy, wine, or stock into the pan.
7. Scrape up all the bits that are stuck to the bottom, put the onions on a small plate, and return the pan to the heat.
8. When the pan is dry (should just

take a few seconds), add the rest of the fat.

9. When the fat is hot, put the breaded liver strips into the fat and fry on each side for about 30 seconds or so, until just brown.

10. Transfer the liver to the plate with the onions, and eat with sauerkraut.

Stir-fry of Pork and Vegetables with Ginger
Serves 2

Lately I have been really enjoying making simple stir-fries. Serve this over steamed rice for a quick and simple meal. It would also be nice with some Quick and Simple Kimchi (page 254) on the side.

1 tablespoon plus 1 teaspoon soy sauce

2 tablespoons mirin or other sweet rice wine

1 large pork chop, cut into a ¾-inch dice

3–4 cups chopped fresh vegetables using a combination of 3 (or more) from this list:

Snap peas or snow peas, stem ends removed

Onions, peeled and cut into half-moons or a ½-inch dice

Broccoli florets, bite sized

Asparagus cut into 1-inch lengths on the diagonal

Shiitake or crimini mushrooms, stems trimmed and cut in quarters

Bok choi, stems slit down the middle and leaves chopped roughly

Carrots, cut in half lengthwise and sliced thinly on the diagonal

Green beans, stem ends removed

Long beans, cut into 2-inch length

Yellow summer squash, cut in half lengthwise and sliced thinly on the diagonal

½ cup pork or chicken stock

1 tablespoon fish sauce

1 tablespoon kuzu root powder or arrowroot powder

3 tablespoons lard or other stable high-heat fat

1 tablespoon minced fresh ginger

1. Before chopping your vegetables, mix 1 tablespoon of the soy sauce with 1 tablespoon of the mirin in a bowl and add the diced pork to this mixture. Mix the pork with the marinade to cover completely. Set aside until you're ready to cook. (You can do this step a day in advance.)

2. Prepare all your fresh vegetables and keep each separate in its own bowl.

3. Mix together the stock and fish sauce with the remaining 1 teaspoon of soy sauce and 1 tablespoon of mirin. Add the kuzu or arrowroot to this mixture and whisk to dissolve.

4. Heat the lard in a wok over medium-high heat, moving the wok

(continued)

Stir-fry of Pork and Vegetables with Ginger
continued

around so that the lard coats the majority of the interior.

5. When the fat is hot, add the ginger and fry for a few seconds, then begin adding the vegetables one by one. Add hardier vegetables—such as broccoli, carrots, and asparagus—first, and delicate vegetables like snow peas and bok choi toward the end. After you add each vegetable, stir and fry for a minute or two.
6. After all the vegetables have been added, lift the pork out of its marinade and add it to the wok. (You may need to add a bit more lard to the wok first if it is too dry.) Stir and fry the pork for a minute until the surface of the pork turns white.
7. Stir the stock mixture again and add it to the wok. Continue to stir as the stock comes to a simmer and thickens. This should take just a minute or two. Turn off the heat.
8. Serve over steamed rice.

Lamb Chops with Meyer Lemon and Mint Gelée
Serves 4–6

Lamb and mint are a classic combination. You don't have to use Meyer lemon for this, but it's nice. You may need to adjust the amount of Sucanat for the degree of sweetness you want.

Gelée

4 large sprigs of fresh spearmint, 5–6 inches long

1 organic Meyer (or other) lemon, washed

¾ cup filtered water

2 teaspoons Bernard Jensen's gelatin (see page 315) or 1 teaspoon Knox gelatin

1 tablespoon Sucanat or Rapadura

¼ teaspoon salt

1. Pull the leaves off the sprigs of mint.
2. Using a vegetable peeler, peel off two or three strips of the lemon peel about 2 inches long. Put the lemon peel and mint stems into a small pan.
3. Add the water to the pan, place over medium heat, and bring to a simmer. Cover and simmer for 5 to 10 minutes.
4. Turn off the heat and remove the lid. Remove the mint stems and lemon peel with a slotted spoon. Add the gelatin to the liquid and stir to dissolve. Pour into a bowl.
5. Add the Sucanat and salt.
6. Juice the lemon and add the juice to the mixture. Allow the mixture to cool.
7. Mince the mint leaves. When the mixture is near room temperature, add the mint to the mixture and stir well.

8. Place the mixture in the fridge and allow it to chill until set—at least an hour.

9. Stir before serving so it is less like Jello and more like a gelée.

Lamb Chops

Sea salt

Freshly ground pepper

1 teaspoon or so minced fresh rosemary

2–4 pounds bone-in lamb chops, figuring at least ½ pound per person, depending on appetites

1–2 tablespoons tallow or other fat

1. Sprinkle salt, pepper, and minced rosemary over both sides of the lamb chops.
2. Heat the tallow or other fat in a cast-iron skillet over medium-high heat.
3. When the fat is hot, put the lamb chops in the pan in a single layer. Brown until dark brown, then turn over and brown on the other side.

You can test the doneness of the chops by pressing with your finger. If they are soft, then they are rare; hard chops are more cooked. I like them rare. You can also cut into them with a sharp knife to see the color inside.

4. Serve the lamb chops with a large dollop of the mint gelée.

Beef Broth
Yield depends on quantity of bones and water

My approach to broth is simple and minimalist. I don't like to add any vegetables, herbs, or salt to it until I use it in a recipe. This makes for a much cleaner and more versatile broth.

A few large beef soup bones or knuckle bones

1–2 tablespoons tallow or other fat

An oxtail, some short ribs, a couple of shanks, or other meaty bones

Filtered water to cover

A tablespoon of white wine (or other) vinegar

I usually make my broth in a 5½-quart Crock-Pot (slow cooker). That way I can let it go for a couple of days without worrying about it. You could easily adapt this to a stockpot.

1. Put the soup or knuckle bones in the Crock-Pot.
2. In a cast-iron or other heavy skillet, heat the tallow or other fat over medium-high heat.

(continued)

Beef Broth
continued

3. When the fat is hot, put the pieces of oxtail, short ribs, or shanks into the skillet and brown on all sides.

4. Turn down the heat and transfer the meaty bones to the Crock-Pot.

5. Pour about 1 cup of filtered water into the hot skillet and scrape up all the flavorful browned bits from the pan. Pour that water into the Crock-Pot.

6. Put enough water in the Crock-Pot to cover all the bones. Add the vinegar. Put the lid on the Crock-Pot and put the heat on high.

7. After the broth comes to a simmer, reduce the heat to low and cook for 36 to 72 hours. I often turn the heat down to warm overnight so I don't wake up to the smell of beef broth, then return the heat to low (or to high for an hour or two and then to low) in the morning.

8. You may need to add a little water each day so the bones stay covered in water and don't brown on top.

9. Strain the broth into a bowl. Pick the meat off the meaty bones and reserve for *Shchi* (page 281) or any other beef soup. You can also pull the meaty bones out of the broth earlier (after half a day or so of cooking), take the meat off, and then return the bones to the broth and keep cooking. This way the meat will be tastier.

10. Using a fat separator, pour the broth into 1-quart jars, with about ½ inch of fat on top of each one (which helps to prevent the broth from spoiling by keeping out air). If you leave at least 2 inches of air space in the top of the jars, you can freeze the broth.

11

SNOW MOON

Our stores are full
Our medicines are strong
Our weapons are worn
Our spirits are glad
Kitche Manitou has been kind.

—From an Anishnabeg (Ojibway) thanksgiving for autumn,
translated from the Anishnabeg

When autumn is becoming winter, we move into the lunar cycle called the Snow Moon in sixteenth-century England. Northern dwellers could expect their first snowfall, and waterways and reservoirs might start to freeze. For many peoples, this was the last opportunity to preserve food and ensure that there would be stores of necessities to last through the winter.

Nowadays we take for granted our ability to freeze and chill food in our own kitchens. But the mechanical refrigerator is an extremely modern invention. The first practical domestic refrigerator was sold in the United States in 1918, so for most of human history cold storage has ranged from elusive, to seasonal, to almost constant, depending on the local climate. Cold needed to be found and used where it was—like a root cellar dug deep in the cool ground. My father-in-law grew up in the 1920s on a Texas farm equipped with a cistern—an underground reservoir for water collected during the rains, used like a well. Dairy products and meat that needed to be kept cold would be lowered in a bucket into the cistern, so that the bucket was just immersed—but not submerged—in the cool underground water. That was their refrigeration.

Some people, of course, didn't need to look far for a source of refrigeration. The Inuit could store their food simply by burying it in the snow or ice. But other peoples often went to great lengths to harvest ice and create the conditions for natural refrigeration. The ancient Romans had snow brought down from the Alps to be used for keeping perishable foods cold. In places where there were cold winters and warm summers, ice would be harvested before the first thaw and stored in insulated icehouses. The icehouse would then be used to preserve food throughout the warm months until the return of the Snow Moon.

The challenges of refrigeration were one of the reasons that our ancestors developed such a wide range of technologies to preserve food. We have a tendency to think that indigenous people ate their food fresh from the forest, farm, or garden, and that processed foods are a modern invention. This misimpression is based on our notion that processed foods means factory-processed foods: chips and other snack foods, cookies and sweets, boxed cold cereals, and everything that falls into the category of junk food. But the staple foods of many traditional diets were actually often quite processed, in the sense that they were taken through a process—sometimes an elaborate series of processes—before they were eaten. The difference lies in how they were processed. While our food processing is mostly done in factories using heavy machinery, traditionally foods were processed on a relatively small-scale basis (what we would now call artisanal), and generally in the context of community.

One example of this is *chuño*, which is eaten in the Andes and relies on the ingenious use of the freezing temperatures at night. Although freeze-drying may strike us as one of the most newfangled ways of preserving food, in *chuño* we see its ancient origins. This is how indigenous people in what is now Peru have been processing their potatoes for millennia:

> The freshly lifted potatoes are washed clean without damaging the skins and laid out on soft turf or straw padding

to be exposed to severe night frost. As soon as they have thawed in the morning they are trodden with bare feet so that the skin remains intact but the fluid resulting from cell rupture is extruded. On the first pressing over 30% of the fluid may be lost. They are left in position and dried by the sun and wind. The process is repeated for five successive days. From the sixth day onwards no further pressing takes place and they are straw-covered to a sufficient depth to prevent further freezing at night. Once dried they are as hard as stone and can be stored indefinitely, and even a minor degree of damp does not seem to damage them unduly. This product is called *chuño*.

The Andeans would travel with a ration of *chuño* and *charqui* (llama jerky), and then reconstitute both by simmering them into a stew on their journeys—a practice that probably contributed to the great Incan migrations throughout South America.

There were many reasons that traditional peoples processed their foods. They preserved them for easy transportation, as in the case of both *chuño* and *charqui*, or because a foodstuff was only available seasonally, or both. Maple sap, for example, was processed into maple sugar both to make it transportable and because it could then be used throughout the rest of the year and traded. Processing food can also increase its nutritional value. While modern factory processing usually dramatically decreases nutrition, traditional processing often greatly enhanced the nutrient density or the accessibility of nutrients in a food. The way grains were processed by soaking, souring, sprouting, or fermentation is one example. This extra step took time, but meant that the grains could be a primary source of nourishment for the community. Similarly, lacto-fermented beverages such as the Waorani *tepae* were full of electrolytes and minerals that increased energy and stamina. In some cases processing was used to increase inebriating, psychoactive, or medicinal properties, or to decrease the poisonous effects of certain foods. And last but not least, foods were processed to create wonderful new flavors. Think about the difference in taste between a glass of fresh milk and a hunk of blue cheese and you'll get the point.

For many of us, the notion of preserving food conjures images of our grandmothers or great-grandmothers filling jar upon steaming jar of tomatoes, corn, peaches, or green beans and then lining them up on pantry shelves. But canning is a recent development, its popularity dating back only to the beginning of the nineteenth century when it was considered a great innovation. Some heat bottling had been practiced previously, but it was not in widespread use until it was patented in 1810 and popularized soon after. Traditional and indigenous food preservation rarely involved high heat. While heat processing kills the enzymes in raw foods and often reduces its nutritional content, traditional approaches actually maximized enzyme and vitamin content.

In Old Europe and northern Asia, the annual ritual of food preservation that took place in the fall centered on the process of pickling. While we think of pickles as cucumbers canned in a vinegary brine, traditional pickling techniques did not use vinegar or heat processing. Rather, a wide range of vegetables (and sometimes fruits, animal products, nuts, seeds, and other ingredients as well) were lacto-fermented using salt (usually), temperature, and a controlled environment for a period of time to create myriad delicacies with complex flavors. Perhaps the most familiar of these to modern Americans is sauerkraut—the German version of cabbage that has been salted and lacto-fermented over a period of weeks into a delicious condiment and side vegetable. Sauerkraut was a crucial part of the winter diet of Europeans, and there are variations in Russia, France, Italy, Hungary, and every other European country. Rich in vitamin C and full of active enzymes, it also appears to have potent anticarcinogenic properties.

In Korea the celebrated kimchi is made in a similar way. Cabbage, other vegetables, and sometimes fruits and seafood are fermented into complex and flavorful condiments that accompany every meal. Making kimchi is still a very important part of the seasonal cycle. Food writer Hi Soo Shin Hepinstall describes the importance of this tradition in Korean life:

Each year, as the month of November approaches, the bustling markets in Korea become even busier than usual, thrown into a frenzy of activity by *kimjang ch'ol*, the kimchi-making season. This traditional culinary event falls between *Ipdong*, the first day of winter, and *Sosol*, the day of the first snowfall. Kimchi is made at other times of year for immediate use (known as "instant kimchi" or "summer kimchi"), but *kimjang* kimchi will sustain a family through the three long months of the harsh Korean winter. *Kimjang ch'ol* is a serious national concern; it is reported on daily, along with current national and international news, supplemented by bulletins on commodity prices, money saving tips, and endless "how to" advice for consumers and suppliers alike. Typically, Korean housewives will exchange daily greetings of "Are you getting ready for *kimjang*?" or "Are you done with your *kimjang*?"

Kimchi is a major part of the Korean diet, and was even more important in the past, as this same writer asserts: "In the days of my childhood, kimchi made up virtually half the daily diet." Similar to sauerkraut, kimchi is the result of a slow, cool fermentation process. The ideal environment for aging both sauerkraut and kimchi is an earthenware crock in a cool place. Hepinstall explains how this was achieved in Korea in times past:

> Our ancestors came up with a sagacious method to maximize *kimchi*'s flavor and longevity: in winter they buried the *kimchi* crocks underground, and in summer placed them in cold caves or in wells. In my childhood home, besides our backyard cave, we had a two-room storage house near the kitchen. In one room, *kimchi* jars were cemented in the floor, with only their necks and covers showing. In the countryside, most folks built temporary straw shelters over their buried *kimchi* jars. Nowadays, most Korean homes have medium-size refrigerators specially designed for *kimchi* only.

A Culture's Culture

Thirteen traditional lacto-fermented vegetables and fruits:

1. Sauerkraut (German cultured cabbage)
2. Kimchi (Korean cultured cabbage and other vegetables)
3. Gundruk (Nepalese preserved greens)
4. Doqq (Moroccan preserved lemons)
5. Nuka-zuke (Japanese rice bran pickles)
6. Achaar (Indian pickles)
7. Kawal (Sudanese preserved cassia leaf)
8. Cortido (Mexican cultured cabbage)
9. Poi (Hawaiian and Polynesian fermented taro)
10. Rosel (Eastern European Jewish fermented beets)
11. Umeboshi (Japanese pickled plums)
12. Kosher dill pickles (Eastern European Jewish pickled cucumbers)
13. Sauerrüben (German cultured turnips)

Northeastern Europeans had a very similar approach in making sauerkraut. While cabbage is the classic main ingredient in both kimchi and Eastern European sauerkraut, both traditions make use of other late-autumn produce as well. Radishes, Asian pears, winter greens, nuts, and seeds are commonly included in kimchi, as are seasonings such as red pepper, ginger, garlic, and green onion. In Eastern European tradition, turnips, beets, carrots, onions, apples, juniper seeds, and caraway seeds are often added to sauerkraut. Additionally, turnips were lacto-fermented to make *sauerrüben*, and beets were similarly processed. Both Koreans and Eastern Europeans also lacto-ferment cucumbers with seasonings to make pickles. In Korea these pickles are simply another kind of kimchi.

All of these traditions serve an important nutritional function. They assure that there will be a supply of vegetables through the frozen winter that are rich not only in vitamins but also in lactic acid—a potent digestive—as well as teeming with active enzymes and beneficial bacteria. Both the Korean and the Eastern European diets rely heavily on stewed meats rich with fat. Probiotic lacto-fermented vegetables help the body to digest these heavy foods. This is why it is traditional to pair sausage and sauerkraut, or to eat your frankfurter topped with pickled relish, or to serve *cornichons* with pâté. The richness of one and the vibrancy and acidity of the other make a combination both delicious and nourishing.

Other cuisines also abound with lacto-fermented vegetables and pickles. In Japan vegetables are pickled in a medium of rice bran, and in India pickles are fermented in mustard seed oil. Some traditional lacto-fermented vegetables are made without any salt at all. In Sudan cassia leaves are pounded to a paste, packed in an earthenware jar that is then buried in a cool shady place, and covered with sorghum leaves. The fermentation is mixed by hand every few days for about two weeks, when the pickled paste—called *kawal*—is formed into balls and dried in the sun. In Nepal, brassica leaves are used to make *gundruk*. The leaves are sun-dried until they are yellowish, then crushed and pounded to shreds in a mortar, stamped down tight into a jar lined with banana leaves, and allowed to ferment for ten days. The contents are then sun-dried again before use.

In places that rely on starchy tubers and roots as staples, vegetables are often pounded and fermented before eating. A classic example is the traditional Hawaiian or Polynesian *poi*. Taro root is cooked, pounded to a paste, and then allowed to sour for two to four days before it is eaten. In Nigeria *fufu* is often made from cassava roots that are steeped in water, fermented, mashed, pressed, sun-dried, and then pounded into flour. Yams are also used to make *fufu*; many other parts of West Africa rely on similar preparations.

Consider the differences between these traditional food-preparation techniques and those currently in use. Today's cold cereals are made using a huge and expensive machine called an extruder that forms them into cute shapes but also destroys nutrients in the grain and can even create toxic effects. In one study, rats fed puffed cereal died more quickly than rats fed the cardboard box the cereal came in. But traditional porridges were made using simple and accessible technologies—such as pounding in a large mortar and fermenting in an earthenware crock—that served to greatly increase the nutritive value of the grain. Both are heavily processed, but to very different effect.

Modern food-processing technologies disconnect us from our food source by separating us from the raw ingredients, keeping us ignorant of what actually happens to them, and ensuring that there is as little human contact with the food as possible. Indigenous counterparts had the opposite outcome. They brought people into close contact with the raw ingredients that were the source of their nourishment, and involved intimate knowledge of every stage of the process through hands-on experience. While packaged modern foods require us to be autonomous consumers in the anonymous environment of the supermarket, traditional foods required the people of the village to be active creators of their foods. Partly because processing food is often hard, repetitive work, these tasks were usually done in groups, often with chanting, singing, or lively discussion. Hi Soo Shin Hepinstall points out that even today, "[k]imchi making remains a laborious, communal task shared among relatives, neighbors, and friends."

Traditional food processing often took on the characteristics of a ritual. Author Malidoma Patrice Somé discusses the important role that chant and song often play in the completion of apparently mundane tasks in West African indigenous life:

> Most work done in the village is done collectively. The purpose is not so much the desire to get the job done but to raise enough energy for people to feel nourished by what they do. The nourishment does not come after the job, it comes before the job and during the job. The notion that you should do something so that you get paid so that then you can nourish yourself disappears. You are nourished first, and then the work flows out of your fullness.
>
> Many areas of work among villagers, including farming, are accompanied by music. Music is meant to maintain a certain state of fullness. People recognize that even if you are full before the work, you can't take that fullness for granted. You have to keep feeding it so that the feeling of fullness continues, so that the work you are doing constantly reflects that fullness in you. It is as if the output of work takes a toll on your fullness, even if it is an expression of your fullness, and you have to be filled again before you can continue. Music and

rhythm are the things that feed someone who is producing something.

Somé describes the toll that work takes and the importance of
refilling yourself as you go along—not just physically, but spiritually
and emotionally as well. Our daily labors need to fill our hunger for
connection as well as our bodies. Somé talks about how this impacts
food-processing tasks:

> I remember my mother uttering very moving, poetic
> chants as she milled grain, grinding for six hours to fill
> only a small bucket. The meal that came out of her
> work contained tremendous energy, the spiritual
> energy of poetry and music as well as the physical
> energy contained in the grain. All of her work was a
> work of art, done so genuinely, with total devotion, that
> it contributed to a profound sense of fullness in the
> family.

Modern women may not relish the thought of spending six hours
grinding grain by hand. But I think we should take seriously the possibility that this kind of work can be deeply satisfying and even be a
form of expression for the soul.

The idea begs an important question. Why have cooking and so many
other food-processing tasks been women's work in so many parts of
the world? What makes certain work women's work and other work
men's work? Some people postulate that these definitions grew out of
innate physical or psychological factors such as men's physical strength
and women's nurturing nature. In 1970 anthropological scholar Judith
K. Brown wrote a brief paper called "A Note on the Division of Labor
by Sex" in which she puts forth a theory that makes much more sense.
In traditional, subsistence-based societies, women are most likely to
participate in those activities most compatible with simultaneous child

care responsibilities. Because women bear and breast-feed children, the majority of child care responsibilities usually falls to them. As Brown puts it:

> Nowhere in the world is the rearing of children prima-
> rily the responsibility of men, and in only a few soci-
> eties are women exempted from participations in sub-
> sistence activities. If the economic role of women is to
> be maximized, their responsibilities in childcare must
> be reduced or the economic activity must be such that
> it can be carried out concurrently with childcare.

Brown goes on to outline four characteristics that distinguish economic activities compatible with child care: First, they do not oblige the participant to range very far from home. Second, the tasks are relatively repetitive and do not require rapt concentration. Third, the work is not dangerous and does not unduly endanger the life of the child. And fourth, the work can be performed despite interruptions and is easily resumed afterward.

In Brown's view it is not ultimately skill or ability that is at issue as certain work comes to be considered women's work, but rather a practical question for the society of how to maximize productivity. The kinds of work that would fit these characteristics may vary somewhat from culture to culture depending on their particular needs, but some activities are obviously better matches than others: spinning and weaving, gardening and gathering, making baskets and pottery, drawing water, doing bead work, dyeing cloth, herbal medicine making, sewing, knitting, cleaning, laundering, and many aspects of food preparation. Tasks that clearly don't fit include hunting, mining, metalsmithing, and heavy fieldwork requiring plows and beasts of burden.

Modern cooking shares only some of these characteristics. It does not require ranging far from home, though kitchens can be somewhat dangerous. But much traditional food processing was relatively repetitive and not in the least dangerous. Shelling beans, winnowing grain, pounding roots, grinding spices, churning butter, shucking corn, brewing beer, preserving fruits, plucking chickens: All are perfect examples of activities that fit all the above qualifications—tasks that are now, for the most part, accomplished commercially by modern machines. Consequently, some of the most beautiful rituals of women bonding in various cultures are the descendants of this legacy: four generations of Mexican women making tamales together at Christmastime, while next door an extended family of Polish women are making pierogi for their celebration.

It's no coincidence that women rebelled against cooking and their role in the kitchen in the middle part of the twentieth century. Two major changes were happening simultaneously. First, the extended family and village social structure had given way to the modern suburban model of a nuclear family living in relative isolation. Cooking became a solitary—rather than a collective—activity. This stripped food preparation of one of its primary pleasures: being in community. Second, factory processing of food had become widespread. This had a number of effects. Most obviously, it made home food preparation and processing less necessary—a wife and mother no longer *had* to spend six hours grinding grain. But even more significantly to my mind, canned, frozen, and packaged foods deprived cooking of all the things that make cooking so rewarding: the creativity, the skill and expertise it requires, the intimacy with the gifts of the Earth, the sense of power and fascination that comes with transforming these gifts into something new and wonderful, the sense of history and pride in carrying on a cultural tradition. All of these were important parts of the culinary traditions that women carried on throughout the world, and factory-processed foods stripped the midcentury kitchen of these considerable satisfactions.

In addition, the twentieth century saw an explosive increase in the use of written recipes. Traditionally, most people learned how to cook from their mothers or other members of their village. They learned by watching, participating, and verbal instruction. They learned by singing and chanting. Malidoma Somé translates for us a song that was sung to an ancestral Dagara woman by a being from the spirit world called a *kontomblé*. The song taught the woman—and all subsequent Dagara women—how to make *dan*, the village's millet beer:

For three days and two nights
let the grain soak in water
under firm ground.
I'm saying it
But I'm not saying anything.
On the third day bring the wet grain
into air below the sky
and let it rest
below a blanket of green leaves
for another three days.
I'm saying it
But I'm not saying anything.
Then separate the grains
one from the other, slowly
and let the sun dry them, slowly.
I'm saying it
But I'm not saying anything.
Pound the dry grains
cook the meal for two days
and drain,
take the juice and add
some ferment.
Let it mix and foam.
I'm saying it
But I'm not saying anything.
When the juice is under a white foaming blanket
enjoy the whole of it.
I said it
But I didn't say anything.

Learning to brew *dan* by learning this chant accomplishes many things at once. The crucial information about the process is conveyed in a memorable way, so there is no need to have a cookbook to look up the recipe—important in an oral culture. But the chant also keeps alive the knowledge that *dan* is a gift, because the voice in the chant is the voice of the spirit who gives it. The chant creates a strong sense of tradition and connection to ancestors: The women who chant as they brew are chanting the same ancient words and tune as their foremothers did. The activity takes on greater meaning when we sense an unbroken line of connectedness back through the generations.

Lastly, the kontomblé's recipe is descriptive without being prescriptive. I can imagine a modern American trying to follow it and all the questions that would immediately be raised: What kind of grain? How much water? How do you get it under the ground? What kind of leaves do you use? How thick is a blanket? How slowly is slowly? How finely should the grains be ground? And so on. We are used to written recipes that are extremely precise, and we are used to following them exactly. But until a little over a century ago there were no such things as measuring cups or spoons. Recipes often gave some idea as to measurement, but it was vague at best. The cook had to rely on her own judgment, skill, and, even more important, on her senses. She had to really look at the food, to watch it, to touch it, to smell it, to taste it, even to listen to it. This brought the food processor into greater relationship with her ingredients, and even into greater relationship with her own embodied sensual self.

Bri Maya Tiwari writes about the importance of this aspect of cooking in Ayurveda:

> In the Vedas, the hands and feet are referred to as the "organs of action." By using our organs of action, we engage in the moment-to-moment remembering of the five elements of our nature. Our hands are vital extensions that enable us to touch, and be in touch with, creation. Ayurveda exhorts us to use our body as the ruler and measuring cup for all our needs. . . .
>
> In keeping with this principle, you need to become comfortable using your hands and eyes for all measuring. In Sanskrit, the term *anjali* refers to the volume that can be held by your two hands cupped together. Two *anjalis* of grain or vegetables from your own hands is designed by Nature to fill your own stomach. . . .

Likewise gauge your spices or accents with your own pinch. Like your handful, it is tailored to provide a suitable amount for your own personal body needs. *Angula* refers to the distance between the joints of each finger. This unit of measure is cosmically designed to gauge spices and herbs, such as cinnamon sticks and ginger.

Sadhana means your participation with everything. Use only those tools that are absolutely necessary. As soon as possible, give up using measuring cups, spoons, and useless kitchen paraphernalia. These adjuncts are distracting and interrupt your direct energetic exchange with the food.

Tiwari describes many traditional food-processing activities as being Ayurvedic forms of spiritual practice, or *sadhanas*. Cleaning grain is a *sadhana* to invite resolve. Rhythmic pounding (as Somé's mother probably did) is a *sadhana* to bring harmony among the body, mind, and heart. Rolling *chapatti* dough is a *sadhana* to invite the Earth's energy to the womb. Making *ghee* is a *sadhana* to induce a sattvic mind. Again, this approach meant that these necessary daily activities were not mere drudgery but filling and fulfilling parts of women's daily lives. They were meaningful tasks with spiritual resonances.

If *sadhana* means participation with everything, then recipes—including their measurements—can actually be helpful for people who didn't grow up cooking. If we were never taught basic culinary skills and principles, following the measurements of a recipe can be greatly empowering—enabling us to cook things that we otherwise never would be able to. I tend to look at recipes as maps. If you fly into a new city and need to get around but don't have a map, you are lost. If you stay there a week or two, you may find that you can get certain places without the map. If you live there for a few years, you may find you can get around quite well without a map. It is the same with recipes. They can be critical when we are first learning to cook, or when we are learning a new cuisine that is foreign to us. But the more familiar with food we become, the less we need to rely on them. We may just glance at a recipe again before beginning to cook dinner, the same way we glance at a map to remind us of a route that we are pretty sure we know well enough to navigate by sight.

Unfortunately, in modern America, many of us don't trust our intelligence, experience, or senses well enough to put down the recipe and cook without it. We become obsessed with following the directions, doing everything just right, rather than experimenting, being creative, and trusting our eyes, nose, fingers, taste buds, and intuition as we work with food. Cooking turns into a sort of a laboratory experiment, with strict procedures and parameters, and becomes too inflexible and unwieldy to be practicable on a daily basis. But part of what makes cooking so much fun for me is that I have the basic skills necessary to come home, look in the fridge, and cook something off the top of my head that I will find delicious and nourishing. I certainly read lots of recipes, but I very rarely (if ever) follow one exactly. It takes the creativity away.

I often find myself surprised when I travel to other countries at how comfortable and familiar people can be with culinary tasks that Americans of my generation consider akin to rocket science. Staying with a friend in Berlin, I was startled to find that her roommate, a photographer in his early thirties, had a small grinder that he used to grind grain for his breakfast porridge. It was apparently not at all unusual for a young, urban person to grind his own cereal on a regular basis. No one considered him a strange, hippie type for doing so—it was commonplace. Here, if people eat porridge at all, it is usually the instant kind. Few people make it from scratch, and if you grind it yourself you are definitely someone who has a special interest in cooking.

All too often, modern Americans are like oversized infants when it comes to food. We are used to having it provided for us. We are like baby birds in a nest with our mouths wide open, squawking for more. But we never grow up into the mama bird that goes and hunts and finds food and provides. We never learn how to feed ourselves, because it is so easy and culturally supported *not* to. People who cook on a daily basis and who like to prepare food from scratch are considered either foodies or health nuts. Cooking is not seen as a universal skill of self-sufficiency and adulthood, like driving a car. We are surprised when someone doesn't know how to drive a car, but we are not at all surprised when someone doesn't know how to cook. Large corporations are more than happy to keep us in this state of helplessness. It creates a huge market for factory-processed products and fast food.

By current cultural standards I would certainly be considered both a foodie and a health nut. A few years ago I began to expand my cooking experience into tasks that few Americans do anymore—traditional food-processing tasks. In addition to simple things like soaking grains before cooking them and simmering bones to make mineral-rich broths, I began to experiment with making yogurt, crème fraîche, and fresh cheeses; grinding grain myself and baking sourdough bread; rendering lard and churning butter; decocting herbs to make old-fashioned ales; and lacto-fermenting vegetables to make sauerkraut, kimchi, and pickles.

I began these adventures out of an interest in better nutrition. I became convinced through my reading and research that in order for food to be truly nourishing, it needs to be processed in these traditional ways. While you can certainly buy sauerkraut in jars in the store nowadays, it is heat processed and preserved in vinegar rather than lacto-fermented. This means that it lacks the digestive enzymes, beneficial bacteria, and lactic acid that old-fashioned sauerkraut had. I believe the lack of probiotic foods in today's diet is one of the reasons so many people have digestive disorders, and that culturing food is an important skill to revive.

Along the same vein, the vast majority of modern breads do not follow the traditional process of using sourdough leaven and a long, slow rising period. So I wanted to learn how to bake my own bread. And while you can buy organic whole-grain flour in the grocery store, you never know when it was ground. Once flour is ground, it begins to oxidize and lose nutrients, and if exposed to too much warmth the oils in it can become rancid. So I bought a grain grinder and began grinding my own flour for my bread. (Maybe I should start singing a song while I do it!)

Even commercial yogurt often has additives other than milk and culture and is often made from the milk of confined dairy cattle. Commercial bubbly drinks are full of sweeteners and lacking in enzymes or electrolytes. Store-bought lard is from confined pigs and usually contains preservatives. So I began to process my own foods at home because I can be assured of the quality of the raw ingredients when I buy them directly from farmers I know and trust, and I know that the process is designed to preserve or enhance nutrient density and to prevent toxicity.

I also wanted to reconnect to my food source and my ancestral knowledge by keeping alive these timeless skills. I want to have the adult knowledge necessary to provide for myself—as well as any hungry baby birds I might find in my midst. Besides, it's fun. I get a huge sense of satisfaction from a loaf of bread that turns out well, or a delicious batch of homemade sauerkraut, or a jar of cottage cheese that I made from scratch.

Learning to make these things put me into greater contact with universal processes of degeneration and regeneration, and with the world of microorganisms. Lacto-fermentation is basically a kind of carefully controlled decay. It is an adventure that is simultaneously magical, mysterious, and slightly dangerous. It is a kind of culinary frontier, and it is exciting to cross it. Because microorganisms aren't perceptible to the naked eye, they are rather alien beings, and most Americans growing up in a largely pasteurized, sterilized world are afraid of this unknown realm.

Working with cultures in my kitchen has become a little like having a microbial family, or a microbial farm. On a regular basis I have to take care of these invisible creatures. At least once a week I have to feed my sourdough starter (it eats whole-grain flour and water). Almost daily I need to feed my kefir cultures either milk or sweetened water. My kombucha mother eats tea and sugar and needs to be fed every ten days or so. In addition to being fed, my microbial family has diverse climate preferences. My sauerkraut bacteria are happy at around 70° F, the crème fraîche cultures thrive at around 75° F, and those in soda are most active at around 85° F. Like a kind of microbial rancher, I am tending all these invisible herds of microorganisms almost daily—feeding them, housing them, protecting them from the elements, and then harvesting and eating them. While I don't have acres of fields or pasture to watch over, I do have lots of crocks and jars full of growing things, and I love having this kind of intimate relationship with the natural world.

Once you begin to process foods at home, preparing meals becomes much easier. When you have jars of beef broth in your freezer and a jar of sauerkraut in your fridge, it is easy to make a simple peasant soup using a few seasonal vegetables. Top it off with some of your homemade crème fraîche and a slice of hearty sourdough bread, and you have a fabulous meal. Once processed, foods like sourdough breads, sauerkraut, raw cheese, or old-fashioned ham or salami become wonderful fast foods, requiring little preparation. In discussing the healthy Swiss villagers he studied, Weston Price writes:

> The nutrition of the people of the Loetschental Valley, particularly that of the growing boys and girls, consists largely of a slice of whole rye bread and a piece of the summer-made cheese (about as large as the slice of bread), which are eaten with fresh milk of goats or cows.

When a village has a rhythm of processing foods, then there are foods ready to eat each day. Meals needn't be created from scratch at every mealtime. There is certainly less variety than we are used to, but greater nourishment—and these old-fashioned foods were delicious and satisfying. This is part of why I have been so attracted to them. As another writer points out:

> The fermentation of vegetables (sauerkraut, kimchi, pickles), grains (sourdough bread, kvass, kiesiel, kisra, koji), beans (miso, natto, tempeh) and fish are experi-

encing renewed interest. . . . As the world's fastest and best quality foods, these are always ready to be consumed, cold or warmed. . . . The truth is, simple folks toiled in the fields long hours, had to be in good health and had little time for preparing moveable-feast style lunches to be quickly consumed in the furrows. These foods often had to stand all morning long in the heat of harvest without the benefit of refrigeration. . . . Sourdough breads, pickled olives, herrings and anchovies, lacto-fermented vegetables and beans and sometimes yoghurt and cheese were the everyday fare. . . . A properly elaborated sourdough loaf acquires an unsurpassed taste and an aroma that no cracker or porridge can ever match. *Sauerkraut* achieves a succulent gourmet savor that cole-slaw never reaches. If you taste Normandy country farm butter, churned from aged fermented sour cream, you will never again eat creamery butter.

Traditionally processed foods were nutrient-dense, easily digested and assimilated, naturally preserved without refrigeration, and full of wonderful flavor. They were healthy and delicious fast foods for hard-working people. They expressed the cultural identity, *terroir*, and collaborative spirit of a particular people living in a particular place on Earth. And they were made with love by human hands.

On the Snow Moon, may we keep in our hearts a vision of a group of villagers laboring together, singing a song while they keep their hands moving. May we feel inspired to experiment in our cooking—to try something new and to use all six of our senses to guide us through the process. May we feel the sense of freedom and power that comes from being able to provide for ourselves. May we find the time to put up a batch of sauerkraut, bake a loaf of bread, or culture some yogurt. And may we welcome the coming winter, knowing that even if the ground is covered with snow or ice, we will be well fed in all ways.

SNOW MOON RECIPES

Sauerkraut and Rot Kohl

Making sauerkraut is an artisanal process—it is both extremely easy and endlessly subtle. Just sprinkling salt on cabbage and crushing it will begin to release juices and culture the cabbage. You can make cultured cabbage that is just a few days old, or sauerkraut that has been culturing for six weeks, and all of it will taste delicious— although its flavor will change dramatically over time. My favorite sauerkraut to make is rot kohl—substituting red cabbage for green yields a beautiful dark red kraut.

Quick Kraut
Makes about 3 cups

4 cups (tightly packed) shredded
   cabbage

1 tablespoon sea salt

1 teaspoon caraway seeds

1. Put the cabbage in a bowl and sprinkle the salt over it. Using your hands, begin to squeeze and massage the cabbage to release the juices.
2. Once it is thoroughly wet, add the caraway seeds.
3. Pack the cabbage into a 1-quart, widemouthed mason jar, pressing down with your hand to release the juices.
4. Fill a 1-pint, narrow jar (or any jar that has a bottom narrow enough to fit in the mouth of the 1-quart jar) with water and screw the lid on. Place this second jar into the mouth of the 1-quart jar and push on it until the liquid from the cabbage rises above the vegetable matter inside.
5. Set this on the counter, with one jar nestled inside the other, and drape a cloth napkin over the top. Keep at room temperature for about a week, pressing down on the weight jar at least once a day and making sure that the liquid stays above the vegetable matter.
6. After a week of fermenting, taste and see if you like it. At this point you can remove the weight jar, screw a lid onto the kraut jar, and transfer it to the refrigerator. You can also experiment with fermenting it for longer as long as you keep a close eye on the liquid level. If too much water has evaporated, mix ½ teaspoon of salt with ⅓ cup filtered water and pour this into the jar.

Slow Kraut
Makes 6–8 quarts

This is how I usually make my kraut. For best results, get a special sauerkraut crock made by the German company Harsch. It comes with a weight to keep the kraut under the brine, and is designed with a water seal lip that lets gases escape but no air in. Mine is a 10-liter size, and these instructions are for that size. You can adapt these amounts to a crock of any size, or use a bucket with any kind of makeshift weight.

15 pounds cabbage, green or red, shredded

½ cup salt, or more to taste

1–2 tablespoons caraway seeds or juniper seeds that have been gently crushed

1. In batches, follow the same procedure as for the Quick Kraut: Put the cabbage in a bowl and sprinkle the salt over it. Using your hands, begin to squeeze and massage the cabbage to release the juices. Once it is wet, sprinkle some of the caraway seeds over it and transfer to the Harsch crock.
2. As you add each layer of cabbage to the crock, gently and rhythmically pound it—using a pestle, a meat tenderizer, a clean hammer, or anything else you can lower into the crock—to break down the cellulose of the cabbage. Repeat with all the cabbage until the crock is fairly full.
3. Lay the weights on top of the kraut and make sure the brine comes above the weights by an inch or so. If not, add enough salty water (1 tablespoon salt to each cup of filtered water) to bring the brine above the weights.
4. Put the lid on and fill the water rim with water.
6. Let it ferment at room temperature for 10 days, and do not lift lid during this time. After this you can check on the kraut, but allow it to ferment for up to 5 more weeks. Then remove the weights, transfer the kraut to mason jars, and store in the fridge.

Quick and Simple Kimchi
Makes about 1 quart

This is an easy starter version of kimchi, but it is delicious. After it is fermented, I make a quick meal by serving it in a bowl topped with soba noodles drizzled with toasted sesame oil, and a well-seasoned beef or chicken broth (such as the one I use for Asian Egg Drop Soup, page 67). You can add some cooked meat or just a sprinkling of scallions for an easy lunch or dinner.

1 head napa cabbage

1 daikon radish

1 black Spanish radish (these are common in local farmer's markets—if you can't find it, just leave it out or replace with another kind of radish)

1 turnip

2 carrots

2 tablespoons sea salt

Filtered water

1 4-inch piece ginger, peeled

3 cloves garlic

1 bunch scallions

1 Thai bird red pepper (Optional. This makes the kimchi quite spicy—you can add 2 if you like it very spicy. You could also just use a pinch of cayenne to add some spice, but not too much.)

1. Rinse the cabbage and cut into ½-inch strips (not the tough core). Cut the radishes, turnip, and carrot in half and then slice thinly on the diagonal. Mix the vegetables together in a bowl and sprinkle generously with sea salt. Cover with filtered water, cover with a towel, and let sit for 3 hours.

2. Meanwhile coarsely chop the garlic, ginger, and scallions. Remove the stem and seeds from the pepper and cut the skin into a few pieces. Put these ingredients into a mortar and pestle (what I use) or a food processor and mash into a paste.

3. Drain the soaking liquid off the cabbage mixture and reserve.

4. Mix the ginger paste in with the cabbage mixture and pack into a mason jar. Press the mixture down repeatedly with your fist until liquid begins to rise up. Then add enough of the soaking water into the jar so that all the vegetables are covered with liquid.

5. Now gently weigh down the top of the mixture, with a smaller jar filled with water as for the Quick Kraut above, so that the liquid rises above the solids. This pushes the vegetables down but allows the liquid to come up over the top.

6. Place the jar with the weight inside on a counter and drape a cloth napkin or tea towel over it.

7. Ferment at room temperature for 1 week, checking daily to make sure the vegetables are submerged in the brine. (If you find that you need more brine, dissolve 1 teaspoon sea salt in ⅓ cup water and pour enough liquid into the jar so that the brine coveres the vegetables.)

8. Remove the plastic lid and weight, screw the top on the jar, and transfer it to the fridge. This will last for several months.

Lacto-fermented Raita
Makes 3–4 cups

This is a very probiotic and digestible version of the classic Indian sauce or salad. Serve with any Indian meal.

3 Armenian cucumbers, peeled and diced, or 3 regular cucumbers, peeled, seeded, and diced

Zest and juice of 1 lemon

2 tablespoons minced scallions

4 teaspoons sea salt

1 teaspoon cumin seeds, toasted in a small cast-iron pan over medium heat until fragrant

1 quart yogurt

5 sprigs mint (about 30 leaves), minced

1. In a bowl, combine the cucumber, mint, lemon zest, lemon juice, scallions, salt, and cumin seeds. Mix thoroughly.
2. Transfer to a 1-quart mason jar. It is a good idea to gently weigh down the top of the mixture so that the liquid rises above the solids. I do this by filling a small, narrow jar with water and setting it inside the other jar. This pushes the vegetables down but allows the liquid to come up over the top.
3. Let sit at room temperature for 24 to 48 hours, depending on how hot it is (24 hours is sufficient if it is hot, 48 hours if it is not). Then transfer to the fridge until ready to assemble.
4. Meanwhile, pour the yogurt into a strainer lined with a couple of layers of cheesecloth and set above a bowl or pot. Allow it to drip at least 12 hours in the fridge until it is thick. You can transfer the yogurt cream to a jar (and keep the whey for future recipes) until ready to assemble.
5. In a bowl, combine the cucumber mixture with the yogurt cream. Add the fresh minced mint and serve.

Lacto-fermented Tabbouleh
Serves 4 as a side dish

Tabbouleh lends itself well to lacto-fermentation. This makes the tabbouleh probiotic and easy to digest. Armenian cucumbers are sold at our farmer's market. Long and curved, they have dense flesh and only a few small seeds. You can substitute a large regular cucumber, seeded. This is a great dish to bring to a picnic or potluck.

1 long Armenian cucumber, peeled, or
  1 large cucumber, peeled and seeded

6 small Early Girl tomatoes

1–2 cloves garlic, minced

½ teaspoon cumin seeds

3 tablespoons yogurt whey
  (page 313)

1 tablespoon salt

2 tablespoons minced red onion
  or scallions

Zest and juice of 1 lemon

1 cup bulgur wheat

1 bunch flat-leafed parsley, minced

1 tablespoon olive oil

1. Cut the cucumber and the tomatoes into a small dice and put in a bowl.
2. Add the minced garlic and the cumin seeds (you can toast the seeds for a few minutes in a cast-iron skillet to make them more fragrant).
3. Add 2 tablespoons of the whey, the salt, the onion, and the lemon zest and juice to the mixture. Stir thoroughly and transfer to a jar. It is a good idea to gently weigh down the top of the mixture so that the liquid rises above the solids. I do this by filling a small, narrow jar with water and setting that inside the other jar. This pushes the vegetables down but allows the liquid to come up over the top.
4. Let sit at room temperature for 24 hours.
5. Meanwhile, soak the bulgur wheat in a cup of filtered water plus the remaining tablespoon of whey. Place in a warm place for 8 to 24 hours.
6. Transfer the bulgur to a pan. Add a fresh ½ cup of filtered water, cover, and bring to a boil. Then turn off the heat and let the mixture steam and finish cooking, covered, for 15 minutes.
7. Strain the brine off the lacto-fermented cucumber-tomato mixture, reserving the brine. (Drink a little shot of it. It should be delicious—and very good for you!)
8. Combine the cucumber-tomato mixture with the minced parsley and olive oil in a bowl.
9. Strain off any liquid remaining on the bulgur and allow to cool to room temperature. Add the bulgur to the bowl and mix thoroughly. Add back as much of the brine as you would like to the tabbouleh.

Lacto-fermented Corn Relish
Makes 1 quart

This is my version of the southern corn relish. The only sweetness in this one is from the corn.

7 ears corn

4 small pimiento red peppers, diced— or substitute 1 large red pepper, or 2 red gipsy peppers

1 teaspoon celery seeds

1 teaspoon mustard seeds

½ white onion, minced

Sea salt

2 heads cabbage

1. Using a sharp knife, cut the kernels off the corn and into a wide-bottomed bowl or casserole dish.
2. Mix the pimientos, celery seeds, mustard seeds, and onion into the corn. Salt to taste.
3. Pull any wilted leaves off the outside of the cabbage and shred it using a sharp knife or food processor. In a large bowl, sprinkle salt generously over the cabbage and begin to massage it with strong hands. This will begin to release the liquid from the leaves. You can also pound it gently using a pestle or wooden meat pounder. If the cabbage is not releasing its liquid, then sprinkle more salt on it. Once it is wet, taste a pinch. It should taste salty but not offensively so.
4. In a 2-quart mason jar, layer about an inch of cabbage followed by some of the corn mixture. Repeat using all of the cabbage and corn mixture and finishing with a layer of cabbage on top.
5. Now weigh down the cabbage. Find a narrow-bottomed jar that fits into the hole at the top of the jar. Fill this smaller jar with water, screw the lid on, and place it in the 2-quart mason jar so that it is pushing the relish down, and the liquid from the relish rises up above the vegetable matter. Then set it on the counter with a cloth over the whole thing.
6. Check the relish daily to make sure the liquid is still above the vegetable matter. (If not, dissolve 1 teaspoon of salt in ⅓ cup of filtered water and pour as much of it into the jar as necessary to raise the brine up above the lid.)
7. After about 10 days at room temperature, remove the weighing jar and the plastic lid, screw the regular lid onto the mason jar, and transfer this to the fridge. Enjoy throughout the winter.

Lacto-fermented Peach Chutney
Makes 1 quart

You can also use this recipe to make Tomato Chutney by simple substituting tomatoes for the peaches. You should use a firm tomato variety such as Early Girl, and you do not need to peel the tomatoes.

2 teaspoons fenugreek seeds

¼ cup boiling filtered water

8–10 peaches

1 lemon, juiced

1 tablespoon whole cumin seeds

2 teaspoons black or brown mustard seeds

1 teaspoon fennel seeds

1 4-inch piece of ginger, peeled

1 teaspoon powdered turmeric or one 1-inch piece fresh turmeric, peeled

1 tablespoon Sucanat or Rapadura

¼ cup yogurt whey (page 313)

4 teaspoons sea salt (1 tablespoon plus 1 teaspoon)

¼ teaspoon cayenne (optional)

1. Put the fenugreek seeds in a small bowl and pour the boiling water over them. Let them soak overnight or for at least 6 hours.
2. Peel the peaches and cut into a small dice. Put the peach pieces into a large bowl. Drain the water off the fenugreek seeds and add them to the peaches.
3. Squeeze the juice of the lemon over the peaches.
4. In a small cast-iron skillet, toast the cumin, mustard, and fennel over medium heat until they begin to smell fragrant. Add the seeds to the peaches.
5. Grate or mince the ginger and add to the peaches.
6. If you're using powdered turmeric, add it to the peaches. If you're using fresh, grate or mince as you did with the ginger.
7. Sprinkle the Sucanat and the yogurt whey over the peaches.
8. Sprinkle the salt over the peaches, and the ¼ teaspoon cayenne. Stir thoroughly and taste. The mixture should be salty but delicious.
9. Transfer to a 2-quart jar. It is a good idea to gently weigh down the top of the chutney so that the liquid rises above the solids. Fill a small, narrow jar with water and set it inside the other jar so that it gently pushes the chutney down but allows the liquid to come up over the top.
10. Ferment at room temperature at least overnight. If it is hot, 24 hours may be enough. If it is cool or just warm, allow to ferment for about 48 hours.
11. Eat right away, or transfer to the fridge and eat within 1 month.

12

MOON OF LONG NIGHTS

I've extinguished the flame:
  There's no more smoke from the lamp.
Only the moon's left:
  There's nothing else.

—From a song by Kabir, translated from the Hindi

The Moon of Long Nights arrives in late autumn as the days grow shorter and the winter solstice approaches. In some parts of the world nights are so long that dawn and dusk occur almost at the same time. It is eerie to contemplate such sunless days, and yet they are an annual reality for many northern dwellers. Even those people living at moderately northern latitudes experience the shortness of the day and the length of the night at this time of year. It is a time of darkness.

Western post-industrial society is not very comfortable with darkness. To the modern Western mind, darkness is a symbol of ignorance, death, danger, depression, and even evil—not a very positive set of connotations. It is no wonder that we have developed so many technologies that dispel it. But the lightbulb is a very recent invention. For the vast majority of human history there was no electricity, and light came from just a few sources: the sun, the moon, the stars, and fire.

Today electric lights are so ubiquitous that cities and suburbs suffer a constant level of light pollution; urban dwellers are shocked at all the stars they can see when they get far enough away from civilization.

Where I live, many people have installed motion-sensitive floodlights in front of their houses, even though our neighborhood is relatively quiet, peaceful, and suburban. When my partner and I walk the dog along the sidewalks at night, we are assaulted by these glaring lights, one after the other. We are a culture that is scared of the dark.

Malidoma Somé describes the very different approach of the West African Dagara people to darkness and the nighttime:

> Among the Dagara, darkness is sacred. It is forbidden to illuminate it, for light scares the Spirit away. Our night is the day of the Spirit and of the ancestors, who come to us to tell us what lies on our life paths. To have light around you is like saying that you would rather ignore this wonderful opportunity to be shown the way. To the Dagara, such an attitude is inconceivable. The one exception is a bonfire. Though they emit a powerful glow, they are not prohibited because there is always drumming around them, and the beat of the drum cancels out the light.
>
> Villagers are expected to learn how to function in the dark. I was given light because I had lost the ability to deal with darkness, and each time people saw the timid light of the shea-oil lamp in my room, they would walk away from it as if it signaled the presence of someone playing with the elements of the cosmos.

What a different perspective! The fact that we very rarely, if ever, experience true darkness in modern America must certainly have a profound psychic effect on our lives. Some scientists believe that it has a strong biological effect as well.

In *Lights Out: Sleep, Sugar, and Survival*, anthropologist T. S. Wiley puts forward a provocative hypothesis. She believes that the rise of degenerative diseases in industrialized countries (especially diabetes, heart disease, cancer, and obesity) can be traced to the invention and wide-spread use of electricity. Her reasoning is that the use of electric lighting, televisions, and computers after the sun goes down (and our consequent ability to stay up later and sleep less) serves to keep our bodies in an artificial state of perpetual summer. This disrupts our natural hormonal functioning and deprives us of a period of semi-hibernation that our pre-agrarian and even many of our agrarian ancestors would have enjoyed: a winter season of long nights and lots of extra sleep.

Wiley believes that this is the cause of our cravings for sugars and carbohydrates. Our ice age hunter-gatherer ancestors would have had, for the most part, access to sugars and carbohydrates during the summer only, and would have lived on proteins and fats throughout the winter. Wiley claims that we crave sugar because our bodies think it is summer all the time, and our bodies have evolved to use carbohy-drates to store up energy for the long, sugarless winter—a winter that never really comes in our modern, electrically lit world.

Wiley discusses the many implications she believes our perpetual summer has on our health. One of them relates in an interesting way to the Dagara injunction against illuminating the darkness and their belief that the night is the time of the Spirit. Wiley describes research showing that when you sleep for fourteen hours a night, as our ances-tors would have done during long winter nights, nine of those four-teen hours consist of sleep as we know it. In the middle of such a long night of sleep, our bodies secrete a hormone called prolactin that puts us into a state that is a kind of quiescent wakefulness. Wiley points out that during this state, "[t]he brain-wave readings were akin to those observed during transcendental meditation." According to Wiley, our bodies release higher levels of endorphins during this state:

> It is statistically proven that ninety or so percent of all babies are born between midnight and 4:00 A.M., the exact time their mothers would, in nature, be in a medi-tative state with high endorphin (painkiller) levels, just like yogis who are able to walk over beds of nails and hot coals without any effect. In this state, an unmedicated

birth would be far more tolerable. It was in this period of time, which we no longer have access to, that we solved problems, reproduced, and transcended the stress, and, most likely, talked to the gods.

So following Wiley, by depriving ourselves of long nights of winter sleep, we are depriving ourselves of a state of meditative healing and spiritual communion, a time when we have access to messages from a higher consciousness. By getting less than a full nine hours of sleep on a regular basis, we are depriving ourselves of the minimal amount of rest our bodies need so that our immune systems can function properly, our blood pressure can regulate itself, we can recover from stressors, our diet is not dictated by cravings, and we don't get depressed. It all has to do with hormones.

Some aspects of Wiley's book don't hold together for me, but I do find nuggets of truth in her argument. I have long regretted that just at the time of year when our bodies and souls want rest, sleep, dreamtime, hibernation, and a turning inward and homeward, we find ourselves in the midst of the holiday season. We are encouraged to be at our busiest: to get out there and shop till we drop, attend office holiday parties, make travel plans, pack up and get on planes, trains, and buses to go to lively celebrations with friends and families. No wonder so many of us get depressed and overwhelmed around the holidays: Our biology says, *Curl up in the back of the cave and gnaw on a buffalo bone, then sleep for fourteen hours*, while our society says, *Run around shopping in brightly lit stores and then stay out late at a party drinking champagne, eating truffles, and being sociable with your coworkers.*

Christmas has become secular and commodified, but this was not always the case. In the traditional Christian calendar, the Moon of Long Nights corresponded to the period of Advent, which means "coming." Advent was a time of penitence, abstinence, and prayer. For those of the Christian faith, the period of long nights is about the expectation of a miracle: the coming of the light. It is not an accident that Christ's Mass—the celebration of the birth of the Son of God—corresponds to the winter solstice—the rebirth of the Sun.

These days an appreciation of the season's darkness and hope is lost in the rush of holiday plans, of shopping and purchasing, of making a list and checking it twice. It is not part of our cultural consciousness to let ourselves be in the dark, to meditate upon that darkness, to listen, to pray. Instead we rush headlong into the light. Many of us zoom past the solstice in a rush of last-minute to-dos, and arrive exhausted on Christmas morning, glad to have survived the ordeal once again.

We have little use for parts of the traditional Christian liturgical calendar such as Lent and Advent that were once so important. There's no money to be made on people fasting and praying and exercising self-restraint. And so we usually skip to the celebration that comes after, and forgo the experience of darkness and renewal.

But Advent is my favorite part of Christmas. A couple of years ago I began keeping an Advent wreath, which holds four candles and sits on your dining room table. The first Sunday in Advent you light one of the candles and pray a special prayer before dinner. The second Sunday you light the first candle plus a second one, and pray again before dinner. You continue this progression through the third and into the fourth Sunday, when you finally have all four candles burning for dinner. It's a simple, lovely ceremony. To me, the Advent ritual symbolizes faith that light comes into the dark places of life. It is not about running away from the darkness, but about deepening our belief that the light will come.

It is no surprise that a culture like ours—which prizes youth and productivity, rationalism and accomplishment, and which generally denies death, magic, mystery, and the irrational—would try to hold on to perpetual long days and skip over the long nights altogether, or fill them up with lots of lights and parties. But ignoring the natural pulse of things must have a real effect on our lives. That cycles of light and dark affect hormone production seems only natural. Scientists have been making the connection between circadian rhythms, melatonin production, and sleep patterns for years now. Is it really so far-fetched that electrical lighting could be having a profound effect on our health, our weight, our psyches, and our diet?

Like many Americans, I find it difficult to rest. I am much more comfortable doing something active than I am with stopping, slowing down, and letting go. Last year—around the Moon of Long Nights— I stopped drinking coffee. I know that coffee is bad for me. It gets me wired and antsy and neurotic. And yet, I love it. I love the smell and the taste of it, and I love the stimulating and focusing effect it has on my mind. Our national addiction to coffee has its reasons. It makes us feel productive and powerful, and gives us the illusion that we can survive without rest, sleep, and the quiescent wakefulness of the deep dark of the night.

Almost immediately after I gave up coffee, I had a dramatic recurrence of eczema. The old rash once again began spreading over my body, and I once again had to see an herbalist. Dr. Tom Cowan classifies eczema, allergies, and asthma as diseases of adrenal insufficiency. Because all of them respond so dramatically to cortisone medications and their derivatives, he believes that they are the result of a weak adrenal cortex. He points out: "The adrenal gland is the processor of stress in our bodies. It is there to help us adapt. When we become exhausted by life, on a mental or physical level, our adrenal glands often fail to keep up, and illness ensues." According to my Chinese acupuncturist, my eczema is a result of *"yin* deficiency." According to an Ayurvedic practitioner, my "Pitta is deranged." All of these diagnoses are just variations on a theme: I need to slow down and cool down, I need rest and recovery, I need the healing energy of the moon and of the deep dark of the night. I think many of us in this driven, industrial, electrically lit world do.

Popular author Leonard Shlain puts forth another theory about the connections among darkness, light, diet, and evolution. In his book *Sex, Time and Power*, Shlain begins with the question of why women menstruate. He points out that there is really no good biological reason that human women should bleed so much each month. Some other primates have a slight menstrual cycle, but so scant as to be negligible. Almost every animal besides humans has a pronounced and obvious period of estrus, or ovulation, when mating occurs. But the human ovulation period is so hidden that most women don't even know when it occurs. Why is it that when we are emphatically *not* ovulating, something dramatic and visible happens to us?

The question takes on even more gravity for Shlain when he considers that menstrual cycles put women on the verge of iron deficiency and anemia. If you take a moment and ponder why women evolved to bleed so heavily every month, and are unable to come up with one good reason, you're not alone. It's a mystery to the evolutionary biologists, too.

Shlain posits that *women evolved to menstruate in order to give human beings a sense of time*. He argues that our understanding of past, present, and future is a unique human consciousness that was sparked by women's menses, and by the fact that our menstrual cycles so closely mirror the phases of the moon. We are, evidently, the only primates whose menstrual cycle averages the same length as the moon cycle.

Shlain further postulates that humans evolved from herbivorous primates into omnivorous hunters to satisfy women's need for a reliable and easily assimilated form of iron in the diet—an evolutionary adaptation that allowed us to survive the ice age. He argues that men began hunting to provide women with the meat they needed to maintain health and strength. This premise leads to a whole bevy of other theories. He has an evolutionary explanation for left-handedness, homosexuality, color-blindness, baldness, language, marriage, female orgasm, misogyny, patriarchy, art, religion, and even love!

While some of Shlain's theories seem a bit far-fetched, at least one point fits in with some of my own experiences and musings. When I decided, reluctantly, to begin eating meat again after ten years of vegetarianism, I began to regain my energy and strength. As I did so, I remember having a kind of shorthand understanding for the reason that meat eating was making me well again: "Blood out; blood in." I began to observe that while some men and postmenopausal women could remain healthy on a vegetarian diet, many young women could not. I became a vegetarian just at the time of life when my body was developing from a girl's into a woman's—before I had even menstruated for the first time—which might explain why I had so many health problems during my ten years of vegetarianism.

Shlain points out that when women are asked to draw a representation of time, they most often draw a circle. Men, asked the same question, usually draw an arrow. He argues that women's menses and their connection to the moon make them more accepting of death, and more attuned to the cycles of life. Shlain cites research to show that women risk death more readily than their male counterparts, and are generally less frightened of dying.

Shlain's hypothesis and Wiley's overlap a bit. The light pollution that Wiley writes about not only affects our sleep cycles, but seems to be having an effect on the synchronicity between women's reproductive cycles and lunar cycles as well. Before the advent of electric lighting, women typically menstruated with the moon. They often bled at the new moon and ovulated at the full, and this synchronicity is why Shlain believes menstruation was the vehicle for human understanding of time. Babies were most often conceived on the full moon and born on the full, exactly nine lunar months after conception. (The average length of a human pregnancy is 265.80 days, and nine lunar months equal 265.77 days.) Women's hormones seem to respond to even the subtle cyclical changes in the light of the moon.

In her book *The Garden of Fertility*, Katie Singer discusses some of the recent experiments relating menstrual cycles to lunar cycles:

> In the late 1960s, writer Louise Lacey realized that being on the Pill took her body away from its natural rhythm. She went off it and subsequently had very irregular cycles. She began reading about circadian rhythm as well as the sexual cycles of some primates, which suggested peaks of sexual activity relating to the lunar cycle. Lacey

wondered if the moon's cycles relate to human reproduction and, if so, how? She wondered if artificial lights
interrupt the moon's effect.

She found that sleeping in complete darkness except
for three nights each cycle . . . triggered ovulation. She
called the technique Lunaception and found that it could
be used to direct her fertility—and that of her women
friends. By avoiding intercourse on the days they slept
with light, Louise Lacey and twenty-seven of her friends
developed regular, healthy menstrual cycles and used
Lunaception to avoid pregnancy effectively until
menopause.

As fertility problems rise, even such anecdotal information can provide clues as to what aspects of our environment may be impacting
our health. If light stimulates chickens to lay eggs, why not humans to
ovulate? Cycles of light and darkness do seem to have profound effects
on hormonal patterns. In addition to promoting a nutrient-dense traditional diet for healthy fertility, Singer suggests eliminating light pollution from the room where you sleep—with the optional exception of
low-level lighting during the time you should be ovulating. She has
seen women reestablish healthy reproductive cycles through this combination of approaches.

All these theories reinforce my sense that much of human physiology
and evolution remains shrouded in mystery. They also make me see
how much food is interconnected with everything else in the web of
life—planetary cycles, sexuality, consciousness, health, biology, and
the environment. We don't eat—or do anything else—in a vacuum. It
is a cliché but it's true: Everything is connected.

So we have to be very careful about looking to food as the sole
cause—and cure—of our modern diseases. I believe that Weston
Price's work shows what a huge impact nutrition can have on quality
of life. But we cannot look at food in isolation, and nutritious food is

not the only foundation of a thriving society. Because the dominant culture seems so clueless as to the importance of nutrient density in growing healthy and well-adjusted individuals, it is easy to become single-minded in our conviction that food is a critical part of what is wrong with today's society. Within the native nutrition movement, heart disease, diabetes, obesity, infertility, and cancer are not the only conditions attributed to poor diet. Alcoholism, violence, and the general breakdown of the social fabric are often also blamed on nutritional deficiencies. But these problems are complex and involve a matrix of different factors.

Most of us know that increasing numbers of American children are being diagnosed with learning disabilities such as autism, Asperger's syndrome, ADD, ADHD, Down syndrome, and dyslexia, but few people in the mainstream consider that there may be a connection between these diagnoses and the degradation of our food supply. People in the native nutrition movement make the important point that food can have a powerful impact on brain development. But the prevalence of these diagnoses raises a bevy of complex and important questions about the way we understand intelligence, normalcy, and disease in this culture. We risk losing the richness of those conversations when we think we have the answer, and the answer is food.

I have a friend who has worked for years as a learning specialist for children diagnosed with learning disabilities, and who is now working to educate parents about the importance of good nutrition and nutrient density. When I mentioned to her that I have a nephew with Asperger's syndrome, she nodded and said that she had a number of students with that diagnosis. I caught the subtle but important difference in her language—I said that he *has Asperger's,* she talked of students who *have that diagnosis.* In other words, these diagnoses are just that—modern science's attempts to categorize something that may be, ultimately, highly complex and subjective. I learned something from her in that exchange. Ironically, since that conversation, doctors are reconsidering whether Asperger's is the right diagnosis for my nephew—he doesn't quite fit the usual parameters of that category.

Some in the native nutrition movement even view the increased visibility of sexual minorities in our culture as a social ill that could be corrected or prevented by proper nutrition. Gay, lesbian, transgendered, intersexual, and other people who don't fit our society's images of normalcy are seen by some as the unfortunate victims of nutritional depletion. But sexual minorities and same-sex behavior have been a part of life in communities throughout the world and throughout history. This attempt to classify what is so obviously a part of human nature as an illness not only rings false, but is a dangerous notion to propagate. The idea of human perfection and normalcy has historically been used to sinister purposes, and we need to be careful how we handle it.

Modern Western thinking has a tendency to respond to difference in one of two ways: We either deny the existence of the difference, thereby negating it, or we pathologize it. By this I mean that when we don't understand something, or when it doesn't fit into our predetermined categories, our culture often labels this thing as a *problem* that has a *scientific, material basis* and *needs to be solved*. We want to try to fix things—even things that another culture would not consider broken. There is a saying that circulates in twelve-step and self-help circles: "Life is not a problem to be solved but a mystery to be lived." Modern Americans need to repeat this to one another because it goes so much against the grain of our culture.

The book *The Spirit Catches You and You Fall Down* by Anne Fadiman is a powerful exploration of the difference between approaching life as a problem to be solved versus a mystery to be lived. In it, Fadiman tells the story of a young Hmong girl born to a recently arrived refugee family. The girl—named Lia—has seizures, and is diagnosed with epilepsy. Fadiman explores the huge chasm between the way that modern American doctors viewed and responded to Lia's seizures and the way that Lia's parents and Hmong culture did. The inability of the two sides to see each other's perspective had tragic consequences. The title of the book comes from the phrase that Hmong people use to describe what we call an epileptic seizure: "the Spirit catches you, and you fall down." This experience was not uncommon in the highlands of

Laos where the Hmong came from, and it was approached with ambivalence. It was seen as an illness, but what that meant for the role of an epileptic in the culture may seem alien to us. As Fadiman explains:

> Hmong epileptics often become shamans. Their seizures are thought to be evidence that they have the power to perceive things other people cannot see, as well as facilitating their entry into trances, a prerequisite for their journeys into the realm of the unseen. The fact that they have been ill themselves gives them an intuitive sympathy for the suffering of others and lends them emotional credibility as healers. Becoming a *txiv neeb* (shaman) is not a choice; it is a vocation. The calling is revealed when a person falls sick, either with *qaug dab peg* [the spirit catches you and you fall down] or with some other illness whose symptoms similarly include shivering and pain. An established *txiv neeb*, summoned to diagnose the problem, may conclude from these symptoms that the person (who is usually but not always male) has been chosen to be the host of a healing spirit, a *neeb*. (*Txiv neeb* means "person with a healing spirit.") It is an offer that the sick person cannot refuse, since if he rejects his vocation, he will die. In any case, few Hmong would choose to decline. Although shamanism is an arduous calling that requires years of training with a master in order to learn the ritual techniques and chants, it confers an enormous amount of social status in the community and publicly marks the *txiv neeb* as a person of high moral character, since a healing spirit would never choose a no-account host. Even if an epileptic turns out not to be elected to host a *neeb*, his illness, with its thrilling aura of the supramundane, singles him out as a person of consequence.

The traditions of shamanism among indigenous cultures help them live the mystery even as they seek to solve problems. Shamans always have an important role not just as healers, but as those who commune with the spirit world. As such there is often something about them that is wounded, or mysterious, or both.

When we resist the temptation to pathologize difference, we are able to look at it through mythological and metaphorical lenses. While in the past few centuries Western culture has viewed sexual minorities as sick, more mythologically literate cultures often saw in sexual difference a touch of the Divine. As Leonard Shlain writes:

> Mythology is a projection of a community's collective beliefs onto the scrim of the cosmos. Therefore, it should come as no surprise that mythical characters who fully manifested both their *anima* [feminine spirit] and *animus* [male spirit] were considered the wisest seers and most powerful deities in ancient cultures. Originating in the myth of the union of Isis and Osiris in Egypt, hermaphroditic sagacity has remained a constant thread connecting many civilizations throughout the ancient world. . . .
>
> Hermes, the Greek god of magic, transformation, and wisdom, was an androgynous god who combined both the essence of the female and the virility of the male. Appropriately, Hermes was the god of the hermaphrodites (Hermes and Aphrodite were the parents of Hermaphroditus, who combined an equal mixture of masculine and feminine in one body). . . .
>
> Among Hindus, Lord Shiva is an androgynous god who is both the creator and destroyer of worlds. His feminine aspect is Durga. Many of the paintings depicting this hermaphroditic deity portray Shiva on the right side and Durga on the left. The Hindu caste system has a special class, called *hidjra*, for homosexuals, transvestites, and intersexes. In Mesopotamia, cultic dancers dressed in costumes to emphasize the hermaphroditic nature of their deities. The right side of their costume signified the male, and the left side represented the

female aspect. The ancient culture of Oman recognized a third sex they called the "zaniths."

Farther east, originating in the same distant era, people began to worship a hermaphroditic deity in China. Quan Yin, born a man but transformed into a woman, is the god/goddess of wisdom and compassion.

In North America many Pueblo Indians—for example, the Zuni and the Hopi—had a special reverence for a man who manifested a strong *anima*. White settlers disparagingly called a man who lived and dressed like a woman a "berdache." The other members of his native tribe often believed a transvestite or gay male possessed magical and intercessionary powers. Often he was the tribe's shaman.

It's not that sexual minorities weren't seen as being different, it's just that the difference was not always pathologized. In some cultures that otherness was seen as a gift, a blessing, a vocation into deeper relationship with the spirit world.

In the fifteenth century, peasant revolt leader Joan of Arc was tried for heresy, and part of the evidence cited against her was her refusal to stop wearing men's clothes and put on women's. She agreed to do so, but after her trial she resumed wearing men's clothes, and was consequently executed for her "relapse into sin." Eventually the Catholic Church canonized her. She was made a saint because she had stayed true to God's calling, even unto death. This story shows our profound ambivalence toward differences that challenge our assumptions about sex and gender.

The work of Temple Grandin, author of *Thinking in Pictures* and *Animals in Translation*, further challenges our notions of pathology. Grandin is autistic, and her autism has given her a special ability to relate to animals. She calls autism a kind of way station on the road from animals to humans, and has been able to see the world through the eyes of animals better than nonautistic humans. As a consequence, she may have done more to ease the suffering of agricultural animals than any other person. Systems she designed changed the way we move and slaughter livestock; audits she created ensure that meatpacking plants operate with a minimum of animal fear and suffering. While these improvements don't make me approve of factory farming, the lives and deaths of millions of animals have been vastly improved by Grandin's contributions. It is impossible to read her books and still consider autism simply a pathology, a tragedy, or a curse. Her work is possible only because of the unique way her mind functions.

In his book *The Biology of Belief*, cellular biologist Bruce Lipton poses some challenges to our materialistic, reductionistic view of health and illness. Having spent decades studying genetics, Lipton has concluded that genetics are not nearly as influential in our well-being as popular science has led us to think. He argues that our environment has a much larger impact on us—even on the molecular level—than is

> ## A Healing Spirit
>
> Thirteen words for shaman from different traditional cultures:
>
> 1. *Saman* (Tungusic)
> 2. *Txiv neeb* (Hmong)
> 3. *Quga bix* (Aleut)
> 4. *Awenydd* (Welsh)
> 5. *Mara'akame* (Huichol)
> 6. *Lhaba* (Ladakhi)
> 7. *Noieta/noiete* (Saami)
> 8. *Marabout* (Berber)
> 9. *Karadji* (Australian Aboriginal)
> 10. *Dibia* (Igbo)
> 11. *Buu* (Mongolian)
> 12. *Naghual* (Aztec)
> 13. *Pajé* (Quechua)

widely believed. This is in keeping with Weston Price, who found that nurture certainly trumps nature in the health of indigenous peoples. But Lipton argues persuasively that consciousness, spirituality, and belief can actually trump both nature *and* nurture. His research—and that of many other scientists, such as quantum physicists—shows the strong influence that supposedly nonmaterial reality can have on what we usually consider to be material reality. Energetic, spiritual, and emotional forces have a profound impact on our physical existence.

While Western science is just beginning to be able to articulate this fact using scientific language, our indigenous souls have understood all along. Shamanism works because energetic shifts can have huge physical repercussions (and traditional peoples all around the world have developed various spiritual approaches to physical healing).

When Weston Price noted the dramatic change in health and psychological well-being between traditional and newly modernized peoples, he focused on the change in diet as the most tangible and concrete cause. As far as I'm concerned, his work proves that a diet based on sugars, refined carbohydrates, and factory-processed foods greatly undermines health while eating nutrient-rich traditional foods greatly supports health. But food was not the only thing that had changed in the lives of the unhealthy modernized communities Price studied. The communities where the health was so poor had just undergone a radical shift from following in the footsteps of their ancestors—living in intimate relationship with the Earth and with their particular place on the planet—to following the path of Progress. They had moved (or been moved) onto reservations, into foreign missions, or into large unfamiliar cities. Not only their food changed; their whole way of life changed. Their spiritual practices, their culture, their language, the daily and seasonal rituals that shaped their daily lives—all were threatened, undermined, or weakened in this move. A profound energetic, emotional, spiritual, and psychic shift had taken place. People who had been largely self-sufficient became, in a short period of time, largely dependent upon and vulnerable to strong outside influences. I do not think we can ignore the importance of this. While Price was able to control for genetic factors in his studies, he was not able to control for these other factors. And these other factors may have also had a important impact.

The shift that happened in people's diet was not only a nutritional loss, *but also a cultural and spiritual loss*. Culinary traditions had deep, long-standing, and multilayered meanings for these communities. Their ancestral foodways were woven together with every other part of their lives. Their nutritional wisdom was part of a proud heritage, and a sense of freedom, self-sufficiency, and empowerment—all of which were undermined by the new circumstances of their lives. It is important to look at the dietary changes that were occurring within this larger context.

At the same time, in discussing and comparing ancient or traditional customs and our own, we must not fall into the trap of thinking that modern Western culture has it all wrong, and traditional peoples had it all right. It's easy to idealize life in the village—to see in it a kind of

Garden of Eden where no one is sick, depressed, or troubled, except due to outside influences. Malidoma Somé warns us against the idea that there is no trouble endemic to the indigenous village:

> For those of you who have begun to construct a romantic picture of indigenous life, let this be a warning. For the indigenous world is not a place where everything flows in harmony, but one in which people must be constantly on the alert to detect and to correct imbalances and illnesses in both communal and individual life.

We can learn from the wisdom of traditional cultures without romanticizing them. Looking at life through a different lens helps us to recognize our subjective biases, and to consider alternatives. It is interesting, for example, to see how a particular indigenous community responds to mental imbalances and illnesses. Somé again:

> In African indigenous culture, just as there is high respect for artists and healers, there is a similar respect for the person who is experiencing a psychological crisis. This crisis is seen as the result of an intense interaction with the Other World, making the person think and act crazily. Resolving that crisis, in an indigenous community, results in releasing that person's gifts to the community—the very gifts won through the person's intense dealings with Spirit. Every time I encounter a modern person who is in crisis, a person whom other people refer to as crazy, I wonder what gifts are being lost to the community.
>
> Countless people wake up in the middle of the night wondering what is going on around and within them. Some think they are crazy, some feel something incredible is happening to them, and others just go insane. This problem is not specific to the modern world, it happens also in Africa. The difference is that in the modern world, errant behavior in a person is regarded as a personal

problem, concerning only that individual. The possibility that there is a larger meaning to be found in the person's experiences, which might translate into something meaningful for that person's community, is rarely considered.

People who have studied native nutrition look at a person talking to himself on the street corner and generally conclude that our nation's poor diet is the root of his crazy behavior. The Dagara take a much wider view, one more in keeping with what Bruce Lipton calls the New Biology:

> In an indigenous view of illness, the disease is always linked to a breakage in relationship. Some connection is loose or completely absent, or has been severed. What the villager sees in the physical disease is simply the aftermath of something that has happened on the level of energy or relationship. The illness is a physical manifestation of a spiritual decay.

Our poor diet is at least partly a physical manifestation of a spiritual decay. By now you've noticed this basic premise in my thinking about food. Most of the connections that we should have to the source of our food are loose, some are absent, and some have been severed. There has been a breakage in relationship—between people and the Earth, between people and the animals and plants that we eat, between people and other people, and between people and the Divine—the source of everything.

We cannot heal ourselves or make up for this loss by simply taking supplements or restricting our diet. We have to heal the relationships and reestablish these primary connections if we want to be healthy and whole. It is not just about self-help, it is about cultural transformation and rebuilding community. Don't get me wrong—I definitely believe we should be concerned with the illnesses we are seeing in our society and their material causes. I also believe that eating nutrient-dense foods, and keeping as many toxins as possible out of our food stream, would alleviate much suffering. But this is just one level of change that needs to happen if we want true healing to occur.

When we begin to heal the broken relationships in our food system, the nutrition of our food begins to improve. Animals are treated humanely when we understand that we are in relationship with them—that they are part of a whole we, too, belong to. Once we accept that we are all connected, and that we want those connections to be strong, flexible, and resilient instead of severed, torn, or frayed, healing becomes profound and multilayered. Ultimately, it is not something that any one of us can do in isolation. Once we begin to acknowledge our interdependence with others, it becomes absurd to think *I am healthy but my community is sick*, or *I am healthy but the world is sick*. We are too much a part of our community and our world is too much a part of us for that to be viable.

We must begin to think about modern diseases in metaphorical and symbolic language, not just the language of physiology, to figure out what connections have been loosened and what relationships have been broken. While degenerative diseases are certainly related to our diet, and perhaps to electric lights, I am convinced that they are also related to our way of being in the world, and to our belief systems. While I think it can only help to turn the lights out a little earlier and to eat more traditional fats and less refined sugars, these changes should be part of a development that is psychospiritual as well as physiological. We live in the material world, but that is not the only level of reality. It is also not the only level of healing.

On the Moon of Long Nights, may we begin to be a little more comfortable with the dark, and the mystery it symbolizes. May we remember to sleep, and to rest, to dream, and to talk to the Divine. May we remember that there is no such thing as human perfection, and show humility in the presence of all the things that surpass understanding. May we remember that both illness and difference can be gifts, or can carry within them gifts of very great measure. Let us not be too arrogant to accept the gift, or to offer the giver a place at our table. And may that table be full of nourishing foods, with plenty to share.

MOON OF LONG NIGHTS RECIPES

Sausage with Potatoes and Cabbage
Serves 2–4

This is one of my favorite wintertime meals. I consider it an eintopf—*the German word for a one-pot meal.*

2 tablespoons bacon drippings, olive oil, lard, or other fat

2 whole fresh sausages in casings

2 leeks, sliced thin, including much of the green part—or 1 large onion, sliced thin

1 small head cabbage or ½ large head cabbage, shredded

½ teaspoon caraway seeds (optional)

½ bunch greens (chard, kale, collards; or mustard, radish, or turnip greens), sliced into ribbons

3 medium potatoes (such as Yukon gold), diced

½ cup hot water or stock, or more as needed

Sea salt and freshly ground pepper to taste

½ cup sauerkraut (optional, page 252)

Sour cream or crème fraîche

1. Heat the bacon drippings, oil, or fat in a large skillet over medium heat. Add the whole sausages and brown on both sides.
2. Add the leeks (or onions) to the pan around the sausage and sauté. When the sausage is cooked through, remove it from the pan and let it cool.
3. Add the shredded cabbage to the pan along with a pinch of salt and the optional caraway seeds. Continue to sauté a few minutes, until the cabbage begins to wilt.
4. Add the greens and stir gently.
5. Add the diced potatoes, another pinch of salt, and the hot water or stock. Cover, reduce the heat somewhat, and steam until potatoes are just tender. Add more water or stock if the pan gets too dry.
6. Slice the sausage into ½-inch-thick pieces and add it back to the pan, stirring to incorporate and heat through. You can also leave the sausage whole or cut it in half.
7. Add plenty of salt and freshly ground pepper. Taste and adjust.
8. Remove from the heat and stir in the optional sauerkraut.
9. Serve in a shallow bowl with a big dollop of sour cream or crème fraîche.

Pot Roast

Serves 2–3 people for every pound of meat

This is how I make my pot roast. It is wonderful with sauerkraut. Quantities can vary with the size of the roast you are cooking and the size of your pot.

1–2 tablespoons tallow, lard, or other fat

1 piece roasting beef, such as a chuck roast, round roast, or brisket, weighing 3–6 pounds

½–1 onion, diced

2–3 stalks celery, diced

1–2 carrots, diced

1 teaspoon sea salt

Lots of freshly ground pepper

1 bouquet garni (page 309)

1–4 cups beef stock (page 231) or filtered water

¼ cup or so red wine (optional)

Potatoes, turnips, parsnips, rutabaga, and/or carrots, cut into large chunks (small vegetables can be left whole)

Salt and pepper to taste

Crème fraîche

2–3 tablespoons parsley or celery leaves, minced

1. Heat a tablespoon of the fat in a heavy-bottomed pot that is deep enough to fit the roast with the lid covering the pot. Have the flame at medium or medium-high heat.
2. When the fat is hot, put the roast in the fat and brown on all sides, turning it in the pan as needed.
3. When the roast is browned, transfer it to a cutting board and add the onion to the fat. (If there isn't enough fat in the pan, add a little more.)
4. When the onion begins to turn translucent, add the celery. After a minute or two add the carrots, and sprinkle generously with salt and pepper.
5. When the vegetables have all sautéed for a few minutes, add the roast to the pot again, add the bouquet garni, then add enough beef stock, water, and/or optional wine so that the roast is about three-quarters of the way submerged in liquid. Bring the liquid to a boil and then reduce heat to a bare simmer. Cover the pot and allow to simmer about 3 hours.
6. Once or twice during the simmering period, turn the pot roast over with a wooden spoon.
7. Transfer the pot roast to a cutting board. Take out the bouquet garni and discard.
8. Using an immersion blender, puree the remaining mixture until smooth. Return the roast to the pot along with starchy vegetables such as potatoes, turnips, parsnips, rutabaga, and carrots. How many vegetables depends on how much room you have in your pot and how many you want to eat or serve!

(continued)

Pot Roast
continued

9. Return the pot to a simmer and cook for another 20 to 30 minutes, or until the vegetables are fork-tender. The pot roast should also be very tender. Add most of the minced parsley or celery to the pot, reserving some for garnish. Taste the gravy and add more salt and pepper to taste.

10. I like to serve a chunk of meat surrounded by vegetables in a shallow bowl with plenty of gravy. Then I sprinkle with the remaining parsley or celery, and top with a dollop of crème fraîche. I often add a big dollop of sauerkraut to the bowl as well.

Pumpkin Mashed Potatoes
Serves 4 as a side dish, or more if part of a larger meal

The word pumpkin, *used in its broad sense, includes all the winter squashes. I use butternut squash here for the pumpkin because it is reliably dense and smooth. You could also get a good baking pumpkin at a farmer's market—just check with the vendor to make sure the flesh will be smooth and not stringy.*

4 cups (1 pound) chopped potatoes such as Yukon gold, washed and cut into big chunks

3 cups combined chopped sweet potatoes and butternut squash (or baking pumpkin), both peeled before chopping

½ cup butter

½ cup cream, sour cream, half-and-half, buttermilk, yogurt, crème fraîche, whole milk, or a combination

Nutmeg, grated

Pinch of mace, if you have it

Pinch of allspice, if you have it

Salt and pepper

1. Bring a pot of water to a boil. Steam the potatoes, sweet potatoes, and squash over simmering water until fork-tender.
2. Pour out the water and pour the vegetables from the steamer into the pan.

3. Mash the vegetables with a potato masher, fork, or whisk and add the butter, dairy, and spices until you like the consistency and flavor.

Cranberry Sauce
Makes 1½ cups

There is no reason to buy canned cranberry sauce for Thanksgiving. It is easy to make and tastes much better.

12 ounces fresh cranberries

⅔ cup maple syrup

⅓ cup water

Pinch of cinnamon and cloves (optional)

Honey to taste, if needed

1. Wash the cranberries and put in a pan. Pour the maple syrup and water over them, add the optional spices, and bring to a simmer.
2. Cook until the cranberries pop open, about 10 minutes. Remove from the heat and cool for about 15 minutes.
3. Stir and taste. If it is too tart, add honey by spoonfuls, stirring, until it is a little bit sweeter than you want because it will lose some of its sweet taste when you chill it.
4. Cool to room temperature, then refrigerate until you're ready to eat.

Shchi (Russian Peasant Soup)
Serves 4

We think of borshcht as being the national soup of Russia, but it is more an Eastern European specialty. Shchi is the Russian soup. It is a wonderful and unusual combination of things, and a great way to enjoy sauerkraut!

¼ cup dried porcini mushrooms

1 cup boiling filtered water

2 tablespoons tallow, olive oil, or other fat

1 onion or 2 leeks, diced

1 stalk celery, diced

1 carrot, diced

2 cups shredded cabbage

2 cups diced tomatoes (canned is fine)

1 bouquet garni (page 309)

Sea salt and pepper to taste

1 quart beef broth (page 231)

Meat from making beef broth (page 231) or any leftover beef (optional)

Minced parsley or celery leaves (at least a tablespoon)

Sauerkraut for serving

Crème fraîche for serving

(continued)

Shchi (Russian Peasant Soup)
continued

1. Put the porcini mushrooms into a bowl, pour the boiling water over them, and let them rehydrate.
2. In a heavy-bottomed soup pot, heat the tallow or other fat. Add the onion or leeks and sauté until they begin to get translucent.
3. Add the celery and then the carrot to the pot and continue sautéing. Then add the cabbage.
4. Strain the mushrooms, reserving the soaking water. Mince the mushrooms and add them to the sauté.
5. When the cabbage has wilted, add the tomatoes to the sauté along with the bouquet garni and a generous pinch of sea salt and freshly ground pepper.
6. Bring the mixture to a simmer and cook for a few minutes.
7. Add the mushroom soaking water (except for the dirt that has settled to the bottom) and the beef broth.
8. Bring the soup to a simmer and cook, covered, over low heat for about 45 minutes.
9. Add the meat to the soup and heat through, then taste for salt and pepper. Add more until it is well seasoned. Add about a tablespoon of minced parsley or celery leaves, reserving a few for garnish.
10. Serve by putting a big dollop of sauerkraut in the bottom of each bowl. Ladle the *shchi* over the kraut, and then put a dollop of crème fraîche on top. Sprinkle a little minced parsley or celery leaves over the top and serve.

New England Clam Chowder
Serves 3–4

I make my fish stock by covering the bones and heads of non-oily white fish (ask the fishmonger for recommendations) with filtered water and adding a tablespoon of white wine vinegar. Then I bring to a simmer and cook over very low heat, covered, for 2 to 3 hours. You can also make it in a Crock-Pot and cook for about 6 hours.

2–3 tablespoons butter, bacon drippings, or other fat

1 onion, diced

3 stalks celery, diced

2 large potatoes, diced into big, bite-sized chunks

Bouquet garni: a bay leaf, plus a few sprigs of parsley stems, thyme, sage, and/or oregano, tied in a bundle with string for ease of removal

Fish stock (½–1 quart)

1 small jar clams with juice (10 oz)

1 tablespoon kuzu root starch or arrowroot starch

½ cup milk

Salt and pepper to taste

½ cup crème fraîche

½ pound fresh clams in their shell (optional)

Celery leaves, minced, for garnish

1. In a heavy-bottomed pan, heat the fat over medium heat. When it is hot, add the onion.
2. When the onion is translucent, add the celery and cook for a few minutes.
3. Add the potatoes and bouquet garni to the pot. Add just enough fish stock to cover the vegetables. Bring to a simmer and cook, covered, for about 20 minutes.
4. Meanwhile, drain the clams and save the liquid. Feel through the clams to make sure there aren't any shells. Add the clams to the chowder along with the clam juice. Check the potatoes to see if they are tender. If not, cook a while longer.
5. Dissolve the kuzu or arrowroot in the milk.
6. Once the potatoes are tender, stir the starch mixture into the chowder and return to a simmer.
7. When chowder is thick, add salt and pepper generously to taste, cover, and remove from the heat.
8. If you're using whole clams, steam the clams over ½ cup simmering water just until they open. Add the simmering water to the chowder and stir.
9. Add the crème fraîche to the chowder and stir until incorporated. Taste again and adjust the seasonings.
10. Serve chowder in a shallow bowl with the open clams floating on top and the whole sprinkled with the minced celery leaves.

13

WOLF MOON

Busy, normal people: the world is here.
Can you hear it wailing, crying, whispering?
Listen: the world is here.
Don't you hear it,
Praying and sighing and groaning for wholeness?
Sighing and whispering: wholeness,
Wholeness, wholeness?

—From "An African Call for Life"

The Wolf Moon comes in the deep dark of winter, when the North is covered with snow. At this time of year our northern ancestors would have taken refuge in their homes, staying close to the fire as the winds and the wolves howled outside. Families lived off the food they had put up in the fall, often supplemented by hunting for wild game. It was these rations that kept the wolf from the door.

The wolf as a metaphor for hunger, appetite, or famine dates back to at least the fifteenth century. Over the past sixty years we have steadily driven the metaphorical wolf from our door, and we have also steadily driven the actual wolf from the land. We have also, perhaps, driven the wildness of the wolf from our hearts. These developments are not unrelated. By the mid-1970s wolves, once the most populous large mammals in North America, had become an endangered species. The development throughout the American West of large tracts of rangeland for cattle and sheep, and the widespread practice on the part of ranchers of shooting predators on sight, contributed to the wolf's demise. Agricultural and urban development also steadily eroded the large, uninterrupted areas of wilderness where wolves thrived.

The same agricultural system that has displaced wolves from the countryside has made food in modern America abundant and cheap—driving the metaphorical wolf from our door. I'm sure many people consider the near extinction of wolves a small price to pay for well-stocked supermarket shelves. But the disappearance of wolves and other species whose habitats have been appropriated for human use is part of a complex, globalized set of developments that may well have dire consequences for human beings. Wolves were just early casualties of a huge experiment in the course of human life on Earth. It is one that is proving unsustainable.

Many signs warn that we cannot sustain our current agricultural model. Our agricultural methods deplete the soil. Pesticides and herbicides destroy the microorganisms that live in the earth and ensure its fertility, and kill many of the beneficial insects, earthworms, bats, owls, birds, and other organisms that help maintain a healthy agrarian ecosystem. Agricultural toxins pollute our water—which all living things need to survive. Fertilizers provide a quick fix to depleted soil, but ultimately further undermine the soil's integrity. Our chemical-intensive approach decreases the soil fertility over time, when we could be maintaining or even enriching it. In depleting the soil we are eroding the very foundation for a healthy agricultural system.

In *Collapse*, Jared Diamond looks at ancient civilizations that exhausted their natural resources and—for a variety of reasons and in a variety of ways—could not change the course of their decline and eventual collapse. He describes how Norse attempts to graze cattle and grow hay eroded the fragile topsoil in Greenland and contributed to the collapse of that culture. Similarly, he points to soil erosion as a factor in the collapse of the Classic Mayan civilization. Diamond also analyzes modern situations in which resource pressure has contributed to terrible living conditions and civil breakdown. He cites topsoil depletion (due to intensive farming) and overpopulation as at least contributing factors in the Rwandan genocide.

In the 1930s, Weston Price paid particular attention to soil quality in the places he studied. Almost sixty years before Diamond laid out his argument in *Collapse*, Price was aware that an approach to farming that consisted of mining the land could have catastrophic consequences for a culture as its population rose:

> It is apparent that the present and past one or two generations have taken more than their share of the minerals that were available in the soil in most of the United States, and have done so without returning them. Thus, they have handicapped, to a serious extent, the succeeding generations, since it is so difficult to replenish the minerals, and since it is practically impossible to accumulate another layer of topsoil, in less than a period of many hundreds of years. This constitutes, accordingly, one of the serious dilemmas, since human beings are dependent upon soil for their animal and plant foods. . . . The vitamin and protein content of plants has been shown to be directly related to availability of soil minerals and other nutriments. A program that does not include maintaining this balance between population and soil productivity must inevitably lead to disastrous degeneration. Over-population means strife and wars. The history of the rise and fall of many of the past civilizations has recorded a progressive rise, while civilizations were using the accumulated nutrition in the topsoil, forest, shrubbery and grass, followed by a progressive decline, while the same civilizations were reaping the results of the destruction of these essential ultimate sources of life.

Ecological farmers who are rebuilding their soil are doing us all a great service. I know one couple who has been farming the same five acres for nearly thirty years. When they bought the property it had only three inches of topsoil. Through composting and cover cropping, the topsoil on their farm is now almost two feet deep. This is a life's work of which they should be very proud.

Our agricultural system's dependence upon petroleum further adds to its unsustainability. Petroleum is a finite, nonrenewable resource. Some of the Earth's petroleum is so difficult to access that we would have to expend more energy to pump it out than we would get from the reserve. That oil is, for all intents and purposes, useless to us. We have mapped the remaining known oil reserves, and the likelihood of discovering unmapped sources of major significance is slight.

Many analysts predict that sometime in the next few decades we will reach Peak Oil, the point at which we will be pumping out more oil than we ever have before—or ever will afterward due to declining availability. Once we reach Peak Oil, it is all downhill. Like a desert hiker who has drunk half of her precious water, we will have to begin to ration very carefully. In fact, the sooner we begin to ration, the better.

But what does oil have to do with food? Everything—in our current system. Gasoline or diesel fuels power the equipment that we use to plant, water, spray, and harvest our crops. Fertilizers and pesticides are synthesized from petroleum products. We rely on petroleum and its derivatives to transport crops, process them, and package them. Plastic, used throughout the entire system, is derived from petroleum. The average plate of food travels fifteen hundred miles to get to our table—and every mile is fueled by petroleum and releases more carbon dioxide into the atmosphere. Even cooking at home—whether using natural gas or electricity—depends on petroleum somewhere along the way. In other words, in just the past sixty years—a blink of the eye in human history—we have built a global food system entirely dependent on petroleum. As we begin to run out of oil, the crucial problem facing humanity is not how we will get to work each day, but rather how we will feed ourselves.

Other earthly resources are in short supply as well. We are depleting our forests faster than we are replanting them, and over-fishing our rivers, seas, and fisheries. We are polluting the air and the water. Climate change will have consequences for our food system that are too complex to predict.

We are going to feel the impact of these problems more acutely in the coming decades. When I worked as director of education programs for the Ferry Plaza Farmers Market in San Francisco, I designed an exhibit called Sustainable Agriculture A to Z. Each letter of the alphabet described a different aspect of ecological farming and food systems: A for Animals Grazing, B for Beneficial Insects, C for Cover Cropping, and so on. The letter S stood for Soil Building—which of course is crucially important. But in retrospect, I wonder if S shouldn't have stood for Survival. The more I learn about the problems of resource depletion we are facing, the more I believe that in the not-so-distant future, ecological farming, carefully managed fishing, grass-based ranching, and human-scale food processing are going to cease to be about niche marketing, and become matters of basic survival—just as they were for our ancestors.

In *How to Cook a Wolf*, M. F. K. Fisher addressed an audience that had been struggling to feed itself through the privations of the Depression, World War II, and food rations. Published in 1942, *How to Cook a Wolf* concerns itself with how to live well in difficult circumstances. But Fisher acknowledges that even her witty advice may sometimes be inadequate:

> There are times when helpful hints about turning off the gas when not in use are foolish, because the gas has been turned off permanently, or until you can pay the bill. And you don't care about knowing the trick of keeping bread fresh by putting a cut apple in the box because you don't have any bread and certainly not an apple, cut or uncut. And there is no point in planning to save the juice from canned vegetables because they, and therefore their juices, do not exist. In other words, the wolf has one paw wedged firmly into what looks like a widening crack in the door.

It is not unthinkable that even those of us in the prosperous West will find ourselves once again experiencing such a crisis, and feel the wolf at the door.

Cultures really do experience ecological crises, and sometimes they collapse. As Jared Diamond points out, Easter Islanders really did cut down all their timber, the Greenland Norse really did eat their very last cow, and the people of both these island cultures starved to death. Clearly, to survive we have to adapt to the natural limits of the place where we live. We must observe what nature gives us and build our systems of food, transport, shelter, and clothing in response to those gifts. Although dairy ranching is ecologically appropriate for the Tibetans living in the Himalayas and the Swiss in the Alps, it was disastrous for the Greenland Norse. The Inuit, who also lived on Greenland, discovered ecologically appropriate strategies: fishing and seal hunting. The technologies they developed reflected an understanding of their landscape. If only the Norse had been willing to learn from the Inuit, they could have survived. But they were, it seems, too sure of themselves, and too wedded to their own cultural assumptions.

> ### Homestead Security
>
> Thirteen culinary traditions that can be practiced at home and without the use of petroleum or industrial technology:
>
> 1. Cheese making
> 2. Grinding grain
> 3. Pickling
> 4. Sun-drying
> 5. Fermenting beverages
> 6. Bread baking
> 7. Sugaring
> 8. Butchering
> 9. Pressing apples, grapes, and other fruit
> 10. Curing meats
> 11. Culturing dairy products
> 12. Smoking
> 13. Rendering

We have much to learn by observing the food systems of peoples that have for millennia endured and thrived in the world's landscapes. It is not romanticism or idealism to learn from their wisdom: It is a matter of survival. We must not waste any time shifting the course of food production, processing, and distribution away from mining the Earth and toward ecologically sustainable technologies—many of which can be gleaned from those who developed agriculture without petroleum or its co-products.

While I propose reconnecting to our food source through buying from small-scale and local farmers, eating seasonally, and shifting from factory-processed to traditionally processed foods, I know that these options are not available to everyone. But this might change radically in the coming decades. Right now it might be more expensive to buy food from local, organic, small farms and humane grass-based ranches than to shop at the supermarket. But as petroleum costs go up, the cost of factory farming will go up, the cost of shipping will go up, and imported and store-bought foods could again become the expensive luxuries they once were.

Right now eating foods that were processed on an artisanal scale might seem costly. Processing them ourselves at home might seem time consuming. But these foods may someday soon be far more economical and practical than their petroleum-intensive, factory-produced alternatives. They are already more sustainable. If the ecological crisis grows dire, knowing farmers in your area, maintaining a garden, knowing how to kill, pluck, and dress a chicken, knowing how to cook, being able to store foods without refrigeration, and knowing how to make medicinal teas and ales from local plants will once again be critical to survival.

It would also serve us well to develop sustainable approaches to harvesting wild foods. While many wild foods are endangered and need to be protected, others could provide important sources of local nutrition. Nettles are a prime example—full of nutrients and prolific, they were enjoyed by many Europeans during World War II when more traditional vegetables were scarce. Edible animals are prolific in some places and could be harvested sustainably. I am writing these words in the heart of West Marin, where a debate is currently raging about what to do with non-native deer that are multiplying rapidly and have no natural predators. Their populations are so high that they are a nuisance to both humans and native species. Many people agree that a percentage of the deer need to be killed in order to stabilize the ecosystem. To avoid wasting life, one rancher I know is pushing for a sustainable harvest of the deer, one that would yield meat packaged for consumption. This makes sense, but USDA and other regulations make it very difficult to carry out in practice. In other parts of the Bay Area, wild boar populations are growing unchecked, with many destructive consequences, and a selective, sustainable harvest would be beneficial. Wild seafoods such as crabs are already being harvested sustainably off the Pacific coast, using traps that minimize impacts on the seafloor and other species, and maintaining reproductive populations. While these sources wouldn't suffice to feed the entire local population of the Bay Area, we would do well to cultivate them and thus reduce our dependence on a doomed food system.

The fewer resources we squander now, the more we conserve, the less we drive, the more we grow our food locally, the better for our own well-being and future generations. The more we begin now to develop practices that can be maintained with minimal external inputs, the better off we will be as our wasteful and polluting infrastructure breaks down. While we need to look at technologies that have worked in the past, we also need to invest in developing new technologies that combine traditional wisdom with modern innovations. We cannot go back to pre-petroleum days; we will have to go forward into post-petroleum days. No matter what, survival will entail curbing our level of consumption. The Earth's resources cannot support a population that consumes at the rate modern Americans now do. As one book on the subject states in its title: The Party's Over.

Not that it was a particularly fun party. We drove around in SUVs, shopped at big-box stores, watched hours of television, and ate prepackaged snack foods, but was it fulfilling? What has all of this consumerism done to our sense of connection and intimacy? Have we substituted factory-produced stuff for the things that really matter? What does all this mining of the planet do to the human heart, and to the wild wolf of our earthly souls? Martín Prechtel challenges us to look at this question seriously:

> Over the last two or three centuries, a heartless culture-crushing mentality has incremented its *progress* on the earth, devouring all peoples, nature, imagination, and spiritual knowledge. Like a big mechanized slug, it has left behind a flat, homogenized streak of civilization wherever it passed. Every human on this earth—African, Asian, European, Islanders, or from the Americas—has ancestors who at some point in their history had their stories, rituals, ingenuity, language, and lifeways taken away, enslaved, banned, exploited, twisted, or destroyed by this force.

Now what is indigenous, natural, subtle, hard to explain, generous, gradual, and village-oriented in each of us is being banished into the ghettos of our hearts, or hidden away from view onto reservations inside the spiritual landscape of the Earth Body. . . .

Meanwhile, our natural souls, which are like Bushmen or rare waterbirds, know that our minds and our souls should be working together to maintain or replaster the crumbling hut of life. Instead, our indigenous souls are being utterly overlooked and pushed aside in the bustle of the minds' competitive activity, until our true beings feel just like a tribesman in a big, trafficky city: unwelcome, lost, and homeless.

Everything we do on a daily basis—from what we eat to how we treat the stranger in the checkout line to how we get to work—is an opportunity to reverse this trend, to salvage our true beings from their sense of homelessness and alienation. When we buy eggs from a local rancher who lets his chickens range freely, we build a relationship and a community, a place where we belong, a home. When we soak our grains or brew our own herbal ale, we are doing something that is indigenous, natural, subtle, and hard to explain. When we ride a bike to the local farmer's market to do our shopping, we are making a change that is generous, gradual, and village-oriented. Not only do such activities help heal our hearts, but they create networks of support, ingenuity, and cooperation that will help us solve the problems we may soon be facing. Our survival may depend upon re-creating the village.

From an evolutionary perspective, the human propensity to organize in cooperative groups, among other things, makes us special among primates. On the Wolf Moon, it is only fitting to point out that this characteristic may have been learned from close habitation with wolves. In her book *Animals in Translation*, Temple Grandin relays interesting recent research into the origins of human community, and the co-evolution of humans and canines:

> If [researcher] Dr. Wayne is right, wolves and people were together at the point when *homo sapiens* had just barely evolved from *homo erectus*. When wolves and humans first joined together people only had a few rough tools to their name, and they lived in very small nomadic bands that probably weren't any more socially complicated than a band of chimpanzees. Some researchers think these early humans may not even have had language. . . .
>
> Going over all the evidence, a group of Australian anthropologists believes that during all those years when early humans were associating with wolves *they learned to act and think like wolves.* Wolves hunted in groups; humans didn't. Wolves had complex social structures; humans didn't. Wolves had loyal same-sex and nonkin friendships; humans probably didn't, judging by the lack of same-sex and nonkin friendships in every other primate species today. . . . Wolves were highly territorial; humans probably weren't—again, judging by how non-territorial all other primates are today.
>
> By the time these early people became truly modern, they had learned to do all these wolfie things. When you think about how different we are from other primates, you see how doglike we are. A lot of the things we do that the other primates don't do are dog things. The Australian group thinks it was the dogs who showed us how. . . .
>
> The Aborigines have a saying: "Dogs make us human." Now we know that's probably literally true.

If this is true, then wolves—as important early teachers—have earned better treatment than what we have given them in modern times. We could, perhaps, honor their legacy by making sure that our complex social structures serve us well. That would mean reviving the importance of communities, and remembering the many ways in which our lives are enriched by the sense of belonging to a village.

I have had many blessings in life, but one that I hold very dear is the blessing of community. I was raised by parents who surrounded our family with friends and loved ones. I am grateful to have been raised in a metaphorical village. My parents' friends became aunts and uncles to me in the village sense, and their children were like my cousins. We also kept in touch with extended family, and I was close to all four of my grandparents. Throughout my youth, the nurturing influence and wisdom of my elders was palpable and real, and I felt held in a web of love and goodness that I sense to this day.

Since moving from the East Coast to the West Coast in my early twenties, I have been able to find and create similar metaphorical villages in my adult life. The restaurant where I was a manager for a number of years, and the arts center where I was a chef both became strong communities of support. At the arts center, I had the experience of cooking and eating in the context of community, and that proved even more fulfilling than I could have imagined. To create food with people who perceived the ingredients to be great gifts, and to share that food with others who perceived our meals to be a true blessing—this was deeply rewarding. There was, in that experience, the strong echo of an ancient rhythm: a clan or a band or even a whole tribe coming together at dusk to share a meal that a few of us had spent hours preparing.

Creating and participating in community life is one of the most important steps on the path to healing. In recent years I have had another nourishing experience of a metaphorical village. In 1997 I was baptized and became a member of a church. It was a profound rite of passage. With that drizzle of water, I experienced a new sense of belonging—a spiritual belonging. I became part of something larger than myself as I was brought into deeper relationship with the congregation at my chosen church, with Christianity, and with God.

Certainly some people will be surprised that—with all my love of indigenous culture and tradition and ecology—I could embrace a tradition that has inflicted so much harm on indigenous peoples throughout the world. But I see at the heart of Christianity—in the work and teachings of Jesus—a radical response to empire, a proclamation of God's unconditional love, a celebration of Creation, and a great cry for justice. I read the Bible as a historical document that contains the sacred stories and indigenous wisdom of ancient Israel, as well as the teachings of Jesus and the struggles of the early Christian movement to live those teachings in the context of community. I experience the scriptures and the rituals of Christian life—baptism, communion, worship, prayer, observance of the liturgical calendar—as thin places: experiences that bring me into deeper relationship with the Divine. I read the Bible through a lens that is metaphorical, sacramental, and relational, not literal, dogmatic, or fundamentalist.

Some people feel that organized religion is inimical to spirituality. But for me organized religion is spirituality plus community plus tradition—all three of which I find deeply nourishing. Of course, tradition has its gifts and its burdens, and to me the trick is to embrace the gifts while acknowledging that the church is constantly in need of reform. The church that I belong to is independent, having been expelled from the national body because of its stand for full inclusion in ministry for gays, lesbians, bisexuals, and transgendered people. Perhaps because of this history, our church is not a complacent place. It is a community where striving to be faithful to the heart of Christianity is part of every day's work. Often it feels like being part of a village—a group of people who are not precisely friends, not exactly family, but who pray together, worship together, and work together to live most fully our vision of how faith, hope, and love can be made manifest in a suffering world.

Participating in my church has also taught me about stewardship. In the Christian context, everything we have—our time, our talents, and our treasure (our wealth)—is a gift from God. Stewardship is about how we choose to use those gifts and our accountability for them. When we tithe to the church, or serve on a committee, or offer our skills to a particular project, we do so knowing we have been given gifts and are called upon to give in return. This is what Lewis Hyde would call keeping the gift moving. It is a very different notion from the secular, market-based notion that if we have wealth it is because we have earned it, and the best thing we can do with it is to invest it and make it accumulate. In a commodity economy, time is money rather than a gift, and talents are assets that can be marketed. But in the context of faith, our time, talents, and treasure are gifts from God, and we are called to steward them wisely, with love and a generous heart. It is the closest thing I have experienced to the gift economy that Hyde writes about so beautifully.

Stewardship is an important notion within the context of sustainable agriculture as well. Ecological farmers often see themselves as stewards of their land. Whether they own or lease the acreage that they farm, they acknowledge that every decision they make—how to control pests, how to build the soil's fertility, how to protect their property's waterways—will have long-term impacts not just for that piece of land but for the bioregion or watershed in which they farm. This goes against the grain of the post–World War II corporate farming model. Visionary farmers and ranchers are reviving a model of wise stewardship in an effort to heal the Earth from the ravages of decades of toxic factory farming.

In many indigenous villages, everyone is expected to be a steward. Helena Norberg-Hodge tells the story of an experience she had living among the Ladakhis in the Himalayas:

> Soon after I had arrived in Ladakh, I was washing some clothes in a stream. Just as I was plunging a dirty dress into the water, a little girl, no more than seven years old, came by from a village upstream. "You can't put your clothes in that water," she said shyly. "People down there have to drink it." She pointed to a village at least a mile farther downstream. "You can use that one over there; that's just for irrigation."
>
> I was beginning to learn how Ladakhis manage to survive in such a difficult environment. I was also beginning to learn the meaning of the word *frugality*. In the

West, frugality conjures up images of old aunts and pad-locked pantries. But the frugality you find in Ladakh, which is fundamental to the people's prosperity, is something quite different. Using limited resources in a careful way has nothing to do with miserliness; this is frugality in its original meaning of "fruitfulness": getting more out of a little.

Through this kind of frugality—this wonderful fruitfulness—and an ethic of universal stewardship, we might just be able to survive whatever ecological crises come our way. By caring for one another, by working together, and by cooperating, we may actually stand a chance.

On the Wolf Moon, may we find ways to keep the metaphorical wolf from our door without driving the literal wolf into extinction. May we celebrate wildness in all its forms, including its presence in our own indigenous souls. As we look carefully at the natural environments that we depend upon for our survival, may we make wise choices about how to use the precious gifts that Earth offers us. May we begin to rebuild the village, to create community, and to nurture a place in our hearts for all the creatures of God's green Earth. May we be blessed with the great fruitfulness that comes with true frugality, and may it serve us well for many—many, many, many—generations yet to come.

WOLF MOON RECIPES

Cream of Butternut Squash Soup
Serves 3–4

This is one of my favorite cold-weather standards. The primary recipe is for an herby, European-style squash soup. Then I offer an Asian-style variation.

2 tablespoons butter or olive oil

2–3 leeks, sliced into rounds

1 fresh seasonal butternut squash, peeled, seeded, and cut into chunks

Chicken stock or filtered water to cover

1 bouquet garni (page 309)

½ cup cream, crème fraîche, or yogurt; or 1 cup buttermilk or half-and-half

Salt and pepper to taste

Crème fraîche or yogurt, for garnish

Finely minced rosemary, thyme, sage, or parsley leaves (or a combination of these herbs); or a grating of nutmeg; or a grind of black pepper, for garnish

1. Heat the butter or oil in a medium-sized soup pot. Add the leeks and sauté until soft.
2. Add the butternut squash, then add stock or filtered water to cover the vegetables by about ½ inch. Add the bouquet garni and bring the pot to a boil.
3. Reduce the heat and simmer until the squash is soft.
4. Turn off the heat and remove the bouquet garni.
5. Puree the soup with an immersion blender (or in a standard blender), adding the yogurt or other dairy, and plenty of salt and pepper as you blend. Taste the soup and adjust the seasonings—adding more salt and pepper if it's too bland.
6. Serve in a shallow bowl with a dollop of crème fraîche (or yogurt) and a sprinkling of herbs, nutmeg, or pepper.

Note: This simple recipe shows off the flavor of a good in-season squash, but might be unimpressive if made with an older, less-flavorful squash—in which case you might want to roast the squash first to bring out the sweetness.

Variation: Butternut Soup with Coconut Milk and Ginger

1. Replace the butter or olive oil with ghee, if you have it.
2. Replace the bouquet garni with 3 to 4 slices fresh gingerroot.
3. Add a tablespoon or so of fish sauce to the soup while it's cooking (reduce the salt).
4. Replace the yogurt (or other dairy) in the puree with coconut milk (you can use a whole 13.5-oz can).
5. Garnish with a dollop of yogurt and a sprinkling of minced scallions.

Chicken Stock
Yields 2–4 quarts

As with my beef stock (page 231), I prefer to make chicken stock without any herbs or vegetables. This makes a light, neutral-tasting broth that can be used in any of the recipes of this book—or in any other recipe! I think vegetables and herbs have a tendency to create a strong, rather muddy flavor, especially if cooked for 12 to 24 hours. If you do want to add herbs or vegetables to this stock, please add them only in the last hour of cooking.

Carcass from one roast chicken, meat removed, such as that used for Simplest Roast Chicken (page 226), or a fresh stewing hen or rooster.

Fresh chicken feet (the more you have, the more gelatin the broth will have)

Chicken neck, gizzards, and heart from the packet inside the chicken

Head of the chicken, if you happen to have it

¼ cup vinegar (use any kind except distilled white vinegar)

Filtered water to cover

1. Remove any herbs that might be stuffed into the cavity of the carcass.
2. Place the carcass, chicken feet, and giblets (excluding the liver) in a stainless-steel stockpot (avoid using aluminum) or Crock-Pot.
3. Cover with cold filtered water. Add the vinegar to the pot.
4. If you're using a stockpot, bring the pot to a boil and reduce the heat to a very low simmer. You can skim the scum off the top of the stock if you like.
5. If you're using a Crock-Pot, put the cover on the pot and turn the pot on to the low setting.
6. Allow the broth to cook for at least a day if possible, preferably 24 hours. You may need to add a bit more water to the pot if the water evaporates and leaves the chicken parts exposed.
7. Strain the stock off the chicken. Use immediately, or let it cool and then transfer to jars or other containers. Refrigerate or freeze until you're ready to use it. If you used a fresh hen or rooster, you can remove the meat and add it to soups such as the following one, Chicken Soup with Wild Rice.

Chicken Soup with Wild Rice
Serves 3–4

This is a hearty, thick, nourishing soup perfect for winter. You can add more broth for a thinner soup.

⅓ cup wild rice

1 cup water

1 tablespoon yogurt

2 tablespoons olive oil, schmaltz, or other fat

1 onion, diced, or 1 large leek, cut into rounds

3 stalks celery, diced

2 carrots, diced

1 quart chicken stock, or more for a thinner soup (you can also thin it with water)

1 bouquet garni (page 309)

½ teaspoon salt

1 cup chicken, either cooked or raw, cut into bite-sized pieces

1. Put the wild rice in a jar and add the water and yogurt. Put in a warm place and let it sit for at least 7 hours.
2. In a heavy-bottomed pot, heat the oil or fat over medium heat. When the fat is hot, add the onion or leek and sauté until it begins to turn translucent.
3. Add the celery and sauté for a minute or two, then add the carrots and continue sautéing for a few minutes.
4. Strain the wild rice and rinse thoroughly. Add to the sauté along with the broth, the bouquet garni, and the salt.
5. Turn the heat to high, bring to a boil, then reduce to a simmer.
6. Simmer, covered, over low heat until the wild rice is tender.
7. Add the chicken and simmer a few minutes more.
8. Remove bouquet garni and add salt and pepper generously to taste.

Dungeness Crab Cakes
Makes 4 crab cakes

Crabs are caught very sustainably off the California coast, where they live full lives in the wild before being caught in humane pots.

1 egg yolk

¼ cup sourdough starter (page 312)

1½ cups Dungeness crab meat, picked through for shells (about 1/2 pound)

1 tablespoon parsley, minced

1–2 tablespoons scallions, onions, or chives, minced

¼ teaspoon salt

Freshly ground pepper

2 tablespoons olive oil or other fat

1. In a bowl, mix the egg yolk and sourdough starter together with a fork until thoroughly combined.
2. Add the crab, parsley, scallions, salt, and pepper. Combine thoroughly.
3. Heat the oil in a cast-iron skillet.
4. Place a large dollop of the crab mixture in the pan and repeat until you've used all the mixture.
5. When the cakes are brown on one side, flip and cook on the other.
6. Serve crab cakes with a generous salad, and maybe a dollop of Olive Oil Mayonnaise (page 118).

Sourdough Cheese Herb Scones
Makes 7 scones

1 cup sourdough (page 312)

¼ cup lard, butter, or combination

¼ cup sprouted spelt flour, or unbleached white flour, plus more as needed

¼ teaspoon baking soda

¼ teaspoon salt

1 tablespoon arrowroot powder

¼ cup packed grated cheddar cheese, preferably sharp

1 teaspoon dried herbs such as oregano, thyme, sage, and marjoram—or 1 tablespoon minced fresh herbs

1. Preheat the oven to 375° F and grease a cast-iron skillet with lard or butter. Put it in the oven to get it hot.
2. In a bowl, cut together the sourdough and fat with a fork, pastry cutter, or two knives, and then mix with a spoon until well combined.
3. In a smaller bowl, mix the flour, baking soda, salt, arrowroot powder, cheese, and herbs. If you're using dried herbs, rub them between the

(continued)

Sourdough Cheese Herb Scones
continued

palms of your hands before adding to the flour—this helps release their flavor.

4. Add the flour mixture to the sourdough mixture and combine gently but thoroughly. If the mixture seems wet, add a bit more flour.

5. Carefully remove the skillet from the oven.

6. Using a ¼-cup measure, put mounds of dough onto the skillet. Return the skillet to the oven.

7. Bake for 25 to 30 minutes or until done. Serve with butter. I like to eat them with scrambled eggs for breakfast.

Homemade Sourdough Crackers
Makes 20–40 crackers depending on how big you cut them

1 cup sourdough, fed with whole-grain flour, such as wheat, spelt, or kamut flour (see page 312, and variations suggested at the end of the recipe)

¼ cup lard rendered from local, free-range pork fat—or 1/4 cup coconut oil

¼ cup sprouted spelt flour or unbleached white flour, or as much as you need to make a stiff dough, plus extra for rolling

½ teaspoon sea salt

¼ teaspoon baking soda

Olive oil for brushing

Coarse salt (such as kosher salt) for sprinkling on top

1. In a large bowl, combine thoroughly the sourdough and the lard.

2. Mix the salt and baking soda in with the ¼ cup flour and add to the sourdough mixture. Knead it all together in the bowl, adding as much flour as necessary to make a stiff dough.

3. Let the dough rest for about 10 minutes. Preheat the oven to 350° F and line a sheet pan with parchment paper.

4. Take a small portion of the dough (about ¼ cup) and roll it out on a floured board using a rolling pin, adding flour if it's too sticky, until it is very thin.

5. Cut into cracker shapes using a dough cutter or sharp knife. Transfer the crackers to the sheet pan, brush with olive oil, and sprinkle with salt. Repeat with another ¼ cup of dough until the sheet pan is filled with crackers. Bake the crackers in batches as necessary for 15 to 20 minutes or until just golden brown.

Variations: Feed your starter with cracked rye for rye crackers, or coarsely ground rice for rice crackers.

Sourdough Pancakes
Serves 2–3

1 egg

¼ cup milk, cream, or half-and-half

1 cup sourdough, preferably fed with whole wheat pastry flour, or spelt or kamut flour

1 tablespoon maple syrup

¼ teaspoon salt

¼ teaspoon baking soda

2 tablespoons melted butter

¼ cup sprouted spelt flour or unbleached white flour, or more if the batter is too thin

1 heaping tablespoon ghee

1 heaping tablespoon coconut oil

Optional: blueberries, banana slices, sliced strawberries, or other fruit

1. In a large bowl, whisk the egg, and add the milk, beating both together.
2. Add the sourdough to the bowl and whisk all together.
3. Whisk in the syrup, salt, baking soda, melted butter, and enough flour to make a batter that is neither too thin nor too thick.
4. Melt the ghee and coconut oil together in a skillet over medium heat. When the ghee and oil are hot but before they begin to smoke, use a ladle or cup measure to pour in the batter in circles about 4 to 5 inches in diameter. At this point you can add some blueberries, banana slices, strawberry slices, or a little of whatever fruit is in season to the pancakes. Cook until bubbles start to show and the pancakes are cooked around the edges, and then flip. Cook until cooked through, transfer to a plate, and top with butter while you cook the remaining pancakes. I like to serve with whole yogurt and jam, though maple syrup is of course the classic topping.

ON THE CUSP OF ANOTHER MOON

And I knew that the spirit that had gone forth to shape the world and make it live was still alive in it. I just had no doubt. I could see that I lived in the created world, and it was still being created. I would be part of it forever.

—WENDELL BERRY, *Jayber Crow*

I t is easy, when contemplating the devastation of the environment, the overall declining health in our society, the breakdown of community life, and the globalization of the corporate-industrial economy, to despair. So many of us give ourselves a pep talk and go about our daily lives trying to make a difference. We make a great effort to become better stewards of the Earth. We buy environmentally friendly products, conserve water, carpool, recycle our batteries, and try to eat locally. Living in the San Francisco Bay Area, I almost take for granted that the people I come in contact with have some consciousness of environmental issues, and make some adjustments in their daily life as a result. But I nevertheless have to acknowledge that we are a countercultural minority in this country.

Sometimes it gets tiresome to have alternative rather than normative values. One of the things I find most fascinating about studying life in indigenous villages is that many of the so-called alternative values I cherish—frugality, stewardship, maintenance of cultural traditions, community life, and a deep ecological awareness, to name a few—are cultural norms rather than countercultural alternatives.

Daily participation in the life of the village expresses, deepens, reinforces, and supports these values. But our society is so vast, so diverse, so young, and so oriented toward economic prosperity, individual freedom, and worldly power that we have not yet developed a set of ecologically sustainable values that are also widely embraced. As a result, anything that expresses an ecological ethic is fixed with a special label and set apart from mainstream society.

As the Wolf Moon gives way once again to the Hunger Moon and the cycle begins anew, the fate of wolves in this country makes an instructive example. By the late 1970s, environmentalists had managed to get federal funding for an effort to protect wolves and reintroduce them into the wild. By the 1990s this effort had been quite successful, and federally funded animal control forces were being called in by ranchers in some states to kill the wolves that other federal funds were protecting. Wolf lovers and conservationists launched a protest against these killings, pointing out that the numbers of livestock lost to predators is minimal compared with those lost to diseases and other factors. They argued that the loss of a limited number of livestock should be a price we are willing to pay for the protection of a magnificent wild animal. Furthermore, wolves are considered an umbrella species: When we protect habitat for wolves, we protect whole ecosystems and countless other species within them. Meanwhile, ranchers defended their right to protect their herds with guns.

One novel innovation to come out of this controversy was a herd management approach called predator-friendly ranching. Certain ranchers began to protect their sheep and cows from predators by using shepherding dogs, llamas, and humans as chaperones for their ruminant herds. These escorts helped minimize the number of livestock taken by predators in certain areas. The ranchers agreed not to kill those predators that still managed to attack livestock, and to accept a certain amount of loss as part of the business. A certification for predator-friendly products was developed, and you can now purchase predator-friendly wool, lamb, and beef to support these ranchers.

This is great. But if you're like me, you bristle at all these labels: *What will they think of next?* We already have songbird-safe coffee, salmon-safe wine, and now predator-friendly beef. Why does everything have to be so complicated? I find myself wishing that the foods I believe in could just be regular, everyday fare. I wish that instead all the special labels were applied to foods produced using dangerous or questionable practices. How different it would be to shop in a grocery store and see labels that read: Sprayed with Pesticides; Grown Where Rain Forest Was Clear-cut; Genetically Modified; Chickens Kept in Cramped Cages with Their Beaks Burned Off; Shipped from the Other Side of the Planet; or Wolves Killed in Order to Protect This Cow. For simplicity's sake we could just cut to the chase with labels like: Toxic, Cruel to Animals, Unnatural, and Earth-unfriendly. If food didn't have any of these labels, you would know it was organically grown, humanely ranched, free of additives, and processed, packaged, and distributed with a sense of wise stewardship.

This frustration may become compounded once you start following the principles of traditional nutrition. Rather than merely free-range beef, you want grass-fed and grass-finished. It is not enough to eat sauerkraut made from organic cabbage, you want it lacto-fermented, preferably slowly in a ceramic crock. You don't just want bread from organically grown wheat, you want to make sure it was sprouted or naturally leavened. It is no longer enough to have organic, nonhomogenized milk, you want it 100 percent raw from cows that ate biodiverse pasture. You're concerned about chickens' beaks being intact but also want to make sure they got to eat lots of bugs and grasses and feed without too much soy in it. Again, life can start to feel very complicated. The healthy indigenous peoples that Weston Price studied didn't have to struggle with these things on an individual level. Over millennia they had evolved a set of foodways that kept their community healthy and their ecosystems thriving. What they ate was their everyday food; it was what everyone they knew, or visited, or invited over, also ate. Their nutritional needs were met by their culture as part of their survival strategy. Similarly, environmental stewardship was integrated into everyday life.

We face a different set of challenges. When you make a decision to eat nutrient-dense foods and traditional fats, you place yourself outside the mainstream of our culture. The same is true when you decide to be an ecological steward. Your family, friends, religious community, coworkers, neighbors, and others might think you are a bit of a weirdo. I think there is always a delicate balance between adhering to your convictions and participating in community. Because I believe community is so important in our lives, I often decide to set aside my nutritional or ecological preferences in order to share meals and other activities with people whom I value being in relationship with. As much as I dislike using ecologically irresponsible products like disposable plates and plasticware, I don't refuse to eat off them. While I soak my grains when cooking at home, I don't expect that others will do this when I eat at their houses. While I carry around a reusable cup that I use if I stop at a coffee shop, I don't lecture those who fail to do this. We each make compromises every day. Purity and perfection are impossible. This is the real world, and we are fallible and human. It takes a lot of energy to swim against the cultural current, and sometimes you just need to go with the flow.

In the next decades we need to change the course of the flow. Or at least to create more and more little tidal pools along the stream—areas of respite from the dominant paradigm. Environmental factors may well cause a sea change in cultural norms, and those of us who have developed some alternative resources, skills, and strategies will be better equipped to cope. But one thing is for sure: None of us can do it alone. As much as this country has been built on the ideals of freedom and independence, the sea change will start with a recognition of our interdependence. We will once again acknowledge that everything is connected; life is a web of mutual indebtedness. Every part of nature, wild or domesticated, animal, vegetable, mineral, or elemental, is a precious and vital part of this web. Even the lowliest, least prized scrap of life—a moldy fungus, or slimy algae, or bit of unimpressive rock—may have some great gift to offer that will help us out of our trouble. But we will never make it on human genius alone.

I believe that there is a great intelligence at work in the universe. I trust it. I believe it works through human beings but not only through human beings. I believe it works through every part of life, and that even the things that I most decry—slavery, war, colonialism, commodification, nutritional degeneration, environmental destruction—are part of this vast and incomprehensible intelligence. These tragedies contain the difficult lessons to be learned if human life on Earth is to continue.

So there is no reason to despair. There is only the opportunity to participate in Creation—to participate as fully as we are able. That we shall die one day is a certainty. So the question is only: How shall we live? How present can we be? How courageous? How trusting? How loving? How thoughtful? How forgiving?

And so my final prayer is for each of you, and for me, too: That we may find within our hearts the faith, hope, and love to live ourselves into a world where action is balanced by relationship, and vision is balanced by tradition. May each of us have the opportunity to make the contribution to the world that we have been called to make. May each of us give the gift that we came here to bear. And may these gifts feed the hunger for connection that is such an enduring part of the human condition, so that we may have that delicious experience of being—at least for a moment—well fed.

RESOURCES

INGREDIENTS

Animal products, humanely raised: The Eat Well Guide (www.eat wellguide.org) is an online directory of farms, stores, restaurants, and mail-order outlets that offer sustainably raised meat, poultry, dairy, and eggs from the United States and Canada.

Bee pollen: Bee pollen is widely available at health food stores and farmer's markets. Look for pollen that is frozen and has not been stored at room temperature.

Beet kvass and rusell: Both beet kvass and rusell are traditional sour fermented liquids (similar to vinegar) made from beets. I follow the beet kvass recipe from *Nourishing Traditions* by Sally Fallon (see New Trends Publishing Company), though I usually use half the salt.

Birch syrup: The cooked-down sap of the birch tree—look for 100 percent pure Alaskan. Try www.juniperridge.com; www.alaskabirch syrup.com; or www.birchboy.com.

Bouquet garni: This is a classical element in French cookery, and I use it all the time. It is a little bundle of herbs tied together. Because you remove it before pureeing or serving, it makes use of the tough stems of herbs and saves the trouble of removing leaves from fresh herbs. You can buy them already made at specialty food stores, but I just make one whenever I'm cooking. The classic herbs in a bouquet garni are:

- Bay leaf
- Parsley (stems with most leaves removed)
- Thyme (stems with or without leaves attached)
- Sage (leaves and/or stems)

You can also add:
- Oregano (stems with or without leaves attached)
- Marjoram (stems with or without leaves attached)
- Rosemary stems (needles removed)—rosemary has a strong
  flavor and I usually only use it for chicken or beef soups or stews.

All of these herbs can be fresh or dried. I just lay a twelve-inch piece of string out on a cutting board and add the bay leaf and whatever other stems I have on hand across it on the perpendicular. (I often don't have parsley stems, so I just skip that herb.) Then I wrap the string around the middle of the bundle a few times and tie in a bow. My usual bundle has just bay leaves, thyme stems, and sage stems and is about as thin as my pinkie finger, if not thinner. A bouquet garni infuses your soup or stew with wonderful flavor. Once you get the hang of it, it is very easy. It is a great way to use herbs from your garden.

Crème fraîche: I always make my own crème fraîche, since it's so easy and satisfying. I put 1 tablespoon of the last batch of crème fraîche (or from a store-bought container) into the bottom of a 1-pint jar. Then I add 1½ cups heavy cream and whisk together gently. I put this in a warm place—I put mine on top of the pilot light on my gas stove—for 24–36 hours, then transfer to the fridge. That's it.

Ginger bug: This culture was traditionally made for ginger beer. I think it is also the best culture for root beer. In a 1-pint, wide-mouth jar, put 1 cup of water. Add 2 teaspoons of white sugar and 2 teaspoons of grated fresh ginger, put on the lid, and shake it up. Set the jar in a warm spot. The next day add the same amount of ginger and sugar and shake and return to the warm spot. Repeat each day until it starts to bubble and come alive. It usually only takes mine 3 or 4 days to do so, but if your spot isn't as warm it might take up to a week.

Grass-fed meats and pastured poultry: Contact a Weston A. Price Foundation chapter leader for a recommendation of a source in your area. The list of leaders can be found online at www.weston aprice.org/localchapters.

Also check out the list on www.eatwild.com.

The American Grassfed Association has a contact list for producers by state at www.americangrassfed.com.

Kefir grains: These little clusters of cauliflower-like grains are actually a community of yeasts and bacteria that will culture (lactoferment) milk or other liquids. When they culture milk, they reproduce and grow, and so extra ones can be harvested and used in sodas. I got my grains from an acquaintance who made kefir, and if you contact your local chapter of the Weston A. Price Foundation you may be able to find someone locally who will share them with you. There are also some people who share them through Internet connections. You can purchase them from G.E.M. Cultures.

Kombucha mother: This community of yeasts looks like a cross between a jellyfish and a pancake. When used to make kombucha, it reproduces—so kombucha mothers are often available from people who regularly make kombucha. If you contact your local chapter of the Weston A. Price Foundation you may be able to find someone locally who will share one with you. There are also some people who share them through Internet connections. You can purchase them from G.E.M. Cultures.

Kuzu: A starch made from the kuzu (kudzu) root in Japan. It is a wonderful, traditional thickener. Available from health food stores or many places online.

Local foods, farms, and ranches: Check out www.localharvest.com for a great nationwide list of small farms, farmer's markets, and more. The site www.newfarm.org/farmlocator can help you find farms near you. And of course check out your local farmer's market.

Native nutrition: To learn more about the nutritional wisdom of traditional peoples, peruse the Weston A. Price Foundation's Web site: www.westonaprice.org. You can also find more links at Jessica's Web site, www.wisefoodways.com.

Palm sugar: The cooked-down sap of the palm tree. You can find it at Asian grocery stores, especially Thai groceries, or online. It comes either as cakes wrapped in plastic or as a hardened mass in a jar. If you have a choice, get the cakes. I think it is easier to cut them than to wrestle it out of a jar. I just shave the sugar off the cake with a knife until I have enough. Coconut sugar is also available and very similar—made from the sap of the coconut palm.

Pickle brine: If you make lactofermented pickles, the brine is a wonderful way to finish many soups and stews. I make pickles following Sandor Ellix Katz's recipe in the book *Wild Fermentation* (Chelsea Green).

Raw milk and cream: Each state has its own laws. Contact a Weston A. Price Foundation chapter leader for a recommendation of a source in your area. The list of leaders can be found online at www.weston aprice.org/localchapters. See also www.realmilk.com.

Sourdough: Sourdough means many different things to different people. This is how to prepare sourdough for the recipes in this book.

Take 1 tablespoon of sourdough starter and mix it together with ½ cup filtered water and 1 cup freshly ground whole wheat (or spelt) flour in a clean jar. Let this sit for 8 hours at room temperature or between 48 hours and 1 week in the refrigerator before using in the recipe. You can use it at room temperature, or cold. Each time you cook with your sourdough, reserve 1 tablespoon of starter, mix with ½ cup water plus 1 cup flour, and store in the fridge for the next recipe. You can keep your starter going indefinitely this way. Mine is about 15 years old.

The best way to get a good sourdough starter is from a friend or an artisanal bakery. There are folks online who will send you some dehydrated starter for next to nothing, which is very generous of them. I don't recommend making a starter with commercial yeast. The great thing about a real sourdough starter is that it is made up of wild yeasts—that's what you want. Try G.E.M. Cultures for sourdough as well.

Sorghum molasses: Sold as sweet sorghum by www.lehmans.com. Type "sorghum" into the search engine or go to the pantry and you'll find it.

Sprouted spelt flour: This is flour made from organic spelt berries that have been sprouted and then dried. It is available online from www.creatingheaven.net. There is also a wonderful hot cereal.

Sucanat: Dehydrated sugar cane juice, also sold as Rapadura. Available at health food stores and natural groceries.

Wise Food Ways: Check out Jessica's Web site at www.wisefood ways.com.

Yogurt whey: To make yogurt whey, simply take a quart of organic, live-culture whole milk yogurt and pour it into a colander or strainer lined with cheesecloth set above a bowl or pot. Let drip for 8 hours or so (I usually put mine in the fridge while it drips). In the bowl or pot will be the whey. In the cheesecloth will be yogurt cream or yogurt cheese, which you can use as you would cream cheese.

INGREDIENT SOURCES AND PUBLISHERS

The American Grassfed Association
P.O. Box 400
Kiowa, CO 80117
877-77GRASS
www.americangrassfed.com

Birch Boy
P.O. Box 637
Haines, AK 99827
907-767-5660
www.birchboy.com

Campaign for Real Milk
www.realmilk.com

Chelsea Green Publishing Company
85 North Main Street, Suite 120
P.O. Box 428
White River Junction, VT 05001
802-295-6300
www.chelseagreen.com
Order many books on sustainable living, including food and agriculture titles. Sandor Katz's *Wild Fermentation* is a wonderful resource on live cultured foods. Check out *This Organic Life* by Joan Dye Gussow, *The Bread Builders* by Daniel Wing and Alan Scott, *American Farmstead Cheese* by Paul Kindstedt, and *The Maple Sugar Book* by Helen and Scott Nearing. Chelsea Green also distributes Joel Salatin's books.

Eat Well Guide
Global Resource Action Center for the Environment (GRACE)
215 Lexington Avenue, Suite 1001
New York, NY 10016
212-726-9161
www.eatwellguide.org

G.E.M. Cultures
30301 Sherwood Road
Fort Bragg, CA 95437
707-964-2922
www.gemcultures.com
Although I have never purchased from them, they are a well-respected source for kefir grains, kombucha mothers, and sourdough starters.

Juniper Ridge
P.O. Box 5535
Berkeley, CA 94705
800-205-9499
www.juniperridge.com

Kahiltna Birchworks
P.O. Box 2267
Palmer, Alaska 99645
800-380-7457
www.alaskabirchsyrup.com

Local Farm Locator
www.newfarm.org/farmlocator

Local Harvest
220 21st Avenue
Santa Cruz, CA 95062
831-475-8150
www.localharvest.com

New Trends Publishing Company
401 Kings Highway
Winona Lake, IN 46590
888-707-1776
www.newtrendspublishing.com
Order books about food and nutrition, including *Nourishing Traditions* by Sally Fallon, *Fourfold Path to Healing* by Thomas Cowan, *The Untold Story of Milk* by Ron Schmidt, *The Yoga of Eating* by Charles Eisenstein, and other wonderful titles.

Radiant Life Wellness Catalog
P.O Box 2326
Novato, CA 94948
888-593-9595
www.radiantlifecatalog.com
A good source for Bernard Jensen's gelatin.

Summers Sprouted Flour Co.
P.O. Box 337
Torreon, NM 87061
877-384-0337
www.creatingheaven.net

ORGANIZATIONS AND GROUPS

American Farmland Trust (AFT)
1200 18th Street NW
Washington, DC 20036
202-331-7300
www.farmland.org
AFT has three strategies for saving America's farmland: to protect the best land through publicly funded agricultural conservation easement programs; to plan for growth with agriculture in mind through effective community planning and growth management; and to keep the land healthy for farmland through encouraging stewardship and conservations practices.

Bioneers and the Collective Heritage Institute
6 Cerro Circle
Lamy, NM 87540
1-877-BIONEER
www.bioneers.org
The Collective Heritage Institute, also known as Bioneers, was conceived to conduct educational and economic development programs in the conservation of biological and cultural diversity, traditional farming practices, and environmental restoration.

The Center for Ecoliteracy
2528 San Pablo Avenue
Berkeley, CA 94702
www.ecoliteracy.org
The Center for Ecoliteracy is dedicated to education for sustainable living.

The Center for Progressive Christianity (TCPC)
99 Brattle Street
Cambridge, MA 02138
617-441-0928
www.tcpc.org

TCPC provides guiding ideas, networking opportunities, and resources for progressive churches, organizations, individuals and others with connections to Christianity. The Center also affirms the variety and depth of human experience and the richness of each person's search for meaning, and encourages the use of sound scholarship, critical inquiry, and all intellectual powers to understand the presence of God in human life.

The Center for Traditional Medicine (CTM)
1001 Cooper Point SW, #140
Olympia, WA 98502
360-586-0117
www.centerfortraditionalmedicine.org
CTM conducts research, education and clinical treatment that integrates traditional systems of indigenous healing with complementary and integrative medicine. The center promotes social change through its activities by and for Native and non-Native peoples worldwide.

The Center for World Indigenous Studies (CWIS)
PMB 214
1001 Cooper Point Road SW, Suite 140
Olympia, WA 98502
360-407-1095
www.cwis.org
CWIS is dedicated to wider understanding and appreciation of the ideas and knowledge of indigenous peoples and the social, economic, and political realities of indigenous nations.

The Center for Visionary Activism
888-741-GODS
www.visionaryactivism.com
Caroline Casey's work is dedicated to the wild blooming of the compassionate trickster heart stirring within all of us everywhere and always and the cultivation of unique, empathic imaginative ingenuity, which encourages this blooming.

The Community Alliance with Family Farmers (CAFF)
36355 Russell Boulevard
Davis, CA 95617
530-756-8518
www.caff.org
CAFF is building a movement of rural and urban people to foster family-scale agriculture that cares for the land, sustains local economies, and promotes social justice.

Cultures on the Edge
www.culturesontheedge.com
Worldwide some 300 million people, roughly 5 percent of the global population, still retain a strong identity as members of an indigenous culture, rooted in history and language, attached by myth and memory to a particular place on the planet. Though their populations are small, these cultures collectively represent as much as half of the intellectual legacy of humanity. Yet increasingly their voices are being silenced, their unique visions of life itself lost in a whirlwind of change and conflict. Cultures on the Edge is dedicated to open dialogue and increasing global awareness about these unique segments of humanity.

The David Suzuki Foundation
2211 West 4th Avenue, Suite 219
Vancouver, BC V6K 4S2
Canada
800-453-1533
www.davidsuzuki.org
The David Suzuki Foundation works to find ways for society to live in balance with the natural world that sustains us. Focusing on four program areas—oceans and sustainable fishing, forests and wild lands, climate change and clean energy, and the web of life—the Foundation uses science and education to promote solutions that help conserve nature.

Echoes of the Ancestors
www.malidoma.org
This organization was created by Malidoma Somé and is dedicated to
the preservation of the Wisdom of the Dagara people of West Africa.

The Ecological Farming Association (EFA)
406 Main Street, Suite 313
Watsonville, CA 95076
831-763-2111
www.eco-farm.org
EFA's programs bring together growers, consumers, educators,
activists, and industry related businesses to exchange the latest
advances in sustainable food production and marketing.

Ecotrust
Jean Vollum Natural Capital Center
721 NW Ninth Avenue, Suite 200
Portland, OR 97209
503-227-6225
www.ecotrust.org
Ecotrust's mission is to build Salmon Nation, a place where people and
wild salmon thrive. Citizens of Salmon Nation want to live in a place
where economic, ecological, and social conditions are improving,
where a "conservation economy" is emerging.

The En'owkin Centre
RR2, S50, C8
Lot 45 Green Mt. Road
Penticton, BC V2A 6J7
Canada
250-493-7181
www.enowkincentre.ca
The Centre was founded by Jeanette Armstrong and is an Indigenous
cultural, educational, ecological, and creative arts post-secondary
institution that practices and implements Indigenous knowledge and
systems.

Flowering Mountain
Martín Prechtel
P.O. Box 28474
Santa Fe, NM 87592
www.floweringmountain.com
Martín Prechtel presents the Teachings of the Flowering Mountain. "Deep in our bones resides an ancient, singing couple who just won't give up making their beautiful, wild noise. The world won't end if we can find them."

GRACE Factory Farm Project
215 Lexington Avenue, Suite 1001
New York, NY 10016
212-726-9161
www.factoryfarm.org
The goal of the Factory Farm Project is to eliminate factory farming in favor of a sustainable food production system that is healthful and humane, economically viable, and ecologically sound.

Heifer International
P.O. Box 8058
Little Rock, AR 72203
800-422-0474
www.heifer.org
Heifer's mission is to work with communities to end hunger and poverty and to care for the earth. They do this by giving families a source of food (such as dairy animals, laying hens, and honey bees) rather than short-term relief. Their strategy is about "passing on the gift"—as people share their animals' offspring with others—along with their knowledge, resources, and skills—an expanding network of hope, dignity, and self-reliance is created that reaches around the globe.

The Humane Farming Association (HFA)
www.hfa.org
HFA's goals are to protect farm animals from cruelty, to protect the public from the dangerous misuse of antibiotics, hormones, and other

chemicals used on factory farms, and to protect the environment from the impacts of industrialized animal factories.

The International Forum on Globalization (IFG)
1009 General Kennedy Avenue, #2
San Francisco, CA 94129
415-561-7650
www.ifg.org
IFG is a North-South research and educational institution composed of leading activists, economists, scholars, and researchers providing analyses and critiques on the cultural, social, political, and environmental impacts of economic globalization.

The International Society for Ecology and Culture (ISEC)
(ISEC UK)
Foxhole
Dartington
Devon TQ9 6EB
United Kingdom
01803-868650

(ISEC USA)
P.O. Box 9475
Berkeley, CA 94709
510-548-4915
www.isec.org.uk
ISEC is concerned with the protection of both biological and cultural diversity, and promoting locally based alternatives to the global consumer culture.

National Family Farm Coalition (NFFC)
110 Maryland Avenue N.E., Suite 307
Washington, DC 20002
202-543-5675
fax 202-543-0978
www.nffc.org

The NFFC represents family farm and rural groups whose members face the challenge of the deepening economic recession in rural communities caused primarily by low farm prices and the increasing corporate control of agriculture.

The Ontario Consultants on Religious Tolerance (OCRT)
(Main office in Canada)
Box 27026
Kingston, ON K7M 8W5
Canada

(USA-P.O. Box only)
P.O. Box 128
Watertown, NY 13601-0128
www.religioustolerance.org
OCRT is an agency that promotes the freedom of individuals to follow the religious path of their choosing, without discrimination or oppression.

Price-Pottenger Nutrition Foundation
P.O. Box 2614
La Mesa, CA 91943
619-462-7600
www.ppnf.org
PPNF is a nonprofit organization that preserves, protects, and disseminates the research of Dr. Weston A. Price, DDS, Dr. Francis M. Pottenger, Jr., MD, and other pioneers in the field of nutrition and care of the environment.

Slow Food USA
20 Jay Street, Suite 313
Brooklyn, NY 11201
718-260-8000
www.slowfoodusa.org
Slow Food USA is an educational organization dedicated to stewardship of the land and ecologically sound food production; to the revival

of the kitchen and the table as centers of pleasure, culture, and community; to the invigoration and proliferation of regional, seasonal culinary traditions; to the creation of a collaborative, ecologically oriented, and virtuous globalization; and to living a slower and more harmonious rhythm of life.

The Sustainability Institute (SI)
3 Linden Road
Hartland, VT 05048
802-436-1277
www.sustainer.org
SI focuses on understanding the root causes of unsustainable behavior in complex systems to help restructure systems and shift mindsets that will help move human society toward sustainability.

Weston A. Price Foundation
PMB 106-380
4200 Wisconsin Avenue NW
Washington, DC 20016
202-363-4394
www.westonaprice.org
The Foundation is dedicated to restoring nutrient-dense foods to the human diet through education, research, and activism. It supports a number of movements that contribute to this objective including accurate nutrition instruction, organic and biodynamic farming, pasture-feeding of livestock, community-supported farms, honest and informative labeling, prepared parenting and nurturing therapies.

SUGGESTED READING

Buhner, Stephen Harrod. *Sacred and Herbal Healing Beers*. Boulder, Colorado: Siris Books, 1988.

Berry, Wendell. *A Place on Earth*. New York: Counterpoint Books, 1983.

———. *Jayber Crow*. New York: Counterpoint Books, 2000.

———. *That Distant Land*. New York: Counterpoint Books, 2004.

———. *Three Short Novels*. New York: Counterpoint Books, 2004.

———. *The Memory of Old Jack*. New York: Counterpoint Books, 1999.

———. *Hannah Coulter*. Emeryville, California: Shoemaker & Hoard, 2004.

Borg, Marcus. *The Heart of Christianity*. San Francisco: Harper San Francisco, 2004.

———. *Reading the Bible Again for the First Time*. San Francisco: Harper San Francisco, 2002.

Cowan, Thomas. *The Fourfold Path to Healing*. Winona Lake, Indiana: New Trends Publishing, 2004.

Davidson, Alan. *The Oxford Companion to Food*. Oxford and New York: Oxford University Press, 1999.

Davis, Wade. *One River*. New York: Simon and Schuster, 1997.

Diamond, Jared. *Guns, Germs, and Steel*. New York: W.W. Norton and Company, 1999.

———. *Collapse*. New York: Viking, 2004.

Fadiman, Anne. *The Spirit Catches You and You Fall Down*. New York: Farrar, Straus and Giroux, 1998.

Fallon, Sally. *Nourishing Traditions*. Winona Lake, Indiana: New Trends Publishing, 2000.

Fisher, M.F.K. *How to Cook a Wolf.* New York: North Point Press, 1988.

Hyde, Lewis. *The Gift*. New York: Vintage, 1983.

Katz, Sandor. *Wild Fermentation*. White River Junction, Vermont: Chelsea Green Publishing, 2003.

Kingsolver, Barbara. *Prodigal Summer.* New York: Harper Perennial, 2001.

Mollison, Bill. *The Permaculture Book of Ferment and Human Nutrition*. Berkeley, California: Ten Speed Press, 1997.

Naylor, Gloria. *Mama Day.* New York: Vintage, 1989.

Norberg-Hodge, Helena. *Ancient Futures*. San Francisco: Sierra Club Books, 1992.

Prechtel, Martín. *Secrets of the Talking Jaguar*. New York: Tarcher, 1999.

———. *Long Life, Honey in the Heart*. Berkeley, California: North Atlantic Books, 2004.

———. *The Toe Bone and the Tooth*. Berkeley, California: North Atlantic Books, 2004.

———. *The Disobedience of the Daughter of the Sun*. Somerville, Massachusetts: Yellow Moon Press, 2001.

Price, Weston A. *Nutrition and Physical Degeneration*. La Mesa, California: Price-Pottenger Nutrition Foundation, 14th printing, 2000. (First published in 1939.)

Shapiro, Laura. *Perfection Salad: Women and Cooking at the Turn of the Century*. New York: Modern Library, 2001.

Smiley, Jane. *The Greenlanders*. New York: Ballantine Books, 1996.

Somé, Malidoma Patrice. *Of Water and the Spirit*. New York: Penguin Books, 1995.

———. *The Healing Wisdom of Africa*. New York: Tarcher, 1999.

Schmidt, Ron. *The Untold Story of Milk*. Winona Lake, Indiana: New Trends Publishing, 2003.

Spyri, Johanna. *Heidi*. New York: Children's Classics, 1998.

Tiwari, Maya. *Ayurveda: A Life of Balance*. Rochester, Vermont: Healing Arts Press, 1994.

Wilder, Laura Ingalls. *Little House* box set. New York: HarperTrophy, 1994.

NOTES

Introduction: Lunar Calendars and Traditional Food Ways

p. xxi *Stars around the beautiful moon:* Anne Carson, trans., *If Not, Winter: Fragments of Sappho.* New York: Vintage Books, 2003.

p. xviv *We have forgotten, it is the Moon When the Clouds Become White:* A. C. Hollis, *Masai: Myths, Tales and Riddles.* New York: Dover Publications, 2003, pp. 98–99. Taken from a study originally published in 1905 called "The Masai: Their Language and Folklore."

Chapter 1: Hunger Moon

p. 9 For an essay by Jeanette Armstrong and more information about the Four Societies, see *Ecological Literacy*, Michael K. Stone and Zenobia Barlow, eds. San Francisco: Sierra Club Books, 2005.

Chapter 2: The Sap Moon

p. 24 *Once again we shall:* Basil Johnston, *Ojibway Heritage.* Lincoln, Nebraska: Bison Books, 1990, p. 145.

p. 25–26 *The season of sugar-making came:* W. J. Hoffman, "The Menomini Indians," 14th Annual Report of the Bureau of Ethnology, Washington, DC, 1896, part I, p. 288.

p. 26 *No more knowledge is necessary:* Benjamin Rush, *An Account of the Sugar Maple-Tree of the United States.* 1792.

p. 26 *Generally, they prefer their maple sugar:* Johann Georg Kohl, *Kitchi-Gami.* Bremen: Schunemann, 1859, p. 140.

p. 27 *Prepare for making maple sugar:* Robert B. Thomas, *The Farmer's Almanack*, 1803.

p. 27 *Make your own sugar:* Ibid., 1805.

p. 27 *two important recommendations:* Zadock Thompson, *History of Vermont.* Burlington: Goodrich, 1842, p. 210.

p. 27 *The earth offers us* soma: Maya Tiwari, *Ayurveda: A Life of Balance.* Rochester, VT: Healing Arts Press, 1995, p. 181.

p. 28 *it provides not only food and drink:* Alan Davidson, *The Oxford Companion to Food.* Oxford: Oxford University Press, 1999, p. 199.

p. 28–29 *Near the colorful Damnoen Saduak floating market:* Kasma Loha-unchit, *It Rains Fishes.* Rohnert Park, CA: Pomegranate Artbooks, 1995, pp. 61–62.

p. 30   *Only during the last century has man's diet:* Sally Fallon (with Mary Enig, PhD), *Nourishing Traditions,* Second Revised Edition. Washington, DC: New Trends Publishing, 2001, p. 21.

p. 31   *When we consume refined sugars and starches:* Ibid., p. 22.

p. 35   *The way we commonly used our sugar while encamped:* James Smith, *An Account of Remarkable Occurences during Captivity with the Indians, 1755–59.* Philadelphia: Grigg, 1831, p. 44.

p. 37   *In short, 'tis to live in a perpetual Noise and Hurry:* Thomas Tryon, *Friendly advice to gentlemen-planters of the East and West Indies.* London, 1700, pp. 201–202.

p. 37   *So rapid was the motion of the mill:* W. L. Mathieson, *British Slavery and Its Abolition.* London: Longmans, Green, 1926, p. 63.

p. 38   *There are great differences between families using ancient wooden machinery:* Sidney Mintz, *Sweetness and Power.* New York: Viking, 1985, p. 52.

p. 39   *To "Barbados" someone became a seventeenth-century verb for stealing humans:* Ibid., p. 52.

Chapter 3: The Egg Moon

p. 48   *I only remember my grandfather would put the egg up:* Eugene S. Hunn, Darryll R. Johnson, Priscilla N. Russell, and Thomas F. Thornton, "Huna Tlingit Traditional Environmental Knowledge, Conservation, and Management of a 'Wilderness' Park," *Current Anthropology* 44, Supplement (2003): S86

p. 54   *Inhumane, fecal-factory, concentration-camp mausoleum houses:* Joel Salatin, "'Sound Science' Is Killing Us," *Acres USA* 34, no. 4 (April 2004).

p. 56   *It is amazing when people find out the truth:* Joel Salatin, "The State of the Eco-Union," *Acres USA* 33, no. 5 (May 2003).

p. 57–58   *Since Viti Levu, one of the islands of this group:* Weston A. Price, *Nutrition and Physical Degeneration,* Price-Pottenger Nutrition Foundation, 1997 (first published in 1939), pp. 110–111.

p. 58–59   *Eggs have provided mankind with high-quality protein:* Sally Fallon (with Mary Enig, PhD), *Nourishing Traditions,* Second Revised Edition. Washington, DC: New Trends Publishing, 2001, p. 436.

p. 59–60   *Johnson started with two chicken houses:* Monte Mitchell, "Poultry Growers at Mercy of Industrialized Agriculture and Short, Tenuous Contracts Drawn Up by Food Giants," *Winston-Salem Journal* (June 20, 2004).

p. 61–62   *Large farming businesses, reluctant to provide outdoor access:* "Raising Organic Chickens, Salmonella, and the Issues of Outdoor Access" by Robert Hadad, director of Farming Systems, Farm Animals and Sustainable Agriculture Section, Humane Society of the United States, p. 1.

p. 62–63 *One of the restaurants we used to sell to had a salmonella outbreak:* Salatin, "The State of the Eco-Union."

Chapter 4: The Milk Moon

p. 70 *My speckled heifer will give me her milk:* From the milking song "Ortha nan Gaidheal" from the *Carmina Gadelica*, Gaelic chants, songs, and poems collected and translated by Alexander Carmichael during the nineteenth century. They can be accessed online at http://www.smo.uhi.ac.uk/gaidhlig/corpus/Carmina/.

p. 70 *I love you, my favorite cow:* From the liner notes to *African Sanctus*, an unorthodox setting of the Latin Mass harmonized with traditional African music, composed and recorded by David Fanshawe on his journeys up the Nile River in 1969–1973. This music is currently available from Fanshawe One World Music, Box 574, Malborough Wilts, SN8 2SP, United Kingdom, or from www.africansanctus.com.

p. 71–72 *Almost every household has goats or cows or both:* Weston A. Price, *Nutrition and Physical Degeneration*, Price-Pottenger Nutrition Foundation, 1997 (first published in 1939), p. 26.

p. 75 *I grew up in an idyllic village not far from the sea:* Maya Tiwari, *Ayurveda: A Life of Balance*. Rochester, VT: Healing Arts Press, 1995, p. 176.

p. 75–76 *Some of my best memories of living closer to nature:* Helena Norberg-Hodge, *Ancient Futures*. San Francisco: Sierra Club Books, 1991, pp. 26–29.

p. 76 *Most milk, oma, is made into butter, mar:* Ibid., p. 30.

p. 77 *Their estimate of a desirable dairy stock is based on quality:* Price, p. 137.

p. 79–80 *The War of 1812 with England resulted in the permanent cutting off:* Ron Schmidt, *The Untold Story of Milk*. Washington, DC: New Trends Publishing, 2003, p. 32.

p. 80–81 *Today in confinement dairies throughout America cows:* Ibid., p. 38.

p. 81–82 *At the midwife's bidding and Ya Lur's command:* Martín Prechtel, *Long Life, Honey in the Heart*. Berkeley, California: North Atlantic Books, 2004, pp.131–132.

p. 82 *I find the very idea of drinking unmodified milk disgusting:* Felipe Fernandez-Armesto, *Near a Thousand Tables*. New York: The Free Press, 2002, p. 71.

p. 84 *I find that on the spiritual level, milk reunites us:* Annemarie Colbin, *Food and Healing.* New York: Ballantine Books, 1986, pp. 156–157.

p. 85 *They wept and wept for life, for the grief of being a person:* Prechtel, p. 253.

p. 85–86 *Only an initiated man or Acha could marry a woman:* Ibid., p. 240–241.

p. 88 *To milk the cow is to praise the hand of God:* Mouth Music, "Milking the Cow," from the album *Mo-Di,* Triple Earth Music, 1993.

Chapter 5: The Moon of Making Fat

p. 95 *Dekar, don't get excited:* Tsering Wangmo and Zara Houshmand, *The Lhasa Moon Tibetan Cookbook.* Ithaca, New York: Snow Lion Publications, 1999, p. 13.

p. 97 *Fats from animal and vegetable sources provide:* Sally Fallon (with Mary Enig, PhD), *Nourishing Traditions,* Second Revised Edition. Washington, DC: New Trends Publishing, 2001, p. 4.

p. 98 *Seal oil provides a very important part of their nutrition:* Weston A. Price, *Nutrition and Physical Degeneration,* Price-Pottenger Nutrition Foundation, 1997 (first published in 1939), p. 70.

p. 98–99 *I have referred to the importance of a high vitamin butter:* Ibid., p. 291.

p. 100 *Running the plant material through an animal was, in fact, a general strategy:* "Nutrient Intake Among Saami People Today Compared with an Old, Traditional Saami Diet" by L. Haglin of the Department of Dietetics, Umea University Hospital, Sweden, 1991. Indexed on PubMed.

p. 107 *American breeders have started selecting for much leaner pigs:* Temple Grandin and Catherine Johnson, *Animals in Translation.* New York: Scribner, 2005, pp. 100–101.

p. 108 *One of the most important food components the body needs:* Thomas S. Cowan, MD, *The Fourfold Path to Healing.* Washington, DC: New Trends Publishing, 2004, p. 279.

p. 109 *The feeling of satiety is designed to tell us:* Ibid., pp. 278–279.

p. 110–111 *Traditionally, this marine diet has made the people of the Arctic Circle:* Marla Cone, "Dozens of Words for Snow, None for Pollution" *Mother Jones Magazine* (January–February 2005).

p. 111 *The average levels of PCBs and mercury in newborn babies' cord blood:* Ibid.

p. 112–113 *We inoculated three mounds of soil:* Paul Stamets, "Earth's Natural Internet: Healing the Planet with Mushrooms," *Whole Earth Magazine* (Fall 1999).

Chapter 6: The Mead Moon

p. 119   *I got a drink of the precious mead:* translated from the Norse by Carolyne Larrington.

p. 119   *It is so ancient a beverage that the linguistic root for mead,* medhu*:* Mikal Aasved, "Alcohol, Drinking, and Intoxication in Preindustrial Society: Theoretical, Nutritional, and Religious Considerations," PhD dissertation, University of California–Santa Barbara, 1988, pp. 410–411.

p. 120   *A Russian study of the inhabitants of the province of Georgia:* Sally Fallon (with Mary Enig, PhD), *Nourishing Traditions,* Second Revised Edition. Washington, DC: New Trends Publishing, 2001, p. 617.

p. 122   *Food and drink in Africa transform rapidly:* Robert A. Leonard, "Notes on Uki, East African Honey Wine," Oxford Symposium 1994. London: Prospect Books, pp. 136–140.

p. 122   *The avowed motive for the ban was to decrease drunkenness:* Ibid.

p. 123–124   *The gods were at war with one another for so long:* Adapted from *The Prose Edda* by Snorri Sturluson. The translation I read was by Jean I. Young, University of California Press, 1964, pp. 100–103.

p. 124   *Many ancient peoples viewed intoxication as an element of worship:* Tamra Andrews, *Nectar and Ambrosia: An Encyclopedia of Food in World Mythology.* Santa Barbara, CA: ABC-CLIO, 2000, p. 2.

p. 125   *Balche is a kind of mead, an intoxicating beverage:* Ibid., p. 15.

p. 125–126   *A typical ritual of the ancient Maya involved:* Ibid.

p. 126   *When shall I dance once more:* Euripides, *The Bacchae.* From *The Complete Greek Tragedies,* Volume IV: *Euripides,* edited by David Grene and Richmond Lattimore. Chicago: University of Chicago Press, 1959, pp. 581–582.

p. 127   *For now I raise the old, old hymn to Dionysus:* Ibid., p. 546.

p. 128   *Of itself* The Bacchae *needs neither apology nor general introduction:* Ibid., from the "Introduction to *The Bacchae*" by William Arrowsmith, p. 530.

p. 128   *What the divinity of Dionysus represents:* Ibid., p. 537

p. 129   *In the ritual of the Maenads is the ambivalence conveyed: Maenad.* Time-Life, 1987.

p. 129   *Alcoholics Anonymous currently estimates their United States membership:* John C. Higgins-Biddle, PhD, and Thomas Babor, PhD, at the Alcohol Research Center at the University of Connecticut Health Center, especially their 1996 report.

p. 135   *The Christian theologian Marcus Borg writes:* Marcus Borg, *The Heart of Christianity.* New York: HarperCollins Publishers, 2003, chapter 8.

Chapter 7: The Wort Moon

p. 141 *If they would eat nettles in March:* Susun Weed, *Healing Wise.* Woodstock, NY: Ash Tree Publishing, 1989, p. 172.

p. 141 *A plant, herb, or vegetable used for food: Compact Oxford English Dictionary,* Second Edition. Oxford: Oxford University Press, 2000, p. 2343, section page number 583.

p. 141 *Woortes, for which wee now:* Verstegan, quoted in ibid.

p. 141 *We find the healing power of worts:* Cockayne, quoted in ibid.

p. 141 *And worts and pansies there which grew:* A. S. Wilson, "Lyric Hopeless Love," quoted in ibid.

p. 142 *The World Health Organization recently estimated that 80 percent of the world's population:* Attributed to Farnsworth et al., "Medicinal Plants in Therapy," *Bulletin of the World Health Organization* 63 no. 6 (1985), pp. 965–981.

p. 145–146 *"Tongue of dog" may have referred to an herb:* Lynn Smythe, "Halloween's Herbal Legends," *Herb Quarterly* (fall 2003).

p. 148 *The infusion of malt or other grain:* OED.

p. 150 *To concoct, contrive, prepare, bring about, cause:* Ibid.

p. 151–152 *A survey of popular ethnic beverages will show:* Sally Fallon (with Mary Enig, PhD), *Nourishing Traditions,* Second Revised Edition. Washington, DC: New Trends Publishing, 2001 pp. 584–585.

p. 152 *Squatting by the fire, [Tomo] drank a calabash:* Wade Davis, *One River.* New York: Touchstone, 1996, pp. 281–282.

p. 153 *Today's sweet bubbly products are the toxic mimics:* I owe the phrase "toxic mimic" to Caroline Casey, who is well known for promoting "visionary activism."

p. 153 *Root beer and ginger ale are two familiar sodas:* Charles Eisenstein "The Real Real Thing," *Wise Traditions* (journal of the Weston A. Price Foundation), Spring 2003.

p. 154 *Spruce beer does not produce drowsiness:* Stephen Harrod Buhner, *Sacred and Herbal Healing Beers.* Boulder, CO: Siris Books, 1998, p. 253.

p. 154 *This drink is very pleasant and allsoe physicall:* Quoted in ibid., p. 248.

p. 154 *The wonderful Russian herbalist, Rita Bykhovsky:* Ibid., pp. 248–249.

p. 157 *Reviving the tradition of the alewife:* Fallon, p. 585.

Chapter 8: The Corn Moon

p. 166 *A 24-hour clock on which one hour represents 100,000 years:* Jared Diamond, "The Worst Mistake in the History of the Human Race," *Discover* (May 1987), pp. 64–66.

p. 166-167 *At Dickson Mounds, located near the confluence of the Spoon and Illinois rivers:* Ibid.

p. 167 *Hunter-gatherers have little or no stored food:* Ibid.

p. 168 *To produce grain in useful quantities requires rich flat land:* Quoted in Ron Schmidt, *The Untold Story of Milk*. Washington, DC: New Trends Publishing, 2003, p. 116.

p. 168 *These included the Swiss villagers in the Loetschental Valley:* Weston A. Price, *Nutrition and Physical Degeneration*, Price-Pottenger Nutrition Foundation, 1997 (first published in 1939), pp. 256–267.

p. 169 *Much farming work is shared, either by the whole community:* Helena Norberg-Hodge, *Ancient Futures*. San Francisco: Sierra Club Books, 1991, p. 53.

p. 171 *When it came time to plan for the next year:* Wendell Berry, *Jayber Crow*. New York: Counterpoint Books, 2000, pp. 184–185.

p. 175–176 *What's this you brought home with you, Honey:* Martín Prechtel, *The Toe Bone and the Tooth*. Berkeley, California: North Atlantic Books, 2004, p. 44.

p. 177 *[C]arbohydrate intake should be intimately related to our level of activity:* Thomas S. Cowan, MD, *The Fourfold Path to Healing*. Washington, DC: New Trends Publishing, 2004, p. 171.

Chapter 9: The Moon When Salmon Return to Earth

p. 187 *Welcome, friend Swimmer:* Franz Boas, *The Religion of the Kwakiutl Indians*, Part I: Texts (in the original Kwakiutl), Part II: Translations. New York: Columbia University Press, 1930, p. 179 of Part I, p. 184–185 of Part II.

p. 187 *More specifically, the Saanich of the Pacific Northwest:* Earle Claxton (author) and John Elliott (author/illustrator), "The Saanich Year," Saanich School Board 63, 1993 (ISBN 1-55036-366-2).

p. 188–189 *After a time, some signal passes between the two principals:* Freeman House, *Totem Salmon: Life Lessons from Another Species*. Boston: Beacon Press, 1999, pp. 25–26.

p. 191–192 *Why exactly was fish regarded as suitable Lenten fare:* Anthea Bell (translator), *History of Food*. Malden, MA: Blackwell Publishers, 2000. p. 313.

p. 194   *The first fish was treated as if it were a high-ranking chief:* Lewis Hyde, *The Gift: Imagination and the Erotic Life of Property.* New York: Vintage Books, 1983, pp. 26–27.

p. 195   *In all of northwestern California, the largest and most elaborate social event:* House, pp. 57–58.

p. 195–196 *In these traps, there get to be a mass of salmon:* Quoted in ibid., p. 58.

p. 197   *That these [indigenous] cultural conservation strategies were successful:* Ibid., p. 61.

p. 198   *A gift makes a connection:* Hyde, p. 56.

p. 198–199 *Because of the bonding power of gifts:* Ibid., pp. 66–67.

p. 199   *Gift exchange brings with it, therefore, a built-in check:* Ibid., p. 27.

p. 199   *The increase is the core of the gift, the kernel:* Ibid., p. 36.

p. 200–202 Kas-limaal, *that's what we call it,* kas-limaal, *mutual indebtedness:* Martín Prechtel, *Long Life, Honey in the Heart.* Berkeley, California: North Atlantic Books, 2004, pp. 347–349.

p. 201   *The idea is to get so entangled in debt that no normal human:* Ibid., p. 349.

Chapter 10: The Blood Moon

p. 209   *Those animals which I use for riding and loading:* Helena Norberg-Hodge, *Ancient Futures.* San Francisco: Sierra Club Books, 1991, p. 31.

p. 214–215 *He shook his head, got up to collect two more logs from the woodpile:* Barbara Kingsolver, *Prodigal Summer.* New York: HarperCollins, 2001, p. 322–323.

p. 215   *Bios is limited life, characterized life, life that dies:* Lewis Hyde, *The Gift: Imagination and the Erotic Life of Property.* New York: Vintage Books, 1983, p. 32.

p. 217   *Following tradition, they perform ritual prayers of gratitude:* Ulrike Koch, *The Saltmen of Tibet.* Documentary film, Zeitgeist Films, 1997.

p. 218   *For the Dagara people, death results in simply a different form:* Malidoma Patrice Somé, *The Healing Wisdom of Africa.* New York: Tarcher/Putnam, 1998, p. 53.

p. 219   *The [Vedic] law book of Manu (200 BC–AD 200):* Dwijendra Narayan Jha, *The Myth of the Holy Cow.* New York: Verso Books, 2004, pp. 91–92.

p. 221   *Light, pleasant, full of flavour, and good for digestion:* From the ancient text Mililidapañho, quoted in ibid., p. 68.

p. 221　*As is well known, throughout its history the religion:* Ibid., p. 72.

p. 221　*Fundamentalism itself—whether Christian, Jewish, or Muslim—is modern:* Marcus Borg, *Reading the Bible Again for the First Time.* San Francisco: Harper San Francisco, 2002, p. 7.

Chapter 11: The Snow Moon

p. 233　*Our stores are full:* Basil Johnston, *Ojibway Heritage.* Lincoln, Nebraska: University of Nebraska Press, 1990, p. 145.

p. 234–235　*The freshly lifted potatoes are washed clean:* Dawn Nelson and Douglas Nelson, "Chuno and Tunta," quoted in *The Oxford Companion to Food,* edited by Alan Davidson. Oxford: Oxford University Press, 1999, p. 185.

p. 237　*Each year, as the month of November approaches:* Hi Soo Shin Hepinstall, *Growing Up in a Korean Kitchen.* Berkeley, CA: Ten Speed Press, 2001, p. 93.

p. 237　*In the days of my childhood, kimchi made up virtually half:* Ibid., p. 94.

p. 237　*Our ancestors came up with a sagacious method to maximize:* Ibid., p. 95.

p. 240　*[k]imchi making remains a laborious, communal task:* Ibid., p. 94.

p. 240–241　*Most work done in the village is done collectively:* Malidoma Patrice Somé, *The Healing Wisdom of Africa.* New York: Tarcher/Putnam, 1999, p. 68.

p. 241　*I remember my mother uttering very moving:* Ibid., p. 69.

p. 242　*Nowhere in the world is the rearing of children primarily the responsibility:* Judith K. Brown, "A Note on the Division of Labor by Sex," *American Anthropologist* 72, no. 1073 (1970).

p. 244　*For three days and two nights:* Malidoma Patrice Somé, *Of Water and the Spirit.* New York: Penguin, 1994, pp. 69–70.

p. 245–246　*In the Vedas, the hands and feet are referred to as:* Maya Tiwari, *Ayurveda: A Life of Balance.* Rochester, VT: Healing Arts Press, 1995, pp. 153–154.

p. 250　*The nutrition of the people of the Loetschental Valley:* Weston A. Price, *Nutrition and Physical Degeneration,* Price-Pottenger Nutrition Foundation, 1997 (first published in 1939), p. 26.

p. 250–251　*The fermentation of vegetables (sauerkraut, kimchi, pickles):* Jacques De Langre, *Seasalt's Hidden Powers.* Quoted in Sally Fallon (with Mary Enig, PhD), *Nourishing Traditions,* Second Revised Edition. Washington, DC: New Trends Publishing, 2001, p. 488.

Chapter 12: The Moon of Long Nights

p. 259 *I've extinguished the flame:* Vinay Dharwadker, trans., *Kabir: The Weaver's Songs.* New Delhi, India: Penguin Books India, 2003, p. 109.

p. 260 *Among the Dagara, darkness is sacred:* Malidoma Patrice Somé, *Of Water and the Spirit.* New York: Penguin, 1994, pp. 175–176.

p. 261 *[t]he brain-wave readings were akin to those observed:* T. S. Wiley, *Lights Out: Sleep, Sugar and Survival.* New York: Pocket Books, 2000, p. 90.

p. 261–262 *It is statistically proven that ninety or so percent of all babies:* Ibid., p. 90.

p. 264 *The adrenal gland is the processor of stress:* Thomas S. Cowan, MD, *The Fourfold Path to Healing.* Washington, DC: New Trends Publishing, 2004, p. 193.

p. 266 *Shlain cites research to show that women risk death more readily:* Leonard Shlain, *Sex, Time, and Power: How Women's Sexuality Shaped Human Evolution.* New York: Viking: 2003, pp. 272–273.

p. 266 *Shlain believes menstruation was the vehicle for human understanding:* Ibid., p. 179.

p. 266–267 *In the late 1960s, writer Louise Lacey realized:* Katie Singer, *The Garden of Fertility.* New York: Penguin, 2004.

p. 270 *Hmong epileptics often become shamans:* Anne Fadiman, *The Spirit Catches You and You Fall Down.* New York: Noonday Press, 1997, p. 21.

p. 271–272 *Mythology is a projection of a community's collective beliefs:* Shlain, pp. 255–256.

p. 275 *For those of you who have begun to construct a romantic picture:* Somé, *Of Water and the Spirit*, p. 62.

p. 275–276 *In African indigenous culture, just as there is high respect:* Malidoma Patrice Somé, *The Healing Wisdom of Africa.* New York: Tarcher/Putnam, 1999, p. 97.

p. 276 *In an indigenous view of illness, the disease is always linked:* Ibid., p. 73.

Chapter 13: The Wolf Moon

p. 284 *Busy, normal people:* Desmond Tutu, *An African Prayer Book.* New York: Doubleday, 1995, p. 110.

p. 286 *It is apparent that the present and past one or two generations:* Weston A. Price, *Nutrition and Physical Degeneration*, Price-Pottenger Nutrition Foundation, 1997 (first published in 1939), p. 417.

p. 288   *There are times when helpful hints about turning off the gas:* M. F. K. Fisher, *How to Cook a Wolf.* New York: North Point Press, 1942, p. 66.

p. 291–292   *Over the last two or three centuries, a heartless culture-crushing mentality:* Martín Prechtel, *Secrets of the Talking Jaguar.* New York: Penguin Putnam, 1998, pp. 281–282.

p. 293   *If [researcher] Dr. Wayne is right, wolves and people:* Temple Grandin and Catherine Johnson, *Animals in Translation.* New York: Scribner, 2005, pp. 304–306.

p. 296–297   *Soon after I had arrived in Ladakh, I was washing some clothes:* Helena Norberg-Hodge, *Ancient Futures.* San Francisco: Sierra Club Books, 1991, pp. 24–25.

INDEX

Note: Entries and page numbers in italics indicate recipes.

A

abundance, 11
acupuncture, 143–146
Addaru, xvi
Advent ritual, 263
AFT (American Farmland Trust), 316
After-dinner Mints, 46–47
agriculture, 166–172
ahimsa, 219, 221
alcoholic beverages
 ales, 155
 balche, 125–126
 beer, 148–149
 honey wine, 121–122
 mead, 123–124
 millet beer, 243–244
 sacred aspects of, 123–129
alcoholism, 129–130
ale recipes
 Lemon Verbena, 158
 Sorghum, 163
 Yarrow, 162
ales, 155
alternative medicine, 141–148, 156–157
alternative values, challenges of, 304–308
American Farmland Trust (AFT), 316
American Grassfed Association, 313
Andrews, Tamra, 124–125
animal products, 309
animals, value of, 217–218, 223–224
antibiotics, 54–55, 173
aquaculture, 193, 195–196, 197–198
Armstrong, Jeanette, 9
 The En'owkin Centre, 319
Asian Egg Drop Soup, 67
Asparagus Frittata, 66
Asperger's syndrome, 268
Avocado and Hard-cooked Eggs with a Lemony Dressing, 69

B

Bacchus, 126–128
balche, 125–126
Beef Broth, 231–232
Beef Liver with Browned Onions, 228–229
beer, 148–149
bees, 120–121

Beet Borscht, 19
beet kvass, 309
Beltane, 70
Berries, Summer with Lavender Crème Anglaise, 140
Berry, Wendell, 170–172
beverage recipes
 Birch Beer, 163
 Herbal Latte, 160
 Hibiscus and Rose Hip Soda, 161
 Honeybee Lemonade, 139
 Hot Coco Cocoa, 46
 I Dream of Peaches and Cream, 139
 Kefir, 92
 Lemon Verbena Ale, 158
 Mellow Mead, 138
 Root Beer, 159
 Sorghum Ale, 163
 Superfood and Kefir Shake, 114
 Yarrow Ale, 162
beverages
 lacto-fermented, 152–155
 traditional, 124
Bioneers and the Collective Heritage Institute, 316
birch beer, 154, 163
Birch Boy, 313
birch syrup, 309
Bisque, Golden Vegetable, 22
Blue Moon, xviii
Borg, Marcus, 135, 221
Borscht, Beet, 19
bouquet garni, 309–310
bread-making, 178–181
breast feeding, 81–82
brining, 236–239, 312
Broth, Beef, 231–232
Brown, Judith K., 241–242
Budín de Maíz, 186
Buhner, Stephen Harrod, 129–130, 154
butter, 97–99
Butternut Squash Soup, Cream of, 298

C

C&H sugar, 39
Cabbage and Potatoes, Sausage with, 278
CAFF (The Community Alliance with Family Farmers), 318
Calabacitas with Herbed Crema, 183

calendars, lunar, xvi, xviii–xx
Campaign for Real Milk, 314
carbohydrates, 30, 176–177
Cardamom and Jaggery Rice Pudding, 44–45
Catholicism, 191–192, 272
cattle, and corn, 172–173
cavities, 31–33
The Center for Ecoliteracy, 316
The Center for Progressive Christianity
   (TCPC), 316–317
The Center for Traditional Medicine
   (CTM), 317
The Center for Visionary Activism, 317
The Center for World Indigenous Studies
   (CWIS), 317
Cheese, Clabbered Cottage, 93
Chelsea Green Publishing Company, 314
Chernin, Kim, 5–6
chewing gum, 36
chicken recipes
   Simplest Roast, 226
   Soup with Wild Rice, 300
   Stock, 299
child care, 242
Chinese medicine, 141–148, 155–156
chowder recipes
   New England Clam, 282–283
   Oyster Plant (Salsify Soup), 20
   Potato-corn, 184
   see also soups
Christianity
   Advent ritual, 263
   Catholicism, 191–192, 273
   The Center for Progressive Christianity
     (TCPC), 316–317
   Christmas, 262–263
   Easter, xix
   and indigenous culture, 295
Christmas, 262–263
chuño, 234–235
Chutney, Lacto-fermented Peach, 258
Clabbered Cottage Cheese, 93
Clam Chowder, New England, 282–283
Coca-Cola, 36
Cocoa, Hot Coco, 46
Coconut and Palm Sugar Semifreddi, 43
Coconut-date Energy Balls, 115
*Coconut Milk and Lemongrass Sauce, Salmon
  Poached in, 208*
coconut palm, 28
Colbin, Annemarie, 84, 212
commodity economies, 198–200, 296
community
   life, 292–295
   origins of, 292–293
   values, 9

The Community Alliance with Family Farmers
   (CAFF), 318
Cone, Marla, 110–111
corn, agricultural role of, 172–175
corn oil, 173
corn, sacred aspects of, 175–176
Cottage Cheese, Clabbered, 93
countercultural values, challenges of, 304–308
Cowan, Thomas
   on diet, 100, 108–109, 176–177
   New Trends Publishing Company, 315
cows, and corn, 172–173
Crab Cakes, Dungeness, 301
Crackers, Homemade Sourdough, 302
Cranberry Sauce, 281
Cream of Butternut Squash Soup, 298
Cream of Parsnip Soup, 18
cream, raw, 312
Creamy Salad Dressing, 94
crème fraîche, 310
crisis, ecological, 289–292
crop diversification, 16
Crumpets, Sourdough, 185
CTM (The Center for Traditional Medicine), 317
Cultures on the Edge, 318
cultures, working with, 249–250
Cured Salmon with Maple and Juniper, 205
CWIS (The Center for World Indigenous
   Studies), 317
cycles, lunar.*see* lunations

D

dairy products
   butter, 97–99
   crème fraîche, 310
   lactose intolerance, 78–79
   Price on, 77
   raw milk and cream, 312
   yogurt, 79, 313
   see also milk
dairy recipes
   Clabbered Cottage Cheese, 93
   Creamy Salad Dressing, 94
   Honeybee Yogurt, 140
   Kefir, 92
   Summer Berries with Lavender Crème Anglaise,
     140
   Superfood and Kefir Shake, 114
   Warm Frothed Milk with Saffron and
     Cardamom, 90
   Yogurt, 89
   Yogurt Cheese Peras with Rosewater Syrup, 91
dams, fish, 195–196
dan, 243–244
darkness, 259–260

Davidson, Alan, 28
The David Suzuki Foundation, 318
Davis, Wade, 152
deer, 290
dental health, 31–33
dessert recipes
    After-dinner Mints, 46–47
    Cardamom and Jaggery Rice Pudding, 44–45
    Coconut and Palm Sugar Semifreddi, 43
    Coconut-date Energy Balls, 115
    I Dream of Peaches and Cream, 139
    Maple-vanilla Panna Cruda, 43–44
desserts, 34–36
Diamond, Jared, 166–167, 285, 289
Dionysus, 126–128
disease
    eggborne, 61–63
    and electricity, 260–262
    heart disease, 96–97
    salmonella, 61–63
doshas, 103
Dungeness Crab Cakes, 301

E

Easter, xix
Easy Hollandaise, 207
Eat Well Guide, 309, 314
eating disorders, 4–7, 108–109
    see also obesity
Echoes of the Ancestors, 319
ecological crisis, 289–292
The Ecological Farming Association (EFA), 319
economies, gift vs. commodity, 198–200, 296
Ecotrust, 319
eczema, 143–146, 264
EFA (The Ecological Farming Association), 319
Egg Drop Soup, Asian, 67
eggs
    eggborne disease, 61–63
    goose, 50
    nutritional value, 58–59, 63
    production of, 49–50, 52, 56
    salmonella, 61–63
    sources of, 52
electricity, 259–262
    and disease, 260–262
Energy Balls, Coconut-date, 115
Enig, Mary, 58–59
The En'owkin Centre, 319
Eostre, xix
epilepsy, 270
Ethiopiam Spiced Ghee (Niter Qibbeh), 117
Euripedes, 126–128

F

factory farming, 59–60, 83, 272–273
Fadiman, Anne, 269–270
Fallon, Sally
    on beverage production, 157
    on eggs, 58–59
    on fats, 97
    on honey, 120
    on lacto-fermentation, 151–152
    New Trends Publishing Company, 315
    on sugar, 30–31
farmer's markets, 11–17, 288
farming, organic, 11
fats
    nutritional qualities of, 96–101
    Price on, 98–99, 106
    sources of, 101
fatty acids, 102
Fernandez-Armesto, Felipe, 82–83
Ferry Plaza Farmers Market, 14, 288
fish dams, 195–196
fish farming, 193, 195–196, 197–198
fish sauce, 191
Fisher, M.F.K., 288
flour, sprouted spelt, 313
Flowering Mountain, 320
food
    and love, 7–9
    obsessions with. *see* eating disorders
    scarcity of, 1
food preparation, 243, 248–250
free range eggs, 53–54, 53–56
Frittata, Asparagus, 66
Fritters, Sourdough Corn, 184–185

G

G.E.M. Cultures, 314
genetically modified organisms (GMOs),
    174–175
ghee, 96
Ghee, Ethiopian Spiced, 117
gift economies, 198–200, 296
ginger bug, 310
gluttony, 108–109
GMOs (genetically modified organisms),
    174–175
Golden Vegetable Bisque, 22
goose eggs, 50
gophers, 213
GRACE Factory Farm Project, 320
grains
    corn, 172–175, 175–176
    history of, 164–165

kefir, 310–311
and Ladakhi people, 168–169, 179
Prechtel on, 175–176, 181
Price on, 168
Grandin, Temple
on community, 292–293
on farm animals, 107
on pathology, 272–273
grass-fed meats, 310
Grohman, Joann, 168
gum, chewing, 36
Gussow, Joan Dye, 105, 314

H
Hærfestmo:nath, xvii
Harvest Moon, xvii
health
Chinese medicine, 155–156
dental, 31–33
and interdependence, 277
Price on, 31–33, 56–58, 71–72, 273–274
heart disease, 96–97
Heidi, 72
Heifer International, 320
Hepinstall, Hi Soo Shin, 236–237, 240
Herb Scones, Sourdough Cheese, 301–302
Herbal Latte, 160
Herbed Creama aith Calabacitas, 183
Herbistmanoth, xvii
herbs, medicinal, 141–143, 156–157
Herstmaand, xvii
HFA (The Humane Farming Association),
320–321
Hibiscus and Rose Hip Soda, 161
Hinduism, ahimsa
Hodesh ha-Aviv, xvii
holiday season, 262–263
Hollandaise, Easy, 207
Homemade Sourdough Crackers, 302
honey, 119–120
honey wine, 121–122
Honeybee Lemonade, 139
Honeybee Yogurt, 140
hormones, and sleep, 261–262, 263–264
hospitality, and vegetarianism, 219–220
Hot Coco Cocoa, 46
House, Freeman, 188–189, 194–196, 197
The Humane Farming Association (HFA),
320–321
Hyde, Lewis, 193–194, 198–200, 215

I
I Dream of Peaches and Cream, 139
indigenous culture, and Christianity, 295
industrial agriculture, 166–172
interdependence, 200–202, 277
The International Society for Ecology and
Culture (ISEC), 321
intoxication, 129–135
Inuit people, 110–112
ISEC (The International Society for Ecology and
Culture), 321

J
Jerusalem artichokes, 14–15
Jha, Dwinjendra Narayan, 219, 221
Joan of Arc, 272
Johnson, Jimmy, 59–60
Jumaada Awal, xvii
Juniper Ridge, 314

K
Kahiltna Birchworks, 315
kefir, *92, 114,* 310–311
kimchi, 236–237, *254*
Kingsolver, Barbara, 213–215
kombucha, 154–155, 311
Kornskurdarmánudr, xvii
Kraut, Quick, 252
Kraut, Slow, 253
kuzu, 311
Kvaser, 124

L
lacto-fermentation, 151–155, 238–239, 249
Lacto-fermented Corn Relish, 257
Lacto-fermented Peach Chutney, 258
Lacto-fermented Raita, 255
Lacto-fermented Tabbouleh, 256
lactose intolerance, 78–79
Ladakhi people
and grain, 168–169, 179
and milk, 75–76
self-sufficiency of, 87
and stewardship, 296–297
Lamb Chops with Meyer Lemon and Mint Gelée,
230–231
Lard, Rendering, 116–117
Latte, Herbal, 160
Lavender Crème Anglaise, with Summer Berries, 140
leavened foods, 178–181
Lemon Verbena Ale, 158

Lemonade, Honeybee, 139
Lemongrass and Coconut Milk Sauce, and
    Poached Salmon, 208
Leonard, Robert, 121–122
life, value of, 215–217
light pollution, 259
lipid hypothesis, 97
Lipton, Bruce, 273, 276
Liver, Beef with Browned Onions, 228–229
Local Farm Locator, 315
Local Harvest, 315
Loha-unchit, Kasma, 28–29
love, and food, 7–9
low-carbohydrate diets, 176–177
lunaception, 267
lunar cycles, and menstruation, 265–267
lunations, xvi

M

Maasai people
    health of, 77
    and honey, 120
    and milk, 87, 96
Maíz, Budín de, 186
Manu, 219–220
manure, chicken, 53–54
Maple-roasted Nuts, 45
maple syrup, 24–29
Maple-vanilla Panna Cruda, 43–44
Mashed Potatoes, Pumpkin, 280
Maui, 39
Max's appetizers, 130–135
Mayonnaise, Olive Oil, 118
mead, 123–124, *138*
Meatballs, Swedish, 227–228
meats, grass-fed, 310
medicinal herbs, 141–143, 156–157
menstruation, 264–267
metaphorical villages, 294
Mexico, trade with, 173–174
microbial cultures, working with, 249–250
midwifery, 150–151
migrant workers, 16
milk
    arguments against, 74–75
    Campaign for Real Milk, 314
    lactose intolerance, 78–79
    and Ladakhi people, 75–76
    pasteurization, 78–79
    raw, 312
    sources of, 74
    Tiwari on, 75
    see also dairy products

millet beer, 243–244
Minestrone, Winter, 21
Mint Gelée and Lamb Chops with Meyer Lemon,
    230–231
Mints, After-dinner, 46–47
Mintz, Sidney, 38–39
molasses, 29, 312
Mountaire Farms, 59–60
Mouth Music, 88
mushrooms, 112–113
music, and work, 240–241, 243–245

N

National Family Farm Coalition (NFFC),
    321–322
native nutrition movement, 11, 268–269, 311
natural sweeteners
    maple syrup, 24–29
    palm sugar, 28–29, 311–312
    sorghum, 29
    sources of, 30
    sucanat, 313
    see also sugar
Nettle Soup, Spring Tonic, 68
New Biology, 276
New England Clam Chowder, 282–283
New Trends Publishing Company, 315
NFFC (National Family Farm Coalition),
    321–322
Niter Qibbeh (Ethiopiam Spiced Ghee), 117
Norberg-Hodge, Helena, 75–76, 168–169,
    296–297
nutritional deficiencies, 268
Nuts, Maple-roasted, 45

O

obesity, 102–103, 108–109
    see also eating disorders
OCRT (The Ontario Consultants on Religious
    Tolerance), 322
Old Farmer's Almanac, xvii
Olive Oil Mayonnaise, 118
The Ontario Consultants on Religious Tolerance
    (OCRT), 322
organic farming, 11, 53–54
Oyster Plant Chowder (Salsify Soup), 20

P

palm oil, 101
palm sugar, 28–29, 311–312
P'an-gu, 48–49

Pancakes, Sourdough, 303
Panna Cruda, Maple-vanilla, 43–44
Parsnip Soup, Cream of, 18
pasteurization, 78–79
pastured poulty, 310
Peach Chutney, Lacto-fermented, 258
Peaches and Cream, I Dream of, 139
Peak Oil, 287, 289
Pekelánew, xvi
pemmican, 35, 95
Peras, Yogurt Cheese with Rosewater Syrup, 91
pesticides, 174, 285
petroleum, dependence upon, 287, 289
pickling, 236–239, 312
pigs, 107–108
Poached Salmon, in a Lemongrass and Coconut Milk
    Sauce, 208
Pollan, Michael, 5
pollution
    effects of, 109–112
    light, 259
    pesticides, 285
Pork, Stir-fry, and Vegetables with Ginger, 229–230
Pot Roast, 279–280
potato recipes
    and Cabbage, Sausage with, 278
    Potato-corn Chowder, 184
    Pumpkin Mashed, 280
potatoes, 234–235
poulty, pastured, 310
Powamuya, 8
Prechtel, Martín
    Flowering Mountain, 320
    on grain, 175–176, 181
    on interdependence, 200–202
    on progress, 291–292
    on tradition, 81–82, 85–86
predator-friendly ranching, 305
Price-Pottenger Nutrition Foundation, 322
Price, Weston A.
    on connection between health and diet,
        56–58, 71–72, 273–274
    on dairy products, 77
    on dental health, 31–33
    on fats, 98–99, 106
    on food preparation, 250
    on grain, 168
    Price-Pottenger Nutrition Foundation, 322
    on soil quality, 285–286
    Weston A. Price Foundation, 323
Pumpkin Mashed Potatoes, 280

Q
Quick and Simple Kimchi, 254
Quick Kraut, 252

R
Rabia Awal, xix
Raita, Lacto-fermented, 255
ranching, predator-friendly, 305
Rapadura, 313
raw milk and cream, 312
recipes, use of, 245–247
red palm oil, 101
refined carbohydrates, 30
refrigeration, 233–234
Reinheitsgebot, 149
relationship, loss of, 10
Relish, Lacto-fermented Corn, 257
Rendering Lard, 116–117
rest, 261–262, 263–264
rice-eating ceremony, 7
Rice Pudding, Cardamom and Jaggery, 44–45
Roast Chicken, Simplest, 226
Roast Salmon, Whole, 204
Roasted Nuts, Maple, 45
Roasted Root Vegetables, 23
Roman Egg Drop Soup (Stracciatella), 67
Root Beer, 159
root cellars, 2
Root Vegetables, Roasted, 23
Rose Hip, and Hibiscus Soda, 161
rusell, 309
Rush, Benjamin, 26
Russian Peasant Soup (Shchi), 281–282

S
sadhanas, 246
Sakipakawpicim, xvii
Salad Dressing, Creamy, 94
salad recipes
    Avocado and Hard-cooked Eggs with A Lemony
        Dressing, 69
    Creamy Salad Dressing, 94
    Lacto-fermented Raita, 255
    Lacto-fermented Tabbouleh, 256
Salatin, Joel
    on egg production, 56, 62–63
    on farming, 53–54, 60
salmon
    restoration work, 202–203
    see also fish farming

salmonella, 61–63
Salsify Soup (Oyster Plant Chowder), 20
SaTsuki, xvi
sauerkraut, 236
Sauerkraut and Rot Kohl, 252
Sausage with Potatoes and Cabbage, 278
Schmidt, Ron, 79–81, 315
Scones, Sourdough Cheese Herb, 301–302
self-sufficiency, of Ladakhi people, 87
Semifreddi, Coconut and Palm Sugar, 43
sexual minorities, 268–269, 271–272
shamanism, 270–273
Shchi (Russian Peasant Soup), 281–282
Shlain, Leonard, 264–266, 271–272
SI (The Sustainability Institute), 323
Simple Salmon Fillets, 206
Simplest Roast Chicken, 226
Singer, Katie, 266–267
slavery, 26–27
sleep, 261–262
    and hormones, 263–264
Slow Food movement, 11, 322–323
Slow Kraut, 253
Soda, Hibiscus and Rose Hip, 161
soil quality, 285 286
soma, 27–28
Somé, Malidoma Patrice
    on darkness, 260
    on death, 218
    Echoes of the Ancestors, 319
    on idealism of indigenous life, 275–276
    on music, 240–241, 243–244
sorghum, 29
Sorghum Ale, 163
sorghum molasses, 312
soup recipes
    Asian Egg Drop Soup, 67
    Beef Broth, 231–232
    Beet Borscht, 19
    Chicken Soup with Wild Rice, 300
    Chicken Stock, 299
    Cream of Butternut Squash Soup, 298
    Cream of Parsnip, 18
    Golden Vegetable Bisque, 22
    New England Clam Chowder, 282–283
    Oyster Plant Chowder (Salsify Soup), 20
    Potato-corn Chowder, 184
    Shchi (Russian Peasant Soup), 281–282
    Spring Tonic Nettle Soup, 68
    Stracciatella (Roman Egg Drop Soup), 67
    Winter Minestrone, 21
sourdough, 312
Sourdough Cheese Herb Scones, 301–302

Sourdough Corn Fritters, 184–185
Sourdough Crackers, Homemade, 302
Sourdough Crumpets, 185
Sourdough Pancakes, 303
spawning, of salmon, 188–189, 194
spelt flour, sprouted, 313
Spring Tonic Nettle Soup, 68
sprouted spelt flour, 313
spruce beer, 154
Spyri, Johanna, 72
squirrels, 177–178
Stamets, Paul, 112–113
stewardship, 295–297, 306–307
Stir-fry of Pork and Vegetables with Ginger, 229–230
Stock, Chicken, 299
Stracciatella (Roman Egg Drop Soup), 67
sucanat, 313
Succotash, Suffer-free, 182
sugar
    C&H sugar, 39
    Fallon on, 30–31
    palm, 28–29, 311–312
    production of, 37–39
    white, 36–40
    see also natural sweeteners
sugar maples, 24–26
Summer Berries with Lavender Crème Anglaise, 140
Summers Sprouted Flour Co., 315
sunchokes, 14–15
Superfood and Kefir Shake, 114
The Sustainability Institute (SI), 323
Swedish Meatballs, 227–228
sweeteners, natural
    maple syrup, 24–29
    palm sugar, 28–29, 311–312
    sorghum, 29
    sources of, 30
    sucanat, 313
    see also sugar

T

Tabbouleh, Lacto-fermented, 256
TCPC (The Center for Progressive Christianity), 316–317
teekvass, 154–155
teeth, 31–33
Thai cooking, 28–29, 35, 191
thirteenth moon, xviii
Tiwari, Maya
    on cooking, 245–246
    on milk, 75
    and soma, 27–28

Toussaint-Samat, Maguelonne, 191–192
tradition, loss of, 10, 274
Tuho'osmuya, xvii

U
uki, 121–122

V
vegetarianism
    challenges of, 210–212
    and fish, 191–192
    and hospitality, 219–223
Viti Levu, 57–58

W
*Warm Frothed Milk with Saffron and
    Cardamom,* 90
Weston A. Price Foundation, 323

whey, yogurt, 313
Whole Roast Salmon, 204
wild honey, 119–120
Wiley, T.S., 260–262
wine, honey, 121–122
Winnemanoth, xvii
Winter Minestrone, 21
winter produce, 17
Wise Food Ways, 313
wolves, 284–285, 305
women, and food preparation, 243
work, 16, 240–245
wort, 141, 142, 148

Y
Yarrow Ale, 162
yin and yang, 83
yogurt, 79, 89, 313
Yogurt Cheese Peras with Rosewater Syrup, 91
Yogurt, Honeybee, 140

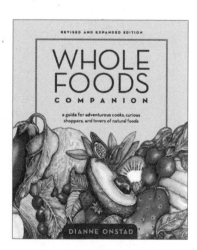